Bertrand Russell

A Bibliography of his Writings

Eine Bibliographie seiner Schriften

1895–1976

Compiled by / Zusammengestellt von

Werner Martin

K·G·Saur

München · New York · London · Paris 1981

Linnet Books · Hamden, Connecticut

CIP-Kurztitelaufnahme der Deutschen Bibliothek

Martin, Werner:
Bertrand Russell : a bibliogr. of his
writings ; 1895 – 1976 / compiled by
Werner Martin. – München ; New York ;
London ; Paris : Saur, 1981.
   ISBN 3-598-10348-4

NE: HST

© 1981 by K. G. Saur Verlag KG, München
Printed in the Federal Republic of Germany
by Pera-Druck KG, Gräfelfing b. München
ISBN 3-598-10348-4

A successful theatrical production is easily enjoyed; the troublesome detailed work of the producer, however, which chiefly makes success possible, remains concealed. The same also applies to a bibliography, that indispensable scien= tific instrument of scholarly investi= gation: A bibliography is consulted with ease, but the painstaking accuracy of its compilation which enters into the most minute detail and which alone makes a bibliography useful, remains concealed.

Eine erfolgreiche Theateraufführung ge= nießt sich leicht, aber die mühevolle Kleinarbeit des Regisseurs, die ihren Erfolg erst möglich macht, die bleibt verborgen. Ähnliches gilt auch von der Bibliographie, dem unentbehrlichen Ar= beitsinstrument wissenschaftlicher Stu= dien: Eine Bibliographie benutzt sich leicht, aber die mühevolle bis ins klein= ste Detail gehende Akribie ihrer Zusam= menstellung, die sie erst brauchbar macht, die bleibt verborgen.

CONTENTS

INHALT

In Lieu of a Foreword

From a letter of the historian Professor
Dr. Golo Mann of 15 June 1979, with per-
mission to publish as presented here –

"Unfortunately, I have to disappoint you as regards your request. I cannot write a foreword for

your Russell-Bibliography, which, by the way,
is excellently, even ingeniously produced.

For all of the foreseeable future I am overbur-
dened with work projects of many different kinds."

With friendly regards

yours

Golo Mann

Statt eines Geleitwortes

Aus einem Brief des Historikers Herrn Prof.
Dr. G o l o M a n n vom 15.6.1979 mit er-
laubter Veröffentlichung in vorliegender Form:

"Leider muß ich Sie, was Ihre Bitte betrifft,
enttäuschen. Ich kann ein Geleitwort für

Ihre übrigens vorzüglich, ja geist-
voll gemachte Russell-Bibliographie

nicht schreiben. Für alle absehbare Zeit bin
ich von Arbeit der verschiedendsten Art über-
wältigt."

Mit freundlichen Grüssen

Ihr

Preliminary Remarks

It should be emphasized at the outset that the Bertrand-Russell-Bibliography (BRB) presented here offers the complete explanatory text (introductions to and comments on most of the main titles) in German and English so as to cater for a larger range of users. These actual introductions and title commentaries are an indispensable extension of the BRB, intended to elucidate Russell's dominant role as a thinker of the West and as an independent universal intellect.

Russell left behind a voluminous literary œuvre, including more than sixty books, many pamphlets and countless contributions to journals and newspapers. Attention to the latter is drawn here through a typical selection. All reprints and translations, in as far as they are listed in the extensive source materials, are recorded in the BRB and in each case occur after the listing of the first publication of individual titles. If, in the case of reprints or translations, the remarks "Excerpt" or "Auszug" is missing, the user is always dealing with the main title which first appeared under ".01" or (if an American title version is involved) under ".02". A compelling reason for the inclusion of reprints was that it offers important material for research into Russell's reception, while the listing of translations evidences the worldwide resonance occasioned by Russell's literary production. The listing of Russell's chief works - editions in English as well as the German translations - includes, for the greater part, their tables of contents in order to demonstrate, over and above the mere title entry, Russell's universal knowledge. Within the bibliography and the alphabetical index of works, the titles of Russell's main writings are reproduced exclusively in capital letters while all other publications appear in normal style. Each independent title is accompanied by its own bibliographical number (BN). The figure before the period counts as the collective bibliographical number whereas the current number after the period indicates the (frequently multiple) subordination under the main title. In so far as a relationship between titles had to be established, this was achieved with the aid of the BNs. Because the original titles of non-English miscellanies, if recorded independently, can be fitted into the alphabetically arranged index only with difficulty the following title transformation was uniformly adopted: "Miscellany/Sammelband in German (or other languages) under the title '........'". The final manuscript of the BRB was produced by myself in its present form. By utilizing the typographic possibilities of the typewriter I have endeavoured not only to arrive at an aesthetically satisfying overall form but also to arrange the necessary groupings and the individual line endings in such a way that, if possible, they correspond with the contents. This was done in order to make optically for a greater legibility than one usually encounters in bibliographies.

The confidence that I was closing a gap with this BRB for the German speaking area and, moreover, for the science of letters has encouraged me not let up in the attempted longterm accomplishment of such a task in spite of all its laborious demands. I hope, in all modesty, to have achieved the goal. In this I received support by many to whom I would like to express my gratitude at this point. Above all I have to thank Mr. Werner Schlick, my German literary friend in faroff Australia (University of Queensland, St. Lucia, Brisbane) for his devotion of time to translate part of the explanatory texts from German into English and vice versa, and for his consultative interest in my BRB to the end, despite his taxing preparations for a doctorate at a German university. To authors, editors and publishers, as recorded inter alia in the list of sources accompanying relevant titles, I have to give thanks for the opportunity to evaluate materials, to quote and to partially reprint (a fact especially referred to in the Introduction, in the 1st to 4th Compensation). To the Embassies of the Federal Republic of Germany in Istanbul and Peking I am grateful for their assistance in the search for information particularly difficult to obtain. The same thanks go to the Lenin University of Moscow for special and helpful information. A comprehensive correspondence of inquiries with universities and Institutions in Germany and abroad yielded much valuable information about many indispensable details for which I would like to thank a host of unknown helpers even if this can be done summarily only.

Abkürzungen und eine kleine Wörterliste
Abbreviations and a small list of words

        Auszüge = Excerpts
        Auszug aus = Excerpt from
        Bd. = Band / vol. = volume
        Bde. = Bände / vols. = volumes
        BN = Bibliographie-Nummer
            = bibliographical number
        BRB = Bertrand-Russell-Bibliographie
        hrsg. = herausgegeben / ed. = edited
        Hrsg. = Herausgeber / Ed. = Editor
        ill. = illustriert
        illus. = illustrated
        Inhalt = Contents
        Kommentar = Commentary
        Neudrucke, Nachdrucke = Reprints
        rev. Ausg. = revidierte Ausgabe
        rev. ed. = revised edition

Vorbemerkungen

Die hier vorliegende Bertrand-Russell-Bibliographie (BRB)
bringt, dies sei eingangs besonders hervorgehoben, den
gesamten erklärenden Text (Einleitungen und Kommentare
zu den meisten Haupt-Titeln) in Deutsch und Englisch, um
damit einem größeren Benutzerkreis entgegenkommen zu können. Die eigentliche Einleitung und die Titelkommentare
sind eine unverzichtbare Erweiterung der BRB, um Russell's dominierende Rolle als Denker des Abendlandes und
unabhängiger universeller Geist zu verdeutlichen.

Russell hinterließ ein umfangreiches schriftstellerisches
Werk, darunter mehr als 60 Bücher, viele Broschüren und
zahllose Beiträge in Zeitschriften und Zeitungen. Letz-
teres wird hier in einer charakteristischen Auswahl zur
Kenntnis gebracht. Alle Neudrucke und Übersetzungen, soweit sie in dem umfangreichen Quellenmaterial nachgewiesen sind, wurden in die BRB aufgenommen und jeweils
den Erstveröffentlichungen der einzelnen Titel nachge-
ordnet. Wenn bei den Neudrucken oder Übersetzungen der
Vermerk Auszug oder Excerpt fehlt, dann handelt es sich
stets um den Haupt-Titel, der erstmalig jeweils unter
".01" oder (handelt es sich um amerikanische Titel-Ver-
sionen) unter ".02" aufgeführt wird. Für den Nachweis der
Neudrucke ergab sich als zwingender Grund, daß damit wichtiges Material für die Rezeptionsforschung angeboten wird,
während der Nachweis der Übersetzungen augenfällig macht,
welche weltweite Wirkung dem Schaffen Russell's beizu-
messen ist. Die Hauptwerke Russell's, sowohl die englischen Ausgaben wie auch die deutschen Übersetzungen,
werden größtenteils mit ihren Inhaltsverzeichnissen nachgewiesen, um damit mehr noch als nur durch die Titelan-
gabe Russell's Universalwissen erkennen zu lassen. Für
die Hauptwerke Russell's erfolgt die Titelschreibung innerhalb der Bibliographie und des alphabetischen Werk-
registers ausschließlich in Großbuchstaben und für alle
anderen Veröffentlichungen in der normalen Schreibweise.
Jeder selbständige Titel führt eine eigene Bibliographie-
Nummer (BN). Als Bibliographie-Sammelnummer gilt die Zahl
vor dem Punkt, während die laufende Nummer nach dem Punkt
die oft mehrfache Unterordnung unter den Haupt-Titel
deutlich macht. Soweit eine Bezogenheit der Titel unter-
einander herzustellen war, wurde dies mit Hilfe der BN
erreicht. Da die Original-Titel außerenglischer Sammel-
bände, wenn sie selbständig geführt werden, in der alphabetischen Registerordnung schwer unterzubringen sind,
wurde folgende einheitliche Titel-Umbildung gewählt:
"Miscellany/Sammelband in Deutsch (oder andere Sprachen)
under the title '.......'". Das Reinschrift-Typoskript
für diese BRB wurde in der vorliegenden Form von mir selbst
hergestellt. Unter Ausnutzung der typographischen Möglichkeiten der Schreibmaschine bemühte ich mich nicht nur
um eine ästhetisch befriedigende Gesamtform, sondern auch
darum, notwendige Gruppierungen und den einzelnen Zeilen-
bruch möglichst inhaltsgemäß durchzuführen, um damit op-
tisch eine leichtere Lesbarkeit zu erreichen, als man sie
gemeinhin in Bibliographien anzutreffen pflegt.

Die Zuversicht, mit dieser BRB für den deutschen Sprach-
bereich und darüber hinaus eine literaturwissenschaftli-
che Lücke zu schließen, hat mich trotz aller mühevollen
Anforderungen ermutigt, in der langfristigen Bewältigung
einer solchen Aufgabe nicht nachzulassen. Ich hoffe in
aller Bescheidenheit, daß ich diese Aufgabe erfüllt habe.
Hierbei habe ich vielfache Unterstützung gefunden, für die
ich an dieser Stelle meinen Dank aussprechen möchte. Ins-
besondere habe ich Herrn Werner Schlick, meinem deutschen
Literaturfreund aus dem fernen Australien (University of
Queensland, St. Lucia, Brisbane) dafür zu danken, daß er
sich, trotz anstrengender Promotions-Vorbereitung an einer deutschen Universität, die Zeit dafür absparte, um mir
einen Teil der erklärenden Texte aus dem Deutschen ins
Englische und umgekehrt zu übersetzen und auch bis zuletzt
an meiner BRB beratenden Anteil nahm. Verfassern, Heraus-
gebern und Verlegern, so wie sie u.a. im Quellennachweis
bei den entsprechenden Titeln angeführt werden, habe ich
für die Möglichkeit der Materialauswertung, des Zitierens
und teilweisen Nachdrucks (auf den in der Einleitung beim
1. - 4. Ausgleich besonders hingewiesen wird) zu danken.
Den deutschen Botschaften in Istanbul und Peking danke ich
dafür, daß sie mich bei besonders schwierigen Ermittlungen
unterstützt haben. Desgleichen danke ich der Lenin-Uni-
versität in Moskau für besondere hilfreiche Auskünfte.
Eine umfangreiche Anfragen-Korrespondenz mit in- und aus-
ländischen Universitäten und Instituten brachte über manche unverzichtbare Einzelheit wertvolle Information, für
die ich vielen unbekannten Helfern danken möchte, wenn es
auch nur summarisch geschehen kann.

Lingen (Ems)   Werner Martin
Frühjahr 1980

Abkürzungen und eine kleine Wörterliste (Forts.)
Abbreviations and a small list of words (Cont'd.)

    Sammelband = Miscellany
    S. = Seite, Seiten / p. = page, pp. = pages
    s.a. = siehe auch / see also
    Teil = Part
    Ü.: Übersetzer / Tr.: = Translator
    Übersetzungen = Translations
    u.d.T. = unter dem Titel / under the title
    Verlagsrecht = (c) copyright
    veröffentlicht = published

    "Mind" = A quarterly review of philosophy
       In Oxford erscheinende
       Quartals-Zeitschrift der Philosophie
    Proceedings Aristotelian Society / Oxford
       Berichte der Aristotel. Gesellschaft

Introduction

Einleitung

Bertrand Russell was born in 1872, on 18 May; he died at the age of ninetyseven on 2 February 1970. Among his public honours were the Order of Merit in 1949 (the most exclusive honour, which it is in the King's George VI. power to bestow), the Nobel Prize for Literature in 1950, in 1957 the UNESCO Kalinga Prize, and in 1960 the Danish Sonning Prize for contributions to European Culture.

Russell, an upright moralist and, in the words of his biographer Alan Wood, a "passionate sceptic" constantly participated in the discussion of worldwide problems and of topical questions; he protested against anything which to him seemed wrong or dangerous. This resulted not only in great popularity for him but also in his being simplistically labelled as "leftist", which gives a completely distorted picture if one compares it with his role as a thinker of the western world and as an independent spirit of universal interests.

Russell is a mathematician, a philosopher, a natural scientist, sociologist, educationist, psychologist, political scientist, historian, moralist and philanthropist. In other words, he is a phenomenon in many areas of science and philosophy, and in all of these he has performed with distinction. In each field by itself, his achievements would have sufficed to earn him greatness. With his works Russell not only addressed the academicians or the professional philosopher but many of his books, written in a brilliant near-scholarly style, were directed at an interested lay-public. During his whole life he was moved by two impulses: to discover if definite cognition was possible, and to do everything in his power to make this world a happier one (see also BN 617.06).

The reprints of many titles, the new publications of miscellanies and of secondary literature (for example "The Life of Bertrand Russell" by Ronald W. Clark, London, 1975, 750 pp.) all confirm to this very day, that Russell as a thinker of the western world is as important now as he used to be during his lifetime. This has to be emphasized clearly in order to counteract the distortion of Russell's image referred to above which is responsible for erroneous opinions of him voiced at the level of daily politics, and for the occasional misuse of Russell's name.

As mentioned before, such misguided practices tend to distort and darken the true image of Russell as a thinker of the western world. To place that image in its true perspective, and to do so emphatically, is a task to which this bibliography would like to contribute.

Bertrand Russell wurde am 18. Mai 1872 geboren; er starb in Alter von 97 Jahren, am 2. Februar 1970. Unter seinen öffentlichen Ehrungen waren 1949 der "Order of Merit" (die exklusivste Ehrung, die der König George VI. zu verleihen hatte), 1950 der Nobelpreis für Literatur, 1957 der Kalinga-Preis der UNESCO und 1960 der dänische Sonning-Preis für Beiträge zur europäischen Kultur.

Russell, aufrechter Moralist und, in der Formulierung seines Biographen Alan Wood, "Skeptiker aus Leidenschaft", hat in ständiger Anteilnahme an weltbewegenden Problemen und Tagesfragen, gegen alles protestiert, was ihm falsch oder gefährlich erschien. Hieraus resultierte nicht nur seine große Popularität, sondern auch seine simplifizierte Einengung als "Linker", was gegenüber seiner dominierenden Rolle als Denker des Abendlandes und unabhängiger universeller Geist ein vollkommen falsches Bild ergibt.

Russell ist Mathematiker, Philosoph, Naturwissenschaftler, Soziologe, Pädagoge, Psychologe, Politologe, Historiker, Moralist und Philanthrop. Mit anderen Worten: Er ist ein Phänomen auf vielen Gebieten der Wissenschaft und Philosophie und hat auf allen Hervorragendes geleistet. Jedes für sich allein hätte genügt, ihn Größe erreichen zu lassen. Russell wandte sich mit seinen Werken nicht nur an Akademiker und Berufsphilosophen, sondern mit vielen seiner in glänzendem Stil geschriebenen populärwissenschaftlichen Büchern auch an ein interessiertes Laienpublikum. Er war sein ganzes Leben hindurch von zwei mächtigen Impulsen bewegt: zu entdecken, ob sichere Erkenntnis möglich sei, und alles nur mögliche zu tun, um diese Welt glücklicher zu machen (siehe auch BN 617.06).

Die bis in die jüngste Zeit erfolgten Neudrucke vieler Titel, die Neuerscheinungen von Sammelbänden und Sekundär-Literatur (z. B. "The Life of Bertrand Russell" von Ronald W. Clark, London, 1975, 750 S.) bestätigen, daß Russell's Bedeutung als Denker des Abendlandes nach wie vor Geltung hat. Dies sei sehr deutlich unterstrichen, um jenem oben erwähnten falschen Russell-Bild entgegenzuwirken, dem ja u.a. auch Tatsachen zuzuschreiben sind, die oft auf einer tagespolitischen und für viele Irrtümer anfälligen Ebene liegen oder gelegentlich auch in einer mißbräuchlichen Ausnutzung von Russell's Namen bestehen.

Solche abseitigen Tatsachen verdunkelten, wie schon mit anderen Worten ausgesprochen, das Bild Russell's als Denker des Abendlandes. Es wieder nachdrücklich aufzuhellen, dazu möchte auch diese Bibliographie ihren Beitrag liefern.

The introduction of a bibliography cannot offer, of course, an exhaustive commentary on Russell's multilayered philosophical œuvre. To make up for this lack, it appeared necessary to make a compensation in four different ways:
1st by a general philosophical startingpoint,
2nd by an insight into Russell's workshop of thinking,
3rd by an insight into Russell's world of ideas, and
4th by orientative aids on individual titles.

1st compensation by a general philosophical starting-point: Reprint of Russell's interpretation of "Philosophy" (excerpt from the Introduction to "A History of Western Philosophy"; 1945, New York: Simon & Schuster; 1946, London: Allen & Unwin)

"Philosophy" is a word which has been used in many ways, some wider, some narrower. I propose to use it in a very wide sense, which I will now try to explain.

Philosophy, as I shall understand the word, is something intermediate between theology and science. Like theology, it consists of speculations on matters as to which definite knowledge has, so far, been unascertainable; but like science, it appeals to human reason rather than to authority, whether that of tradition or that of revelation. All definite knowledge - so I should contend - belongs to science; all dogma as to what surpasses definite knowledge belongs to theology. But between theology and science there is a No Man's Land, exposed to attack from both sides; this No Man's Land is philosophy. Almost all the questions of most interest to speculative minds are such as science cannot answer, and the confident answers of theologians no longer seem so convincing as they did in former centuries. Is the world divided into mind and matter, and, if so, what is mind and what is matter? Is mind subject to matter, or is it possessed of independent powers? Has the universe any unity or purpose? Is it evolving towards some goal? Are there really laws of nature, or do we believe in them only because of our innate love of order? Is man what he seems to the astronomer, a tiny lump of impure carbon and water impotently crawling on a small and unimportant planet? Or is he what he appears to Hamlet? Is he perhaps both at once? Is there a way of living that is noble and another that is base, or are all ways of living merely futile? If there is a way of living that is noble, in what does it consist, and how shall we achieve it? Must the good be eternal in order to deserve to be valued, or is it worth seeking

Es ist selbstverständlich, daß man in einer Bibliographie-
Einleitung keinen annähernd erschöpfenden Kommentar über
das vielschichtige philosophische Werk Russell's zu geben
vermag. Deshalb erscheint es zwingend notwendig, für dieses Unvermögen einen vierfachen Ausgleich anzubieten:
1. durch einen allgemeinen philosophischen Ausgangspunkt,
2. durch einen Einblick in Russell's Denkwerkstatt,
3. durch einen Einblick in Russell's Gedankenwelt und
4. durch Orientierungshilfen zu Einzel-Titeln.

1. Ausgleich durch einen allgemeinen philosophischen
   Ausgangspunkt: Nachdruck von Russell's Interpretation der 'Philosophie' (Auszug aus
   der Einführung zur "Philosophie des Abendlandes"; 1950, Zürich, Europa Verlag).

"Philosophie" ist ein Wort, das in mannigfaltiger Weise
verwendet worden ist, zuweilen umfassender, zuweilen
enger begrenzt. Ich beabsichtige, es in sehr weitem
Sinne zu gebrauchen, was zu erklären ich nun versu-
chen will.

Die Philosophie ist nach meiner Auffassung ein Mittel-
ding zwischen Theologie und Wissenschaft. Gleich der
Theologie besteht sie aus der Spekulation über Dinge,
von denen sich bisher noch keine genaue Kenntnis ge-
winnen ließ; wie die Wissenschaft jedoch beruft sie
sich weniger auf eine Autorität, etwa die der Tradition
oder die der Offenbarung, als auf die menschliche Vernunft. Jede sichere Kenntnis, möchte ich sagen, gehört
in das Gebiet der Wissenschaft; jedes Dogma in Fragen,
die über die sichere Kenntnis hinausgehen, in das der
Theologie. Zwischen der Theologie und der Wissenschaft
liegt jedoch ein Niemandsland, das Angriffen von beiden Seiten ausgesetzt ist; dieses Niemandsland ist die
Philosophie. Fast alle Fragen von größtem Interesse
für spekulative Köpfe vermag die Wissenschaft nicht zu
beantworten, und die zuversichtlichen Antworten der
Theologen wirken nicht mehr so überzeugend wie in
früheren Jahrhunderten. Besteht die Welt aus Geist und
Materie, und wenn ja, was ist dann Geist und was Materie? Ist der Geist an die Materie gebunden oder wird
er von unabhängigen Kräften beherrscht? Liegt dem Universum etwas Einheitliches zugrunde? Wohnt ihm ein
Zweck inne? Strebt es in seiner Entwicklung einem Ziel
zu? Gibt es tatsächlich Naturgesetze, oder glauben wir
nur dank der uns eingeborenen Ordnungsliebe daran? Ist
der Mensch, wie die Astronomen meinen, nur eine Win-
zigkeit aus unreinem Kohlenstoff und Wasser, die ohn-
mächtig auf einem kleinen, unbedeutenden Planeten um-
herkriecht? Oder ist er das, was Hamlet in ihm sieht?
Ist er vielleicht beides zugleich? Kann man ein edles
oder ein minderwertiges Leben führen, oder ist es überhaupt belanglos, wie man lebt? Wenn es eine edle Le-
bensführung gibt, woraus besteht sie und wie können
wir dazu kommen? Muß das Gute unvergänglich sein, um
Wertschätzung zu verdienen, oder ist es erstrebenswert,

even if the universe is inexorably moving towards death? Is there such a thing as wisdom, or is what seems such merely the ultimate refinement of folly? To such questions no answer can be found in the laboratory. Theologies have professed to give answers, all too definite; but their very definiteness causes modern minds to view them with suspicion. The studying of these questions, if not the answering of them, is the business of philosophy.

Why, then, you may ask, waste time on such insoluble problems? To this one may answer as a historian, or as an individual facing the terror of cosmic loneliness.

The answer of the historian, in so far as I am capable of giving it, will appear in the course of this work. Ever since men became capable of free speculation, their actions, in innumerable important respects, have depended upon their theories as to the world and human life, as to what is good and what is evil. This is as true in the present day as at any former time. To understand an age or a nation, we must understand its philosophy, and to understand its philosophy we must ourselves be in some degree philosophers. There is here a reciprocal causation: the circumstances of men's lives do much to determine their philosophy, but, conversely, their philosophy does much to determine their circumstances. This interaction throughout the centuries will be the topic of the following pages.

There is also, however, a more personal answer. Science tells us what we can know, but what we can know is little, and if we forget how much we cannot know we become insensitive to many things of very great importance. Theology, on the other hand, induces a dogmatic belief that we have knowledge where in fact we have ignorance, and by doing so generates a kind of impertinent insolence towards the universe. Uncertainty, in the presence of vivid hopes and fears, is painful, but must be endured if we wish to live without the support of comforting fairy tales.

It is not good either to forget the questions that philosophy asks, or to persuade ourselves that we have found indubitable answers to them. To teach how to live without certainty, and yet without being paralysed by hesitation, is perhaps the chief thing that philosophy, in our age, can still do for those who study it.

selbst wenn das Universum sich unerbittlich seinem Untergange nähert? Gibt es so etwas wie Weisheit oder ist das, was uns als Weisheit erscheint, nur letzte, höchste Torheit? Die Antwort auf derartige Fragen finden wir nicht im Laboratorium. Die Theologen haben behauptet, sie allesamt mehr als genau beantworten zu können; aber eben ihre Entschiedenheit veranlaßt moderne Köpfe, solche Antworten mißtrauisch zu betrachten. Die Untersuchung dieser Fragen, wenn schon nicht ihre Beantwortung, ist Sache der Philosophie.

Warum aber, wird der Leser vielleicht fragen, Zeit an derartige unlösbare Probleme verschwenden? Darauf kann man als Historiker antworten oder als Mensch, der sich in seinem entsetzlichen kosmischen Verlassensein sieht.

Was der Historiker darauf zu antworten hat, wird sich im Verlauf dieses Werkes zeigen, soweit ich eine solche Antwort zu geben vermag. Seit die Menschen fähig wurden, unabhängig zu denken, war ihr Handeln stets in zahllosen wichtigen Punkten durch ihre Welt- und Lebensanschauung, ihre Ansichten über Gut und Böse bedingt. Das gilt für die Gegenwart wie für die gesamte Vergangenheit. Um ein Zeitalter oder ein Volk verstehen zu können, müssen wir seine Philosophie verstehen, und um seine Philosophie zu begreifen, müssen wir selbst bis zu einem gewissen Grade Philosophen sein. Wir haben es hier mit einer wechselseitigen Ursächlichkeit zu tun: die Lebensumstände der Menschen bestimmen weitgehend ihre Philosophie; während umgekehrt auch ihre Philosophie in hohem Maße ihre Lebensumstände bedingt. Diese Wechselwirkung durch die Jahrhunderte zu verfolgen ist das Thema der nächsten Seiten.

Es gibt jedoch auch eine persönlichere Antwort. Durch die Wissenschaft erfahren wir, was wir wissen können, doch ist das nur wenig; wenn wir aber vergessen, wieviel wir nicht wissen können, werden wir unempfänglich für viele Dinge von sehr großer Bedeutung. Die Theologie andererseits vermittelt die dogmatische Überzeugung, daß wir wissen, wo wir in Wahrheit nicht wissen, und züchtet auf diese Weise so etwas wie eine Anmaßung dem Universum gegenüber. Bei lebhaften Hoffnungen und Befürchtungen ist Ungewißheit qualvoll; sie muß jedoch ertragen werden, wenn wir ohne die Unterstützung tröstlicher Märchen leben wollen.

Es tut weder gut, die von der Philosophie aufgeworfenen Fragen zu vergessen, noch uns selbst einzureden, wir hätten über jeden Zweifel erhabene Antworten darauf gefunden. Wie man ohne Gewißheit und doch auch ohne durch Unschlüssigkeit gelähmt zu werden, leben kann, das zu lehren ist vielleicht das Wichtigste, was die Philosophie noch für diejenigen tun kann, die sich mit ihr beschäftigen.

2nd compensation by an insight into Russell's workshop of thinking: Excerpts from "Russell's Philosophy: a Study of its Development" by Alan Wood (appended to "My Philosophical Development" by B. Russell; 1959, London: Allen & Unwin) and from "Bertrand Russell. The Passionate Sceptic." by Alan Wood; 1956, London: Allen & Unwin.

The further Russell's thoughts advanced, the more was found of increasing subtle distinction and complex changes of viewpoint. One cannot sum up his philosophy by attaching his name to one single specific doctrine.

In spite of all the apparently conflicting statements to be found in the total of Russell's philosophical writings, in spite of the number of cases where he champions different opinions at different times, there is throughout a consistency of purpose and direction, and a consistency of method.

"I wanted certainty", Russell wrote in retrospect, "in the kind of way in which people want religious faith." I believe the underlying purpose behind all Russell's work was an almost religious passion for some truth that was more than human, independent of the minds of men, and even of the existence of men.

And there may be a subsidiary explanation, once again, in human and easily understandable terms. Less than halfway through his career he had already achieved immortality; his place was secure as a thinker who had made the greatest advances in logic since Greek times. He was therefore under no incentive, conscious or unconscious, to create some distinctive Russellian doctrine to be made secure against all attacks.

It may now be easier to understand why Russell's writings are so complex, subtle and intricate. In fact there is no great philosopher since Plato whose ideas are harder to sum up in a short space. His philosophy was a battleground on which he fought a losing battle against himself; sometimes going one way, sometimes another. A. N. Whitehead once described Russell as a Platonic dialogue in himself.

2. Ausgleich durch einen Einblick in Russell's Denkwerkstatt: Auszüge aus "Die Philosophie Bertrand Russell's, Fragmente einer Studie über ihre Entwicklung" von Alan Wood (im Anhang zu "Philosophie. Die Entwicklung meines Denkens" von B. Russell; 1973, München, Nymphenburger Verlagshandlung) u n d aus "Bertrand Russell, Skeptiker aus Leidenschaft" von Alan Wood; 1959, Ott-Verlag, Thun/München.

Je weiter sich Russell's Gedanken entwickelten, desto mehr feindifferenzierte Unterscheidungen und komplex begründete Änderungen von Auffassungen fanden sich. Man kann nicht eine Summe aus seiner Philosophie ziehen und seinen Namen mit einer einzelnen besonderen Lehre verknüpfen.

Ungeachtet all der scheinbar widersprüchlichen Äußerungen, denen man in Russell's Gesamtwerk begegnet, und ungeachtet der zahlreichen Fälle, in denen er zu verschiedenen Zeitpunkten miteinander unverträgliche Standpunkte hat, durchläuft das Ganze doch ein roter Faden - die konsequent durchgehaltene Zielsetzung, die einheitliche Ausrichtung, die innere Konsistenz (Beständigkeit) der Methode.

"Ich hatte das Bedürfnis nach Gewißheit" heißt es bei Russell in einem Rückblick, "und zwar auf die gleiche Weise wie ein religiöser Mensch, der in seinem Glauben gefestigt sein möchte." Ich glaube, daß seinem ganzen Werk ein von einer nahezu religiösen Inbrunst getragenes Streben zugrundeliegt, zu einer Wahrheit zu kommen, die über das Maß des bloß Menschlichen hinausreicht und vom Bewußtsein, ja sogar von der Existenz des Menschen völlig unabhängig ist.

Und daneben mag es noch eine weitere, ganz einfach menschliche und leichtverständliche Erklärung geben. Weniger als die Hälfte seines Weges war durchschritten, als er schon Unsterblichkeit erlangt hatte. Sein Platz war gesichert als der eines Denkers, der seit dem griechischen Altertum die größten Fortschritte auf dem Gebiete der Logik gemacht hatte. Er stand daher, weder bewußt noch unbewußt, unter keinem Anreiz, irgend eine hervorragende Russellsche Lehre zu schaffen, um sich gegen alle Angriffe zu sichern.

Vielleicht ist es für den Leser jetzt schon etwas leichter einzusehen, warum Russell's Schriften so komplex, subtil und intrikat (heikel, knifflig) sind. Tatsächlich gibt es seit Plato kaum einen bedeutenden Philosophen, dessen Ideen sich so schwer auf eine Formel bringen lassen. Russell's Philosophie ist ein Schlachtfeld, auf dem er gegen sich selbst gekämpft hat, einmal in dieser Richtung einmal in einer anderen. A. N. Whitehead hat Russell einmal einen platonischen Ein-Mann-Dialog genannt.

3rd compensation by an insight into Russell's world of ideas: Reprint of a table of contents consisting of 81 individual titles, and of the brief commentaries accompanying his XVII summary titles, taken from "The Basic Writings of Bertrand Russell"; 1961, New York: Simon & Schuster; London: Allen & Unwin; 736 pp. A complete rendering of this book in German does not exist. In connection with each of the 81 individual titles the corresponding number in the bibliography is referred to: those titles which have been translated into German are identified by the additional symbol (g).

I.
Autobiographical Asides

The clarity and succingtness one expects from the works of Russell are well illustrated by his own reference to his attempt to advance the demonstrative methods of mathematics and science into regions conventionally assigned to vague speculation. As Russell says by way of characteristic autobiographical aside: "I like precision. I like sharp outlines. I hate misty vagueness."

He reveals that even at the age of eleven he refused to accept what tradition had made appear as indestructible as granite. His brother consented to teach him geometry which, Russell had heard, "proved things". When his brother told him that Euclidian axioms cannot be proved, his hopes to find some certain knowledge all but vanished.

1. My Religious Reminiscences 432.02
2. My Mental Development 495.03
3. Adaption: An Autobiographical Epitome 617.04
4. Why I Took to Philosophy 617.04

II.
The Nobel Prize Winning Man of Letters
(Essayist and Short Story Writer)

Few Nobel Prize winners in literature have set forth so revealing an account of how they write as we have here. Russell ever displays a mastery of detail and a precision of presentation that leaves no doubt of his position whether one agrees or disagrees. The clarity of thinking of an ever lucubrating mind is apparent in all he has done. The characteristic style follows naturally. Recognition through the Nobel Prize thus came as no surprise.

3. Ausgleich durch einen Einblick in Russell's Gedankenwelt: Nachdruck des aus 81 Einzel-Titeln
bestehenden Inhaltsverzeichnisses und der
seinen XVII Sammel-Titeln beigegebenen Kurz-
Kommentaren aus "The Basic Writings of Bertrand Russell"; 1961, New York: Simon & Schuster; London: Allen & Unwin; 736 S. Von diesem Buch gibt es keine deutsche Gesamtaus-
gabe. Bei allen 81 Einzel-Titeln wird auf
die entsprechende Bibliographie-Nr. verwie-
sen, und diejenigen Titel, die ins Deutsche
übersetzt worden sind, erhielten ein (d)-
Kennzeichen.

I.
Autobiographisches
Die Klarheit und Prägnanz, die man von Russell's Arbeiten erwartet, werden durch seinen
eignen Hinweis auf seinen Versuch verdeutlicht,
die anschaulichen Methoden der Mathematik und
Wissenschaft auf Gebiete zu übertragen, auf die
gewöhnlich eine vage, spekulative Betrachtung
angewandt wird. Eine charakteristische autobio-
graphische Aussage lautet:"Ich liebe Präzision.
Ich liebe scharfe Umrisse. Ich hasse verschwom-
mene Unklarheiten."
Er berichtet, daß er schon im Alter von elf
Jahren sich weigerte, etwas hinzunehmen, was
Tradition so unzerstörbar wie Granit erscheinen
ließ. Sein Bruder hatte eingewilligt, ihm Geometrie zu lehren, die, so hatte Russell gehört,
"Dinge bewiese". Als sein Bruder ihm erklärte,
daß Euklid's Axiome nicht bewiesen werden können, verschwand beinahe seine ganze Hoffnung,
einiges zuverlässiges Wissen zu finden.

1. Meine religiösen Erinnerungen . . . .
2. Meine geistige Entwicklung . . . . . .
3. Anpassung: Ein autobiographischer Abriß
4. Warum ich mich mit Philosophie befasse

II.
Der Nobelpreisträger für Literatur
(Essayist und Kurzgeschichtenschreiber)
Wenige Nobelpreisträger für Literatur haben
eine so aufschlußreiche Darstellung von der
Art und Weise ihres Schreibens gegeben, wie es
hier geschieht. Russell entfaltet immer wieder
eine Meisterschaft des Details und eine Präzision der Darstellung, die keinen Zweifel an
seinem Standpunkt erlaubt, ob man übereinstimmt
oder nicht übereinstimmt. Die Klarheit des Denkens seines allzeit gelehrten Verstandes ist,
in allem was er getan hat, offenkundig. Der
charakteristische Stil geht daraus wie natürlich hervor. Die Anerkennung durch den Nobelpreis kam also nicht überraschend.

While Russell asserts that he no longer thinks well of his most popular essay, "A Free Man's Worship", no Russell anthology would be complete without it and an anthology of the best twentieth-century prose would be hard put to justify its exclusion.

III.
The Philosopher of Language

Closely related to the advances made in contemporary thought in the fields of logic and mathematical philosophy are the increasingly important strides made in semantics and the philosophy of language. Russell has played a prominent and pivotal part in this advance, although he is not in accord with some of the lengths to which the analytic philosophers have gone.

IV.
The Logician and Philosopher of Mathematics

The impact of "Principia Mathematica" on twentieth-century mathematics, logic, and philosophy was both enormous and paradoxical. On the one hand, this ten-year cooperative labour (Russell/Whitehead), in its aim to codify relational inferences, is viewed as one of the world's greatest contributions to knowledge and, on the other hand, there are few, outside of professional specialists, who have read, much less understood, particularly the latter parts of this work. At Russell's own suggestion, we include here none of the symbolic expositions, but merely introductory sections which are explanatory of the scope and aim of the work.

The reduction of mathematics to logic and the critical view of traditional logic are the theme of Russell's other important works in the field as illustrated here. We have also given one side of one of the most provocative running debates in contemporary philosophic literature, that between Russell and J. Dewey.

Während Russell behauptet, daß er sein populärstes Essay "Eines freien Mannes Gottesdienst" nicht mehr für gut hält, würde keine Russell-Anthologie ohne dieses Essay vollständig sein und eine Anthologie der besten Prosa des 20. Jahrhunderts könnte sein Fehlen schwer rechtfertigen.

III.
Der Sprachphilosoph

Nah verwandt mit den Fortschritten, die im zeitgenössischen Denken im Bereich der Logik und der mathematischen Philosophie gemacht wurden, sind die zunehmend wichtiger werdenden Schritte in der Semantik und der Sprachphilosophie. Russell hat bei diesen Fortschritten eine prominente und angelpunktbildende Rolle gespielt, obwohl er mit mancher Ansicht, zu der analytische Philosophen kamen, nicht übereinstimmte.

IV.
Der Logiker und Philosoph der Mathematik

Die Einwirkung der "Principia Mathematica" auf die Mathematik, Logik und Philosophie des 20. Jahrhunderts war sowohl enorm als auch paradox. Einerseits wird diese zehnjährige Zusammenarbeit (Russell/Whitehead), in ihrer Absicht, Beziehungsschlüsse zusammenzufassen, als einer der Welt größten Beiträge zum Wissen angesehen, andererseits gibt es wenige, außer professionelle Spezialisten, die besonders die letzten Teile dieses Werkes gelesen, geschweige denn es verstanden haben. Auf Russell's eigenen Vorschlag hin bringen wir hier keine der symbolischen Darstellungen, sondern lediglich einführende Teile, die den Bereich und das Ziel des Werkes erklären.

Die Rückführung der Mathematik zur Logik und die kritische Sicht traditioneller Logik sind das Thema von Russell's anderen Hauptarbeiten in dem hier aufgezeigten Bereich. Außerdem geben wir eine der herausfordernsten Debatten in der zeitgenössischen philosophischen Literatur wieder, die zwischen Russell und John Dewey.

V.

The Epistemologist

Since ancient Greece, theories of knowledge have run the gamut between the crudely simple and the ultra imaginative. Before the nineteenth century, the attempt to humanize the cosmos had been the preoccupation of almost every major philosopher. The impact of science has changed this view. Modern theories of knowledge are no longer concerned with inventing comforting answers but rather with the problem of gaining new insights.

A study of Russell's theories in the field of epistemology reveals an important aspect of his philosophic contributions. His concern in this area is indicative of his continued interest in the variety of views presented in this century as is evidenced by the three contributions which follow, taken from works spanning over forty years. They also show once more the dynamics of continued reflection as opposed to static adherence to a view originally advanced.

VI.

The Metaphysician

Since the beginning of Western Civilization philosophers have been vitally concerned with the enormous questions raised by metaphysics. Few philosophers have, however, supplied even a brief glimpse of the vast problems to be explored. Perhaps Russell's most distinctive contribution to metaphysics is his novel view of "Atomism".

V.
Der Erkenntnistheoretiker

Seit dem alten Griechenland wetteifert alles von der unreif-einfachen bis zur übertrieben ideenreichen Theorie des Wissens miteinander. Vor dem 19.Jahrhundert war der Versuch, den Kosmos menschlicher zu machen, die Haupttätigkeit von fast jedem bedeutenden Philosophen gewesen. Die Einwirkung der Wissenschaft hat diese Sicht geändert. Moderne Theorien des Wissens befassen sich nicht länger damit, tröstliche Antworten zu finden, sondern vielmehr mit dem Problem, neue Einsichten zu erringen.

Ein Studium von Russell's Theorien im Bereich der Epistemologie (Erkenntnistheorie) enthüllt einen wichtigen Aspekt seiner philosophischen Beiträge. Seine Beschäftigung mit diesem Bereich zeigt ein fortgesetztes Interesse an der Vielfalt der Ansichten dieses Jahrhunderts, wie die drei folgenden Beiträge beweisen, entnommen aus Werken einer Zeitspanne von über vierzig Jahren. Sie zeigen noch einmal die Dynamik fortgesetzter Überlegungen im Gegensatz zum statischen Festhalten an ursprünglich formulierten Ansichten.

VI.
Der Metaphysiker

Seit dem Beginn westlicher Zivilisation haben sich die Philosophen intensiv mit den von der Metaphysik aufgeworfenen bedeutungsvollen Fragen befaßt. Wenige Philosophen jedoch haben auch nur einen flüchtigen Einblick in die zu erforschenden riesigen Probleme vermittelt. Vielleicht ist Russells neue Ansicht des "Atomismus" sein bezeichnendster Beitrag zur Metaphysik.

While critics have taken him to task for his refusal to abandon this view, none has yet succeeded in finding convincing arguments against his logical atomism. The last of the three selections which follow is particulary searching and revelatory of Russell's fundamental approach.

VII.
Historian of Philosophy
"Many histories of philosophy exist and I should not wish to add one the their number", wrote Russell in the preface to his own "A History of Western Philosophy", but he wrote that monumental survey and followed it by the more recent, more current, "Wisdom of the West". In both of these volumes and in other essays in the field, he not only ably expounds what each philosopher thought but also exhibits what a leading philosopher thinks of each philosopher reviewed.
Historians of philosophy in the past have been prone to make philosophy even more dull in its historical setting than it already appeared in its technical attire. Russell's works succeed in showing that philosophy can be both interesting and instructive to the general reader.

VIII.
The Psychologist
Certainly no psychologist today takes seriously the Platonic doctrine that there is a sharp and irreducible dichotomy between mind and matter. The ancient view that there is an absolute division between these two entities finds no support in modern physics and psychology. Both mind and matter ars outmoded terms which should be abandoned. Russells own view is that both are composed of groups or series of events.

Während Kritiker ihn wegen seiner Weigerung, diesen Standpunkt aufzugeben, Vorwürfe machten, hat bislang keiner ein überzeugendes Argument gegen diesen logischen Atomismus gefunden. Der letzte von den drei folgenden Abschnitten ist besonders tiefgründig und erschließt Russell's fundamentale Methode.

VII.
Historiker der Philosophie

"Es existieren viele Geschichten der Philosophie, und es sollte nicht meine Absicht sein, noch eine hinzuzufügen", schrieb Russell im Vorwort seiner eigenen "Philosophie des Abendlandes", jedoch - er schrieb diesen monumentalen Überblick und ließ das neuere, aktuellere "Denker des Abendlandes" folgen. In beiden Werken und in anderen Essays über dieses Gebiet erklärt er nicht nur gekonnt, was jeder Philosoph dachte, sondern zeigt auch, was ein führender Philosoph über jeden der besprochenen Philosophen denkt.

Historiker der Philosophie haben in der Vergangenheit dazu geneigt, die Philosophie in ihrer historischen Entwicklung noch schwerverständlicher darzustellen, als sie in ihrem fachlichen Gewand schon ist. Russell's Arbeiten zeigten erfolgreich, daß Philosophie sowohl interessant als auch lehrreich für den allgemeinen Leser sein kann.

VIII.
Der Psychologe

Sicherlich nimmt kein heutiger Psychologe die platonische Doktrin ernst, daß es eine scharfe und nicht verwandelbare Zweiteilung zwischen Geist und Materie gibt. Die alte Ansicht, daß es eine absolute Trennung zwischen diesen beiden Bereichen gibt, findet in der modernen Physik und Psychologie keine Unterstützung. Sowohl Geist als auch Materie sind unmoderne Begriffe, die man aufgeben sollte. Russell's eigene Ansicht ist, daß beide aus Gruppen oder Serien von Ereignissen zusammengesetzt sind.

A mind and a piece of matter, therefore, are structurally the same. The only significant difference is that there is a variance in arrangement, like considering people according to geographical order or chronological order. Some samples of his application of psychological theory follow.

IX.
The Moral Philosopher

Perhaps no philosopher in modern times has been subject to more scathing criticism of his views on ethics than Russell. Few major thinkers have, however, dared to utter opinions that were so out of tune with current stereotyped beliefs. Whether history will later confirm or deny the wisdom of Russell's views on ethics, his desire to champion unpopular ideas and to question any idea which seemed irrational deserves admiration. Those who see morality as a settled body of knowledge will obviously derive no pleasure from reading Russell's terse criticism of traditional beliefs, many of which have deep roots in ancient superstitious.

It is, of course, on the topic of sex that Russell has encountered most unfavourable criticism for here he strikes deeply at superstitions. But sex is not the whole subject-matter of ethics as the selections which follow amply demonstrate. Russell, as a scientific humanist, has had deep concern for the problems of human conduct and the theories of their solution for the individual and society, the more so since he finds these solutions outside of organized religion. In this field of moral theory, we finde once more a gradual change and development of viewpoint as his ideas of language, logic and philosophy in general have altered over the years.

Ein Geist und ein Stück Materie sind daher struk-
turell das Gleiche. Der einzige bedeutsame Un-
terschied ist, daß es eine Abweichung in der
Anordnung gibt, wie es z. B. Menschen nach
geographischer oder chronologischer Ordnung zu
betrachten. Einige Proben von Russell's Anwendung der psychologischen Theorie folgen.

IX.
Der Moralphilosoph

Wahrscheinlich ist in neuerer Zeit kein Philosoph wegen seiner Ansichten über Ethik mehr
Gegenstand verletzender Kritik gewesen, als
Russell. Wenige bedeutende Denker haben es jedoch gewagt, Meinungen zu äußern, die mit dem
zeitgenössischen stereotypen Glauben so wenig
übereinstimmten. Ob nun die Geschichte später
die Weisheit der Ansichten Russell's über Ethik
bestätigt oder verneint, sein Verlangen, unpo-
puläre Ideen zu verteidigen und jede Idee, die
vernunftwidrig erscheint, zu bezweifeln, ver-
dient Bewunderung. Jene, die Moral als einen
festen Bestandteil des Wissens ansehen, werden
offensichtlich wenig Freude daran haben, Russell's starke Kritik an traditionellen Glau-
bensäußerungen, von denen viele ihre tiefen
Wurzeln in altem Aberglauben haben, zu lesen.
Es ist natürlich, daß Russell bei dem Thema
Sex auf die meiste ungünstige Kritik gestoßen
ist, da er hier auf tiefen Aberglauben trifft.
Aber Sex ist nicht das ganze Thema der Ethik,
wie die folgende Auswahl ausführlich demon-
striert. Russell, als wissenschaftlicher Humanist, zeigte tiefes Interesse für die Probleme
menschlichen Verhaltens und für die Theorien
über deren Lösung für das Individuum und die Gesellschaft, um so mehr, als er diese Lösungen außerhalb der institutionellen Religion fand. In
diesem Bereich der Moraltheorie finden noch
einmal eine allmähliche Änderung und Entwicklung von Ansichten statt, weil sich im Laufe
der Jahre seine Ideen über Sprache, Logik und
Philosophie im allgemeinen geändert haben.

X.
The Philosopher of Education

Theories and practices in education have been both varied and numerous. Any philosophy of education will, however, ultimately be tested by the degree to which it coincides with objective evidence of the worth of its proffered ideal.

The selections that follow are indicative of the import of Russell's philosophy of education and the great value Russell places upon the function of a teacher and the vital significance of a sound education in a troubled world.

XI.
The Philosopher of Politics

Few technical philosophers have shown such keen insight and astute observance of political theories and trends as Russell. The title of his Nobel Prize Acceptance Speech was "Politically Important Desires", and as the "New York Times" observed, it was "as witty as it was penetrating".

Russell, even in his earliest writings, displayed an uncanny foresight in being able to predict with remarkable accuracy events that would follow. In his first book, "German Social Democracy", published in 1896, he acutely observed the seeds which later developed into Germany's future of dictatorship and war. This book showed what was to become Russell's most characteristic asset, his ability to discuss any problem in a scientific, objective and dispassionate way. When Russell changed his views, as he frequently did, he always held steadfastly to the belief that any approximation of truth can only be obtained by examining the available evidence at the moment.

The analysis of power has been Russell's key concept in the theory of politics. To his thinking in this area he has brought to bear his critical acumen which serves to point to the fallacious theories that abound in Fascism and Communism.

X.
Der Pädagoge

Theorien und Praktiken der Erziehung waren
sowohl unterschiedlich als auch zahlreich.
Gleichwohl wird jede Erziehungsphilosophie zu
guter letzt daran gemessen, inwieweit sie durch
objektiven Beweis mit dem Wert des von ihr an-
gebotenen Ideals übereinstimmt.

Die folgenden Abschnitte sind bezeichnend
für die Bedeutung von Russell's Erziehungsphilosophie und für den großen Wert, den Russell
der Funktion einer Lehrperson zuschreibt sowie
für die vitale Bedeutung einer soliden Erziehung in einer unruhigen Welt.

XI.
Der Politologe

Wenige Fachphilosophen haben eine so große
Einsicht in und scharfsinnige Beobachtung von
politischen Theorien und Richtungen gezeigt
wie Russell. Der Titel seiner Rede anläßlich der
Annahme des Nobelpreises lautete "Politisch
bedeutsame Wünsche" und war, wie die 'New York
Times' bemerkte, "ebenso geistreich wie ein-
dringlich".

Schon in seinen frühesten Schriften entfal-
tete Russell eine unheimliche Fähigkeit, kom-
mende Ereignisse mit bemerkenswerter Genauig-
keit vorauszusagen. In seinem ersten Buch "Die
Deutsche Sozialdemokratie", 1896 publiziert,
bemerkte er scharfsinnig den Keim, aus dem später in Deutschland Diktatur und Krieg hervor-
gehen sollte. Dieses Buch zeigte, was Russell's
charakteristischer Aktivposten werden sollte,
seine Fähigkeit, jedes Problem in einer wissenschaftlichen, objektiven und leidenschaftslo-
sen Weise zu diskutieren. Wenn Russell seine
Ansichten änderte, was er häufig tat, hielt er
stets an dem Glauben fest, daß jede Annäherung
an die Wahrheit nur durch das Untersuchen der
augenblicklich verfügbaren Beweise erreicht
werden kann.

Die Analyse der Macht war Russells Schlüssel-
konzept in der Theorie der Politik. Bei seinen Gedanken auf diesem Gebiet hat er seinen kritischen
Scharfsinn angewandt, der dazu diente, die trüge-
rischen Theorien hervorzuheben, die im Faschismus und Kommunismus reichlich vorhanden sind.

He has long been outspoken not only as a political theorist but as an analyst of the practical import of these theories in the daily political scene.

XII.
The Philosopher in the Field of Economics

Despite the fact that Russell has made no major contribution to economic theory his views on economics have not gone unnoticed. As far back as 1896, when his first hostile criticism of Marx was published, Russell had shown a keen interest in economic problems. He has repeatedly stressed the fact that an exclusively economic point of view is an oversimplification.

Although some of his views have undergone "repeated changes", as he admits in his preface to this volume ("The Basic Writings of Bertrand Russell"), he has at times held steadfast to some of his earlier views. For example, he has always disagreed with Marx's theory of surplus value and his rigid doctrine that all historical events have been motivated by class conflicts.

The selections that follow indicate his recognition of the psychological and other factors which bear upon man's activities in the economic as well as other spheres.

XIII.
The Philosopher of History

Despite Russell's own admission that he is not a professional historian and that he approaches the subject with "considerable trepidation", he does show keen insight into some of the crucial problems of history. Russell was intensely interested in history as a youth and ever kept alive this fascination in later life. With such an intense interest in the panorama of history, it is not surprising to find the philosopher early turning to the philosophy of history.

Schon frühzeitig war er freimütig, nicht nur
als politischer Theoretiker, sondern auch als
Analytiker der praktischen Bedeutung dieser
Theorien in der Tagespolitik.

XII.
Der Philosoph auf dem Gebiete der Wirtschaft

Trotz der Tatsache, daß Russell keinen be-
deutenderen Beitrag zur Wirtschaftstheorie geleistet hat, ist seine Meinung darüber nicht
unbemerkt geblieben. Zurück bis 1896, als seine erste feindliche Kritik an Marx publiziert
wurde, zeigte Russell ein eifriges Interesse
an wirtschaftlichen Problemen. Er hat wieder-
holt die Tatsache unterstrichen, daß ein ausschließlich wirtschaftlicher Gesichtspunkt eine übertriebene Gleichmacherei sei.

Obwohl sich manche seiner Auffassungen "wie-
derholt änderten", wie er im Vorwort dieses
Buches ("The Basic Writings of Bertrand Russell")
zugibt, gab es Zeiten, in denen er unerschüt-
terlich an einigen früheren Standpunkten fest-
hielt. Zum Beispiel hat er mit der Mehrwert-
theorie von Marx und dessen starrer Doktrin, daß
alle historischen Ereignisse durch Klassenkon-
flikte motiviert sind, nie übereingestimmt.

Die folgende Auswahl zeigt seine Anerkennung
von psychologischen und anderen Einwirkungen,
die menschliche Aktivitäten sowohl in der Wirtschaft als auch auf anderen Gebieten beein-
flussen.

XIII.
Der Geschichtsphilosoph

Trotz Russell's eigenem Zugeständnis, daß
er kein professioneller Historiker sei und sich
dem Thema mit "beträchtlichem Zittern" nähert,
zeigt er einen scharfen Einblick in einige ent-
scheidende Probleme der Geschichte. Russell war
als junger Mensch an Geschichte sehr interessiert
und ihre Faszination hielt auch in seinem späteren Leben an. Bei einem so intensiven Interesse am Geschichtspanorama überrascht es nicht,
daß sich der Philosoph früh der Geschichts-
philosophie zuwandte.

In addition to this interest in history for philosophers of history, Russell thinks that history should be of concern not only to academicians but that it should be "an essential part of the furniture" of any educated mind. The man whose interests are governed by the short span between his birth and death has a myopic vision and limitation of outlook. On the other hand, one with a sense of history can foresee the tragedy of repeated blunders and face with stoic endurance the follies of the present. The selections that follow also show Russell's critical appraisal of theories of history and the practice of the writing of history.

XIV.
The Philosopher of Culture: East and West

Philosophers for the most part are not world travellers. Few have observed, first hand, the atmosphere of even their own continent; Kant, for instance, never travelled more than forty miles beyond the limits of his native Königsberg. Among the major philosophers of the twentieth century, few have travelled as extensively and understood so well the diverse economic and political problems of culture East and West.

Russell has taught and lectured on four continents. Following his travels in Russia, Japan and China in the early twenties and his frequent trips and extended stays in the United States, he wrote informatively of what he saw and critically of what each civilization boded.

XV.
The Philosopher of Religion

The finest minds will always be attracted to ultimate questions that remain unsolved. Lesser minds are content with "answers" to questions for which there is no evidence.

Since his youth, Russell has found no reason to change his agnostic position in religion. It was while reading John Stuart Mill's "Autobiography" at the age of eighteen that he became convinced of the fallacy in the argument of the First Cause.

Außer diesem Interesse der Geschichtsphilosophen an Geschichte, ist es Russell's Ansicht, daß Geschichte nicht nur eine Angelegenheit für Akademiker ist, sondern daß sie auch "ein wesentlicher Teil der Ausstattung" jedes gebildeten Geistes sein sollte. Dem Menschen, dessen Interessen durch die kurze Spanne zwischen Geburt und Tod gelenkt werden, bleibt für seine Auffassungen nur eine kurze Einsicht und Begrenzung. Andererseits kann ein Mensch mit Sinn für Geschichte die Tragödie wiederholter Fehler voraussehen und den Torheiten der Gegenwart mit gleichmütiger Geduld entgegensehen. Die folgende Auswahl zeigt auch Russell's kritische Abschätzung der Geschichtstheorien und die Praxis der Geschichtsschreibung.

XIV.
Der Kulturphilosoph: Ost und West

Philosophen sind meist keine Weltreisenden. Wenige haben die Atmosphäre selbst ihres eigenen Kontinents beobachtet. Kant z. B. reiste niemals weiter als vierzig Meilen außerhalb der Grenzen seiner Heimatstadt Königsberg. Unter den größten Philosophen des 20. Jahrhunderts sind wenige ausgedehnt gereist, um die verschiedenen wirtschaftlichen und politischen Probleme der östlichen und westlichen Kultur gut zu verstehen.

Russell hat in vier Kontinenten gelehrt und Vorlesungen gehalten. Im Anschluß an seine Reisen nach Rußland, Japan und China in den frühen 20er Jahren und an seine häufigen Trips u. ausgedehnten Aufenthalte in den USA, schrieb er informativ von dem, was er sah, und kritisch von dem Zukünftigen jeder Zivilisation.

XV.
Der Religionsphilosoph

Die gebildesten Geister werden immer durch letzte, ungelöst gebliebene Fragen angezogen. Kleinere Geister sind mit "Antworten" zufrieden, für die keine Beweise vorliegen.

Seit seiner Jugend fand Russell keinen Grund, seinen agnostischen Standpunkt über Religion zu ändern. Als er im Alter von achtzehn Jahren John Stuart Mill's "Autobiographie" las, wurde er von dem Irrtum in der Beweisführung über die erste Ursache überzeugt.

His concern with religious problems and the philosophy of religion has been active over the years.

Any critic of religion is, of course, prone to attack from all sides. What is particularly significant perhaps is that religious apologists are especially fervent in their attacks upon eminent intellectuals. Philosophers in the twentieth century have, for the most part, tended to avoid expressing any view which touched the core of religious sensitivity. Whether thinkers like Russell are right or wrong, perhaps only history can decide. Anyone who can keep an open mind, or who is permitted to keep an open mind, in this controversial area can gain much from the frank and fearless articles Russell has contributed to the subject.

XVI.
The Philosopher and Expositor of Science

Philosophers in our time are no longer concerned with inventing vast systems of philosophy from crude imagination. Since the seventeenth century science has gradually whittled away the mortar between the bricks of the foundations erected by the dogmatic philosophers. Perhaps philosophic progress will always lag behind scientific achievements because of the kind of problems with which philosophy is concerned. But one thing now seems clear: advance in philosophy will probably be based upon the same kind of evidence that has made science so successful. In the beginning philosophy prodded science, now science prods philosophy.

Russell, as the selections that follow indicate, has ever been conscious of this relationship between science and philosophy, but he also has ever been mindful of the limitations of science and the ethical import of its application. He is one of our most lucid expositors of the far reaches of contemporary scientific theory.

Sein Interesse an religiösen Problemen und der Religionsphilosophie war über Jahre hinweg aktiv.

Jeder Kritiker der Religion ist natürlich Angriffen von allen Seiten ausgesetzt. Besonders bedeutend ist vielleicht, daß Religionsverteidiger in ihren Angriffen gegen hervorragende Intellektuelle außergewöhnlich heiß sind. Philosophen des 20. Jahrhunderts haben zumeist jede Ansicht vermieden, die den Kern religiöser Empfindlichkeit berührte. Ob Denker wie Russell recht oder unrecht haben, kann vielleicht nur die Geschichte entscheiden. Jeder, der einen offenen Geist bewahrt, oder dem erlaubt ist, einen offenen Geist zu bewahren, kann von den freien und furchtlosen Artikeln, die Russell diesem strittigen Gebiet gewidmet hat, viel lernen.

XVI.
Der Philosoph und Naturwissenschaftler

Philosophen unserer Zeit befassen sich nicht mehr damit, weite philosophische Systeme aus unreifen Einbildungen zu ersinnen. Seit dem 17. Jahrhundert hat die Wissenschaft nach und nach den Mörtel zwischen den durch dogmatische Philosophen errichteten Fundamentsteinen geschwächt. Vielleicht wird philosophischer Fortschritt immer hinter wissenschaftlichen Erkenntnissen zurückbleiben aufgrund der Problemart, mit der die Philosophie sich befaßt. Aber eines scheint jetzt klar: Fortschritt in der Philosophie wird wahrscheinlich auf derselben Art von Beweisen basieren, die die Wissenschaft so erfolgreich machten. In ihren Anfängen trieb die Philosophie die Wissenschaft voran, jetzt treibt die Wissenschaft die Philosophie voran.

Russell hat, wie die folgende Auswahl zeigt, immer bewußt auf diese Verwandtschaft zwischen Philosophie und Wissenschaft hingewiesen, aber er war sich auch immer der Begrenzung der Wissenschaft und der ethischen Bedeutung ihrer Anwendung bewußt. Er ist einer unserer klarsten Darsteller der großen Reichweite heutiger wissenschaftlicher Theorien.

XVII.
The Analyst of International Affairs
　　　　　Any cursory attempt to assess international
affairs is, of course, only indulged in by the
uneducated. The analyst of world problems in
the second half of the twentieth century is
faced with a peculiar dilemma. The turbulence
of the period and the unpredictability of human
behaviour make even the most exhaustive attempt
exceedingly uncertain. Mistakes in science and
business are both costly and deplorable but
continued mistakes in international affairs
today could result in the destruction of civilization as we know it.
　　　　Russell has, perhaps more than other thinkers
in our time, successfully seen through the maze
of conflicting fanaticisms, and with his
characteristic sobriety pointed out fallacies
in the arguments of proposed saviours. He was
among the earliest of severe critics of Marxism
and of its Soviet manifestations, but not
without a recognition of the realities which
require a world perspective for the solution
of the problems confronting us in this nuclear
age.

XVII.
Der Analytiker internationaler Affären

      Jede oberflächliche Einschätzung internationaler Vorgänge geschieht natürlich nur durch Ungebildete. Der Analytiker von Weltproblemen wird in der zweiten Hälfte des 20. Jahrhunderts einem seltsamen Dilemma gegenübergestellt. Die Turbulenz der Zeit und das unberechenbare menschliche Verhalten machen selbst den erschöpfendsten Versuch außerordentlich unzuverlässig. Irrtümer in Wissenschaft und Wirtschaft sind sowohl kostspielig als auch beklagenswert, aber fortgesetzte Fehler in internationalen Affären könnten heute die Zerstörung der uns vertrauten Zivilisation zur Folge haben.

      Russell hat, vielleicht mehr als andere Denker unserer Zeit, erfolgreich durch das Labyrinth fanatischer Auffassungen geblickt, und mit seiner charakteristischen Nüchternheit wies er auf die Trugschlüsse in den Argumenten erhoffter Retter hin. Er war einer der frühesten ernsthaften Kritiker des Marxismus und seiner sowjetischen Manifestationen, aber nicht ohne Anerkennung der Realitäten, die für die Lösung der Probleme, denen wir in diesem Atomzeitalter gegenübergestellt sind, Weltperspektiven verlangen.

4th compensation
by orientative aids on individual titles:

Commentaries to some of the main titles within the following bibliography and was compiled from "Bertrand Russell. The Passionate Sceptic." by Alan Wood (London 1956) with the exception of a few other sources.

Russell himself mentions the book by Alan Wood in his prefatory note to his work "My Philosophical Development" (London 1959): "Mr. Alan Wood, whose book 'The Passionate Sceptic' won widespread and well-deserved applause ..."

4. Ausgleich

durch Orientierungshilfen zu Einzel-Titeln:

Kommentare zu einigen Haupt-Titeln innerhalb der nachfolgenden Bibliographie, bis auf wenige Ausnahmen zusammengestellt aus "Bertrand Russell, Skeptiker aus Leidenschaft" von Alan Wood (Thun, München 1959).

Russell erwähnt das Buch von Alan Wood in seiner Vorbemerkung zu seinem Werk "Philosophie. Die Entwicklung meines Denkens." (München 1973): "Mr. Alan Wood, dessen Buch 'Skeptiker aus Leidenschaft' so verbreiteten und verdienten Beifall fand ..."

BIBLIOGRAPHIE

BIBLIOGRAPHY

Review of G. Heymans'
"Die Gesetze und Elemente
des Wissenschaftlichen Denkens"

1895 in "Mind", vol. 4, p. 245-249 . . . . 001.00

German Social Democracy
as a Lesson in Political Tactics

1896 (Feb. 14) Lecture to the Fabian Soc., London.
Unpublished manuscript in Russell Archives,
McMaster University, Hamilton/Ontario. 18 pp. 002.01

    T r a n s l a t i o n s
    Deutsch .... 1972 in BN 703/I:1 . . . . 002.02

The A Priori in Geometry

1896 in "Proceedings Aristotelian Society",
    vol. 3, p. 97-112
    London: Williams & Norgate 003.00

The Logic of Geometry

1896 in "Mind", vol. 5, p. 1-23 . . . . 004.00

Review of G. Lechalas'
"Étude sur l'espace et le temps"

1896 in "Mind", vol. 5, p. 128 . . . . 005.00

Review of A. Hannequin's '
"Essai critique sur l'hypothese des atoms
dans la Science contemporaine"

1896 in "Mind", vol. 5, p. 410-417 . . . . 006.00

GERMAN SOCIAL DEMOCRACY

1896 London, New York, Bombay: Longmans, Green &
    Company. 204 pp. 007.01
    C o n t e n t s
    I. Marx and the Theoretic Basis of the Social
    Democracy. II. Lassalle. III. History of
    German Socialism from the Death of Lassalle
    to the Passing of the Exceptional Law, 1878.
    IV. Social Democracy under the Exceptional
    Law, 1878-1890. V. Organization, Agitation,
    Tactics, and Programme of Social Democracy
    since the Fall of the Socialist Law. VI. The
    Present Position of Social Democracy.
    Appendix: Social Democracy and the Woman
    Question in Germany by Alys Russell.

    C o m m e n t a r y
    Russell and his wife made two visits to Ger-
    many in 1895, and the second was largely with
    the object of studying the German Socialist
    movement. This was a rather unconventional.

if not shocking, interest for a young English aristocrat. After returning to England he reported his conclusions in a lecture to the Fabian Society (BN 2), and in a series of six lectures to the newly-foundet "London School of Economics" (Feb./Mar. 1896) the latter being published in 1896 as "German Social Democracy", the first on the long list of Russell's books. These different lectures still have a fascinating interest to-day. It is not only that they foreshadow, with uncanny foresight, Germany's future of dictatorship and war. They are a characteristic example of the attempt to discuss any political problem in a scientific, rational and dispassionate way.

K o m m e n t a r
Russell und seine Frau reisten 1895 zweimal nach Deutschland, das zweitemal hauptsächlich in der Absicht, die deutsche sozialistische Bewegung zu studieren. Das war ein recht ungewöhnliches, wenn nicht sogar empörendes Interesse für einen jungen englischen Aristokraten. Nach seiner Rückkehr nach England berichtete Russell der Fabian Society in einer Vorlesung (BN 2) über seine Schlußfolgerungen. In der neugegründeten "London School of Economics" hielt er eine Reihe von sechs Vorträgen (Februar/März 1896); diese letztgenannten wurden 1896 als "German Social Democracy" veröffentlicht, das erste auf der langen Liste von Russell's Büchern. Diese verschiedenen Vorlesungen sind auch heute noch von packendem Interesse. Nicht nur, weil sie in geheimnisvoller Vorahnung die Schatten von Deutschlands diktatorischer und kriegerischer Zukunft sichtbar machen. Sie sind ein scharf geprägtes Beispiel für den Versuch, ein politisches Problem in wissenschaftlicher, vernünftiger und leidenschaftsloser Art zu diskutieren.

R e p r i n t s
1965 London: Allen & Unwin 007.02
1965 New York: Simon & Schuster 007.03

T r a n s l a t i o n s
Chinesisch:
    "Deguo shehui minzhudang"
    (Im Bestand des Instituts für Philosophie der Akademie für Sozialwissenschaften in Peking. Erscheinungsort und -jahr waren nicht zu ermitteln.) 007.04

Deutsch:
Auszüge
1972 in BN 703/I:2 . . . . 007.05
"Die deutsche Sozialdemokratie"
, Herausgegeben und vollständig übersetzt
von Achim von Borries
1978 Bonn: Verlag J. H. W. Dietz Nachf. 007.06
I n h a l t
Einleitung. I. Marx und die demokratische Grundlage der Sozialdemokratie.
II. Lassalle. III. Die Geschichte der
deutschen Sozialdemokratie vom Tode
Lassalles bis zum Erlaß des Ausnahme-
gesetzes. IV. Das Ausnahmegesetz. V.
Organisation, Agitation, Taktik und
Programm der Sozialdemokratie seit dem
Fall des Sozialistengesetzes. VI. Die
derzeitige Position der Sozialdemokratie. Anhang: (a) Die Sozialdemokratie
und die Frauenfrage in Deutschland von
Alys Russell. (b) Die deutsche Sozialdemokratie in englischer Beleuchtung
von Eduard Bernstein.
Italienisch:
"La Socialdemocrazia Tedesca"
Tr.: Jean Sanders
1970 Rom: Newton Compton Editori . . . 007.07
Russisch:
"Germanskaja social-demokratija"
1906 St. Petersburg: Nevskij kn. skl. 007.08
"Očerki iz istorii germanskoj social-
demokratičeskoj rabočej partii: Šest
lekcij."
1906 St. Petersburg 007.09

Review of L. Couturat's
"De l'infini mathematique"
1897 in "Mind", vol. 6, p. 112-119 . . . . 008.00

On the Relations of Number and Quantity
1897 in "Mind", vol. 6, p. 326-341 . . . . 009.00

AN ESSAY ON THE FOUNDATIONS OF GEOMETRY
1897 Cambridge: University Press. XVI, 201 pp. . 010.01
C o n t e n t s
Introduction. Our Problem Defined by its Re-
lation to Logic, Psychology and Mathematics.
I. A Short History of Metageometry. II.
Critical Account of Some Previous Philo-
sophical Theories of Geometry. III: A. The
Axioms of Projective Geometry. B. The Axioms
of Metrical Geometry. IV. Philosophical
Consequences.

Commentary
In 1896 the Russells went to America for some
months. He visited Walt Whitman's house and
gave lectures at the John Hopkins University
and Bry Mawr, based on his Dissertation on
"The Foundations of Geometry" (Aug. 1895).
Russell revised nad published the Dissertation under the title "An Essay on the Foundations of Geometry" in 1897. After his
travels in Germany and America he settled
down in England, living mostly in a small
cottage in Sussex, and continued the laborious and austere work on mathematical philosophy which was the foundation of his fame.

Kommentar
Im Jahre 1896 gingen die Russells für einige
Monate nach Amerika. Er besuchte das Walt-
Whitman-Haus und hielt Vorlesungen an der
John-Hopkins-Universität und am Bryn Mawr
College; als Basis dieser Vorlesungen benutz-
te er seine Dissertation über "Die Grundlagen
der Geometrie" (August 1895). Russell über-
arbeitete und veröffentlichte die Dissertation 1897 unter dem Titel "An Essay on the
Foundations of Geometry". Nach seinen Reisen
in Deutschland und Amerika ließ er sich end-
gültig in England nieder; meist lebte er in
einem kleinen Häuschen in Sussex und setzte
dort die mühsame und spröde Arbeit an seiner
mathematischen Philosophie fort, die später
seinen Ruhm begründete.

Reprints
1956 New York: Dover Publications.
     Forword by Morris Kline. XVI, 201 pp. .   010.02

Translations
Französisch:
     "Essai sur les fondements
     de la Géométrie"
     Tr.: Albert Cadenat
     1901 Paris: Gautier-Villars 010.03
Spanisch:
     "Ensayo sobre los Fundamentos
     de la Geometria"
     1973 in BN 706 . . . .   010.04

Les Axiomes Propres à Euclide Sont-Ils Empiriques?

1898 in "Revue de Métaphysique et de Morale",
     vol. 6, p. 759-776 . . . .   011.00

Review of A. E. H. Love's "Theoretical Mechanics:
an Introductory Treatise on the Theory of Mechanics"

1898 in "Mind", vol. 7, p. 404-411 . . . .   012.00

Review of E. Goblot's
"Essai sur le classification des sciences"
1898 in "Mind", vol. 7, p. 567-568 . . . . 013.00

Sur les Axiomes de la Géométrie
1899 in "Revue de Métaphysique et de Morale",
vol. 7, p. 684-707 . . . . 014.00

Review of A. Meinong's
"Über die Bedeutung des Weberschen Gesetzes"
1899 in "Mind", vol. 8, p. 251-256 . . . . 015.00

The Classification of Relations
1899 Unpublished manuscript in Russell Archives,
McMaster University, Hamilton/Ontario. 20 pp. 016.00

Necessity and Possibility
1900 (ca.) Unpubl. manuscript in Russell Archives,
McMaster University, Hamilton/Ontario. 33 pp. 017.00

Review of J. Schulz's
"Psychologie der Axiome"
1900 in "Mind", vol. 9, p. 120-121 . . . . 018.00

A CRITICAL EXPOSITION OF THE PHILOSOPHY OF LEIBNIZ:
With an Appendix of leading Passages.
1900 Cambridge: University Press. XVI, 311 pp. . 019.01
     London: Clay 019.02
     C o n t e n t s
     Preface. I. Leibniz's Premisses. II. Ne-
     cessary Propositions and the Law of Contra-
     diction. III. Contingent Propositions and
     the Law of Sufficient Reason. IV. The Con-
     ception of Substance. V. The Identity of
     Indiscernibles and the Law of Continuity,
     Possibility and Compossibility. VI. Why Did
     Leibniz Believe in an External World? VII.
     The Philosophy of Matter: (a) As the Outcome
     of the Principles of Dynamics. VIII. The
     Philosophy of Matter: (b) As Explaining Con-
     tinuity and Extension. IX. The Labyrinth of
     the Continuum. X. The Theory of Space and
     Time and Its Relation to Monadism. XI. The
     Nature of Monads in General. XII. Soul and
     Body. XIII. Confused and Unconscious Per-
     ception. XIV. Leibniz's Theory of Knowledge.
     XV. Proofs of the Existence of God. XVI.
     Leibniz's Ethics. Appendix.

     C o m m e n t a r y
     Russell's main approach to philosophy re-
     mained through mathematics. Next there was a

fortunate accident. McTaggart, who was going to lecture on Leibniz at Cambridge in 1899, wanted to visit his family in New Zealand: and Russell acted as deputy, his lectures being published as "A Critical Exposition of the Philosophy of Leibniz" (later: "The Philosophy of Leibniz"). By sheer intellectual analysis in his study, he offered a completely original interpretation of Leibniz's philosophy; and soon afterwards had the happy experience of having his views confirmed by the discovery of some of Leibniz's manuscripts which had never been published.

K o m m e n t a r
Russell's wichtigster Weg zur Philosophie blieb die Mathematik. Als Nächstes kam ein glücklicher Zufall. McTaggart, der 1899 in Cambridge Vorlesungen über Leibniz halten sollte, wollte gern seine Familie in Neuseeland besuchen, und Russell wirkte als sein Vertreter. Seine Vorlesungen wurden als "A Critical Exposition of the Philosophy of Leibniz" (später: "The Philosophy of Leibniz") veröffentlicht. Einzig durch sein analysierendes Denken beim Studium bot er eine vollkommen originelle Darstellung der Leibnizschen Philosophie. Bald danach hatte er das beglückende Erlebnis, seine Auffassungen durch die Entdeckung einiger bisher unveröffentlichter Manuskripte von Leibniz bestätigt zu sehen.

R e p r i n t s
1937 London: Allen & Unwin, under the title
    "The Philosophy of Leibniz" 019.03
1937 New York: Macmillan 019.04
1951 New York: Humanities Press 019.05
1959 London: Allen & Unwin 019.06
1967 "   : "   " " 019.07
1975 "   : "   " " 019.08

T r a n s l a t i o n s
Französisch:
    "La philosophie de Leibniz"
    Tr.: J. et R. Ray
    1908 Paris: Alcan 019.09
    1970 Paris, New York: Gordon & Breach 019.10
Italienisch:
    "Esposizione critica
    della filosofia di Leibniz"
    Tr.: Elena Bonna Cucco
    1971 Mailand: Longanesi 019.11
    "La filosofia di Leibniz"
    Tr.: Roberto Cordeschi
    1972 Rom: Newton Comton Editori . . . 019.12

Japanisch:
"Leibniz no tetsugaku"
Tr.: Tadasu Hosokawa
1959 Tokio: Kobundo 019.13
Spanisch:
"Exposición Critica
de la Filosofia de Leibniz"
1973 in BN 706 . . . . 019.14

Recent Works on the Principles of Mathematics

1901 (July) in "The International Monthly",
vol. 4, p. 83-101 . . . . 020.01
1917 under the title
"Mathematics and the Metaphysicians"
in "Mysticism and Logic": V (BN 172) . 020.02

Translations
Deutsch . . . . . . 1952 in BN 172.22 . . . . . 020.03
Französisch ... 1922 in BN 172.23 . . . . . 020.04
Italienisch ... 1964 in BN 172.24 . . . . . 020.05
Japanisch . . . . . 1959 in BN 172.27 . . . . . 020.06
Portugiesisch . 1957 in BN 172.29 . . . . . 020.07
Schwedisch . . . . 1954 in BN 172.30 . . . . . 020.08
Spanisch . . . . . . 1973 in BN 172.31 = 706 . . 020.09
Sp./Catalanisch 1969 in BN 172.32 . . . . . 020.10
Türkisch . . . . . . 1970 in BN 172.34 . . . . . 020.11

L'idée de l'ordre et la position absolue dans l'espace et dans le temps

1901 Paris: Colin. III, p. 241-277 . . . . 021.00
(1st International Congress of Philosophy,
Paris, 1900)

On the Notion of Order

1901 in "Mind", vol. 10, p. 30-51 . . . . 022.00

Review of P. Boutroux's "L'imagination et les mathématiques selon Descartes"

1901 in "Mind", vol. 10, p. 274 . . . . 023.00

Is Position in Time and Space Absolute or Relative?

1901 in "Mind", vol. 10, p. 293-317 . . . . . . 024.00

Review of W. Hastie's translation of Kant's "Cosmogony"

1901 in "Mind", vol. 10, p. 405-407 . . . . . . 025.00

Recent Italian Work on the Foundations of Mathematics

1901 Unpublished manuscript in Russell Archives,
McMaster University, Hamilton/Ontario. 28 pp. 026.00

Sur la logique des relations avec des applications
à la théorie des séries

1901 in "Revue de Mathématiques" (Turin),
    vol. 7, p. 115-148 . . . .   027.01
    1956 under the title "The Logic of Relations"
      in "Logic and Knowledge" (BN 616) . .   027.02

    T r a n s l a t i o n s
    Italienisch ... 1961 in BN 616.08 . . . . .   027.03
    Portugiesisch . 1974 in BN 616.09 . . . . .   027.04
    Spanisch ...... 1966 in BN 616.10 . . . . .   027.05

Geometry, Non-Euclidean.

1902 in "The New Volumes of the Encyclopaedia
    Britanica". 10th ed., IV, p. 664-674
    London: Black; New York: Encyclopaedia Bri-
    tanica 028.00

On finite and infinite cardinal numbers
(Section III of "On Cardinal Numbers"
by A. N. Whitehead)

1902 in "American Journal of Mathematics",
    24, p. 378-383 . . . .   029.00

Théorie générale des séries bien-ordonnées

1902 in "Revue de Mathématiques" (Turin),
    vol. 8, p. 12-43 . . . .   030.00

Letter to Frege

1902 in "From Frege to Gödel: A Source Book in
    Mathematical Logic, 1879-1931", ed. by Jean
    van Heijenoort. Cambridge, Mass.: Harvard
    University Press, 1967, p. 124-125 . . . .   031.00

The Teaching of Euclid

1902 in "Mathematics Gazette", vol. 2, p. 165-167   032.00

Recent Works on the Philosophy of Leibniz

1903 in "Mind", vol. 12, p. 177-201 . . . . . .   033.00
    Critical notice of L. Couturat's "La Logique
    de Leibniz d'après des documents inédits"
    and E. Cassierer's "Leibniz' System in sei-
    nen wissenschaftlichen Grundlagen.".

Review of K. Geissler's
"Die Grundsätze und das Wesen des Unendlichen
in der Mathematik und Philosophie"

1903 in "Mind", vol. 12, p. 267-269 . . . . . .   034.00

Definitions of "cause", "contenu", "convergence".

1903 in "Société Française de Phil., Bulletin".
    Paris, vol. 3, p. 163, 192-193, 197 . . . .   035.00

A/THE FREE MAN'S WORSHIP

1903 (Dec.) in "The Independent Review",
vol. 1, p. 415-424 . . . . 036.01

C o m m e n t a r y
For a time he was an Imperialist and supported
the Boer War. But early in 1901, according to
one of his broadcasts: "I had an experience
not unlike what religious people call conversion. ... In the course of a few minutes
I changed my mind about the Boer War, about
harshness in education and in the Criminal
Law, and about combativeness in private relations." - Russell's "conversion" in 1901
followed from his becoming "suddenly and viv-
idly aware of the loneliness in which most
people live, and passionately desirous of
finding ways of diminishing this tragic iso-
lation". The result of this feeling, on the
personal side, was reflected in what is probably the best known of all Russell's essays,
his "A Free Man's Worship". - In Russell's
later years he became more and more of a
preacher, using the word in the best but not
the conventional sense. He surprised some of
his hearers on his lecture tour of Australia
(1950), for instance, by saying that: "The
root of the matter is a very simple and old-
fashioned thing, a thing so simple that I am
almost ashamed to mention it, for fear of the
derisive smile with which wise cynics will
greet my words. The thing I mean, is love,
Christian love or compassion." It was not a
conventional case of a sceptic softening with
advancing years. Russell was merely repeating
in different words what he had preached in
"A Free Man's Worship" in 1903, and in his
"Principles of Social Reconstruction"in 1916.

K o m m e n t a r
Einige Zeit lang war Russell Imperialist und
unterstützte den Burenkrieg. Doch zu Beginn
des Jahres 1901 geschah etwas, wie er selbst
einmal am Radio sagte: "Ich machte eine Erfahrung, so etwa wie das, was religiöse Leute Bekehrung nennen. .... Innerhalb weniger
Minuten änderte ich meine Ansicht über den
Burenkrieg, über Strenge in der Erziehung und
im Strafgesetz und über Machtkämpfe in pri-
vaten Beziehungen." - Russell's "Bekehrung"
1901 war eine Folge davon, daß "ihm plötzlich
und sehr lebhaft die Einsamkeit, in der die
meisten Menschen leben, bewußt wurde und er
leidenschaftlich wünschte, Wege ausfindig zu
machen, um diese tragische Vereinsamung zu

verringern". In persönlicher Beziehung spie-
gelt sich das Ergebnis dieses Gefühls in Russell's "A Free Man's Worship", dem wahrscheinlich bekanntesten aller seiner Essays. - Im Alter wurde Russell immer mehr ein Prediger, der
das Wort im besten, nicht aber im konventio-
nellen Sinne verwendete. Er überraschte zum
Beispiel etliche seiner Hörer, als er auf seiner Vortragsreise in Australien (1950) sagte:
"Die Wurzel der Dinge ist eine sehr einfache
und altmodische Sache, eine Sache, so einfach
daß ich mich fast schäme, sie hier zu erwäh-
nen, aus Angst vor dem abschätzigen Lächeln,
mit dem weise Zyniker meine Worte begrüßen
werden. Die Sache, die ich meine, ist Liebe,
christliche Liebe oder Mitleid." Es war nicht
der übliche Fall des Skeptikers, der im vor-
gerückten Alter milde wird. Russell wieder-
holte nur in anderen Worten, was er 1903 in
"A Free Man's Worship" und 1916 in seinen
"Principles of Social Reconstruction" gepre-
digt hatte. - Siehe auch Golo Mann's auf-
schlußreichen "Versuch über Bertrand Russell"
als Nachwort zur deutschen Ausgabe von R.'s
"Autobiography I" ("Mein Leben", I, 1872 -
1914. Zürich: Europa Verlag, 1967, S. 332).
In diesem siebenundzwanzig Seiten umfassen-
den Nachwort bringt Golo Mann auch eine re-
lativ ausführliche Würdigung von Russell's
Essay, das zu "seinen berühmtesten und am
höchsten bewunderten Schriften gehört."

R e p r i n t s
1904 under the title "An Ethical Approach"
     in "Ideals of Science and Faith",
     New York: Longmans, Green & Co. 036.02
     London: George Allen, p. 157-169 . . .   036.03
1910 in "Philosophical Essays": II (BN 100)   036.04
1917 in "Mysticism and Logic": III (BN 172)   036.05
1923 "A Free Man's Worship",
     with a special preface by B. Russell.
     Portland, Maine: Mosher, XVII, 28 pp.
     (2nd ed. 1927) 036.06
1927 in "Selected Papers of Bertrand Russell"
     (BN 317) 036.07
1927 "What Can A Free Man Worship?"
     Girard, Kansas: Haldeman-Julius Publ.   036.08
1928 in "Further Adventures in Essay Reading"
     New York: Harcourt, p. 517-528 . . . .   036.09
1929 in "Essays from Five Centuries",
     Boston: Houghton Mifflin, p. 404-412 .   036.10
1929 in "Essays toward Truth",
     New York: Henry Holt & Co., p. 175-185 . 036.11
1930 in "Familiar Essays",
     New York: Prentice-Hall, p. 498-508 .   036.12

1930 in "Modern Writers at Work",
  New York: Macmillan, p. 9-22 . . . . . 036.13
1933 in "Fifty Modern English Writers",
  New York: Doubleday, p. 1294-1302 . . 036.14
1934 Excerpt in "Golden Book Magazine",
  vol. 19, Feb., p. 156 . . . . 036.15
1935 in "Pageant of Prose",
  New York: Harper, p. 257-263 . . . . . 036.16
1936 in "Fifty Essays",
  New York: Little Brown & Co., p. 320-331 036.17
1936 in "Modern Reader",
  New York: Heath, p. 417-424 . . . . . 036.18
1948 in "Toward Liberal Education",
  New York: Rinehart & Co., p. 625-631 . . 036.19
1957 in "Why I AM Not a Christian and Other
  Essays" (BN 625) 036.20
1959 in "Two Modern Essaya on Religion",
  Hanover, New Hampshire: Westholm Publ. 036.21
1961 in "The Basic Writings of B. Russell":
  II/6 (BN 659) 036.22
1972 "What Can A Free Man Worship?"
  in "Atheism. Collected Essays." (BN 700) 036.23

T r a n s l a t i o n s
Dänisch . . . . 1966 in BN 625.11 . . . . . 036.24
Deutsch . . . . 1952 in BN 172.22 . . . . . 036.25
Französisch . . . 1922 in BN 172.23 . . . . . 036.26
Italienisch . . . 1960 in BN 625.19 . . . . . 036.27
"   . . . 1964 in BN 172.24 . . . . . 036.28
"   . . . 1972 in BN 100.10 . . . . . 036.29
Japanisch . . . . . 1959 in BN 172.27 . . . . . 036.30
"   . . . . . 1959 in BN 625.21 . . . . . 036.31
Koreanisch . . . . 1960 in BN 625.23 . . . . . 036.32
Niederländisch 1966 in BN 625.26 . . . . . 036.33
Norwegisch . . . . 1947 in BN 172.28 = 519 . . 036.34
Persisch . . . . . . 1970 in BN 625.28 . . . . . 036.35
Portugiesisch . 1957 in BN 172.29 . . . . . 036.36
"   . 1960 in BN 625.30 . . . . . 036.37
Schwedisch . . . . 1954 in BN 172.30 . . . . . 036.38
"   . . . . 1958 in BN 625.32 . . . . . 036.39
Spanisch . . . . . . 1958 in BN 625.33 . . . . . 036.40
"   . . . . . . 1968 in BN 100.12 . . . . . 036.41
"   . . . . . . 1973 in BN 172.31 = 706 . . 036.42
Sp./Catalanisch 1969 in BN 172.32 . . . . . 036.43
Türkisch . . . . . . 1966 in BN 625.36 . . . . . 036.44
"   . . . . . . 1972 in BN 172.34 . . . . . 036.45

THE PRINCIPLES OF MATHEMATICS

1903 Cambridge: University Press. XXIX, 534 pp. 037.01
  C o n t e n t s
  Part I. The Indefinables of Mathematics.
    I. Definition of Pure Mathematics.   II.
    Symbolic Logic.   III. Implication and
    Formal Implications.   IV. Proper Names,
    Adjectives and Verbs.   V. Denoting.   VI.

Appendix.
   A. The Logical and Arithmetical Doctrines
   of Frege. B. The Doctrine of Types.
C o m m e n t a r y
Russell planned his "Principles of Mathematics", to establish his thesis that mathematics nad logic are fundamentally the same.
The book was to be in two volumes, the second
consisting of a riged argument worked out in
symbols, the first a kind of commentary and
introduction in ordinary language. The first
volume was published in 1903. By this time
Russell and A. N. Whitehead had decided to
collaborate in their future work. The result
turned out to be, not simply a second volume
of the "Principles of Mathematics", but the
three massive volumes of "Principia Mathematica", the first of which was not published until 1910 (BN 101.01).

K o m m e n t a r
Russell entwarf seine "Principles of Mathematics", um seine These festzulegen, daß Mathematik und Logik grundsätzlich das gleiche sind. Das Buch war in zwei Bänden geplant,
wovon der zweite in einer strikten, in mathematischen Zeichen ausgeführten Beweisführung
bestehen sollte; der erste war als eine Art
Erläuterung und Einführung in gewöhnlicher
Sprache gedacht. Der erste Band wurde 1903
veröffentlicht. Inzwischen hatten Russell
und A. N. Whitehead beschlossen in Zukunft
zusammenzuarbeiten. Was dann dabei herauskam,
war allerdings nicht einfach ein zweiter Band
der "Principles of Mathematics", sondern die
drei gewaltigen Bände der "Principia Mathematica", deren erster erst 1910 erschien
(BN 101.01).

R e p r i n t s
1937 London: Allen & Unwin,
     with a new introduction, p. V-XIV . . 037.02
1937 New York: Norton & Co. 037.03
1938 "   "   : "   " " 037.04
1943 "   "   : "   " " 037.05
1948 "   "   : "   " " 037.06
1948 London: Allen & Unwin 037.07
1950 "   : "   " " 037.08
1950 New York: Norton & Co. 037.09
1953 "   "   : "   " " 037.10
1956 London: Allen & Unwin 037.11
1961 Excerpt:
     "Symbolic Logis" (I:II)
     in "The Basic Writings of B. Russell":
     IV/13 (BN 659) 037.12

```
1964 London: Allen & Unwin . . . . . . . .  037.13
1964 New York: Norton & Co. . . . . . . . .  037.14
1972 London: Allen & Unwin . . . . . . . .  037.15
```

T r a n s l a t i o n s
Chinesisch:
    "Shuli luoji"
    1921 Peking 037.16
Italienisch:
    "I principi della matematica"
    Tr.: L. Geymont

```
1951 Mailand: Longanesi . . . . . . .  037.17
1963  "       : "         . . . . . . .  037.18
1970  "       : "         . . . . . . .  037.19
1971 Rom: Newton Compton Editori . . .  037.20
```

Spanisch:
    "Los Principios de le Matemática"

```
1948 Madrid, Buenos Aires: Espasa Calpe  037.21
1967  "      ,  "      "    : "        "    037.22
1973 in BN 706 . . . . . . . . . . . .  037.23
```

Literature of the Fiscal Controversy

1904 (Jan.) in "Independent Review",
    vol. 1, p. 684-688 . . . . 038.00
    Review of Ashley's "The Tariff Problem"
    and Pigou's "The Riddle of the Tariff".

Mr. Charles Booth's Proposals for Fiscal Reform

1904 (Feb.) in "Contemporary Review",
    vol. 85, p. 198-206 . . . . 039.00

Review of G. E. Moore's "Principia Ethica" (The Meaning of Good)

1904 (Mar.) in "Independent Review",
    vol. 2, p. 328-333 . . . . 040.00

On History

1904 (July) in "Independent Review",
    vol.3, p. 207-215 . . . . 041.01
    1961 in "The Basic Writings of B. Russell":
    XIII/56 (BN 659) 041.02

The Axiom of Infinity

1904 (July) in "Hibbert Journal",
    vol. 2, p. 809-812 . . . . 042.01
    1973 in "Essays in Analysis": V/11 (BN 705) 042.02

Non-Euclidian Geometry

1904 (Oct. 29) in "Athenaeum",
    no. 4018, vol. 124, p. 592-593 . . . . . . 043.00
    Reply Russell's to criticism of his "Essay
    on the Foundation of Geometry" (BN 10).

Review of L. Couturat's
"Opuscules et fragments inédits de Leibniz"
1904 in "Mind", vol. 13, p. 131-132 . . . . . .   044.00

Review of L. J. Delaporte's
"Essai philosophique
sur les geometries non-Euclidiennes"
1904 in "Mind", vol. 13, p. 132-133 . . . . . .   045.00

Meinong's Theory of Complexes and Assumptions
1904 in "Mind", vol. 13, p. 204-219, p. 336-354,
    p. 509-524 . . . . : 046.01
    1973 in "Essays in Analysis": II/1 (BN 705) 046.02

Review of C.H.Hinton's
"The Fourth Dimension"
1904 in "Mind", vol. 13, p. 573-574 . . . . . .   047.00

Tariff Controversy: Bibliog.
1904 in "Edinburgh Review" (Published anonymously)
    vol. 199, p. 149-196 . . . .   048.00

Letters to Meinong
1904-1907 in "Philosophenbriefe aus der wissen —
    schaftlichen Korrespondenz von Alexius Mei-
    nong", ed. by Rudolf Kindinger.
    1965 Graz: Akademische Druck- und Verlags-
    anstalt, p. 150-153 . . . .   049.00

On Functions, Classes and Relations
1904 Unpublished manuscript in Russell Archives,
    McMaster University, Hamilton/Ontario. 18 pp.   050.00

On Meaning and Denotation
1905 (?) Unpubl. manuscript in Russell Archives,
    McMaster University, Hamilton/Ontario.100 pp.   051.00

Points about Denoting
1905 (?) Unpubl. manuscript in Russell Archives,
    McMaster University, Hamilton/Ontario. 17 pp.   052.00

On the Meaning and Denotation of Phrases
1905 (?) Unpubl. manuscript in Russell Archives,
    McMaster University, Hamilton/Ontario. 24 pp.   053.00

The Existential Import of Propositions
1905 in "Mind", vol. 14, p. 398-401 . . . . . .   054.01
    1973 in "Essays in Analysis": III/4 (BN 705)   054.02

Review of H. Poincaré's
"Science and Hypothesis"
1905 in "Mind", vol. 14, p. 412-418 . . . . . . 055.00
(see also BN 68)

ON DENOTING
1905 in "Mind", vol. 14, p. 479-493 . . . . . . 056.01

C o m m e n t a r y
Russell's most important single contribution
to philosophy was the Theory of Descriptions.
"'The Theory of Description'", said G.E.Moore,
"was something quite new. It was R.'s greatest
philosophical discoversy." The false assumption, exposed by Russell, was that a sentence
about golden mountains was saying something about golden mountains, and that there -
fore such things must have being, or they
could not be talked about. Russell's analysis
proved this assumption wrong: and it also
suggested that there may be many other ways
in which we can be misled by words and the
form of sentences. The theory was put forward
in an article called "On Denoting", first
published in 1905 in "Mind", the leading
British philosophical journal.

K o m m e n t a r
Russell's bedeutendster, ganz allein erar-
beiteter Beitrag zur Philosophie war die Theorie der Beschreibungen. "'Die Theorie der
Beschreibungen'", sagte G.E.Moore, "war etwas ganz Neues. Es war Russell's größte philosophische Entdeckung." Die von Russell auf-
gedeckte irrige Annahme war, daß ein Satz
über goldene Berge etwas über goldene Berge
aussagte und daß darum etwas derartiges existieren müßte, sonst könnte man nicht darüber
sprechen. Russell's Analyse erwies diese Annahme als falsch, zugleich legte sie den Gedanken an mancherlei andere Möglichkeiten na-
he, durch die wir von Worten und Satzformen
irregeführt werden können. Die Theorie **wurde**
bekannt gemacht in einem Artikel "On Denoting", der zuerst 1905 in "Mind", der führenden philosophischen Zeitschrift Englands,
veröffentlicht wurde.

R e p r i n t s
1949 in "Readings in Philosophical Analysis".
    New York: Appleton-Century-Crofts,
    p. 103-115 . . . . 056.02
1956 in "Logic and Knowledge" (BN 616) . . 056.03
1973 in "Essays in Analysis": III/5 (BN 705) 056.04

T r a n s l a t i o n s
Deutsch .... 1971 in BN 696 . . . . . . 056.05
Französisch:
    "De la dénotation"
    in "L'Age de la science"
    1970 Paris, p. 171-185 . . . . 056.06
Italienisch ... 1961 in BN 616.08 . . . . . 056.07
Portugiesisch . 1974 in BN 616.09 . . . . . 056.08
Spanisch ...... 1962 in BN 665 . . . . . . 056.09
"   ...... 1966 in BN 616.12 . . . . . 056.10
Tschechisch ... 1967 in BN 680/A:1 . . . . 056.11

On Fundamentals

1905 Unpublished manuscript in Russell Archives.
McMaster University,Hamilton/Ontario. 40 pp.   057.00
(Russell also noted: "Pp. 18ff. contain the
reasons for the new Theory of denoting." =
Russell bemerkt: "Pp. 18 ff. enthalten die
Gründe für die neue Theorie der Bezeichnung.")

Review of A. Meinong's
"Untersuchungen
zur Gegenstandstheorie und Psychologie"

1905 in "Mind", vol. 14, p. 530-538 . . . . . . 058.01
    1973 in "Essays in Analysis": II/2(BN 705) 058.02

Sur la relation des mathématiques à la logistique

1905 in "Revue de Métaphysique et de Morale",
    vol. 13, p. 906-917 . . . . 059.01
    1973 under the title
    "On the Relation of Mathematics to Logic"
    in "Essays in Analysis": V/12 (BN 705) 059.02

Definition of "evidence"

1905 in "Société Française de Phil., Bulletin".
    Paris, vol. 5, p. 235 . . . . 060.00

On Substitution

1905 (Dec.) Unpublished manuscript in R. Archives,
    McMaster University, Hamilton/Ontario. 13 pp. 061.00

Review of G. Santayana's
"Reason in Science"

1906 (Apr. 7) in "Speaker", vol. 14, p. 14-15 . 062.00

Freethought, Ancient and Modern

1906 in "Speaker", vol. 14, p. 402-403 . . . . . 063.00

On Substitution

1906 (Apr./May) Unpubl. manuscript in R. Archives,
    McMaster University,Hamilton/Ontario.146 pp. 064.00

The Paradox of the Liar

1906 (Sept.)Unpublished manuscript in R. Archives,
McMaster University,Hamilton/Ontario.120 pp.   065.00

The Theory of Implication

1906 in "American Journal of Mathematics",
vol. 28, p. 159-202 . . . .   066.00

On Some Difficulties in the Theory
of Transfinite Numbers and Order Types

1906 in "Proceedings London Mathematical Society",
series 2, vol. 4, p. 29-53 . . . .   067.01
1973 in "Essays in Analysis": IV/7 (BN 705)   067.02

Reply to Poincaré's Letter, Note.

1906 in "Mind", vol. 15, p. 143 . . . .   068.00
(see also BN 55)

Review of H. MacColl's
"Symbolic Logic and Its Applications"

1906 in "Mind", vol. 15, p. 255-266 . . . . . .   069.00

Review of A. Pastore's
"Logica formale dedotta dalla considerazione
di modelli meccanici"

1906 in "Mind", vol. 15, p. 277 . . . .   070.00

Review of A. Meinong's
"Über die Erfahrungsgrundlagen unseres Wissens"

1906 in "Mind", vol. 15, p. 412-415 . . . . . .   071.00

The Nature of Truth

1906 in "Mind", vol. 15, p. 528-533 . . . . . .   072.01
1910 a revised version
in "Philosophical Essays" (BN 100),
first two sections as
"VI. The Monistic Theory of Truth"
and third section rewritten as
"VII. On the Nature
of Truth and Falsehood" 072.02

Les paradoxes de la logique

1906 in "Revue de Métaphysique et de Morale",
vol. 14, p. 627-650 . . . .   073.01
1973 under the title
"On 'Insolubilia'
and their Solution by Symbolic Logic"
in "Essays in Analysis": IV/9 (BN 705)   073.02

Religion and Metaphysics

1906 in "Independent Review", vol. 9, p. 109-116   074.00

Review of H. H. Joachim's
"The Nature of Truth"

1906 in "Independent Review", vol. 9, p. 349-353   075.00

On the Nature of Truth

1907 in "Proceedings Aristotelian Society",
    vol. 7, p. 28-49 . . . .   076.00

The Study of Mathematics

1907 (Nov.) in "New Quarterly", vol. 1, p. 29-44   077.01
1910 in "Philosophical Essays": III (BN 100)   077.02
1917 in "Mysticism and Logic": IV (BN 172)   077.03

    T r a n s l a t i o n s
    Deutsch .... 1952 in BN 172.22 . . . . .   077.04
    Französisch ... 1922 in BN 172.23 . . . . .   077.05
    Italienisch ... 1964 in BN 172.24 . . . . .   077.06
    "   ... 1972 in BN 100.11 . . . . .   077.07
    Japanisch ..... 1959 in BN 172.27 . . . . .   077.08
    Portugiesisch . 1957 in BN 172.29 . . . . .   077.09
    Schwedisch .... 1954 in BN 172.30 . . . . .   077.10
    Spanisch ...... 1968 in BN 100.13 . . . . .   077.11
    "   ...... 1973 in BN 172.31 = 706 . .   077.12
    Sp./Catalanisch 1969 in BN 172.32 . . . . .   077.13
    Türkisch ...... 1972 in BN 172.34 . . . . .   077.14

Review of A. Meinong's
"Über die Stellung der Gegenstandstheorie
im System der Wissenschaften"

1907 in "Mind", vol. 16, p. 436-439 . . . . . .   078.01
1973 in "Essays in Analysis": II/3 (BN 705)   078.02

The Development of Morals

1907 in "Independent Review", vol. 12, p. 204-210   079.00

Metaphysics for the Man of Action

1907 in "Nation" (London), vol. 1, p. 44-45 . .   080.00

Transatlantic "Truth"

1908 (Jan.) in "Albany Review",
    vol. 2, no. 10, p. 393-410 . . . .   081.01
1910 under the title
        "William James's Conception of Truth",
        in "Philosophical Essays": V (BN 100)   081.02

    T r a n s l a t i o n s
    Italienisch ... 1972 in BN 100.11 . . . . .   081.03
    Spanisch ...... 1968 in BN 100.13 . . . . .   081.04
    "   ...... 1973 in BN 100.14 = 706 . .   081.05

Liberalism and Women's Suffrage

1908 (July) in "Contemporary Review",
    vol. 94, p. 11-16 . . . . 082.00

Determinism and Morals

1908 (Oct.) in "Hibbert Journal",
    vol. 7, p. 113-121 . . . . 083.01
    1910 under the title
      "The Elements of Ethics"
      in "Philosophical   ": I (BN 100) 083.02

    T r a n s l a t i o n s
    Italienisch ... 1972 in BN 100.11 . . . . . 083.03
    Spanisch ...... 1968 in BN 100.13 . . . . . 083.04
    "   ...... 1973 in BN 100.14 = 706 . . 083.05

Mathematical Logic as Based on the Theory of Types

1908 in "American Journal of Mathematics",
    vol. 30, p. 222-262 . . . . 084.01
    1956 in "Logic and Knowledge" (BN 616) . . 084.02

    T r a n s l a t i o n s
    Deutsch .... 1976 in BN 711 . . . . . . 084.03
    Italienisch ... 1961 in BN 616.08 . . . . . 084.04
    Portugiesisch . 1974 in BN 616.09 . . . . . 084.05
    Spanisch ...... 1966 in BN 616.10 . . . . . 084.06

Mr. Haldane on Infinity

1908 in "Mind", vol. 17, p. 238-242 . . . . . . 085.00

"If" and "Imply"

1908 in "Mind", vol. 17, p. 300-301 . . . . . . 086.00
    (A reply to Mr. MacColl, see also BN 69)

Space and Mathematical reasoning

1908 in "Mind", vol. 17 . . . . 087.00

Review of L. Bloch's
"La Philosophie de Newton"

1908 in "Nature", vol. 78, p. 99-100 . . . . . . 088.00
    (Unsigned, but verified as Russell's)

Review of
"Essays Philosophical and Psychological
in Honor of William James'"

1908 in "Hibbert Journal", vol. 7, p. 203-204 . . 089.00

Pragmatism

1909 (Apr.) in "Edinburgh Review",
    vol. 209, p. 363-388 . . . . 090.01
    1910 in "Philosophical Essays": IV (BN 100) 090.02

Review
of James "The Will to Believe and Pragmatism",
of F. C. S. Schiller's "Philosophical Essays"
    and "Studies in Humanism"
of Dewey's "Studies in Logical Theory" and
    "Columbia University Essays, Philosophi-
    cal, and Psychological in Honor of William
    James", 1908.
T r a n s l a t i o n s
Deutsch .... 1971 in BN 696 . . . . . . 090.03
Italienisch ... 1972 in BN 100.11 . . . . . 090.04
Spanisch ...... 1968 in BN 100.13 . . . . . 090.05
    "   ...... 1973 in BN 100.14 = 706 . . 090.06

Review of Paul Carus's
"The Foundations of Mathematics"

1909 in "Mathematical Gazette", vol. 5, p.103-104   091.01
1910 in "Monist", vol. 20, p. 64-65 . . . .   091.02

Review of A. Reymond's
"Logique et Mathématiques"

1909 in "Mind", vol. 18, p. 299-301 . . . . . .   092.00

Anti-Suffragist Anxieties

1910 London: "People's Sufrage Federation" . . .   093.00

Ethics

1910 in "New Quarterly", vol. 3,
    (Feb.) p. 21-34, (May) p. 131-143 . . . . .   094.01
1910 under the title
        "The Elements of Ethics"
    in "Philosophical Essays": I (BN 100)   094.02
1952 in "Readings in Ethical Theory",
        ed. by W. Sellars and J. Hospens.
        New York, p. 1-34 . . . .   094.03
T r a n s l a t i o n s
Italienisch ... 1972 in BN 100.11 . . . . .   094.04
Spanisch ...... 1968 in BN 100.13 . . . . .   094.05
    "   ...... 1973 in BN 100.14 = 706 . .   094.06

The Philosophy of William James

1910 (Oct.) in "Living Age", vol. 267, p. 52-55   095.01
1910 in "Nation" (London), vol. 7, p. 793-794   095.02

Some Explanations in Reply to Mr. Bradley

1910 in "Mind", vol. 19, p. 373-378 . . . . . .   096.00
    (Reply to a review
    of "The Principles of Mathematics",
    1903/BN 37)

Review of G. Mannoury's
"Methodologisches und Philosophisches
zur Elementar-Mathematik"

1910 in "Mind", vol. 19, p. 438-439 . . . . . . 097.00

La théorie des types logiques

1910 in "Revue de Metaphysique et de Morale",
    vol. 18, p. 263-301 . . . . 098.01
    1910 under the title
        "Theory of Logical Types"
        in "Principia Mathematica": Introd./II
        (BN 101.01) 098.02
    1973 under the title
        "The Theory of Logical Types"
        in "Essays in Analysis": IV/10 (BN 705) 098.03

    T r a n s l a t i o n s
    Deutsch . . . . 1932 in BN 101.07:II . . . 098.04
    Tschechisch . . . 1967 in BN 101.09 = 680:A/3 098.05

Spinoza

1910 in "Nation" (London), vol. 8, p. 278, 280 . 099.00

PHILOSOPHICAL ESSAYS

1910 London: Allen & Unwin 100.01
    London, New York, Bombay and Calcutta:
    Longmans, Green & Co., VI, 185 pp 100.02
    C o n t e n t s
      I. The Elements of Ethics . . . . . (1908/83)
     II. The Free Man's Worship . . . . . (1903/36)
   III. The Study of Mathematics . . . (1907/77)
    IV. Pragmatism . . . . (1909/90)
     V. W. Jame's Conception of Truth (1908/81)
    VI. The Monistic Theory of Truth (1906/72)
  VII. On the Nature
       of Truth and Falsehood . . . . . (1906/72)

    R e p r i n t s
    1917 Excerpts:
        "The Free Man's Worship" (II)
        "The Study of Mathematics" (III)
        in "Mysticism and Logic": III, IV
        (BN 172) 100.03
    1961 Excerpt:
        "The Free Man's Worship" (II)
        in "The Basic Writings of B. Russell":
        II/6 (BN 659) 100.04
    1966 London: Allen & Unwin, rev. ed. . . . 100.05
    1966 New York: Simon & Schuster 100.06
    1967 "   " : "   " " 100.07
    1968 "   " : "   " " 100.08

T r a n s l a t i o n s
Deutsch:
   "Was der freie Mensch verehrt" (II)
   "Das Studium der Mathematik" (III)
   1952 in BN 172.22 . . . . 100.09
   "Der Pragmatismus" (IV)
   "Über die Natur
   von Wahrheit und Falschheit" (VII)
   1971 in BN 696 . . . . 100.10
Italienisch:
   "Filosofia e scienza"
   Tr.: Chiara Lefons
   1972 Rom: Newton Compton Editori . . . 100.11
   1974 " : " " " . . . 100.12
Spanisch:
   "Ensayos Filisóficos"
   1968 Madrid: Alianza Editorial 100.13
   1973 in BN 706 . . . . 100.14

PRINCIPIA MATHEMATICA

in collaboration with Alfred North Whitehead

1910 Cambridge: Univ. Press, vol. I, XLVI,674 pp. 101.01
1912 " : " " , " II, XXXI,742 pp. 101.02
1913 " : " " , " III, VIII,491 pp. 101.03
C o n t e n t s : vol. I
Preface. Alphabetical List of Propositions
   Referred to by Names.
Introduction. I. Preliminary Explanation of
   Ideas and Notations. II. Theory of Logi-
   cal Types (1910/98). III. Incomplete Sym-
   bols.
Part I.
   Mathematical Logic. Summary of Part I.
   A. The Theory of Deduction. B. Theory of
   Apparent Variables. C. Classes and Rela-
   tions. D. Logic of Relations. E. Products
   and Sums of Classes.
Part II.
   Cardinal Arithmetic. Summary of Part II.
   A. Unit Classes and Couples. B. Sub-
   Classes, Sub-Relations and Relative Types.
   C. One-Many, Many-One, and One-One Rela-
   tions. D. Selections. E. Inductive Re-
   lations.
Appendix.
   A. The Theory of Deduction for Proposi-
   tions Containing Apparent Variables. B.
   Mathematical Induction. C. Truth-Func-
   tions and Others. List of Definitions.
C o n t e n t s : vol. II
Prefatory Statement of Symbolic Conception.
Part III.
   Cardinal Arithmetic. Summary of Part III.
   A. Definition and Logical Properties of

Cardinal Numbers. B. Addition, Multipli-
cation and Exponentiation. C. Finite and
Infinite.
Part IV.
Relation Arithmetic. Summary of Part IV.
A. Ordinal Similarity and Relation Num-
bers. B. Additions of Relations and the
Product of Two Relations. C. The Princi-
ple of First Differences and the Multi-
plication and Exponentiation of Relation.
D. Arithmetic of Relation Numbers.
Part V.
Series. Summary of Part V.
A. General Theory of Series. B. On Sec-
tions, Segments, Stretches, and Deriva-
tives. C. On Convergence, and the Limits
of Function.
C o n t e n t s : vol. III
D. Well Ordered Series. E. Finite and
Infinite Series and Ordinals. F. Compact
Series, Rational Series, and Continuous
Series.
Part VI.
Quantity. Summary of Part VI.
A. Generalization of Number. B. Vector-
Families. C. Measurement. D. Cyclic
Families.

C o m m e n t a r y
Russell and A. N. Whitehead had decided to
collaborate in their future work. The result
turned out to be, not simply a second volume
of Russell's "Principles of Mathematics"
(BN 37), but the three massive volumes of
"Principia Mathematica", the first of which
was not published until 1910. - The collaboration was arranged in this way: Russell had
mapped out the general scheme of the work in
a course of lectures at Cambridge. Different
parts were then divided between himself and
Whitehead. As for Whitehead, it seems that
he was Russell's superior as an ordinary
mathematician, and he was more adept at the
art of inventing logical symbols. But, since
Whitehead was only free from fulltime University teaching during vacations, the bulk
of the work inevitably fell on Russell, and
I think it is fair to say that, but for Russell, "Principia Mathematica" would never
have been completed. - There is little doubt
about it being one of the supreme achievements of the human mind, into which Russell
poured his most intense intellectual energy
over a period of many years; but probably not
more than twenty people have ever read it

right through. Like most classics, it is
now taken for granted rather than studied,
even by those who should be professionally
concerned with it. - The enormous importance of the knowledge gained for contemporary philosophy in "Principia Mathematica"
will be found, above all, in Russell's proof
that all mathematical axioms can be traced
back to logical principles. By this the iden-
tity is proved of logic and mathematics and
a clear answer is given to the old question
as to the character of mathematics. According to Russell mathematics is a system of
purely analytical clauses, e. g. they are
valid for all possible worlds - just as the
logical clauses - independent of existence
and reality and of any real being generally.

K o m m e n t a r
Russell und A. N. Whitehead beschlossen, in
Zukunft zusammenzuarbeiten. Was dann dabei
herauskam, war allerdings nicht einfach ein
zweiter Band von Russell's "Principles of
Mathematics" (BN 37), sondern die drei gewaltigen Bände der "Principia Mathematica",
deren erster erst 1910 erschien. - Die Zusammenarbeit wurde auf folgende Art organisiert:
Russell hatte den allgemeinen Plan der Arbeit
im Laufe einer Reihe von Vorlesungen in Cambridge skizziert. Die verschiedenen Teile
wurden dann zwischen ihm und Whitehead auf-
geteilt. Bei Whitehead scheint es, daß er
Russell als reiner Mathematiker überlegen war
und gewandter in der Kunst, logische Symbole zu erfinden. Doch da Whitehead nur während
der Ferien von seiner vollamtlichen Lehrtä-
tigkeit an der Universität frei war, fiel die
Hauptmasse der Arbeit Russell zu; und ich
denke, es ist richtig zu betonen, daß ohne
Russell die "Principia Mathematica" nie fertig geworden wäre. - Unzweifelhaft handelt
es sich um eine der großartigsten Schöpfun-
gen des menschlichen Geistes; viele Jahre
hindurch ließ Russell seine aufs höchste an-
gespannten Geisteskräfte in dieses Werk ein-
strömen. Doch, wahrscheinlich haben es nicht
mehr als zwanzig Leute jemals vollständig
gelesen. Wie die meisten Klassiker wird es
jetzt zwar als gesichert hingenommen, nicht
aber wirklich studiert; das gilt sogar für
solche, die sich eigentlich berufsmäßig dafür interessieren sollten. - Die große Bedeutung der in der "Principia Mathematica"
gewonnenen Erkenntnisse für die Philosophie
der Gegenwart liegt vor allem in Russell's

Beweis, daß sämtliche mathematischen Axiome
auf logische Principien zurückgeführt werden können. Damit ist die Identität von Logik und Mathematik nachgewiesen und eine ein-
deutige Antwort auf die alte Frage nach dem
Wesen der Mathematik gegeben. Die Mathematik
ist nach Russell ein System rein analytischer
Sätze, das heißt, sie gelten, wie die logischen, unabhängig von Dasein und Wirklichkeit und von jeder wirklichen Welt überhaupt,
für alle möglichen Welten.

R e p r i n t s
1925-1927 with e new introduction.
    Cambridge: University Press 101.04
1959-1960 Cambridge: University Press . . .   101.05
1961 Excerpts:
    "Preface" . . . . from vol. I
    "Introduction" . . . . . from vol. I
    "Summary of Part III" from vol. II
    "Summary of Part IV" from vol. II
    "Summary of Part V" from vol. II
    "Summary of Part VI" from vol. III
    "Introduction to the 2nd ed." (1925)
    in "The Basic Writings of B. Russell":
    IV/15, 16, 17, 18, 19, 20, 21 (BN 659) . 101.06

T r a n s l a t i o n s
Deutsch:
    Auszug aus Bd. I:
    "Einführung in die Mathematische Logik"
    (Einleitung der "Principia Mathematica")
    Ü.: Hans Mokre
    1932 München: Drei Maskenverlag . . .   101.07
    I n h a l t
    Vorwort.
    Einleitung.
      I. Vorläufige Erklärungen über Be-
        griffe und Zeichen.
     II. Die Theorie der logischen Typen.
    III. Unvollständige Symbole.
    Einleitung zur zweiten Auflage (1925).
Spanisch:
    Excerpts from vol. I:
    "Prefacio"
    "Introducciòn"
    "Resumen de la parte I - VI"
    "Intrucción a la segunda edición"
    1973 in BN 706 . . . .   101.08
Tschechisch:
    Excerpt from vol. I:
    "Theorie logických typu"
    (Introduction: II.)
    1967 in BN 680 . . . .   101.09

Knowledge by Acquaintance
and Knowledge by Description

1911 in "Proceedings Aristotelian Society",
    vol. 11, p. 108-128 . . . .   102.01
    1912 in "The Problems of Philosophy": V,
    (BN 118) 102.02
    1917 in "Mysticism and Logic": X (BN 172)   102.03
    1961 in "The Basic Writings of B. Russell":
    V/26 (BN 659) 102.04
    T r a n s l a t i o n s
    Arabisch ...... 1960 in BN 118.19 . . . . .   102.05
    Chinesisch .... 1920 in BN 118.20 . . . . .   102.06
    Deutsch .... 1926 in BN 118.23 . . . . .   102.07
    " .... 1952 in BN 172.22 . . . . .   102.08
    " .... 1976 in BN 711.00 . . . . .   102.09
    Finnisch ...... 1969 in BN 118.28 . . . . .   102.10
    Französisch ... 1922 in BN 172.23 . . . . .   102.11
    " ... 1923 in BN 118.29 . . . . .   102.12
    Hebräisch ..... 1938 in BN 118.32 . . . . .   102.13
    Italienisch ... 1922 in BN 118.34 . . . . .   102.14
    " ... 1964 in BN 172.24 . . . . .   102.15
    Japanisch ..... 1959 in BN 172.27 . . . . .   102.16
    " ..... 1964 in BN 118.37 . . . . .   102.17
    Koreanisch .... 1958 in BN 118.39 . . . . .   102.18
    Niederländisch. 1967 in BN 118.40 . . . . .   102.19
    Norwegisch .... 1964 in BN 118.41 . . . . .   102.20
    Polnisch ...... 1913 in BN 118.42 . . . . .   102.21
    Portugiesisch . 1957 in BN 172.29 . . . . .   102.22
    " . 1959 in BN 118.43 . . . . .   102.23
    Russisch ...... 1914 in BN 118.44 . . . . .   102.24
    Schwedisch .... 1922 in BN 118.45 . . . . .   102.25
    " .... 1954 in BN 172.30 . . . . .   102.26
    Spanisch ...... 1928 in BN 118.49 . . . . .   102.27
    " ...... 1973 in BN 172.31 = 706 . .   102.28
    Sp./Catalanisch 1969 in BN 172.32 . . . . .   102.29
    Türkisch ...... 1936 in BM 118.53 . . . . .   102.30
    " ...... 1972 in BM 172.34 . . . . .   102.31

The Basis of Realism

1911 (Mar. 16) in "Journal of Philosophy,
    Psychology, and Scientific Method",
    vol. 8, no. 6, p. 158-161 . . . .   103.00

L'importance philosophique de la logistique

1911 in "Revue de Metaphysique et de Morale",
    vol. 19, p. 281-294 . . . .   104.01
    (Lecture delivered in French at Ecole des
    Hautes Etudes Sociales, Mar. 22, 1911)
    1913 (Oct.) under the title
        "The Philosophical Importance of Mathe-
        matical Logic"
        in "Monist", vol. 23, p. 481-493 . . .   104.02

1973 under the title
"The Philosophical Implications
of Mathematical Logic"
in "Essays in Analysis": V/14 (BN 705)   104.03

Review of Williams James's
"Memories and Studies"

1911 (Nov. 16) in "Cambridge Review",
vol. 33, p. 118 . . . .   105.00

Le réalisme analytique

1911 in "Société Française de Phil., Bulletin",
Paris, vol. 11, p. 55-82 . . . .   106.00

Sur les axiomes de l'infini et du transfini

1911 in "Société mathématique de France. Comptes
rendus des Séances de 1911", no. 2, p. 22-35   107.00

Review of C. Mercier's
"A New Logic"

1912 (Mar. 23) in "The Nation" (London),
vol. 10, p. 1029-1030 (Unsigned) 108.00

Review of F. C. S. Schiller's
"Formal Logic"

1912 (May 18) in "The Nation" (London),
vol. 11, p. 258-259 . . . .   109.00

The Philosophy of Bergson

1912 (July) in "Monist", vol. 22, p. 321-347 . .   110.01
     1913 (Mar. 11) Read before the Heretics in
          Trinity College 110.02
     1913 (Apr. 26)
          "Mr. Wildon Carr's Defence of Bergson"
          in "The Cambridge Magazine" (Reply to
          Carr's Article in "The Cambridge Maga-
          zine", Apr. 12, 1913) 110.03
     1914 "The Philosophy of Bergson"
          (with BN 110.03)
          London: Macmillan 110.04
          Glasgow: MacLehose 110.05
          Cambridge: Bowes & Bowes. 36 pp. . . .   110.06
                    Published for "The Heretics"
          1945 reprinted in "History of Western
          Philosophy": Book Three/XXVIII (BN 504)   110.07
T r a n s l a t i o n s   see BN 504.13 ff.

C o m m e n t a r y
One event worth mentioning here is Russell's
celebrated lecture on Bergson, to the Cambridge society called "The Heretics". Bergson's mystical philosophy of evolution was

then enjoying a tremendous vogue, which Russell set out to demolish; there was an eager audience to hear him, and everyone had a sense of a great occasion. The lecture can be found reprinted in Russell's "History of Western Philosophy" (BN 504); to enjoy its savour, the reader must imagine it delivered in Russell's dry, precise and ironic voice, and punctuated by the laughter and applause which greeted his sallies. It was an event of some importance in Russell's life, helping to reestablish him as one of the leading figures in Cambridge; and especially because it was his first big success as a public speaker.

K o m m e n t a r
Ein erwähnenswertes Ereignis ist hier noch Russell's berühmter Vortrag über Bergson vor einer Cambridger Gesellschaft mit dem Namen "The Heretics". Bergsons mystische Evolutionsphilosophie erlebte damals einen gewaltigen Modeerfolg, und Russell machte sich daran, ihn zu vernichten. Eine eifrig interessierte Zuhörerschaft hatte sich eingefunden, und jedermann hatte das Gefühl eines großen Ereignisses. Der Vortrag findet sich im Druck in Russell's "History of Western Philosophy" (BN 504); um seinen Reiz voll zu genießen, muß der Leser ihn sich in Russell's trockener, exakter, ironischer Stimme vorgetragen denken, akzentuiert von dem Gelächter und dem Beifall, die seine witzigen Seitensprünge begrüßten. In Russell's Leben war es ein Geschehnis von einiger Bedeutung; einmal verhalf es ihm dazu, seine Stellung als einer der führenden Köpfe von Cambridge neu zu festigen, dann aber auch, weil es sein erster großer Erfolg als öffentlicher Redner war.

Review of H. S. Macran's
"Hegel's Doctrine of Formal Logic"
1912 (Aug. 17) in "The Nation" (London),
vol. 11, p. 739-740 (Unsigned) 111.00

When Should Marriage Be Dissolved?
1912 (Aug.) in "The English Review",
vol. 12, p. 133-141 . . . . 112.00

The Essence of Religion
1912 (Oct.) in "Hibbert Journal", vol. 11, p. 46-62   113.01
    1961 in "The Basic Writings of B. Russell":
        XV/61 (BN 659) 113.02
    T r a n s l a t i o n s
    Italienisch ... 1968 in BN 686 . . . . . . 113.03

On the Relation of Universals and Particulars

1912 in "Proceedings Aristotelian Society",
       vol. 12, p. 1-24 . . . . 114.01
       1956 in "Logic and Knowledge" (BN 616) . . 114.02

       T r a n s l a t i o n s
       Deutsch . . . . 1976 in BN 711 . . . . . . 114.03
       Italienisch . . . 1961 in BN 616.08 . . . . . . 114.04
       Portugiesisch . 1974 in BN 616.09 . . . . . . 114.05
       Spanisch . . . . . . 1966 in BN 616.10 . . . . . . 114.06

Review of W. James's
"Essays in Radical Empiricism"

1912 in "Mind", vol. 21, p. 571-575 . . . . . . 115.00

Response a M. Koyre

1912 in "Revue de Metaphysique et de Morale",
       vol. 20, p. 725-726; in response to Koyre's
       "Sur les nombres de B. Russell", p. 722 - 724 116.00

Review of H. Bergson's
"Laughter" (The Professor's Guide to Laughter)

1912 in "The Cambridge Review", vol. 33, p. 193-194 117.00

THE PROBLEMS OF PHILOSOPHY

1912 London: Williams & Norgate. VIII, 255 pp. . 118.01
       New York: Henry Holt & Co. 118.02
       London: Oxford University Press 118.03
       C o n t e n t s
       Preface. I. Appearance and Reality. II. The
       Existence of Matter. III. The Nature of Mat-
       ter. IV. Idealism. V. Knowledge by Ac-
       quaintance and Knowledge by Description (1911/
       102). VI. On Induction. VII. On Our Knowl-
       edge of General Principles. VIII. How "a pri-
       ori" Knowledge Is Possible. IX. The World of
       Universals. X. On Our Knowledge of Univer-
       sals. XI. On Intuitive Knowledge. XII. Truth
       and Falsehood. XIII. Knowledge, Error and
       Probable Opinion. XIV. The Limits of Philo-
       sophical Knowledge. XV. The Value of Phi-
       losophy. Index.

       C o m m e n t a r y
       Russell's own philosophical views at this
       period were explained with marvellous lu-
       cidity in his "Problems of Philosophy", writ-
       ten for the Home University Library at Gil-
       bert Murray's suggestion. It was an important
       book in its own right, which also remains by
       far and away the best introduction to the sub-
       ject. It is somewhat disappointing to the be-
       ginner, however, when he has read it and been

delighted to discover that he can understand it all, to find that Russell completely changed his mind afterwards about many points in it. There is no similar short statement of his later ideas available, because the further his thoughts advanced, the more was found of increasing subtle distinction and complex changes of viewpoint. One cannot sum up his philosophy by attaching his name to one single specific doctrine.

K o m m e n t a r
Russell's eigene philosophische Auffassungen in jener Zeit wurden mit bewundernswerter Klarsichtigkeit in seinen "Problems of Philosophy" auseinandergesetzt, die auf Gilbert Murray's Veranlassung für die Home University Library geschrieben wurden. Es war ein an sich wichtiges Buch, das zu dem weit und breit die beste Einführung in den Gegenstand bleibt. Es ist jedoch für den Anfänger einigermaßen enttäuschend, wenn er es gelesen und hocherfreut entdeckt hat, daß er alles verstehen kann, schließlich zu finden, daß Russell über viele Punkte darin hinterher seine Ansicht völlig geändert hat. Von seinen späteren Ideen gibt es keine ähnlich knappe Zusammenstellung; denn je weiter sich seine Gedanken entwickelten, desto mehr feindifferenzierte Unterscheidungen und komplex begründete Änderungen von Auffassungen fanden sich. Man kann nicht eine Summe aus seiner Philosophie ziehen und seinen Namen mit einer einzelnen besonderen Lehre verknüpfen.

R e p r i n t s
1919 New York: Henry Holt & Co. Rev. edition. 118.04
London: Williams & Norgate. "   "   118.05
1921 London: "   " " 118.06
1929 London: Butterworth 118.07
1943 London, New York: Oxford Univ. Press . 118.08
1946 "   ,   "   "   : "   "   "   . 118.09
1948 "   ,   "   "   : "   "   "   . 118.10
1950 "   ,   "   "   : "   "   "   . 118.11
1951 "   ,   "   "   : "   "   "   . 118.12
1952 "   ,   "   "   : "   "   "   . 118.13
1956 "   ,   "   "   : "   "   "   . 118.14
1959 "   ,   "   "   : "   "   "   . 118.15
1961 Excerpts:
"On Induction" (VI)
"Knowledge by Acquaintance
and Knowledge by Description" (V)
in "The Basic Writings of B. Russell" :
IV/14, V/26 (BN 659) 118.16
1967 London, New York: Oxford Univ. Press . 118.17
1973 "   ,   "   "   : "   "   "   . 118.18

T r a n s l a t i o n s
Arabisch:
    "Al-falsafah binaẓraḥ 'ilmiyyah"
    Tr.: Zakī Najīb Mahmud
    1960 Kairo:
        Maktabit al-Anglo al-Miṣriyyah . 118.19
Chinesisch:
    "Zhexue wenti"
    1920 Peking 118.20
    1935 Shanghai 118.21
    1959 Peking 118.22
Deutsch:
    "Die Probleme der Philosophie"
    Ü: Paul Hertz
    1926 Leipzig: F. Meiner 118.23
        Erlangen: Weltkreis 118.24
    Ü: Amethe Gräfin Zeppelin
    1950 Wien, Stuttgart: Humboldt-Verlag 118.25
    Ü: Eberhard Bubser
    1967 Frankfurt: Suhrkamp (ed. s. 207) 118.26
    1976 "   : "   6. Auflage . 118.27
    I n h a l t
    Vorbemerkung. 1. Erscheinung und Wirk-
    lichkeit. 2. Die Existenz der Materie.
    3. Die Natur der Materie. 4. Der Idea-
    lismus. 5. Erkenntnisformen: Bekannt-
    schaft und Beschreibung. 6. Über In-
    duktion. 7. Unsere Erkenntnis allge-
    meiner Prinzipien. 8. Wie apriorische
    Erkenntnis möglich ist. 9. Die Welt der
    Universalien. 10. Unsere Erkenntnis
    von Universalien. 11.Intuitive Erkennt-
    nis. 12. Wahrheit und Falschheit. 13.
    14. Die Grenzen philosophischer Erkennt-
    nis. 15. Der Wert der Philosophie. -
    Nachwort von E. Bubser.
Finnisch:
    "Filosofian ongelmat"
    Tr.: Pellervo Oksala
    1969 Helsinki: Otava 118.28
Französisch:
    "Les problèmes de la philosophie"
    Tr.: J. F. Renauld
    1923 Paris: Alcan 118.29
    Tr.: Solange-Marie Guillemin
    1965 Paris: Payot (Petite Biblioth. 79) 118.30
    1975 "   : "   ("   "   79) 118.31
Hebräisch:
    "Baayot ha-filosofya"
    Tr.: M. Sternberg
    1938 Jerusalem 118.32
    1966 Jerusalem: Magnes Press 118.33

Italienisch:
  "I problemi della filosofia"
  Tr.: B. Ceva
  1922 Mailand: Sonzogno 118.34
  Tr.: Elena Spagnol
  1959 Mailand: Feltrinelli 118.35
  1965 "   : " 118.36
Japanisch:
  "Tetsuga nyûmon"
  Tr.: Nakamura Hidekichi
  1964 Tokio: Shakai Sisosha 118.37
  Tr.: Ikimatsu Keizô
  1965 Tokio: Kadokawa Shoten 118.38
Koreanisch:
  "Cheolhak iran mueosinga"
  Tr.: Kang Bong Sik
  1958 Seoul: Sinyangsa 118.39
Niederländisch:
  "Problemen der Filosofie"
  Tr.: J. de Vries
  1967 Meppel: Boom en Zoon 118.40
Norwegisch:
  "Filosofiens problemer"
  Tr.: K. E. Tranøy
  1964 Oslo: Gyldendal 118.41
Polnisch:
  "Zagnadnienia Filozofii"
  Tr.: Ludwig Silberstein
  1913 Warschau: E. Wende i Ska 118.42
Portugiesisch:
  "Os problemas da filosofia"
  Tr.: Antônia Sérgio
  1959 (2nd ed.) Coimbra: A. Amado . . . 118.43
Russisch:
  "Probltmy filosofii"
  1914 St. Petersburg 118.44
Schwedisch:
  "Filosofins problem"
  1922 Stockholm: Tiden 118.45
  Tr.: Andres Byttner
  1958 Stockholm: Natur och Kultur . . . 118.46
  1968 "   : "   "   " . . . 118.47
  1974 "   : "   "   " . . . 118.48
Spanisch:
  "Los problemos de la filosofia"
  Tr.: Joaquin Xirau
  1928 Barcelona, Buenos Aires: Ed. Labor 118.49
  1937 "   , "   " : "   " 118.50
  1953 "   , "   " : "   " 118.51
  1970 "   : Labor 118.52
  1973 "   : " 118.53
  1973 in BN 706 . . . . 118.54

Türkisch:
"Felsefe meseleri"
Tr.: Abdülhak Adnan-Adivar
1936 Istanbul: Remzi Kitabevi 118.55
1963 (3rd ed.) Istanbul: Remzi Kitabevi   118.56

On the Notion of Cause

1913 in "Proceedings Aristotelian Society",
vol. 13, p. 1-26 . . . .   119.01
1917 in "Mysticism and Logic": IX (BN 172) .   119.02
1965 in "On the Philosophy of Science": V/I
(BN 672) 119.03

T r a n s l a t i o n s
Deutsch . . . .   1952 in BN 172.22 . . . . .   119.04
Französisch . . .   1922 in BN 172.23 . . . . .   119.05
Italienisch . . .   1964 in BN 172.24 . . . . .   119.06
Japanisch . . . . .   1959 in BN 172.27 . . . . .   119.07
Portugiesisch .   1957 in BN 172.29 . . . . .   119.08
Schwedisch . . . .   1954 in BN 172.30 . . . . .   119.09
Spanisch . . . . . .   1973 in BN 172.31 = 706 . .   119.10
Sp./Catalanisch   1969 in BN 172.32 . . . . .   119.11
Tschechisch . . .   1967 in BN 172.33 = 680/C:7   119.12
Türkisch . . . . . .   1972 in BN 172.34 . . . . .   119.13

The Place of Science in a Liberal Education

(Orig. title: "Science As An Element in Culture")

1913 (May 24, 31) in "The New Statesman and Nation"
vol. 1, p. 202-204, 234-236 . . . .   120.01
1917 in "Mysticism and Logic": II (BN 172) .   120.02
1929 in "Contemporary Essays"
New York: Scribner, p. 250-262 . . . .   120.03
1931 in "Essays for Our Day"
New York: W. W. Norton, p. 249-258 . .   120.04
1965 in "On the Philosophy of Science": VI/I
(BN 672) 120.05

T r a n s l a t i o n s
Deutsch . . . .   1952 in BN 172.22 . . . . .   120.06
Französisch . . .   1922 in BN 172.23 . . . . .   120.07
Italienisch . . .   1964 in BN 172.24 . . . . .   120.08
Japanisch . . . . .   1959 in BN 172.27 . . . . .   120.09
Norwegisch . . . .   1947 in BN 519.00 . . . . .   120.10
Portugiesisch .   1957 in BN 172.29 . . . . .   120.11
Schwedisch . . . .   1954 in BN 172.30 . . . . .   120.12
Spanisch . . . . . .   1973 in BN 172.31 = 706 . .   120.13
Sp./Catalanisch   1969 in BN 172.32 . . . . .   120.14
Türkisch . . . . . .   1972 in BN 172.34 . . . . .   120.15

The Nature of Sense-Data

(A Reply to Dr. Dawes Hicks)

1913 in "Mind", vol. 22, p. 76-81 . . . .   121.00

Metaphysics and Intuition

1913 in "Cambridge Review", vol. 34, p. 376 - 377   122.00

Review of A. Ruge's
"Encyclopaedia of the Philosophical Sciences"

1913 in "Cambridge Review", vol. 35, p. 161 . .   123.01
    1914 in "The Nation" (London),
       vol. 14, p. 771-772 . . . .   123.02

Preface to Henri Poincaré's
"Science and Method"

1914 London, New York: T. Nelson & Sons, p. 5-8   124.00
   (Tr.: Francis Maitland)

On the Nature of Acquaintance

1914 in "Monist"; vol. 24; Jan.: p. 1-16,
    Apr.: p. 160-187, July: p. 435-453 . . . .   125.01
    1956 in "Logic and Knowledge" (BN 616) . .   125.02

    T r a n s l a t i o n s
    Deutsch .... 1976 in BN 711.00 . . . . .   125.03
    Italienisch ... 1961 in BN 616.08 . . . . .   125.04
    Portugiesisch . 1974 in BN 616.09 . . . . .   125.05
    Spanisch ...... 1966 in BN 616.10 . . . . .   125.06

Mr. Balfour's Natural Theology

1914 (Mar. 4) in "Cambridge Review",
    vol. 35, p. 338-339 . . . .   126.00

Mysticism and Logic

1914 (July) in "Hibbert Journal",
    vol. 12, p. 780-803 . . . .   127.01
    1917 in "Mysticism and Logic": I (BN 172) .   127.02
    1927 in "Selected Papers of Bertrand Russell"
      (BN 317) 127.03

    T r a n s l a t i o n s
    Deutsch .... 1952 in BN 172.22 . . . . .   127.04
    Französisch ... 1922 in BN 172.23 . . . . .   127.05
    Italienisch ... 1964 in BN 172.24 . . . . .   127.06
    Japanisch ..... 1959 in BN 172.27 . . . . .   127.07
    Portugiesisch . 1957 in BN 172.29 . . . . .   127.08
    Schwedisch .... 1954 in BN 172.30 . . . . .   127.09
    Spanisch ...... 1973 in BN 172.31 = 706 . .   127.10
    Sp./Catalanisch 1969 in BN 172.32 . . . . .   127.11
    Türkisch:
       "Mistilik ve mantik"
       Tr.: Yusuf Serif
       1935 Istanbul. 55 pp. 127.12
    Türkisch ...... 1972 in BN 172.34 . . . . .   127.13

The Relation of Sense-Data to Physics

1914 (July) in "Scientia", vol. 16, p. 1-27 . . 128.01
1917 in "Mysticism and Logic": VIII (BN 172) 128.02

Translations
Deutsch .... 1952 in BN 172.22 . . . . . 128.03
" .... 1976 in BN 711.00 . . . . . 128.04
Französisch ... 1922 in BN 172.23 . . . . . 128.05
Italienisch ... 1964 in BN 172.24 . . . . . 128.06
Japanisch ..... 1959 in BN 172.27 . . . . . 128.07
Portugiesisch . 1957 in BN 172.29 . . . . . 128.08
Schwedisch .... 1954 in BN 172.30 . . . . . 128.09
Spanisch ...... 1973 in BN 172.31 = 706 . . 128.10
Sp./Catalanisch 1969 in BN 172.32 . . . . . 128.11
Türkisch ...... 1972 in BN 172.34 . . . . . 128.12

Definitions and Methodological Principles
in Theory of Knowledge

1914 (Oct.) in "Monist", vol. 24, p. 582-593 . . 129.00

Scientific Method in Philosophy

1914 Oxford: The Clarendon Press. 30 pp. 130.01
    (Delivered Nov. 18, 1914, as a Herbert
    Spencer Lecture)
    1916 in "Decennial Volume", Oxford,
       at the Clarendon Press 130.02
    1917 in "Mysticism and Logic": VI (BN 172) 130.03

Translations
Deutsch .... 1952 in BN 172.22 . . . . . 130.04
Französisch ... 1922 in BN 172.23 . . . . . 130.05
Italienisch ... 1964 in BN 172.24 . . . . . 130.06
Japanisch ..... 1959 in BN 172.27 . . . . . 130.07
Portugiesisch . 1957 in BN 172.29 . . . . . 130.08
Schwedisch .... 1954 in BN 172.30 . . . . . 130.09
Spanisch ...... 1973 in BN 172.31 = 706 . . 130.10
Sp./Catalanisch 1969 in BN 172.32 . . . . . 130.11
Türkisch ...... 1972 in BN 172.34 . . . . . 130.12

Why Nations Love War

1914 (Nov.) in "War and Peace" 131.01
    1916 in "Justice in War-Time": 4 (BN 158) . 131.02

War, the Offspring of Fear.

1914 London: Union of Democratic Control.
    Pamphlets no. 3. 11 pp. 132.01
    1915 London: Union of Democratic Control 132.02
    1916 "   : "   " "   " 132.03

    Translations
    Deutsch:
    "Der Krieg, ein Kind der Furcht"
    Ü.: Fel. Beran
    1915 Zürich: Rascher. 22 S. 132.04

OUR KNOWLEDGE OF THE EXTERNAL WORLD
AS A FIELD FOR SCIENTIFIC METHOD IN PHILOSOPHY

1914 London: Allen & Unwin 133.01
Chicago, London: Open Court. IX, 245 pp. . . . 133.02

C o n t e n t s
Preface. I. Current Tendencies. II. Logic
as the Essence of Philosophy. III. On Our
Knowledge of the External World. IV. The
World of Physics and the World of Sense. V.
The Theory of Continuity. VI. The Problem
of Infinity Considered Historically. VII.
The Positive Theory of Infinity. VIII. On the
Notion of Cause, with Application to the
Free-Will Problem. Index.

C o m m e n t a r y
Russell's "Our Knowledge of the External
World" was written for the Lowell Lectures in
Boston in 1914; but he gave the lectures first
in Cambridge (Mass.), at the beginning of the
year, as a kind of preliminary try-out. At
that time C. K. Ogden was the editor of the
"Cambridge Magazine". He saw that people knew
about Russell's lectures in advance, with the
result that sixty or seventy people came to
hear them, Russell, only used to tiny classes for his ordinary University lectures,
was still so shy and diffident as a speaker
that, when he arrived and saw the size of his
audience, he was seen to hesitate and nearly
retreat. When Russell got going, the reception which greeted some early touches of wit
gradually put him at his ease; and the lectures had the same success later at Harvard.

K o m m e n t a r
Russell's "Our Knowledge of the External
World" wurde für die 1914 in Boston (Mass.)
gehaltenen Lowell Vorlesungen geschrieben; er
hielt aber die Vorlesungen das erstemal schon
Anfang 1914 in Cambridge (Mass.) als eine Art
Generalprobe. Damals war C.K.Ogden Herausgeber des "Cambridge Magazine". Er sah, daß die
Leute vorher von Russell's Vorlesungen erfahren hatten, mit dem Erfolg, daß sich nun sech-
zig bis siebzig Hörer einstellten. Russell,
der von seinen üblichen Universitätsvorle —
sungen her nur an kleine Hörergruppen gewöhnt
war, zeigte sich immer noch so scheu und wenig
selbstsicher als Redner, daß er beim Herein-
kommen, als er die große Menschenmenge gese-
hen hatte, einen zögernden Eindruck machte
- fast als wollte er sich zurückziehen. Als
Russell in Gang kam und seine bald aufsprü-
henden Geistesblitze den Kontakt herstellten,

lockerte er sich allmählich; in Harvard später hatten die Vorlesungen den gleichen Erfolg.

R e p r i n t s
1920 New York: W. W. Norton 133.03
1922 London: Allen & Unwin 133.04
1926 "   : "   " "   , rev. ed. . . . 133.05
1927 Excerpt:
"Current Tendencies" (I)
in "Selected Papers of Bertrand Russell"
(BN 317) 133.06
1929 New York: W. W. Norton 133.07
1929 London: Allen & Unwin 133.08
1949 "   : "   " " 133.09
1952 "   : "   " " 133.10
1953 New York: Humanities Press 133.11
1960 "   "   : New American Library 133.12
1961 London: Allen & Unwin 133.13
1965 Excerpt:
"The World of Physics
and the World of Sense" (IV)
in "On the Philosophy of Science": II/I
(BN 672) 133.14
1972 London: Allen & Unwin 133.15

T r a n s l a t i o n s
Chinesisch:
"Zhexue zhong zhi kexue fangfa"
1921 Shanghai 133.16
Deutsch:
"Unser Wissen von der Außenwelt
als Gebiet wissenschaftlicher Methodik
in der Philosophie"
Ü.: Walter Rothstock
1926 Leipzig: F. Meiner 133.17
I n h a l t
Vorwort des Verfassers.   I. Tendenzen
der gegenwärtigen Philosophie.   II.
Die Logik als wesentlicher Bestandteil
der Philosophie. III. Über unser Wissen
von der Außenwelt. IV. Die Welt der Naturwissenschaft und die Sinnenwelt. V.
Die Kontinuitätstheorie.   VI. Die Geschichte des Unendlichkeitsproblems.
VII. Die positive Theorie des Unendlichen. VIII. Über den Ursachbegriff und
seine Anwendung auf das Problem des
freien Willens. Register.
Französisch:
"La méthode scientifique en philosophie
et notre connaissance
du monde exterieur"
Tr.: Philippe Devaux
1929 Paris: Vrin 133.18
1971 Paris: Payot 133.19

Italienisch:
"La conoscenza del mondo esterno
Tr.: Maria Camilla Ciprandi
1966 Mailand: Longanesi 133.20
Tr.: Maurizio Destro
1971 Rom: Newton Compton Editori . . .   133.21
Portugiesisch:
"Nosso conhecimento do mundo exterior".
Tr.: R. J. Haddock, Lobo Netto
1966 Sao Paulo: Edit. Nacional 133.22
Spanisch:
"Nuestro conocimiento del mondo externo"
Tr.: R. J. Velzi
1946 Buenos Aires: Ateneo 133.23
"Conocimiento del mundo exterior"
Tr.: Maria Teresa Cárdenas
1964 Buenos Aires: Fabril 133.24
"Nuestro conocimiento del mundo exterior
como campo para el método cientifico en
filosofia"
1973 in BN 706 . . . .   133.25

Sensation and Imagination

1915 (Jan.) in "Monist", vol. 25, p. 28-44 . . .   134.00

The Ethics of War

1915 (Jan.) in "International Journal of Ethics"
vol. 25, p. 127-142 . . . .   135.01
1916 in "Justice in War-Time": 2 (BN 158)   135.02

Is a Permanent Peace Possible?

1915 (Mar.) in "Atlantic Monthly",
vol. 115, p. 127-142 . . . .   136.01
1916 in "Justice in War-Time": 6 (BN 158)   136.02

On the Experience of Time

1915 (Apr.) in "Monist", vol. 25, p. 212-233 . .   137.00

The Ultimate Constituents of Matter

1915 (July) in "Monist", vol. 25, p. 399-417 . .   138.01
1917 in "Mysticism and Logic": VII (BN 172)   138.02

Translations
Deutsch . . . . 1952 in BN 172.22 . . . . .   138.03
Französisch . . . 1922 in BN 172.23 . . . . .   138.04
Italienisch . . . 1964 in BN 172.24 . . . . .   138.05
Japanisch . . . . . 1959 in BN 172.27 . . . . .   138.06
Portugiesisch . 1957 in BN 172.29 . . . . .   138.07
Schwedisch . . . . 1954 in BN 172.30 . . . . .   138.08
Spanisch . . . . . . 1973 in BN 172.31 = 706 . .   138.09
Sp./Catalanisch 1969 in BN 172.32 . . . . .   138.10
Türkisch . . . . . . 1972 in BN 172.34 . . . . .   138.11

The Future of Anglo-German Rivalry

1915 (July) in "Atlantic Monthly",
vol. 116, p. 127-133 . . . .   139.01
1916 in "Justice in War-Time": 5 (BN 158)   139.02

War and Non-Resistance

1915 (Aug.) in "Atlantic Monthly",
vol. 116, p. 266-274 . . . .   140.01
1915 (Oct.) in "Internat. Journal of Ethics"
vol. 26, p. 23-30 . . . .   140.02
1916 in "Justice in War-Time": 3 (BN 158)   140.03

On Justice in War-Time.
An Appeal to the Intellectuals of Europe.

1915 in "International Review",
vol. 1, no. 4, 5, p. 145-151, 223-230 . . .   141.01
1916 in "Justice in War-Time": 1 (BN 158)   141.02
T r a n s l a t i o n s
Deutsch . . . . 1972 in BN 703/II:3 . . . .   141.03

The Philosophy of Pacifism

A paper read at the Conference upon the Pacifist
Philosophy of Life, Caxton Hall, London, July 1915

1915 London: League of Peace and Freedom. 16 pp.   142.01
T r a n s l a t i o n s
Deutsch . . . . 1922 in BN 239/II:4 . . . .   142.02

The Nature of the State
in View of the External Relations

1915-16 in "Proceedings Aristotelian Society",
vol. 16, p. 301-310 . . . .   143.00

Danger to Civilization

1916 (Mar.) in "Open Court", vol. 30, p. 170-180   144.01
1916 in "Justice in War-Time": 7 (BN 158)   144.02

Religion and the Churches

1916 (Apr.) in "Unpopular Review",
vol. V, p. 392-409 . . . .   145.01
1916 in "Principles of Social Reconstruction"
VII (BN 159) 145.02

T r a n s l a t i o n s
Chinesisch . . . . 1959 in BN 159.21 . . . . .   145.03
Deutsch . . . . 1921 in BN 159.23 . . . . .   145.04
Französisch . . . 1924 in BN 159.27 . . . . .   145.05
Ind./Hindi . . . . 1963 in BN 159.28 . . . . .   145.06
Ind./Marathi . . 1969 in BN 159.29 . . . . .   145.07
Italienisch . . . 1968 in BN 159.30 = 686 . .   145.08
Japanisch . . . . . 1966 in BN 159.32 . . . . .   145.09
Polnisch . . . . . . 1932 in BN 159.33 . . . . .   145.10
Portugiesisch . 1958 in BN 159.34 . . . . .   145.11
Spanisch . . . . . . 1975 in BN 159.35 . . . . .   145.12

The Case of Ernest F. Everett

1916 Pamphlet: "No Conscription Fellowship" . .   146.00
(The discussion of the case of a conscientious objector which led to the prosecution
of Bertrand Russell)

Letter to the Times of London

1916 (May 17) Letter refering
to the Everett case pamphlet 147.01
1942 in "Bertrand Russell: A College Controversy of the Last War" by G. H. Hardy,
Cambridge, at the Univ. Press, p. 33 .   147.02

War as an Institution

1916 (May) in "Atlantic Monthly",
vol. 117, p. 603-613 . . . .   148.01
1916 in "Principles of Social Reconstruction"
III (BN 159) 148.02

Translations
Chinesisch .... 1959 in BN 159.21 . . . . .   148.03
Deutsch .... 1921 in BN 159.23 . . . . .   148.04
Französisch ... 1924 in BN 159.27 . . . . .   148.05
Ind./Hindi .... 1963 in BN 159.28 . . . . .   148.06
Ind./Marathi .. 1969 in BN 159.29 . . . . .   148.07
Italienisch ... 1968 in BN 159.30 = 686 . .   148.08
Japanisch ..... 1966 in BN 159.32 . . . . .   148.09
Polnisch ...... 1932 in BN 159.33 . . . . .   148.10
Portugiesisch . 1958 in BN 159.34 . . . . .   148.11
Spanisch ...... 1975 in BN 159.35 . . . . .   148.12

Rex versus Bertrand Russell

1916 Pamphlet: "No Conscription Fellowship",
23 pp. Speech in own defense. A suppressed
pamphlet. (Report of the Proceedings before
the Lord Mayor at the Mansion House Justice
Room, 5 June 1916) 149.01
1919 in "Living Age" (Feb. 15),
vol. 300, p. 385-394 . . . .   149.02

Education as a Political Institution

1916 (June) in "Atlantic Monthly",
vol. 117, p. 750-757 . . . .   150.01
1916 in "Principles of Social Reconstruction"
V (BN 159) 150.02
1927 in "Selected Papers of Bertrand Russell"
(BN 317) 150.03
1928 in "Essays of Our Times",
New York: Century Comp., p. 359-374 .   150.04
1933 in"Challenging Essays in Modern Thought"
New York: Century Comp., p. 182-199 .   150.05

```
1950 in "The World's Best"
     New York: Dial Press, p. 447-456 . . .    150.06
1961 in "The Basic Writings of B. Russell":
     X/45 (BN 552)  . . . . . . . . . . . .    150.07
```

T r a n s l a t i o n s
```
Chinesisch .... 1959 in BN 159.21 . . . . .   150.08
Deutsch ....... 1921 in BN 159.23 . . . . .   150.09
"       ....... 1974 in BN 707.00 . . . . .   150.10
"       ....... 1975 in BN 710.00 . . . . .   150.11
Französisch ... 1924 in BN 159.27 . . . . .   150.12
Ind./Hindi .... 1963 in BN 159.28 . . . . .   150.13
Ind./Marathi .. 1969 in BN 159.29 . . . . .   150.14
Italienisch ... 1968 in BN 159.30 = 686 . .   150.15
Japanisch ..... 1966 in BN 159.32 . . . . .   150.16
Polnisch ...... 1932 in BN 159.33 . . . . .   150.17
Portugiesisch . 1958 in BN 159.34 . . . . .   150.18
Spanisch ...... 1975 in BN 159.35 . . . . .   150.19
```

Marriage and the Population Question

```
1916 (July) in "International Journal of Ethics"
     vol. 26, p. 443-461 . . . . . . . . . . . .   151.01
1916 in "Principles of Social Reconstruction"
     VI (BN 159)  . . . . . . . . . . . . .        151.02
1925 in "Selected Articles on Marriage and
     Divorce", reprinted in part as 'Marriage'
     New York: H. W. Wilson Comp., p. 51-54        151.03
```

T r a n s l a t i o n s
```
Chinesisch .... 1959 in BN 159.21 . . . . .   151.04
Deutsch ....... 1921 in BN 159.23 . . . . .   151.05
Französisch ... 1924 in BN 159.27 . . . . .   151.06
Ind./Hindi .... 1963 in BN 159.28 . . . . .   151.07
Ind./Marathi .. 1969 in BN 159.29 . . . . .   151.08
Italienisch ... 1968 in BN 159.30 = 686 . .   151.09
Japanisch ..... 1966 in BN 159.32 . . . . .   151.10
Polnisch ...... 1932 in BN 159.33 . . . . .   151.11
Portugiesisch . 1958 in BN 159.34 . . . . .   151.12
Spanisch ...... 1975 in BN 159.35 . . . . .   151.13
```

Freedom of Speech in England

```
1916 (Oct. 21) in "School & Society",
     vol. 4, p. 637-638 . . . . . . . . . . . .    152.00
```

Open Letter to President Wilson

```
1916 (Dec. 30) in "Survey", vol. 37, p. 372-373    153.00
```

Personal Statement

```
1916 (Dec.) in "Open Court", vol. 30, p. 766-767   154.00
```

Making Martyrs
of "Conscientious Objectors" in England

```
1916 in "Current Opinion", vol. 61, p. 257 . . .   155.00
     (Quoting from Russell's "Defense". BN 149.1)
```

Bertrand Russell's Plea for the Child
as the Vital Factor in Modern Education

1916 in "Current Opinion", vol. 61, p. 46 . . . 156.00

Policy of the Entente, 1904-1914.
A Reply to Professor Gilbert Murray.

1916 Manchester, London:
    The National Labour Press. 86 pp. 157.01
    1916 in "Justice in War-Time": 8 (BN 158) 157.02

JUSTICE IN WAR-TIME

1916 Chicago, London: Open Court. IX, 243 pp. . . 158.01
    London: Allen & Unwin 158.02
    C o n t e n t s
    1. An Appeal
       to the Intellectuals of Europe (1915/141)
    2. The Ethics of War . . . . (1915/135)
    3. War and Non-Resistance . . . . . . (1915/140)
    4. Why Nations Love War . . . . (1914/131)
    5. Future of Anglo-German Rivalry (1915/139)
    6. Is a Permanent Peace Possible? (1915/136)
    7. The Danger to Civilization . . (1916/144)
    8. The Entente Policy of 1904-1915 (1916/157)
    R e p r i n t s
    1917 Chicago: Open Court 158.03
    1924 London: Allen & Unwin 158.04
    1974 New York: Haskell 158.05
    1975 Nottingham: B. R. Peace Foundation . . 158.06
    T r a n s l a t i o n s
    Chinesisch:
       "Zhanshi zhi zhengyi"
       (Im Bestand des Instituts für Philoso-
       phie der Akademie für Sozialwissenschaf-
       ten in Peking. Erscheinungsort und -jahr
       waren nicht zu ermitteln.) 158.07
    Deutsch:
       Auszug: "Ein Appell
       an die Intellektuellen Europas" (1)
       1972 in BN 703/II:3 . . . . 158.08

PRINCIPLES OF SOCIAL RECONSTRUCTION

1916 London: Allen & Unwin. 251 pp. 159.01
    1917 under the title
       "Why men fight; a Method of Abolishing
       the International Duel"
       New York: The Century Co. 272 pp. . . 159.02
    C o n t e n t s
    I. The Principles of Growth. II. The State.
    III. War as an Institution (1916/148). IV.
    Property. V. Education (1916/150). VI.
    Marriage and the Population Question (1916/
    151). VII. Religion and the Churches (1916/
    145). VIII. What We Can Do.

Commentary
Russell continued with his pacifist propaganda: preparing for publication, under the
title "Principles of Social Reconstruction",
a series of lectures delivered in the begining
of 1916. In these he had put forward radical
ideas not only about the war, but also about
education, marriage, and other subjects. He
insisted that a book like his "Principles of
Social Reconstruction" "was not intended as
a contribution to learning, but had an entirely practical purpose". He did not write
it as a philosopher, but "as a human being
who suffered from the state of the world".
The book is still of outstanding importance
today. The publication of the book was something of a landmark in Russell's career, because it was the first to show he could have
a wide sale among ordinary readers. For the
rest of his life he was not only a philosopher writing books for dons, but a prophet
appealing to the people and pleading for
human happiness.

Kommentar
Russell setzte seine pazifistische Propaganda
fort: eine Reihe von Vorlesungen, die er Anfang 1916 gehalten hatte, bereitete er unter dem Titel "Principles of Social Reconstruction" zur Veröffentlichung vor. Darin
trat er mit radikalen Ideen nicht nur über
den Krieg hervor, sondern auch über Erziehung,
Ehe und andere Fragen. Er betonte, daß ein
Buch wie seine "Principles of Social Reconstruction" "nicht einen Beitrag zur Bildung
liefern wollte, sondern einen durchaus praktischen Zweck hätte". Er schrieb es nicht als
Philosoph, sondern "als ein Mensch, der unter
dem Zustand der Welt litt". Das Buch ist auch
heute noch von überragender Bedeutung. Die
Veröffentlichung dieses Buches war eine Art
Grenzstein in Russells Laufbahn, denn es zeigte sich zum ersten Male, daß er breiten Ab-
satz beim großen Lesepublikum finden konnte.
Für den Rest seines Lebens war er nicht mehr
allein der Philosoph, der Bücher für Akademiker schrieb, er war zugleich ein Prophet,
der sich an das Volk wandte und für das Glück
der Menschen kämpfte.

Reprints
1917 London: Allen & Unwin 159.03
1919 "   : "   " " 159.04
1920 "   : "   " " 159.05

1920 New York: The Century Co. 159.06
1925 Excerpt:
     "Marriage" (VI)
     in "Selected Articles
     on Marriage and Divorce".
     New York: H. W. Wilson Comp., p. 51-54 159.07
1927 London: Allen & Unwin 159.08
1927 Excerpts:
     "The State" (II)
     "Education" (V)
     in "Selected Papers of Bertrand Russell"
     (BN 317) 159.09
1930 New York: A. & C. Boni 159.10
1946 Excerpt:
     "The State as Organized Power" (II)
     in "Leviathan in Crisis"
     New York: Viking Press, p. 44-55 . . . 159.11
1950 Excerpt:
     "Education" (V)
     in "The World's Best"
     New York: Dial Press, p. 447-456 . . . 159.12
1950 London: Allen & Unwin 159.13
1954 "   : "   " " 159.14
1960 "   : "   " " 159.15
1961 Excerpts:
     "Property" (IV)
     "Education" (V)
     in "The Basic Writings of B. Russell":
     XII/53, X/45 (BN 659) 159.16
1971 London: Allen & Unwin 159.17
1971 New York: Garland Publ. 159.18
     Freeport, N. Y.: Books for Libraries Pr. 159.19
1972 London: Allen & Unwin 159.20
T r a n s l a t i o n s
Chinesisch:
     "Shehui gaizao de yuanli"
     1959 Shanghai 159.21
     "Shê Hui Ch'ung Chien Yüan Li"
     Tr.: Chêng Wei Min
     1973 Taipeh: Horizon 159.22
Deutsch:
     "Grundlagen
     für eine soziale Umgestaltung"
     Tr.: Margarete Hethey
     1921 München: Drei Masken Verlag . . . 159.23
     I n h a l t
     Vorwort des Verfassers. I. Das Prinzip
     der Entwicklung. II. Der Staat. III.
     Krieg als Institution. IV. Besitz. V.
     Erziehung. VI. Ehe und Bevölkerungs-
     frage. VII. Religion und die Kirchen.
     VIII. Was wir tun können.

Deutsch:
    Auszüge:
    "Grundlagen
    für eine soziale Umgestaltung"
    1972 in BN 703/II:4 . . . . 159.24
    Auszug:
    "Erziehung
    als politische Institution" (V)
    1974 in BN 707/II:1 . . . . 159.25
    1975 in BN 710/I 159.26
Französisch:
    "Principes de reconstruction sociale."
    Tr.: E. de Clermont-Tonnerre
    1924 Paris: Payot 159:27
Ind./Hindi:
    "Samajik punarnirman ke siddhant"
    Tr.: Muniš Saksena
    1963 Delhi: Rajkamal Prakašan 159.28
Ind./Marathi:
    "Samajik punarrachanechi mulatattve"
    Tr.: Suman Dabholkar, L. M. Bhingare
    1969 Poona: Samaj prabodhan samstha . 159.29
Italienisch:
    "Principi di reforma sociale"
    1968 in BN 686 . . . . 159.30
    Tr.: R. Zangari
    1970 Rom: Newton Compton Editori . . . 159.31
Japanisch:
    "Shakai kaizô no sho genri"
    Tr.: Ichii Saburô
    1966 Tokio: Kawade shobô shinsha . . . 159.32
Polnisch:
    "Przebudowa Spozeczna"
    Tr.: Antoni Panski
    1932 Warschau: Roj 159.33
Portugiesisch:
    "Princípios de reconstrução social"
    Tr.: Lôlio Lourenço de Oliveira
    1958 Sao Paulo: Ed. Nacional 159.34
Spanisch:
    "Principios de reconstrucción social"
    1975 Madrid: Espasa-Calpe 159.35

For Conscience Sake

1917 (Jan. 15) in "Independent", vol. 89, p.101-103   160.00

Two Ideals of Pacifism

1917 (Jan.) in "War and Peace",
    vol. 4, no. 40, p. 58-60 . . . . 161.00

Political Ideals

1917 (Feb.) in "North American Review",
    vol. 205, p. 248-259 . . . . 162.01
    1917 in "Political Ideals": I (BN 171) . . 162.02

1931 in "Essays in Contemporary Civilization"
   New York: Macmillan, p. 464-477 . . .   162.03
1933 in "Modern Essays",
   Lahore: Careers, p. 141-155 . . . . .   162.04
T r a n s l a t i o n s
Chinesisch ,... 1927 in BN 171.09 . . . . .   162.05
Deutsch .... 1922 in BN 239/IV:17 . . .   162.06
Französisch:
   "Ideals politiques"
   Tr.: Roger Lévi
   in "Les Forgerons"
   1917 Paris, 16 rue Monsieur-le-Prince   162.07
Ind./Marathi .. 1966 in BN 171.13 . . . . .   162.08
Italienisch ... 1963 in BN 171.14 . . . . .   162.09
Japanisch ..... 1963 in BN 171.15 . . . . .   162.10
Schwedisch .... 1963 in BN 171.16 . . . . .   162.11
Spanisch ...... 1963 in BN 171.17 . . . . .   162.12
Türkisch ...... 1966 in BN 171.18 . . . . .   162.13

Liberty and National Service

1917 (Feb. 22) in "Tribunal", no. 48, p. 2 . . .   163.00

The Position of the Absolutists

1917 (Mar. 1) in "Tribunal", no. 49, p. 2 . . .   164.00

War and Individual Liberty

1917 (Mar. 8) in "Tribunal", no. 50, p. 2 . . .   165.01
   T r a n s l a t i o n s
   Deutsch:
      "Krieg und persönliche Freiheit"
      1922 in BN 239/II:5 . . . .   165.02

Resistance and Service

1917 (May 3) in "Tribunal", no. 57, p. 2 . . . .   166.00

National Independence and Internationalism

1917 (Mai) in "Atlantic Monthly",
   vol. 119, p. 622-628 . . . .   167.01
1917 in "Political Ideals": V (BN 171) . .   167.02

   T r a n s l a t i o n s
Chinesisch .... 1927 in BN 171.09 . . . . .   167.03
Ind./Marathi .. 1966 in BN 171.13 . . . . .   167.04
Italienisch ... 1963 in BN 171.14 . . . . .   167.05
Japanisch ..... 1963 in BN 171.15 . . . . .   167.06
Schwedisch .... 1963 in BN 171.16 . . . . .   167.07
Spanisch ...... 1963 in BN 171.17 . . . . .   167.08
Türkisch ...... 1966 in BN 171.18 . . . . .   167.09

Individual Liberty and Public Control

1917 (July) in "Atlantic Monthly",
   vol. 120, p. 112-120 . . . .   168.01

1917 in "Political Ideals": IV (BN 171) . . 168.02
T r a n s l a t i o n s
Chinesisch .... 1927 in BN 171.09 . . . . . 168.03
Ind./Marathi .. 1966 in BN 171.13 . . . . . 168.04
Italienisch ... 1963 in BN 171.14 . . . . . 168.05
Japanisch ..... 1963 in BN 171.15 . . . . . 168.06
Schwedisch .... 1963 in BN 171.16 . . . . . 168.07
Spanisch ...... 1963 in BN 171.17 . . . . . 168.08
Türkisch ...... 1966 in BN 171.18 . . . . . 168.09

Pacifism and Revolution

1917 (July 19) in "Tribunal",Suppl., no. 67 . . 169.01
T r a n s l a t i o n s
Deutsch:
    "Pazifismus und Revolution"
    1922 in BN 239/II:6 . . . . 169.02

Idealism on the Defensive

1917 in "Nation" (London), vol. 21, p. 588, 590. 170.00

POLITICAL IDEALS

1917 New York: The Century Co., 172 pp. 171.01
C o n t e n t s
    I. Political Ideals .... (1917/162)
    II. Capitalism
        and the Wage System .... (1917/171)
    III. Pitfalls in Socialism ..... (1917/171)
    IV. Individual Liberty
        and Public Control .... (1917/168)
    V. National Independence
        and Internationalism ...... (1917/167)

R e p r i n t s
1919 New York: The Century Co. 171.02
1931 Excerpt:
    "Political Ideals" (I)
    in "Essays in Contemporary Civilization"
    New York: Macmillan, p. 464-477 . . . 171.03
1933 in "Modern Essays",
    Lahore: Careers, p. 141-155 . . . . . 171.04
1963 London: Allen & Unwin 171.05
1963 New York: Barnes & Noble 171.06
1964 "   "   : Simon & Schuster 171.07
1977 London: Allen & Unwin 171.08
T r a n s l a t i o n s
Chinesisch:
    "Zhengzhi lixiang"
    1927 Shanghai 171.09
Deutsch:
    Auszüge:
    "Politische Ideale" (I)
    1922 in BN 239/IV:17 . . . . 171.10

Deutsch:
    Auszüge:
    "Der Kapitalismus u.d. Lohnsystem" (II)
    "Schwächen des Sozialismus" (III)
    u. d. Titel. "Politische Ideale"
    1972 in BN 703/II:5 . . . . 171.11
Französisch:
    Auszug:
    "Ideals politiques" (I)
    Tr.: Roger Lévi
    in "Les Forgerons"
    1917 Paris, 16 Rue Monsieut-le-Prince. 171.12
Ind./Marathi:
    "Rajkiya dhyeye"
    Tr.: Suman Dabhōlkar
    1966 Poona: Samaj Prabodhan Samstha . 171.13
Italienisch:
    "Le mie idee politiche"
    Tr.: Adriana Pellegrini
    1863 Mailand: Longanesi 171.14
Japanisch:
    "Seiji risô"
    Tr.: Tsutomu Makino
    1963 Tokio: Risô-sha 171.15
Schwedisch:
    "Politiska ideal"
    Tr.: Anders Byttner
    1963 Stockholm: Natur og Kultur . . . 171.16
Spanisch:
    "Ideales políticos"
    Tr.: Juan Novella Domingo
    1963 Madrid: Aguilar 171.17
Türkisch:
    "Siyasal idealler"
    Tr.: Mehmet Harmanci
    1966 Istanbul: May Matbaasi 171.18

MYSTICISM AND LOGIC AND OTHER ESSAYS

1917 London: Allen & Unwin, VII, 234 pp 172.01
     Garden City, N. Y.: Doubleday, 226 pp . . . 172.02
1918 New York: Longmans, Green & Co.,
     VII, 234 pp. 172.03
C o n t e n t s
    I. Mysticism and Logic . . . . . . (1914/127)
   II. The Place of Science
       in a Liberal Education . . . (1913/120)
  III. A Free Man's Worship . . . . . . (1903/036)
   IV. The Study of Mathematics . . (1907/077)
    V. Mathematics
       and the Metaphysicians . . . . (1901/020)
   VI. On Scientific Methods
       in Philosophy . . . . (1914/130)
  VII. The Ultimate Constituents
       of Matter . . . . (1915/138)

1917

Commentary
This is the great paradox of Russell: All his
instincts were on the side of the "rational-
ists": his greatest hatred was for those who
exalted emotion, or any sort of mystic intuition, at the espense of reason. But because
Russell was the greatest rationalist of all,
he had to admit that reason cannot prove the
mystics wrong. In fact, in some private moods
he was a mystic himself. (Though one of a most
unusual kind: a mystic who hated mysteries,
and devoted his lif to dispelling them.) This
side of his nature was often unsuspected,
although he wrote in "Mysticism and Logic"
that "The greatest men who have been philosophers have felt the need both of science
and of mysticism". - When Russell's "Mysticism
and Logic" was published towards the end of
the First World War, he declared that the
only review of it which showed any understanding was that by T. S. Eliot in the "Nation".

Kommentar
Das ist der große Widerspruch bei Russell:
Alle seine Instinkte waren auf Seiten der
"Rationalisten"; sein größter Hass galt denen, die auf Kosten der Vernunft Gefühle oder
irgendeine mystische Intuition verherrlich-
ten. Aber weil Russell der größte aller Rationalisten war, mußte er zugeben, daß die Vernunft den Irrtum der Mystiker nicht beweisen
kann. Ja manchmal in gewissen Stimmungen war
er selbst ein Mystiker. (Obwohl ein recht
seltsamgearteter: ein Mystiker, der mystische
Vorstellungen haßte und es sich zur Lebens-
aufgabe machte, sie zu zerstören.) An diese
Seite seines Wesens dachte man meist nicht,
obwohl er selbst in "Mysticism and Logic"
schrieb: "Die größten unter den Philosophen
haben gefühlt, daß beides nottut: Wissenschaft und Mystizismus". - Als Russells "Mysticism and Logic" gegen Ende des Ersten Welt-
krieges erschien, erklärte er, daß T.S.Eliots
Besprechung in "Nation" die einzige Kritik
sei, die Verständnis zeigte.

R e p r i n t s
1927 Excerpts:
    "Mysticism and Logic" (I)
    "A Free Man's Worship" (III)
    in "Selected Papers of Bertrand Russell"
    (BN 317) 172.04
1929 New York: Norton & Co., VII, 234 pp. . . 172.05
1932 London: Allen & Unwin 172.06
1936 "   : "   " " 172.07
1949 "   : "   " " 172.08
1950 "   : "   " " 172.09
1951 "   : "   " " 172.10
1953 Baltimore: Penguin 172.11
1957 Garden City, N.Y.: Doubleday 172.12
1959 London: Allen & Unwin 172.13
1959 New York: Barnes & Noble 172.14
1961 Excerpts:
    "A Free Man's Worship" (III)
    "Knowledge by Acquaintance
    and Knowledge by Description" (X)
    in "The Basic Writings of B. Russell":
    II/6, V/26 (BN 659) 172.15
1963 London: Allen & Unwin 172.16
1965 Excerpts:
    "The Place of Science
    in a Liberal Education" (II)
    "On the Notion of Cause" (IX)
    in "On the Philosophy of Science":
    VI/I, V/I (BN 672) 172.17
1969 London: Allen & Unwin 172.18
1970 "   : "   " " 172.19
1971 New York: Barnes & Noble 172.20
1976 under the title
    "A Free Man's Worship and Other Essays."
    London: Allen & Unwin 172.21
T r a n s l a t i o n s
Deutsch:
    "Mystik und Logik". Ü: Erwin Heinzel.
    1952 Wien,Stuttgart: Humboldt-Verlag . 172.22
    I n h a l t
    I. Mystik und Logik.
    II. Die Stellung d. Naturwissenschaf-
        ten in einer modernen Erziehung
    III. Was der freie Mensch verehrt.
    IV. Das Studium der Mathematik.
    V. Die Mathematik u.d. Metaphysiker.
    VI. Über die wissenschaftliche Methode
        in der Philosophie.
    VII. Die letzten Bestandteile d. Materie
    VIII. Das Verhältnis der Sinneswahrneh-
        mungen zur Physik.
    IX. Über den Begriff der Ursache.
    X. Kenntnis durch Bekanntschaft und
        Kenntnis durch Beschreibung.

Französisch:
"Le mysticisme et la logique"
Tr.: Jean de Menasce
1922 Paris: Payot 172.23
Italienisch:
"Misticismo e logica e altri saggi"
Tr.: L. Pavolini
1964 Mailand: Longanesi 172.24
Tr.: Jean Sanders, Leonardo Breccia
1970 Rom: Newton Compton Editori . . . 172.25
1972 " : "   "   "   . . . 172.26
Japanisch:
"Shiupi Shugi to Ronri"
Tr.: Minosuke Emori
1959 Tokio: Misuzu-shobo 172.27
Norwegisch:
Excerpts:
"Vitenskapens plase
i en fri oppdragelse" (II)
"En fri manns tro" (III)
in "Frihet og fornuft"
1947 in BN 519 . . . . 172.28
Portugiesisch:
"Misticismo e lógica"
Tr.: Wilson Velloso
1957 Sao Paulo: Ed. Nacional 172.29
Schwedisch:
"Mystik och logik och andra essäer"
Tr.: A. Byttner
1954 Stockholm: Natur och Kultur . . . 172.30
Spanisch:
"Misticismo y Lógica"
1973 in BN 706 . . . . 172.31
Sp./Catalanisch:
"Misticisme i logica"
Tr.: Francesco Forceisas
1969 Barcelona: Edicions 62 . . . . . 172.32
Tschechisch:
Excerpt:
"O pojmu příčiny" (IX)
1967 in BN 680/C:7 . . . . 172.33
Türkisch:
"Mistisizm ve mantik"
Tr.: Ayseli Usluata
1972 Istanbul: Varlik Kitabevi 172.34

The German Peace Offer
1918 (Jan. 3) in "Tribunal", no, 90, p. 1 . . . 173.01
The basis for the second prosecution of B.
Russell as a result of which he was impris-
oned for six months, during which time he
wrote his "Introduction to Mathematical Philosophy".
1968 in "Autobiography II". London: A. & U. 173.02

Pure Reason at Königsberg

Review of Norman Kemp Smith's
"A Commentary to Kant's 'Critique of Pure Reason'"
1918 (July 20) in "The Nation" (London),
    vol. 23, no. 16, p. 426 and 428 . . . . . . 174.00

Review of C. D. Broad's
"Perception, Physics and Reality"
1918 in "Mind", vol. 27, p. 492-498 . . . . . . 175.00

Man's War with the Universe
in the Religion of Bertrand Russell
1918 in "Current Opinion", vol. 65, p. 45-46 . . 176.00
    (Contains quotations from
    "A Free Man's Worship" - 1903/ BN 36)

ROADS TO FREEDOM:
SOCIALISM, ANARCHISM AND SYNDICALISM
1918 London: Allen & Unwin, XVIII, 215 pp. . . . 177.01
    C o n t e n t s
    Preface. Introduction.
    Part I. Historical.
        I. Marx and Socialist Doctrine. II. Ba-
        kunin and Anarchism. III. The Syndicalist
        Revolt.
    Part II. Problems of the Future.
        IV. Work and Pay. V. Government and Law.
        VI. International Relations. VII. Science
        and Art Under Socialism. VIII. The World
        as It Could Be Made. Index.

    R e p r i n t s
    1919 London: Allen & Unwin 177.02
    1919 under the title
        "Proposed Roads to Freedom: Socialism,
        Anarchism and Syndicalism"
        New York: Holt & Co. XVIII, 218 pp. . . . 177.03
    1920 London: Allen & Unwin 177.04
    1927 Excerpts:
        "Science and Art under Socialism"(VII),
        "The World as It Could Be Made" (VIII)
        in "Selected Papers of Bertrand Russell"
        (BN 317) 177.05
    1931 New York: Blue Ribbon Book 177.06
    1933 London: Allen & Unwin 177.07
    1949 " : " " " 177.08
    1954 " : " " " 177.09
    1966 " : " " " 177.10
    1966 New York: Barnes & Noble 177.11
    1977 London: Allen & Unwin 177.12

T r a n s l a t i o n s
Arabisch:
    "Sobol Al Horria"
    Tr.: Abd El Kerim Ahmed
    1957 Kairo: Dar Al Kahira Liltiba'at . 177.13
Chinesisch:
    "Ziyou zhi lu"
    1959 Peking 177.14
Deutsch:
    Auszug:
    "Kunst, Wissenschaft und der Sozialis-
    mus" (VII)
    1921 Berlin: 'Der Syndikalist', 15 S.   177.15
    Unter dem Titel
    "Politische Ideale" (BN 177.01: I-VIII)
    1922 in BN 239/III:7-10, IV:12-16   177.16
    "Wege zur Freiheit: Sozialismus,
    Anarchismus, Syndikalismus."
    1971 Frankfurt: edition suhrkamp, 447. 177.17
    I n h a l t
    Vorbemerkung. Einleitung.
    Teil I. Geschichte.
        1. Marx und der Sozialismus. 2. Ba-
        kunin und der Anarchismus. 3. Die
        syndikalistische Revolte.
    Teil II. Fragen der Zukunft.
        4..Arbeit und Lohn. 5. Regierung und
        Gesetz. 6. Internationale Beziehun-
        gen. 7. Wissenschaft und Kunst im
        Sozialismus. 8. Wie die Welt gemacht
        werden könnte.
Französisch:
    "Le Monde qui pourrait être"
    Tr.: M. de Cheveigné
    1973 Paris: Denoël 177.18
Ind./Tamil:
    "Sudhandira cuvadugal"
    Tr.: K. S. Srinivasen
    .... Madras: Sudhandiva prasuralayam 177.19
Italienisch:
    "Socialismo, Anarchismo, Sindicalismo"
    Tr.: Camillo Pellizzi
    1946 Mailand: Longanesi 177.20
    "Strade per la libertà"
    Tr.: P. Stampa
    1971 Rom: Newton Compton Editori . . . 177.21
Japanisch:
    "Jiyû eno michi"
    Tr.: Takeo Kurihara
    1953 Tokio: Kadokawa shoten 177.22
Polnisch:
    "Drogi DoWolnosci.
    Socializm, Anarchizm, Syndykalizm."
    Tr.: Amelja Kurlandzka
    1935 Warschau: Roj 177.23

Portugiesisch:
"Caminhos para a liberdade"
Tr.: Brenno Silveira
1955 Sao Paulo: Ed. Nacional 177.24
Spanisch:
"Los čaminos de la libertad: el socia-
lismo, el anarquismo y el sindicalismo"
Tr.: Garcia Paladini
1932 Madrid: Aguilar 177.25
1966 Buenos Aires 177.26

PHILOSOPHY OF LOGICAL ATOMISM

(See also "Logical Atomism", 1924/BN 265)

1918 (Oct.) in "Monist", vol. 28, p. 495-527
1919 (Jan.) "   "   , "   29, "   33- 63
     (Apr.) "   "   , "   29, " 190-222
     (July) "   "   , "   29, " 344-380 . .   178.01
C o n t e n t s
I. Facts and Propositions. II. Particulars,
Predicates and Relations.   III. Atomic and
Molecular Propositions. IV. Proposition and
Facts with More and One Verb, Belief, etc.
V. General Propositions and Existence. VI.
Descriptions and Incomplete Symbols.   VII.
The Theory of Types and Symbolism. VIII. Ex-
cursus into Metaphysics: What there Is.

C o m m e n t a r y
Russells "Philosophy of Logical Atomism" is
the first attempt at a theory of an ontolo-
gical description of the world taking into
account the demands mathematical logic (which
itself is strongly influenced by Russell)
would make upon such a description. Central
to it are the relationships between the world
which is viewed as the aggregate of all facts,
and a logically perfect, or ideal, language.
Russell developed his theory initially in
"Our Knowledge of the External World" (1914/
BN 133), then more fully in "Philosophy of
Logical Atomism" (1918/19) and, finally, once
again in a more concise form and with certain
modifications, in "Logical Atomism" (1924/
BN 265). In "My Philosophical Development"
(1959/BN 648) he says, however, that he had
taken the view of logical atomism as early
as his renunciation of idealism around 1900,
and that all later modifications in his
thinking had been merely of an evolutionary
nature as against this fundamental change
from idealism to realism. The Atomism, in
the narrower sense of the abovementioned publications of 1914, 1918/19 and 1924, is the
result of discussions between Wittgenstein

and Russell in the field of philosophical
logic on the occassion of the appearance of the
"Principia Mathematica", vol. I(1910/BN 101).
The logical atomism of Russell and Wittgenstein has become the model for a series of
theories. Special questions of logical atomism
concerning the theory of language such as
denotation, proper nouns or types are, now
as before, the subject of discussions.

K o m m e n t a r
Russells "Philosophy of Logical Atomism" ist
der erste Versuch einer Theorie einer onto-
logischen Beschreibung der Welt unter Berücksichtigung der Ansprüche, die die von
Russell selbst stark beeinflußte mathematische Logik einer solchen Beschreibung stellen würde. Im Mittelpunkt stehen die Beziehungen zwischen der Welt, die als die Menge aller Tatsachen betrachtet wird, und einer logisch perfekten oder idealen Sprache.
Russell entwickelte diese Theorie erstmals
in "Our Knowledge of the External World"
(1914/BN 133), dann ausführlicher in "Philosophy of Logical Atomism" (1918/19) und
schließlich noch einmal in kürzerer Form und
mit gewissen Modificationen in "Logical
Atomism" (1924/BN 265). In "My Philosophical
Development" (1959/BN 648) sagt er allerdings, daß er den Standpunkt des logischen
Atomismus bereits seit seiner Abkehr vom Idealismus um 1900 vertrete und daß alle späteren Modifikationen gegenüber diesem grund-
legenden Wandel vom Idealismus zum Realismus
in seinem Denken lediglich evolutionärer Natur gewesen seien. Der Atomismus im engeren
Sinne jener angeführten Publikationen von
1914, 1918/19 und 1924 ist das Ergebnis von
Diskussionen zwischen Wittgenstein und Russell auf dem Gebiete der philosophischen Logik anläßlich des Erscheinens der "Principia
Mathematica", vol. I (1910/BN 101). Der logische Atomismus von Russell und Wittgenstein
ist das Vorbild für eine Reihe von Theorien
geworden. Spezielle sprachtheoretische Fragen des logischen Atomismus, wie die Beschreibungen, Eigennamen oder Typen, stehen nach
wie vor zur Diskussion.

R e p r i n t s
1956 in "Logic and Knowledge", BN 616 . . .   178.02
1959 (ca.) Minneapolis: University of Minne-
    sota, Department of Philosophy. 65 pp.   178.03
1972 in "Russell's Logical Atomism", BN 697   178.04

1918/1919

T r a n s l a t i o n s
Deutsch:
"Philosophie des logischen Atomismus"
Ü.: Johannes Sinnreich
1976 in BN 711 . . . . 178.05
I n h a l t
1. Tatsachen und Aussagen. 2. Indivi-
duen, Prädikate, Relationen. 3. Atoma-
re und molekulare Aussagen. 4. Tatsachen und Aussagen mit mehr als einem
Verb. 5. Generelle Aussagen und Existenz. 6. Beschreibungen und sonstige
unvollständige Symbole. 7. Typen,Sym-
bole, Klassen. 8. Zur metaphysischen
Frage: Was gibt es?
Italienisch ... 1961 in BN 616.08 . . . . . 178.06
Portugiesisch . 1974 in BN 616.09 . . . . . 178.07
Spanisch ..... 1966 in BN 616.10 . . . . . 178.08
Spanisch:
"La filosofia del atomismo lógica"
in"Conception analitica de la filosofia"
1974 Madrid: Alianza Editorial. 2 vols.
(vol. I, p. 139-211) 178.09

On Propositions:
What They Are and How They Mean
1919 in "Proceedings Aristotelian Society",
Sup. vol. II, p. 1-43 . . . . 179.01
1956 in "Logic and Knowledge", BN 616 . . . 179.02
T r a n s l a t i o n s
Italienisch ... 1961 in BN 616.08 . . . . . 179.03
Portugiesisch . 1974 in BN 616.09 . . . . . 179.04
Spanisch ..... 1966 in BN 616.10 . . . . . 179.05

Review of J. Dewey's
"Essays in Experimental Logic"
1919 (Jan. 2) in "The Journal of Philosophy",
vol. 16, no. 1, p. 5-26 . . . . 180.00

Note on C. D. Broad's
"A General Notation for the Relation of Numbers"
1919 in "Mind", vol. 28, p. 124 . . . . 181.00

Democracy and Direct Action
1919 (May) in "English Review", vol.28, p.396-403 182.00

Economic Unity and Political Division
1919 (June 28) in "Dial", vol. 66, p. 629-631 . 183.00

Democracy and Efficiency
1919 in "Athenaeum", p. 270 . . . . 184.00

Philosophy and Virtue

1919 in "Athenaeum", p. 270 . . . . 185.00

The Mystic Vision

1919 in "Athenaeum", p. 487-488, 599 . . . . . . 186.00

Review of N. O. Lossky's
"The Intuitive Basis of Knowledge"

1919 in "Athenaeum", p. 524-525 . . . . 187.00

Review of C. E. M. Joad's
"Essays in Common-Sense Philosophy"

1919 in "Aţhenaeum", p. 652-653 . . . . 188.00

A Microcosm of British Philosophy

Review of "Proceedings of Aristotelian Society"

1919 (Nov. 7) in "Athenaeum", vol. 19,
no. 4671, p. 1149-1150 . . . . 189.00

The Anatomy of Desire

1919 in "Athenaeum",
p. 1340-1341, 1372-1373, 1402-1403 . . . . 190.00

INTRODUCTION TO MATHEMATICAL PHILOSOPHY

1919 London: Allen & Unwin, VIII, 208 pp. 191.01
New York: Macmillan, VIII, 208 pp. 191.02
C o n t e n t s
Preface. Editor's Note.
1. The Series of Numeral Numbers. 2. Defi-
nition of Number. 3. Finitude and Mathe-
matical Induction. 4. The Definition of Or-
der. 5. Kinds of Relations. 6. Similarity
of Relations. 7. Rational, Real and Complex
Numbers. 8. Infinite Cardinal Numbers. 9.
Infinite Series and Ordinals. 10. Limits and
Continuity. 11. Limits and Continuity of Func-
tions. 12. Selections and the Multiplicative
Axiom. 13. The Axiom of Infinity and Logical
Types. 14. Incompatibility and the Theory of
Deduction. 15. Proposition Functions. 16.
Description. 17. Classes. 18. Mathematics
and Logic. Index.

C o m m e n t a r y
I will mention what I think was the most important idea which Wittgenstein shared with
Russell at this time, and which I think must
undoubtedly be attributed to Russell, since
its origin can be found in "Principia Mathematica" and earlier. This is the emphasis on

"structure". .. One example, previously mentioned, is the theory about a sentence having
the same structure as the reality which it
describes. But the idea is of wider importance
than this. To quote from Russell's "Introduction to Mathematical Philosophy": "It is
often said .... that phenomena (or "appear-
ances") are subjective, but are caused by
things in themselves. ... Where such hypotheses are made, it is generally supposed that
we can know very little about the objective
counterparts. In actual fact, however, if the
hypotheses as stated were correct, the objective counterparts would form a world having
the same structure as the phenomenal world,
and allowing us to infer from phenomena the
truth of all propositions that can be stated
in abstract terms, and are known to be true
of phenomena." This idea was not so important
from the point of view of Russell's philosophy
at the time; but it became of great importance
on reverting to the ordinary view of an external world which causes our perceptions.
Such knowledge as we have from our perceptions
is knowledge of its structure, only express-
ible in abstract mathematical formulae. Here
again we are in the fascinating realm where
philosophy and science meet.

K o m m e n t a r
Ich möchte auf die meines Erachtens wichtige
Idee hinweisen, die Wittgenstein damals mit
Russell teilte und die, wie ich glaube, zweifellos Russell zuzuschreiben ist, da ihre
Anfänge schon in "Principia Mathematica" und
selbst noch früher zu finden sind. Das ist
das Gewicht, daß er auf die "Struktur" legt.
Ein früher erwähntes Beispiel ist die Theorie,
daß ein Satz dieselbe Struktur hat wie die
Wirklichkeit, die er beschreibt. Doch die Idee
hat eine weiterreichende Bedeutung. Ich zi-
tiere aus Russells "Introduction to Mathematical Philosophy": "Es wird oft behauptet
... daß Phänomene (oder "Erscheinungen") sub-
jektiv sind, aber durch Dinge an sich verursacht werden ... Wo solche Hypothesen aufgestellt werden, wird allgemein angenommen, daß
wir über die objektiven Entsprechungen sehr
wenig wissen können. In Wirklichkeit aber
würden die objektiven Entsprechungen, falls
die aufgestellten Hypothesen richtig wären,
eine Welt von der gleichen Struktur bilden,
wie die Welt der Erscheinungen sie besitzt.
Das würde uns gestatten, aus den Erscheinungen die Wahrheit aller Sätze abzuleiten, die

in abstrakten Begriffen aufgestellt werden
können und von denen man weiß, daß sie auf
die Erscheinungen zutreffen." Diese Idee war
von Russells damaligem philosophischen Standpunkt aus nicht so wichtig; aber sie gewann an
Bedeutung, sobald man sich wieder der üblichen Ansicht von einer äußeren Welt zuwandte,
die unsere Wahrnehmungen verursacht. Die aus
unseren Wahrnehmungen gewonnene Kenntnis ist
eine Kenntnis der Struktur, ausdrückbar in
abstrakten mathematischen Formeln. Hier kommen wir wieder auf das fesselnde Gebiet, wo
Philosophie und Naturwissenschaft sich be-
gegnen.

R e p r i n t s
1920 London: Allen & Unwin 191.03
1924 "   : "   " " 191.04
1924 New York: Macmillan 191.05
1927 Excerpt:
     "Definition of Number" (2)
     in "Selected Papers of Bertrand Russell"
     (BN 317) 191.06
1948 London: Allen & Unwin 191.07
1951 "   : "   " " 191.08
1952 "   : "   " " 191.09
1956 "   : "   " " 191.10
1961 Excerpt:
     "Mathematics and Logic" (18)
     in "The Basic Writings of B. Russell":
     IV/22 (BN 659) 191.11
1965 Excerpt:
     "Mathematic and Logic" (18)
     in "On the Philosophy of Science": I/II
     (BN 672) 191.12
1967 London: Allen & Unwin 191.13
1970 "   : "   " " 191.14
1971 New York: Simon & Schuster 191.15
1975 London: Allen & Unwin 191.16

T r a n s l a t i o n s
Arabisch:
     "Uṣūl al-Riyāḍiyyāt"
     Tr.: Muḥamad Mursi Aḥmad
     1959 Kairo: Dār al-Ma'ārif 191.17
Chinesisch:
     "Lu Su Suan Li Che Hsüeh"
     Tr.: Fu Shih Ming
     1967 Taipeh: Wen Pub. Service 191.18
Deutsch:
     "Einführung
     in die mathematische Philosophie"
     Ü.: E. J. Gumbel, W. Cordon
     1923 München: Drei Masken Verlag . . . 191.19
     1930 "   : "   "   "   . . . 191.20

1953 Darmstadt, Genf: Holle 191.21
I n h a l t
Einleitung.
1. Die Folge der natürlichen Zahlen.
2. Die Definition der Zahl. 3. End-
lichkeit und mathematische Induktion.
4. Die Definition der Ordnung. 5. Die
Beziehungen. 6. Ähnlichkeit von Beziehungen. 7. Rationale, reale und kom-
plexe Zahlen. 8. Unendliche Kardinal-
zahlen. 9. Unendliche Folgen und Or-
dinalzahlen. 10. Limes und Stetigkeit.
11. Limes und Stetigkeit bei Funktionen.
12. Die Theorie der Auswahlen und das
multiplikative Axiom. 13. Das Axiom der
Unendlichkeit und die logischen Typen.
14. Die Unverträglichkeit und die Theorie der Deduktion. 15. Satzfunkti-
onen. 16. Beschreibungen. 17. Mengen.
18. Mathematik und Logik.
1975 Wiesbaden: Vollmer 191.22
Französisch:
"Introduction
à la philosophique mathématique"
Tr.: G. Moreau
1928 Paris: Payot 191.23
1961 Paris: Payot 191.24
Italienisch:
"Introduzione
alla filosofia matematica"
Tr.: Enrico Carone
1946 Mailand: Longanesi 191.25
1962 " : " 191.26
1970 Rom: Newton Compton Editori . . . 191.27
Japanisch:
"Sûri-tetsugaku josetsu"
Tr.: Tomoji Hirano
.... Tokio: Iwanami shoten 191.28
Polnisch:
"Wstep do filozofi matematyki"
Tr.: Czeslaw Znamierowski
1958 Warschau: Panstw. Wydawn. Naukowe 191.29
Portugiesisch:
"Introdução
à filosofia da matemática"
Tr.: Giasone Rebuá
1963 Rio de Janeiro: Zahar 191.30
Spanisch:
"Introducción
a la Filosofiá Matemática"
1945 Buenos Aires: Losada 191.31
1956 in BN 615 . . . . 191.32
1973 in BN 706 . . . . 191.33

Tschechisch:
    Excerpts:
    "Popisy" (16)
    "Matematika a logika" (18)
    1967 in BN 680: A/2, A/4 . . . . 191.34

Review of H. H. Joachim's
"Immediate Experience and Mediation"

1920 in "Athenaeum", p. 43 . . . . 192.00

Relativity Theory of Gravitation

1920 (Jan.) in "English Review", vol.30, p.11-18 193.00

Bertrand Russell Prophesies
the Speedy Triumph of Socialism

1920 in "Current Opinion", vol. 68, p. 813-814 . . 194.00

Dreams and Facts

1920 (Feb.) in "Dial", vol. 68, p. 214-220 . . . 195.01
    1928 in "Sceptical Essays": II (BN 331) . . 195.02
    1933 in "Prose Patterns", N.Y.: Harcourt . 195.03
    T r a n s l a t i o n s
    Chinesisch .... 1932 in BN 331.16 . . . . . 195.04
    Deutsch .... 1930 in BN 331.19 . . . . . 195.05
    Französisch ... 1933 in BN 331.23 . . . . . 195.06
    Italienisch ... 1953 in BN 331.25 . . . . . 195.07
    Japanisch ..... 1963 in BN 331.29 . . . . . 195.08
    Polnisch ...... 1937 in BN 331.33 . . . . . 195.09
    Portugiesisch . 1955 in BN 331.35 . . . . . 195.10
    Schwedisch .... 1950 in BN 331.36 . . . . . 195.11
    Spanisch ...... 1956 in BN 331.39 = 615 . . 195.12

The Why and Wherefore of Wishing for Things

1920 (Feb. 28) in "Living Age",
    vol. 304, p. 528-533 . . . . 196.00

Religious Evolution

1920 in "Nation" (London), vol. 27, p. 116, 118 . 197.00

Review of B. Bosanquet's
"Implication and Linear Inference"

1920 (Mar. 27) in "Nation" (London),
    vol. 26, p. 898, 900 (Unsigned) 198.01
    1920 (Apr. 16) in "Athenaeum",
        no. 4694, p. 514-515 (signed B.R.) . . 198.02

What I Etat

A symposium compiled by Felix Grendon
1920 (Apr.) in "McCall's Magazine", vol. 17, p.24 199.00

1920

Democracy and Revolution
1920 (May/June) in "Liberatur", vol. 3,
    May: p. 10-13, June: p. 23-25 . . . . 200.00

Socialism and Liberal Ideals
Lecture delivered for the National Guilds League
at Kingsway Hall, London, Feb. 26, 1920.
1920 (May/June) in "English Review", vol. 30,
    p. 449-455, 499-508 . . . . 201.01
    1920 (July 10) in "Living Age", vol. 306 . 201.02

Impressions of Bolshevik Russia
1920 (July 10 - Aug. 7) in "Nation" (London),
    vol. 27, p. 460-462, 493-494, 520-521,
    547-548, 576-577 . . . . 202.00
    C o n t e n t s
    The Rule of the Proletariat.   The Puritan
    Parallel.   Plato's Guardians.   An Aristo-
    cracy.   As Internationalists.   Evil of the
    Revolutionary Theory.   Lenin   as   Interna-
    tionalist.   The Evolution   of   Bolshevism.
    Lenin, Trotzky and Gorki (see also BN 203/IV,
    BN 207/I:Ⅲ). Communism and the Soviet Con-
    stitution (see also BN 203/III, BN 207/I:V).
    Town   and   Country   (see   also   BN 203 / VI,
    BN 207/I:VIII).   Bolshevism and the Inter-
    national Situation (see also BN 203/V).

Soviet Russia - 1920
1920 (July 31 - Aug. 7) in "Nation" (New York),
    vol.111, p. 121-126, 152-154 . . . . 203.00
    C o n t e n t s
    I. The Problem. II. Bolshevist Theory.   III.
    Communism and   the Soviet Constitution (see
    also BN 202, BN 207/I:V).   IV. Lenin, Trotzky
    and Gorky (BN 202, BN 207/I:III).   V. The In-
    ternational Situation (see also BN 202).   VI.
    Town and Country (see also BN 202,.BN 207/
    I:VIII).

Bolshevik Theory
1920 (Sept. 15, Nov. 3, 17) in "New Republic",
    vol. 24, p. 67-69, 239-241, 296-298 . . . . 204.00
    C o n t e n t s
    I. The Materialistic Concept of History (see
    also BN 207/II:I).   II. Revolution and Dic-
    tatorship (see also BN 207/II:IV).   III. Me-
    chanism and the Individual (see also BN 207/
    II:V).

The Meaning of Meaning

Symposium: F. C. S. Schiller, B. R., H. H. Joachim.

1920 (Oct.) in "Mind",
    vol. 29, p. 398-404 (Russell's contribution) 205.00

Mathematical Philosophy

1920 in "Science Progress", vol. 15, p. 101 .... 206.00

THE PRACTICE AND THEORY OF BOLSHEVISM

1920 London: Allen & Unwin, 188 pp. 207.01
    Under the title:
    "Bolshevism: Practice and Theory"
    New York: Harcourt, Brace and Howe, 192 pp. 207.02
    C o n t e n t s
    Preface
    Part I. The Present Condition of Russia.
        I. What is Hoped for from Bolshevism.   II.
        General Characteristics. III. Lenin, Trotz-
        ky and Gorky (see also BN 202, BN 203/IV).
        IV. Art and Education (this chapter was
        written by Miss D.W.Black). V. Communism
        and the Soviet Constitution (see also BN
        202, BN 203/III). VI. The Failure of Rus-
        sian Industry. VII. Daily Life in Moscow.
        VIII. Town and Country (see also BN 202,
        BN 203/VI). IX. International Policy.
    Part II. Bolshevik Theory.
        I. The Materialistic Theory of History
        (see also BN 204/I). II. Deciding Forces
        in Politics. III. Bolshevik Criticism of
        Democracy. IV. Revolution and Dictator-
        ship (see also BN 204/II). V. Mechanism
        and the Individual (see also 204/III).
        VI. Why Russian Communism Failed. VII.
        Conditions for the Success of Communism.

    C o m m e n t a r y
    Russell's visit of Soviet Russia came in the
    summer of 1920, when he was invited to go as
    an unofficial member of a Labour-Delegation.
    She was in Russia from May 19 to June 16.
    Not being an official delegate, Russell could
    miss some og the functions and meet ordinary
    people in the streets and villages. Russell
    proceeded to write a considered critical ana-
    lysis, the "Practice and Theory of Bolshevism".
    Russell was able to reprint this book, virtu-
    ally without alteration, in 1949, an aston-
    ishing example of political observation and
    prediction standing up to the passage of time.
    Russell's book gives at first the impression
    of a strange alternation between damnation
    and praise for the Bolsheviks, owning to his

determination to present both the bad and
good sides fairly. - Russell's analysis was
a criticism which raised the whole problem
of the intellectual in politics: how to com-
bine love of truth with corporate political
activity. "Throughout my life", he said once,
"I have longed to feel that oneness with large
bodies of human beings. I have imagined myself
in turn a Liberal, or a Socialist, or a pacifist, but I never have been any of these things
in a profound sense. Always the sceptical intellect, when I have most wished it silent,
has whispered doubts to me."

K o m m e n t a r
Russell's Besuch Sowjetrußlands fiel in den
Sommer 1920. Er war aufgefordert worden, als
inoffizielles Mitglied einer Labour-Delega-
tion mitzugehen. Sie war vom 19. Mai bis
zum 16. Juni in Rußland. Da Russell nicht
offizieller Delegierter war, konnte er etwas
von dem Programm auslassen und Leute auf den
Straßen und in den Dörfern kennen lernen.
Russell machte sich daran, eine wohlfundierte
kritische Analyse zu schreiben, "Practice and
Theory of Bolshevism". Er konnte 1949 dieses
Buch, praktisch unverändert, im Neudruck erscheinen lassen - ein erstaunliches Beispiel
für politische Beobachtungsgabe und Voraussage, die vor der Zeit Bestand haben. Zuerst
hat man den Eindruck einer seltsamen Mischung
von Anerkennung und Verurteilung der Bolsche-
wiken; das ist auf seine Absicht zurückzufüh-
ren, beides gerecht darzustellen, die guten
und die schlechten Seiten. - Russell's Analyse war eine Kritik, die das Problem des In-
tellektuellen in der Politik in seiner Ganz-
heit aufwarf: wie läßt sich Wahrheitsliebe
mit parteigebundener politischer Tätigkeit
vereinen. "Mein ganzes Leben hindurch" sagte er einmal, "habe ich mich danach gesehnt,
dieses Einssein mit großen Gruppen von Menschen zu fühlen. Nacheinander habe ich mir
eingebildet, ein Liberaler, ein Sozialist,
ein Pazifist zu sein, doch im tiefsten Sinne bin ich nie etwas von alledem gewesen. Immer gerade dann, wenn ich es am schweigsam-
sten gewünscht hätte, flüsterte mir der skep-
tische Verstand Zweifel zu."

R e p r i n t s
1921 London: Allen & Unwin 207.03
1927 Excerpt:
     "Deciding Forces in Politics" (II:II)
     in "Selected Papers of Bertrand Russell"
     (BN 317) 207.04

1949 London: Allen & Unwin 207.05
1949 New York: Macmillan 207.06
1951 London: Allen & Unwin 207.07
1954 "   : "   " " 207.08
1961 Excerpt:
     "The Materialistic Theory
     of History" (II:I)
     in "The Basic Writings of B. Russell":
     XIII/57 (BN 659) 207.09
1962 London: Allen & Unwin 207.10
1963 "   : "   " " 207.11
1964 New York: Simon & Schuster 207.12
1972 "   " : Arno Press 207.13
1975 London: Allen & Unwin 207.14

T r a n s l a t i o n s
Arabisch:
     "Al moumarash al balchafiah"
     Tr.: Samir Abdou
     1966 Damaskus: Eds. Abbasiah 207.15
Deutsch:
     Auszüge:
     "Praxis und Theorie des Bolschewismus"
     1972 in BN 703/III:6 . . . . 207.16
Französisch:
     "Théorie et pratique du bolchevisme"
     Tr.: A. Pierre
     1921 Paris: Ed. de la Sirène 207.17
     "Pratique et théorie du bolchevisme"
     1969 Paris: Mercure de France 207.18
Ind./Hindi:
     "Bolshevism vyavhar aur siddhant."
     Tr.: N. C. Jamindar
     1964 Indore: Sahityalay Prakasan . . . 207.19
Italienisch:
     "Teoria e pratica del bolscevismo"
     Tr.: Annamaria Peluchi
     1963 Mailand: Sugar 207.20
     Tr.: Jean Sanders, Leonardo Breccio
     1970 Rom: Newton Compton Editori . . . 207.21
Japanisch:
     "Bolshevism no Jissen to Riron"
     Tr.: Teruhiko Egami
     1959 Tokio: Shakai Shiso Kenkyu
          Kai Shuppan-bu 207.22
Spanisch:
     "Teoría y prática del bolchevismo"
     Tr.: Juan C. Garcia
     1969 Barcelona: Ariel 207.23
Türkisch:
     "Bolsevizm"
     Tr.: N. Sel
     1967 Istanbul: Habora Kitabevi 207.24

The Happiness of China

1921 (Jan. 8) in "Nation" (London),
vol. 28, p. 505-506 . . . . 208.00

Industry in Undeveloped Countries

1921 (June) in "Atlantic Monthly",
vol. 127, p. 787-795 . . . . 209.00

Sketches of Modern China

1921 (Dec. 3-17) in "Nation and Athenaeum",
vol. 30, p. 375-376, 429-430, 461-463 . . . . 210.01
1921 under the title
"Modern China"
(Dec. 14-28) in "Nation",
vol. 113, p. 701-702, 726-727, 756-757 210.02
1922 in "The Problem of China": IV (BN 238) 210.03

T r a n s l a t i o n s
Deutsch . . . . 1925 in BN 238.08 . . . . . 210.04
Französisch . . . 1968 in BN 238.10 . . . . . 210.05
Japanisch . . . . . 1971 in BN 238.11 . . . . . 210.06

Higher Education in China

1921 (Dec.) in "Dial", vol. 71, p. 693-698 . . . 211.01
1922 in "The Problem of China": XIII (BN 238) 211.02

T r a n s l a t i o n s
Deutsch . . . . 1925 in BN 238.08 . . . . . 211.03
Französisch . . . 1968 in BN 238.10 . . . . . 211.04
Japanisch . . . . . 1971 in BN 238.11 . . . . . 211.05

Some Traits in the Chinese Character

1921 (Dec.) in "Atlantic Monthly",
vol. 128, p. 771-777 . . . . 212.00

THE ANALYSIS OF MIND

1921 London: Allen & Unwin. 310 pp. 213.01
New York: Macmillan Co. 310 pp. 213.02
C o n t e n t s
Preface. I. Recent Criticisms of "Conscious-
ness". II. Instinct and Habit. III. Desire
and Feeling. IV. Influence of Past History
on Present Occurrences in Living Organisms.
V. Psychological and Physical Causal Laws.
VI. Introspection. VII. The Definition of
Perception. VIII. Sensation and Images.
IX. Memory. X. Words and Meaning. XI.
General Ideas and Thought. XII. Belief.
XIII. Truth and Falsehood. XIV. Emotions
and Will. XV. Characteristics of Mental
Phenomena. Index.

C o m m e n t a r y

Simultaneously (1918) he was working towards a philosophy whereby not only were the thoughts of his mind hardly free, but his mind did not even exist in the commonly accepted sense, and any difference in kind between mind and matter was declared illusory. Put more precisely, his thesis in "The Analysis of Mind" was "Matter is not so material and mind not so mental as is generally supposed". ... "Both mind and matter seem to be composite, and the stuff of which they are compounded lies in a sense between the two, in a sense above them both, like a common ancestor." This kind of philosophy, developed in America as "neutral monism", owed a great deal to William James. Russell's object in "The Analysis of Mind" was, he said, "to subject Mind to the same kind of analysis as I applied to Matter in "Our Knowledge of the External World". In this he had treated a piece of "matter" as a logical construction based on "sense data". He now decided that mind was a logical construction based on "sensations", and decided that sensations and sense data were the same.

K o m m e n t a r

Zu gleicher Zeit (1918) arbeitete R. auf eine Philosophie hin, bei der nicht nur die Gedanken seines Geistes alles andere als frei waren, sondern sein Geist im Sinne der üblichen Auffassung nicht einmal mehr existierte; jede grundsätzliche Verschiedenheit zwischen Geist und Materie wurde für illusorisch erklärt. Genauer gesagt, war seine These in "The Analysis of Mind", "Materie ist nicht so materiell und Geist nicht so geistig, wie man allgemein annimmt" ... "Sowohl Geist wie Materie scheinen zusammengesetzt zu sein, und der Stoff, aus dem sie gefügt sind, liegt in einem Sinne zwischen beiden, in einem andern Sinne über beiden, gleich einem gemeinsamen Vorfahren." Diese Art Philosophie, die in Amerika als "Neutraler Monismus" entwickelt wurde, ist in hohem Maße William James verpflichtet. Russell's Anliegen in "The Analysis of Mind" war, wie er sagte, dies: "den Geist der gleichen Analyse zu unterziehen, die ich in 'Our Knowledge of the External World' auf die Materie angewandt hatte". Darin hatte er ein Stück "Materie" als eine logische Konstruktion behandelt, die auf "Sinnesdaten" basiert. Jetzt stellte er fest, daß Geist eine logische Konstruktion sei, basiert auf "Empfindungen", und das "Empfindungen" und Sinnesgegebenheiten das gleiche seien.

R e p r i n t s
1924 New York: Macmillan 213.03
1927 Excerpt:
"Words and Meaning" (X)
in "Selected Papers of Bertrand Russell"
(BN 317) 213.04
1961 London: Allen & Unwin 213.05
1961 Excerpts:
"Psychological and
Physical Causal Laws" (V),
"Truth and Falsehood" (XIII)
in "The Basic Writings of B. Russell":
VIII/ 37, 38 (BN 659) 213.06
1965 Excerpt:
"(Characteristics of)
Mental Phenomena" (XV)
in "On the Philosophy of Science": IV/I
(BN 672) 213.07
1968 New York: Humanities Press 213.08
1968 London: Allen & Unwin 213.09
1971 " : " " " 213.10
T r a n s l a t i o n s
Chinesisch:
"Xin zhi fenxi"
1921 Peking 213.11
"Xin de fenxi"
1936 Shanghai 213.12
1958 Peking 213.13
"Hsin Ti Fên Hsi"
Tr.: Li Ch'i
1970 Taipeh: K'ai Shan Book Co. . . . 213.14
Deutsch:
"Die Analyse des Geistes"
Ü.: Kurt Grelling
1927 Leipzig: Felix Meiner. VII, 407 S. 213.15
I n h a l t
Vorwort des Verfassers. I. Neuere Kritik des "Bewußtseins". II. Instinkt
und Gewohnheit. III. Begehren und Fühlen. IV. Der Einfluß der Vergangenheit
auf die gegenwärtigen Vorgänge beim le-
benden Organismus. V. Kausale Gesetze
der Psychologie und der Physik. VI. Innere Wahrnehmung. VII. Die Definition
der Wahrnehmung. VIII. Empfindungen und
Vorstellungen. IX. Erinnerung. X. Wort
und Bedeutung. XI. Allgemeine Begriffe
und Denken. XII. Glauben. XIII. Wahrheit und Falschheit. XIV. Emotionen und
Wille. XV. Die Unterscheidungsmerkmale
der psychischen Erscheinungen. Reg.
Französisch:
"Analyse de l'esprit"
Tr.: M. Lefebvre
1926 Paris: Payot 213.16

Ind./Urdu:
 "Tajziya nafs"
 Tr.: Shujaat Hussain Bokhari
 1964 Lahore: Majlis traqqi-adab. . . 213.17
Italienisch:
 "Analisi della mente"
 Tr.: Bona della Volpe Longo
 1955 Florenz: Editrice Universitaria . 213.18
 Tr.: Jean Sanders, Leonar de Breccia
 1969 Rom: New Compton Editori 213.19
Persisch:
 "Tahlil-e Zehn"
 Tr.: Manuchehr-e Bozorgmehr
 1970 Teheran: Khārazmi 213.20
Portugiesisch:
 "Análise do espírito"
 Tr.: Zora Maria Ursola Valencio,
  JoaoAlves dos Santos
 1958 Sao Paulo: Ed. Nacional 213.21
Spanisch:
 "Análisis del espiritu"
 Tr.: Eduardo Prieto
 1949 Buenos Aires: Paidos 213.22
 1958 "   " : " 213.23
 1962 "   " : " 213.24

How Washington Could Help China

1922 (Jan. 4) in "The New Republic",
 vol. 29, p. 154-155 . . . . 214.00

Hopes and Fears as Regards America

1922 (Mar. 15-22) in "The New Republic"
 vol. 30, p. 70-72, 99-101 . . . . 215.01
 1936 in "New Republic Anthology", p.160-164 215.02

Chinese Civilization and the West

1922 (Apr. 22) in "Dial", vol. 72, p. 356-364 . 216.01
 1922 under the title
   "Chinese and
   Western Civilization Contrasted"
   in "The Problem of China": XI (BN 238) 216.02
 1927 in "Selected Papers of Bertrand Russell"
   (BN 317) 216.03

 T r a n s l a t i o n s
 Deutsch . . . . 1925 in BN 238.08 . . . . . 216.04
 Französisch . . . 1968 in BN 238.10 . . . . . 216.05
 Japanisch . . . . . 1971 in BN 238.11 . . . . . 216.06

What Makes a Social System Good or Bad?

1922 (May) in "Century", vol. 104, p. 14-21 . . 217.01
 1923 in "The Prospects of
   Industrial Civilization": VIII (BN 263) 217.02

```
T r a n s l a t i o n s
Deutsch ....... 1928 in BN 263.09 . . . . . 217.03
Italienisch ... 1973 in BN 263.12 . . . . . 217.04
Polnisch ...... 1933 in BN 263.13 . . . . . 217.05
Spanisch ...... 1962 in BN 263.14 . . . . . 217.06
```

Socialism in Undeveloped Countries

```
1922 (May) in "Atlantik Monthly",
    vol. 129, p. 664-671 . . . . . . . . . . . 218.01
    1923 in "The Prospects of
        Industrial Civilization": VI (BN 263)  218.02

    T r a n s l a t i o n s
    Deutsch ....... 1928 in BN 263.09 . . . . . 218.03
    Italienisch ... 1973 in BN 263.12 . . . . . 218.04
    Polnisch ...... 1933 in BN 263.13 . . . . . 218.05
    Spanisch ...... 1962 in BN 263.14 . . . . . 218.06
```

How Can Internationalism Be Brought About?

```
1922 (June) in "Century", vol. 104, p. 195-202  . 219.01
    1923 under the title
        "The Transition to Internationalism"
        in "The Prospects of
        Industrial Civilization": V (BN 263) 219.02

    T r a n s l a t i o n s
    Deutsch ....... 1928 in BN 263.09 . . . . . 219.03
    Italienisch ... 1973 in BN 263.12 . . . . . 219.04
    Polnisch ...... 1933 in BN 263.13 . . . . . 219.05
    Spanisch ...... 1962 in BN 263.14 . . . . . 219.06
```

Bring Us Peace - On Nationalism

```
1922 (Oct. 7) in "The New Student",
    vol. II, National Student Forum, p. 1-2 . . 220.00
```

Toward an Understanding of China

```
1922 (Oct.) in "Century", vol. 104, p. 912-916 . 221.00
```

The Outlook for China

```
1922 (Nov.) in "Century", vol. 105, p. 141-146 . 222.01
    1922 in "The Problem of China": XV (BN 238) 222.02

    T r a n s l a t i o n s
    Deutsch ....... 1925 in BN 238.08 . . . . . 222.03
    Französisch ... 1968 in BN 238.10 . . . . . 222.04
    Japanisch ..... 1971 in BN 238.11 . . . . . 222.05
```

Instinct and the Unconscious

```
1922 (Nov. 3) in "New Leader" (London),
    vol. 1, no. 5, p. 12 . . . . . . . . . . . 223.00
```

Physics and Perception

```
1922 in "Mind", vol. 31, p. 478-485
    A reply to C. A. Strong . . . . . . . . . . 224.00
```

The Difficulties of Bishops
1922 in "Rationalist Annual" 225.00

Review of J. M. Keynes's
"A Treatise on Probability"
1922 in "Mathematical Gazette", vol. II, p.119-125 226.00

Review of G. E. Moore's
"Philosophical Studies"
and of K. Stephen's
"The Misuse of Mind"
1922 in "Nation & Athenaeum", vol. 31, p. 538-539 227.00

Philosophic Idealism at Bay
1922 in "Nation & Athenaeum", vol. 31, p. 625-626 228.00

Review of A. A. Luce's
"Bergson's Doctrine of Intuition"
1922 in "Nation & Athenaeum", vol. 31, p. 770 . . 229.00

Relativity, Scientific and Metaphysical
1922 in "Nation & Athenaeum", vol. 31, p. 796-797 230.00

What is Morality?
1922 in "Nation & Athenaeum", vol. 32, p. 254-255 231.00

Review of J. A. Gunn's
"Modern French Philosophy"
1922 in "Nation & Athenaeum", vol. 32, p. 426 . . 232.00

The Philosophy of Conservatism
1922 in "New Republic", vol. 32, p. 309-310 . . . 233.00

Review of G. Santayana's
"Soliloquies in England"
1922 in "Dial", vol. 73, p. 559-562 . . . . . . 234.00

Dr. Schiller's Analysis of "The Analysis of Mind"
1922 in "Journal of Philosophy",
        vol. 19, p. 645-651 . . . . 235.00

Free Thought and Official Propaganda
1922 New York: B. W. Huebsch. 56 pp. 236.01
     London: Allen & Unwin 236.02
     London: Watts & Co. 236.03
     (This is the Conway Memorial Lecture, de-
     livered by B. Russell at South Place Insti-
     tute, London, 24 March, 1922)

```
1928 in "Sceptical Essays": XII (BN 331)  .  236.04
1941 in "Let the People Think" (BN 464) . . 236.05
1958 in "The Will to Doubt" (BN 638) . . . 236.06
T r a n s l a t i o n s
Chinesisch .... 1932 in BN 331.16 . . . . . 236.07
Deutsch ....... 1930 in BN 331.19 . . . . . 236.08
Französisch ... 1933 in BN 331.23 . . . . . 236.09
Italienisch ... 1953 in BN 331.25 . . . . . 236.10
Japanisch ..... 1963 in BN 331.29 . . . . . 236.11
Norwegisch .... 1947 in BN 331.32 = 519 . . 236.12
Polnisch ...... 1937 in BN 331.33 . . . . . 236.13
Portugiesisch . 1955 in BN 331.35 . . . . . 236.14
Schwedisch .... 1950 in BN 331.36 . . . . . 236.15
Spanisch ...... 1956 in BN 331.39 = 615 . . 236.16
```

Introduction to Ludwig Wittgenstein's
"Tractatus logico-philosophicus" (1)

```
1922 London: Routledge & Kegan Paul, engl./deutsch
     Tr.: F. P. Ramsey . . . . . . . . . . . . .   237.01
     1922 New York: Harcourt, Brace & Co., p. 7-23 237.02
     1933 London: Routledge & Kegan Paul . . . .   237.03
     1949 "      : "          " "        "   . . . . 237.04
     1955 "      : "          " "        "   . . . . 237.05
     1961 "      : "          " "        "   . . . . 237.06
     1961 New York: Humanities Press . . . . . .   237.07
     1975 "Tractatus logico-philosophicus"
          Tr.: D. F. Pears and B. F. McGuinnes
          London: Routledge & Kegan Paul
          With the introduction by B. Russell
          Rev. ed.; XXII, 89 pp. . . . . . . . .   237.08
     T r a n s l a t i o n s
     Deutsch:
          "Vorwort zum
          Tractatus logico-philosophicus"
          in Beiheft 1 (S. 68-81) zu
          Wittgenstein's "Schriften I-VI"
          1960 Frankfurt: Suhrkamp . . . . . . .   237.09
          1969/72: 2. Auflage  . . . . . . . . .   237.10
     Französisch:
          "Tractatus logico-philosophicus"
          Introduction de Bertrand Russell
          1961 Paris: Gallimard  . . . . . . . .   237.11
          1972 "      : "          . . . . . . . .  237.12
     Spanisch:
          "Tractatus logico-philosophicus"
          Introducción por Bertrand Russell
          1957 Madrid: Revista de Occidente  . .   237.13
```

```
(1)  "Tractatus logico-philosophicus"
     1921 Leipzig: Ostwald's 'Annalen der
          Naturphilosophie', 44. letzter Bd.
     1960 in L. Wittgenstein's "Schriften",
          Frankf.: Suhrkamp. Bd. I, S. 5-83
     1969/72 Frankfurt: Suhrkamp. 2. Auflage
     1973 Frankf.: Suhrkamp. Einzelausgabe.
          ed. suhrkamp 12. 1978, 82. - 86.Tsd.
```

THE PROBLEM OF CHINA

1922 London: Allen & Unwin. 260 pp. 238.01
New York: The Century Co. 276 pp. 238.02

C o n t e n t s
I. Questions. II. China Before the 19th Century. III. China and the Western Powers.
IV. Modern China (1921/210). V. Japan Before the Restoration. VI. Modern Japan. VII.
Japan and China Before 1914. VIII. Japan and China During the War. IX. The Washington Conference. X. Present Forces and Tendencies in the Far East. XI. Chinese and Western Civilization Contrasted (1922/216). XII. The Chinese Character. XIII. Higher Education in China (1921/211). XIV. Industrialism in China. XV. The Outlook for China (1922/222). Appendix. Index.

C o m m e n t a r y
The result of Russell's visit to the Far East (1920) was "The Problem of China", as shrewd in its observation and analysis as "The Practice and Theory of Bolshevism", and which has stood up equally well to the test of time. One of the leading present-day authorities on China, Professor C. P. FitzGerald, has describet it to me as "a remarkable book by any standard", a book of "shrewd and astute foresight". Russell stressed the future importance of China in world affairs at a time when most people in Whitehall, the Foreign Office included, eould hardly be induced to take any interest in it.

K o m m e n t a r
Das Ergebnis von Russells Fahrt nach dem fernen Osten (1920) war "The Problem of China", in Beobachtung und Analyse ebenso scharfsichtig wie "The Practice and Theory of Bolshevism", und auch dieses Buch hat den Test der Zeit bestanden. Einer der führenden Kenner Chinas von heute, Professor C.P.FitzGerald, schilderte es mir als "ein jeder Prüfung standhaltendes, beachtenswertes Buch", ein Buch, "scharfsichtig und klug in seinem Weitblick". Russell betonte die künftige Bedeutung Chinas für die Weltpolitik zu einer Zeit, als die meisten Leute in Whitehall, einschließlich des Außenministeriums, kaum dazu gebracht werden konnten, sich irgendwie dafür zu interessieren.

R e p r i n t s
1927 Excerpts:
"Questions" (I)

"Chinese and
Western Civilization Contrasted" (XI)
"The Chinese Character" (XII)
in "Selected Papers of Bertrand Russell"
(BN 317) 238.03
1938 Excerpt"
"Chinese Character" (XII)
in "Opinions and Attitudes in the Twen-
tieth Century", ed. by S. S. Morgan and
W. H. Thomas, p. 306-316
New York: Nelson 238.04
1961 Excerpt:
"Chinese and
Western Civilization Contrasted" (XI)
in "The Basic Writings of B. Russell":
XIV/59 (BN 659) 238.05
1966 London: Allen & Unwin 238.06
1972 " : " " " 238.07
T r a n s l a t i o n s
Deutsch:
"China und das Problem
des fernen Ostens"
Tr.: Margarete Hethey
1925 München: Drei Masken Verlag. . . 238.08
I n h a l t
I. Fragen. II. China vor dem 19. Jahr-
hundert. III. China und die westlichen
Mächte. IV. Das moderne China. V. Ja-
pan vor der Restauration. VI. Das mo-
derne Japan. VII. Japan und China vor
1914. VIII. Japan und China während des
Krieges. IX. Die Konferenz von Washing-
ton. X. Gegenwärtige Kräfte und Ten-
denzen in Fern-Ost. XI. Gegenüberstel-
lung chinesischer und westlicher Kultur.
XII. Der chinesische Charakter. XIII.
Das höhere Bildungswesen in China. XIV.
Industrialismus in China. XV. Die Aus-
sichten für China. Register.
Auszüge:
"China
und das Problem des fernen Ostens"
1972 in 703/IV:7 . . . . 238.09
Französisch:
"La Chine"
Tr.: Sandra Estreich
1968 Paris: Ed. Planète 238.10
Japanisch:
"Chûgoku no mondai"
Tr.: Makino Tsutomu
1971 Tokio: Risôsha 238.11

1922/1923

Miscellany/Sammelband in Deutsch
unter dem Titel
"Politische Ideale"

1922 Berlin: Deutsche Verlagsgesellschaft
für Politik und Geschichte. 201 S.
Aus dem Englischen übertragen und eingelei-
tet von E. J. Gumbel. Mit einem Vorwort von
Prof. Albert Einstein. 239.00
I n h a l t
  I. Einleitung
    1. Vorwort (A. Einstein)
    2. Russell's wissenschaftliche Bedeu-
      tung (E. J. Gumbel)
  II. Das Problem des Krieges
    3. Russell und die englischen Pazifi-
      sten (E. J. Gumbel)
    4. Die Philosophie des Pazifismus (The
      Philosophy of Pacifism .. 1915/142)
    5. Krieg und persönliche Freiheit (War
      and Individual Liberty .. 1917/165)
    6. Pazifismus und Revolution (Pacifism
      and Revolution .... 1917/169)
  III. Wege zur Freiheit
    7. Allgemeine Bemerkungen (Introduc-
      tion .... 1918/177)
    8. Marx und die sozialistische Lehre
      (M. and Socialist Doctrine 1918/177)
    9. Bakunin und der Anarchismus (Bakunin
      and Anarchism .... 1918/177)
    10. Die Revolte der Syndikalisten (The
      Syndicalist Revolt ...... 1918/177)
    11. Russell's Stellungnahme zum Bolsche-
      wismus (E. J. Gumbel)
  IV. Probleme der Zukunft
    12. Arbeit u. Lohn (Work and Pay 1918/177)
    13. Regierung und Gesetz (Government and
      Law .... 1918/177)
    14. Internationale Beziehungen (Inter-
      national Relations ...... 1918/177)
    15. Kunst und Wissenschaft unterm Sozi-
      alismus (Science and Art Under So-
      cialism .... 1918/177)
    16. Was können wir
      aus der Welt machen? (The World as
      It Could Be Made .... 1918/177)
    17. Politische Ideale (Political
      Ideals .... 1917/162)

Lord Balfour on Methodological Doubt

1923 (Jan. 6) in "Nation and Athenaeum",
vol. 32, p. 542-544 . . . . 240.00

The Case of Margaret Sanger

1923 (Jan. 27, Feb. 10) in "Nation and Athenaeum"
    vol. 32, p. 645, 719 . . . . 241.00

Tolstoy's Domestic Problems

1923 (Jan. 31) in "The Freeman",
    vol. 6, p. 501-502 . . . . 242.00

China and Chinese Influence

1923 (Feb. 28) in "The Freeman",
    vol. 6, p. 585-587 . . . . 243.00

On Vagueness

1923 in "The Australasian Journal of Psychology
    and Philosophy", vol. I, p. 84-92 . . . . . 244.00

Freedom in Education: A Protest Against Mechanism

1923 (Feb.) in "Dial", vol. 74, p. 153-164 . . . 245.00

Sources of Power

1923 (May 2-16) in "The Freeman",
    vol. 7, p. 176-179, 200-202, 224-226 . . . 246.00

Review of George Santayana's
"Life of Reason"

1923 (May 5 in "Outlook", vol. 51, p. 365-368 . . 247.00

Review of C.K.Ogden's and I.A.Richards'
"The Meaning of Meaning" (The Mastery of Words).

1923 in "Nation and Athenaeum", vol. 33, p. 87-89 248.01
    1926 (Aug.) in "Dial", vol. 81, p. 114-121. 248.02

What Constitutes Intelligence

1923 (June 9) in "Nation and Athenaeum",
    vol. 33, p. 330-331 . . . . 249.00

Review of G. Santayana's
"Scepticism and Animal Faith"

1923 in "Nation and Athenaeum", vol. 33, p. 457. 250.01
    1923 in "New Statesman", vol. 21, p. 596 . 250.02

Science and Metaphysics

1923 in "Nation and Athenaeum", vol. 33, p. 716 251.00

Review of Hu Shih's
"The Development of the Logical Method
in Ancient China"

1923 in "Nation and Athenaeum", vol.33, p.778-779 252.00

Slavery or Self-Extermination:
A Forecast of Europe's Future

1923 (July 11) in "Nation", vol. 117, p. 32-34 . 253.00

Biology and Religion

1923 in "Nation and Athenaeum",vol.34, p.223-224 254.00

Philosophy in India and China
Reviews of S. Radhakrishnan's "Indian Philosophy"
and J. Percy Bruce's "Chu Hsi and His Masters."

1923 (Sept. 15) in "Nation and Athenaeum",
    vol. 34, p. 748-749 . . . . 255.00

Leisure and Mechanism

1923 (Aug.) in "Dial", vol. 75, p. 105-122 . . . 256.01
    1933 in "Types of Prose Writing"
        Boston: Houghton, p. 210-228 . . . . . 256.02

The Revival of Puritanism

1923 (Oct. 17) in "The Freeman", vol.8,p.128-130 257.00

Life as an Art

1923 in "Outlook" (London), vol. 52, p. 213-214. 258.00

The Recrudescence of Puritanism

1923 (Oct. 20) in "Outlook", vol. 52, p.300-302.   259.01
    1928 in "Sceptical Essays": X (BN 331) . .   259.02

    T r a n s l a t i o n s
    Chinesisch .... 1932 in BN 331.16 . . . . .   259.03
    Deutsch .... 1930 in BN 331.19 . . . . .   259.04
    Französisch ... 1933 in BN 331.23 . . . . .   259.05
    Italienisch ... 1953 in BN 331.25 . . . . .   259.06
    Japanisch ..... 1963 in BN 331.29 . . . . .   259.07
    Norwegisch .... 1947 in BN 331.32 = 519 . .   259.08
    Polnisch ...... 1937 in BN 331.33 . . . . .   259.09
    Portugiesisch . 1955 in BN 331.35 . . . . .   259.10
    Schwedisch .... 1950 in BN 331.36 . . . . .   259.11
    Spanisch ...... 1956 in BN 331.39 = 615 . .   259.12

Where Is Industrialism Going?

1923 (Nov.) in "Century Magazine",
    vol. 107, p. 141-149 . . . .   260.01
    1925 in "College Readings on Current
        Problems".
        Boston: Houghton, p. 327-341 . . . . .   260.02
    1928 in "Modern Life and Thought".
        New York: Century Comp. 260.03

Truth-Functions and Meaning-Functions
1923 (ca) Unpublished manuscript in R. Archives,
     McMaster University, Hamilton/Ontario. 5 pp.   261.00

Can Men Be Rational?
1923 in "Rationalist Annual" 262.01
     1928 in "Sceptical Essays": IV (BN 331) . .   262.02
     1941 in "Let the People Think" (BN 464) . .   262.03
     1947 Girard, Kansas: Haldeman-Julius Publ.   262.04
     1958 in "The Will to Doubt" (BN 638) . . .   262.05
     1972 in "Atheism" (BN 700) 262.06

     T r a n s l a t i o n s
     Chinesisch .... 1932 in BN 331.16 . . . . .   262.07
     Deutsch .... 1930 in BN 331.19 . . . . .   262.08
     Französisch ... 1933 in BN 331.23 . . . . .   262.09
     Italienisch ... 1953 in BN 331.25 . . . . .   262.10
     Japanisch ..... 1963 in BN 331.29 . . . . .   262.11
     Norwegisch .... 1947 in BN 331.32 = 519 . .   262.12
     Polnisch ...... 1937 in BN 331.33 . . . . .   262.13
     Portugiesisch . 1955 in BN 331.35 . . . . .   262.14
     Schwedisch .... 1950 in BN 331.36 . . . . .   262.15
     Spanisch ...... 1956 in BN 331.39 = 615 . .   262.16

THE PROSPECTS OF INDUSTRIAL CIVILIZATION
(In collaboration with Dora Russell)
1923 New York, London: The Century Co. 287 pp. .   263.01
     London: Allen & Unwin. 283 pp. 263.02
     C o n t e n t s
     Preface
     Part I
         I. Causes of Present Chaos. II. Inherent
         Tendencies of Industrialism. III. Indus-
         trialism and Private Property. IV. In-
         teractions of Industrialism and Nation-
         alism. V. The Transition to Internation-
         alism (1922/219). VI. Socialism in Unde-
         veloped Countries (1922/218). VII. So-
         cialism in Advanced Countries.
     Part II
         VIII. What Makes a Social System Good or
         Bad (1922/217)? IX. Moral Standarts and
         Social Well-Being. X. The Sources of
         Power. XI. The Distribution of Power.
         XII. Education. XIII. Economic Organi-
         zation and Mental Freedom.

     C o m m e n t a r y
     The point between Socialism and Capitalism
     was not so important, perhaps, as the belief
     that industrialism was essential one way or
     the other. Russell gave his own suggestions
     for solving the problem - that of combining

scientific techniques with a respect for human values - in "The Prospects of Industrial Civilization", written in collaboration with Dora Black. This book was inspired by their separate visits to Russia, and by their mutual journey to China.

K o m m e n t a r
Die Frage, ob Sozialismus oder Kapitalismus, war vielleicht nicht so wichtig wie die Überzeugung, daß die Industrie auf jeden Fall von grundsätzlicher Bedeutung war. Russell gab seine eigenen Ideen für die Lösung des Problems - die Kombination von wissenschaftlichen Methoden mit gleichzeitiger Berücksichtigung menschlicher Werte - in "The Prospects of Industrial Civilization", das er in Zusammenarbeit mit Dora Black verfaßte. Dieses Buch war angeregt durch ihre getrennten Besuche in Rußland und ihre gemeinsame Reise nach China.

R e p r i n t s
1925 London: Allen & Unwin 263.03
1927 Excerpts:
     "Causes of Present Chaos" (I)
     "Moral Standarts
     and Social Well-Being" (IX)
     in "Selected Papers of Bertrand Russell"
     (BN 317) 263.04
1931 Excerpt:
     "Moral Standarts
     and Social Well-Being" (IX)
     in "Essays in Contemporary Civilization"
     New York: Macmillan 263.05
1939 Same Excerpt
     in "Century Readings in the English Essay"
     New York: Appleton-Century, p. 513-541 263.06
1959 London: Allen & Unwin 263.07
1970 London: Allen & Unwin 263.08

T r a n s l a t i o n s
Deutsch:
     "Die Kultur des Industrialismus
     und ihre Zukunft"
     Ü.: Clara Margolin
     1928 München, Berlin: Drei Masken Verlag. XI, 336 S. 263.09
     I n h a l t
     Vorwort
     Teil I
          I. Die Ursachen des gegenwärtigen Chaos. II. Die Tendenzen des Industrialismus. III. Industrialismus und Privateigentum. IV. Wechselwirkungen von Industrialismus und

Nationalismus. V. Der Übergang zum
Internationalismus. VI. Der Sozia-
lismus in unentwickelten Ländern.
VII. Der Sozialismus in fortgeschrit-
tenen Ländern.
Teil II
VIII. Wodurch wird ein soziales Sy-
stem gut oder schlecht? IX. Das Ni-
veau der Moral und sozialen Wohl-
fahrt. X. Die Quellen der Macht.
XI. Die Verteilung der Macht. XII.
Erziehung. XIII. Wirtschaftliche
Organisation und geistige Freiheit.
Auszüge:
"Die Kultur des Industrialismus
und ihre Zukunft"

Auszug:
"Erziehung
in der Industriegesellschaft" (XII),
Italienisch:
"Prospective di civiltà industriale"
Tr.: Renato Paveto
Polnisch:
"Perspektyny Przenyslowej Cyvilizacji"
Tr.: Amelja Kurladzka
Spanisch:
"Perspectivas
de la civilizacion industrial"
Tr.: Juan Novella Domingo

THE ABC OF ATOMS

C o n t e n t s
I. Introduction. II. The Periodic Law. III.
Electrons and Nuclei. IV. The Hydrogen Spec-
trum. V. Possible States of the Hydrogen
Atom. VI. The Theory of Quanta. VII. Re-
finements of the Hydrogen Spectrum. VIII.
Rings of Electrons. IX. Rays. X. Radio-
Activity. XI. The Structure of Nuclei. XII.
The New Physics and the Wave Theory of Light.
XIII. The New Physics and Relativity. Appen-
dix: Bohr's Theory of the Hydrogen Spectrum.

C o m m e n t a r y
"The ABC of Atoms", published in 1923, is
still remarkable for its early predictions
of atomic energy. Russell wrote that "If this

source of energy can be utilized commercially,
it will probably in time supersede every
other ... It is impossible to exaggerate the
revolutionary effect which it may have both
in the practice of industry and in the theory
of physics." And Russell, referring to work
on the structure of the atom, said: "It is
probable that it will ultimately be used for
making more deadly explosives and projectiles
than any yet invented." And so, in December
1954, Russell made one of his most moving
broadcasts, on the subject of the hydrogen
bomb. He ended: "I appeal as a human being
to human beings: remember your humanity, and
forget the rest. If you can do so the way
lies open to a new paradise; if you cannot,
nothing lies before you but universal death."

K o m m e n t a r
"The ABC of Atoms", 1923 veröffentlicht, ist
noch heute bemerkenswert, weil es so früh
schon die Atomenergie voraussagte. Russell
schrieb: "Wenn diese Energiequelle geschäft-
lich nutzbar gemacht werden kann, wird sie
wahrscheinlich mit der Zeit jede andere er-
setzen. ... Es ist unmöglich, die revolutionäre Wirkung zu überschätzen, die sie sowohl
für die Praxis in der Industrie als auch für
die Theorie der Physik haben könnte." Und in
bezug auf die Arbeiten der Atomstruktur sagte
Russell: "Es ist anzunehmen, daß sie schließlich dazu verwendet wird, noch verheerendere
Sprengstoffe und Geschosse zu fabrizieren als
alle bisher erfundenen." So gab er im Dezember
1954 eine seiner eindruckvollsten Radiosen-
dungen über das Thema der Wasserstoffbombe.
Er schloß: "Als Mensch rufe ich die Menschen
auf: denkt an eure Menschlichkeit und ver-
geßt alles übrige. Wenn ihr das tun könnt, so
liegt der Weg für ein neues Paradies offen;
könnt ihr es nicht, so liegt nichts vor euch
als all-umfassender Tod."

R e p r i n t s
1925 New York: E. P. Dutton & Co 264.03
1925 London: Kegan Paul 264.04
1932 London: Routledge & Kegan Paul 264.05
1961 Excerpt:
     "The New Physics and Relativity" (XIII)
     in "The Basic Writings of B. Russell":
     XVI/68 (BN 659) 264.06

Translations
Deutsch:
"ABC der Atome"
Ü.: Werner Bloch
1925 Stuttgart: Franckh'sche
    Verlagshandlung. 109 S. 264.07
Inhalt
1. Einleitung. 2. Das periodische System. 3. Elektronen und Kerne. 4. Das
Wasserstoffspektrum. 5. Die verschiedenen möglichen Zustände des Wasser-
stoffatoms. 6. Die Quantentheorie. 7.
Der feinere Aufbau des Wasserstoffspektrums. 8. Elektronenringe. 9. Rönt-
genstrahlen. 10. Radioaktivität. 11.
Der Aufbau der Kerne. 12. Die neue Physik und die Wellentheorie des Lichtes.
13. Die neue Physik und die Relativitätstheorie. Anhang: Bohr's Theorie des
Wasserstoffspektrums.

LOGICAL ATOMISM

(see also "Philosophy of Logical Atomism", 1918/
BN 178 with Commentary)

1924 in "Contemporary Britisch Philosophy: Per-
    sonal Statements". First Series.
    London: Allen & Unwin 265.01
    New York: Macmillan, p. 356-386 . . . . .   265.02
    1956 in "Logic and Knowledge", BN 616 . . .   265.03
    1972 in "Russell's Logical Atomism", BN 697 265.04

    Translations
    Deutsch . . . . 1971 in BN 696 . . . . . .   265.05
    Italienisch . . . 1961 in BN 616.08 . . . . .   265.06
    Portugiesisch . 1974 in BN 616.09 . . . . .   265.07
    Spanisch:
        "El automismo lógico"
        Tr.: Sari Ali Jafella
        in "Revista de Filosofia", 15/16-78
        1964 La Plata 265.08
    Spanisch . . . . . . 1966 in BN 616.1 . . . . .   265.09
    Tschechisch . . . 1967 in BN 680/C:6 . . . .   265.10

Does Ethics Influence Life?

1924 in "Nation & Athenaeum", vol. 34, p. 635-636 266.00

Styles in Ethics

1924 in "Our Changing Morality: A Symposium"
    New York: Albert & Charles Boni, p. 1-24 . .   267.01
    1924 (Apr. 30) under the title "New Morals
    for Old: Styles in Ethics"
    in "Nation", vol. 118, p. 497-499 . .   267.02
    1961 in "The Basic Writings of B. Russell"
    IX/40 (BN 659) 267.03

Preface to Jean Nicod's
"La Geometrie dans le Monde Sensible"
1924 Paris: Alcan 268.01
  1924 (Nov.-Dec.) in "Revue Philosophique",
    vol. 98, p. 450-454 . . . .   268.02
  1962 Paris: Presses Universitaires de France   268.03
  1930 under the title
    "Foundations of Geometry and Induction"
    London: Kegan Paul, Trench & Trubner .   268.04
    New York: Harcourt, Brace 268.05
  1970 under the title
    "Geometry and Induction"
    London: Routledge and Kegan Paul . . .   268.06
    Berkeley: University of Calif. 268.07

Dogmatic and Scientific Ethics

1924 (Jan. 5) in "Outlook", vol. 53, p. 9-10 . .   269.00

Need for Political Scepticism

1924 (Feb. 23) in "The Freeman", vol.8, p.124-126   270.01
  1928 in "Sceptical Essays": XI (BN 331) . .   270.02

  T r a n s l a t i o n s
  Chinesisch .... 1932 in BN 331.16 . . . . .   270.03
  Deutsch .... 1930 in BN 331.19 . . . . .   270.04
  Französisch ... 1933 in BN 331.23 . . . . .   270.05
  Italienisch ... 1953 in BN 331.25 . . . . .   270.06
  Japanisch . . . 1963 in BN 331.29 . . . . .   270.07
  Polnisch ...... 1937 in BN 331.33 . . . . .   270.08
  Portugiesisch . 1955 in BN 331.35 . . . . .   270.09
  Schwedisch .... 1950 in BN 331.36 . . . . .   270.10
  Spanisch ...... 1956 in BN 331.39 = 615 . .   270.11

Psychology and Politics

1924 (Mar. 22) in "Outlook", vol. 53 . . . . . .   271.01
  1926 (Mar.) in "Dial", vol. 80, p. 179-188   271.02
  1928 in "Sceptical Essays": XV (BN 331) . .   271.03

  T r a n s l a t i o n s
  Chinesisch .... 1932 in BN 331.16 . . . . .   271.04
  Deutsch .... 1930 in BN 331.19 . . . . .   271.05
  Französisch ... 1933 in BN 331.23 . . . . .   271.06
  Italienisch ... 1953 in BN 331.25 . . . . .   271.07
  Japanisch ..... 1963 in BN 331.29 . . . . .   271.08
  Polnisch ...... 1937 in BN 331.33 . . . . .   271.09
  Portugiesisch . 1955 in BN 331.35 . . . . .   271.10
  Schwedisch .... 1950 in BN 331.36 . . . . .   271.11
  Spanisch ...... 1956 in BN 331.39 = 615 . .   271.12

Machines and the Emotions

1924 (Mar. 22) in "Outlook", vol. 53 . . . . . .   272.01
  1928 in "Sceptical Essays": VI (BN 331) . .   272.02

```
T r a n s l a t i o n s
Chinesisch  ....  1932  in  BN  331.16  . . . . .  272.03
Deutsch  .......  1930  in  BN  331.19  . . . . .  272.04
Französisch  ...  1933  in  BN  331.23  . . . . .  272.05
Italienisch  ...  1953  in  BN  331.25  . . . . .  272.06
Japanisch  .....  1963  in  BN  331.29  . . . . .  272.07
Polnisch  ......  1937  in  BN  331.33  . . . . .  272.08
Portugiesisch .  1955  in  BN  331.35  . . . . .  272.09
Schwedisch  ....  1950  in  BN  331.36  . . . . .  272.10
Spanisch  ......  1956  in  BN  331.39 = 615  . .  272.11
```

A Motley Pantheon

1924 (Mar.) in "Dial", vol. 76, p. 243-245 . . . 273.00

The Effect of Science on Social Institutions

1924 (Apr. 1) in "Survey", vol. 52, p. 5-11 . . 274.00

If We Are to Prevent the Next War

1924 (May) in "The Century", vol. 108, p. 3-12 . 275.01
1926 in "War - Cause and Cure", p. 161-177 275.02

Democracy and Imperialism

1924 (June) in "World Tomorrow",
vol. 7, p. 173-174(Interview by A.Rochester) 276.00

The American Intelligentsia

1924 (Oct. 11) in "Nation and Athenaeum",
vol. 36, p. 50-61 . . . . 277.00

Philosophy in the Twentieth Century

1924 (Oct.) in "Dial", vol. 77, p. 271-290 . . . 278.01
1928 in "Sceptical Essays": V (BN 331) . . 278.02
1943 in "Twentieth Century Philosophy"
Toronto: McLeod, p. 225-249 . . . . . 278.03
1961 in "The Basic Writings of B. Russell":
VII/32 (BN 659) 278.04

```
T r a n s l a t i o n s
Chinesisch  ....  1932  in  BN  331.16  . . . . .  278.05
Chinesisch:
   "Erh Shih Chê Hsioh"
   Tr.: Hu Tung-yeh
   1950 Teipeh: Hwa Kuo Pub. service  . .  278.06
Deutsch  .......  1930  in  BN  331.19  . . . . .  278.07
Französisch  ...  1933  in  BN  331.23  . . . . .  278.08
Italienisch  ...  1953  in  BN  331.25  . . . . .  278.09
Japanisch  .....  1963  in  BN  331.29  . . . . .  278.10
Polnisch  ......  1937  in  BN  331.33  . . . . .  278.11
Portugiesisch .  1955  in  BN  331.35  . . . . .  278.12
Schwedisch  ....  1950  in  BN  331.36  . . . . .  278.13
Spanisch  ......  1956  in  BN  331.39 = 615  . .  278.14
  "        ......  1962  in  BN  665  . . . . . .  278.15
```

British Labor and Chinese Brigands
1924 (Nov. 5) in "Nation", vol. 119, p. 503-506   279.00

Freedom or Authority in Education
1924 (Dec.) in "Century", vol.109, p.138-139 . .   280.00

British Labor's Lesson
1924 (Dec. 31) in "The New Republic",
    vol. 41, p. 138-139 . . . .   281.00

Government By Propaganda
1924 in vol. I "These Eventful Years: The Twen-
    tieth Century in the Making."
    London: The Encyclopedia Britanica, p.380-385   282.00

ICARUS OR THE FUTURE OF SCIENCE
1924 New York: E. P. Dutton & Co. 64 pp. 283.01
    London: Kegan Paul. 64 pp. 283.02
    1925 London: Kegan Paul 283.03
    1926 New York: E. P. Dutton & Co. 283.04
    1927 London: Kegan Paul 283.05
    1959 "The Future of Science" (Identical?)
        New York: Philosophical Library. With a
        "self-portrait" of the author. 86 pp.   283.06
    1973 "Icarus or the Future of Science"
        Fancsimele of 1924 ed.
        Nottingham: B. R. Peace Foundation . .   283.07

    T r a n s l a t i o n s
    Chinesisch:
        "Kexue de jianglai"
        1928 Shanghai 283.08
        "Kexue zhi jianglai"
        1931 Shanghai 283.09
    Deutsch:
        "Ikarus oder
        Die Zukunft der Wissenschaft"
        Ü.: Franz Arens
        1926 München: Drei Masken Verlag. 55 S.   283.10
    Russisch:
        "Dedal i Ikar"
        1926 Leningrad, Moskau 283.11

How to be Free and Happy
1924 New York:
    The Rand School of Social Science. 46 pp. .   284.01
    (Lecture delivired under auspices of Free
    Youth at Cooper Union, New York, on May 28)
    1924 (Nov.) Summarized in "Playground",
        vol. 18, p. 486 . . . .   284.02

Bolshevism and the West

1924 London: Allen & Unwin. 78 pp. 285.01
New York: The League of public discussion   285.02
A debate on the resolution: "That the Soviet form of government is applicable to
western civilization". Scott Nearing: af-
firmative; Bertrand Russell: negative.
Eine Debatte über die Entschließung, "daß
die sowjetische Regierungsform auf die west-
liche Zivilisation anwendbar ist". - Scott
Nearing: bejahend; B. Russell: verneinend.

Translations
Deutsch:
Auszug unter dem Titel
"Der Bolschewismus und der Westen"
1972 in BN 703/IV:9 . . . . 285.03

Materialism : Past and Present.

1925 Introduction in F. A. Lange's
"The History of Materialism"
Third (English) Edition, three vols. in one.
New York: Harcourt, Brace & Co. 286.01
London: Kegan Paul, p. V-XIV 286.02
1961 in "The Basic Writings of B. Russell":
VI/29 (BN 659) 286.03

Introduction to Mrs. Stan Harding's "The Underworld of State"

1925 London: Allen & Unwin, p. 11-28 . . . . . . 287.00

Life in the Middle Ages

Review of Eileen Power's "Medieval People" and
Johan Huizinga's "The Waning of the Middle Ages"

1925 (Apr.) in "Dial", vol. 78, p. 295-298 . . . 288.01
1957 in "Why I Am Not a Christian and Other
Essays" (BN 625) 288.02

Translations
Dänisch .... 1966 in BN 625.11 . . . . . 288.03
Deutsch .... 1963 in BN 625.12 . . . . . 288.04
Italienisch ... 1960 in BN 625.19 . . . . . 288.05
Japanisch ..... 1959 in BN 625.21 . . . . . 288.06
Koreanisch .... 1960 in BN 625.23 . . . . . 288.07
Niederländisch 1966 in BN 625.26 . . . . . 288.08
Persisch ...... 1970 in BN 625.28 . . . . . 288.09
Portugiesisch . 1960 in BN 625.30 . . . . . 288.10
Schwedisch .... 1958 in BN 625.32 . . . . . 288.11
Spanisch ...... 1958 in BN 625.33 . . . . . 288.12
Türkisch ...... 1966 in BN 625.36 . . . . . 288.13

The Dogmas of Naturalism
1925 in "Nation and Athenaeum", vol. 37, p. 326   289.00

British Policy in China
1925 in "Nation and Athenaeum", vol.37, p.480-482   290.00

Mind and Matter
1925 in "Nation and Athenaeum", vol. 38, p. 323   291.00

Socialism and Education
1925 (Sept.) in "Harper's Monthly Magazine",
     vol. 151, p. 413-417 . . . .   292.01
     T r a n s l a t i o n s
     Deutsch:
       "Sozialismus und Erziehung"
       1974 in BN 707/II:2 . . . .   292.02

WHAT I BELIEVE
(Not identical with BN 342/1929 and BN 364/1931)

1925 New York: E. P. Dutton & Co. 87 pp. 293.01
     London: Kegan Paul. 95 pp. 293.02
     1927 London: Kegan Paul 293.03
     1928 "   : "   " 293.04
     1928 New York: E. P. Dutton & Co. 293.05
     1929 "   "   : " "   "   "   " 293.06
     1933 "   "   : " "   "   "   " 293.07
     1957 in "Why I Am Not a Christian and Other
       Essays" (BN 625 with Commentary) . . .   293.08
     1961 in "The Basic Writings of B. Russell":
       IX/43 (BN 659) 293.09

     T r a n s l a t i o n s
     Chinesisch:
       "Wo de xinyang"
       1927 Shanghai 293.10
       "Wo de renshengguan"
       1936 Nanking 293.11
     Dänisch . . . . 1966 in BN 625.11 . . . . .   293.12
     Deutsch . . . . 1963 in BN 625.12 . . . . .   293.13
     Französisch . . . 1960 in BN 625.16 . . . . .   293.14
     Italienisch . . . 1960 in BN 625.19 . . . . .   293.15
     Japanisch . . . . . 1959 in BN 625.21 . . . . .   293.16
     Koreanisch . . . . 1960 in BN 625.23 . . . . .   293.17
     Niederländisch 1966 in BN 625.26 . . . . .   293.18
     Persisch . . . . . . 1970 in BN 625.28 . . . . .   293.19
     Portugiesisch . 1960 in BN 625.30 . . . . .   293.20
     Schwedisch . . . . 1958 in BN 625.32 . . . . .   293.21
     Spanisch . . . . . . 1958 in BN 625.33 . . . . .   293.22
     Türkisch . . . . . . 1966 in BN 625.36 . . . . .   293.23

THE ABC OF RELATIVITY

1925 New York, London: Harper & Brothers. 232 pp.   294.01
London: Kegan Paul. 237 pp. 294.02

C o n t e n t s
I. Touch and Sight: The Earth and the Heavens.
II. What Happens and What is Observed.   III.
The Velocity of Light.   IV. Clocks and Foot
Rules. V. Space-Time. VI. The Special Theory
of Relativity. VII. Intervals in Space-Time.
VIII. Einstein's Law of Gravitation.   IX.
Proofs of Einstein's Law of Gravitation.   X.
Mass, Momentum, Energy and Action.   XI. Is
the Universe Finite?   XII. Conventions and
Natural Laws. XIII. The Abolition of "Force".
XIV. What is Matter? XV. Philosophical Con-
sequences?

C o m m e n t a r y
Prof. J. E. Littlewood was rather disturbed
when he heard that Russell was writing a popular book on Relativity ("The ABC of Relativity") and cautioned him about some of the
difficulties. At the end he agreed that Russell had succeeded in simplifying without
falsifying, and in providing what is still
the easiest introduction to the subject.

K o m m e n t a r
Prof. J. E. Littlewood war einigermaßen be-
unruhigt, als er hörte, daß Russell dabei
war, ein populäres Buch über Relativität zu
schreiben ("The ABC of Relativity"), und er
warnte ihn vor den Schwierigkeiten. Zum Schluß
aber gab er zu, daß es Russell geglückt war,
zu vereinfachen, ohne zu verfälschen und die
auch heute noch verständlichste Einführung
in das Thema zu geben.

R e p r i n t s
1925 (July 18) Excerpts
      in "Nation and Athenaeum", vol. 37,
      p. 619-620, 651-652, 685-686, 712-713.   294.03
1927 Excerpt:
      "Touch and Sight:
      The Earth and the Heavens" (I)
      in "Selected Papers of Bertrand Russell"
      (BN 317) 294.04
1931 London: Kegan Paul 294.05
1932 London: Routledge 294.06
1958 London: Allen & Unwin. Rev. ed. . . .   294.07
1958 New York: New American Library 294.08
1959 "   "   : "   "   "   . . .   294.09
1959 Fair Lawn, N.J.: Essential Books . . .   294.10
1959 Toronto: Nelson 294.11
1960 New York: New American Library 294.12

1964 London: Allen & Unwin 294.13
1969 "   : "   " " 294.14
1969 New York: New American Library 294.15
1971 London: Allen & Unwin 294.16
1977 "   : "   " " 294.17

T r a n s l a t i o n s
Arabisch:
    "Alif Ba'al-Nisbīyah=
    Tr.: Fu'ād Kāmil
    1965 Kairo:
        Markaz Kutub al-Sharq al-Awsat . 294.18
Deutsch:
    Auszug unter dem Titel
    "Das ABC der Relativität"
    1927 in "Monistische Bibliothek", 41 f.
        Hamburg: Hamburger Verlag 294.19
    "Das ABC der Relativitätstheorie"
    Ü.: Kurt Grelling
    1928 München: Drei Masken Verl. 260 S. 294.20
    Tr.: Uta Dobl, Erhard Seiler
    1970 München: Nymphenburger Verlagsh. 294.21
    1973 Ebenda. 2. Auflage (Russell
        Studienausgabe) 294.22
    I n h a l t
    1. Greifen und Sehen: Erde und Himmel.
    2. Was sich ereignet und was man beob-
    achtet. 3. Die Lichtgeschwindigkeit.
    4. Uhren und Maßstäbe. 5. Das Raum-Zeit-
    Kontinuum. 6. Die Spezielle Relativi-
    tätstheorie. 7. Raum-zeitliche Abstän-
    de. 8. Einstein's Gravitationsgesetz.
    9. Beweise für Einstein's Gravitations-
    gesetz. 10. Masse, Impuls, Energie und
    Wirkung. 11. Das expandierende Univer-
    sum. 12. Konventionen und Naturgesetze.
    13. Die Abschaffung der "Kraft".   14.
    Was ist Materie?   15. Philosophische
    Konsequenzen.
Französisch:
    "ABC de la relativité"
    Tr.: Pierre Clinquart
    1965 Paris: Union générale d'éditions. 294.23
Ind./Marathi:
    "Einsteinchya
    sapeksatavadachi multattve"
    Tr.: Vasant J. Joši
    1971 Nagbur: the translator 294.24
Italienisch:
    "L'ABC della relatività"
    Tr.: Luca Pavolini
    1960 Mailand: Longanesi 294.25
Japanisch:
    "Sotaisei riron eno ninshik"
    Tr.: Kaneko Tsutomu, Satake Seiya
    1971 Tokio: Hakuyô Sha 294.26

Norwegisch:
   "Relativitetsteoriens ABC"
   Tr.: E. K. Broch
   1965 Oslo: Gyldendal 294.27
Portugiesisch:
   "ABC da relatividade"
   Tr.: Giasone Rebuá
   1960 Rio de Janeiro: Zahar 294.28
   1963 "   "   "   : " 294.29
   1966 "   "   "   : " 294.30
   Tr.: Augusto Pastor Fernandes
   1969 Lissabon: Europa-America 294.31
Schwedisch:
   "Relativitetsteorins ABC"
   Tr.: Anders Byttner
   1960 Stockholm: Natur och Kultur . . . 294.32
Serbokroatisch:
   "ABC teorije relativnosti"
   Tr.: Ilija Marinkovič
   1962 Belgrad: Savremena škola 294.33
Spanisch:
   "El ABC de la relatividad"
   Tr.: Ernesto Sábato
   1943 Buenos Aires: Ed. Imán 294.34
   Tr.: Manuel Simas
   1964 Buenos Aires:
      Compania general fabril editora . 294.35

On Non-Euclidean Geometries

1926 in "Encyclopaedia Britanica: Thirteenth Ed."
   vol. 11, p. 724-730
   New York: The Encyclopaedia Britanica . . . 295.01
   London: "   "   " . . . 295.02

Theory of Knowledge

1926 in "Encyclopaedia Britanica: Thirteenth Ed."
   vol. 30, p. 642-645
   New York: The Encyclopaedia Britanica . . . 296.01
   London: "   "   " . . . 296.02

Philosophical Consequences of Theory of Relativity

1926 in "Encyclopaedia Britanica: Thirteenth Ed."
   vol. 31, p. 331-332
   New York: The Encyclopaedia Britanica . . . 297.01
   London: "   "   " . . . 297.02

Review of C. D. Broad's
"The Mind and Its Place in Nature"

1926 in "Mind", vol. 35, p. 72-80 . . . . 298.00

Freedom in Society

1926 (Mar.) in "Harper's Monthly Magazine",
    vol. 152, p. 438-444 . . . . 299.01
    1928 in "Sceptical Essays": XIII (BN 331) . 299.02

    T r a n s l a t i o n s
    Chinesisch..... 1932 in BN 331.16 . . . . . 299.03
    Deutsch .... 1930 in BN 331.19 . . . . . 299.04
    Französisch ... 1933 in BN 331.23 . . . . . 299.05
    Italienisch ... 1953 in BN 331.25 . . . . . 299.06
    Japanisch ..... 1963 in BN 331.29 . . . . . 299.07
    Norwegisch .... 1947 in BN 331.32 = 519 . . 299.08
    Polnisch ...... 1937 in BN 331.33 . . . . . 299.09
    Portugiesisch . 1955 in BN 331.35 . . . . . 299.10
    Schwedisch .... 1950 in BN 331.36 . . . . . 299.11
    Spanisch ...... 1956 in BN 331.39 = 615 . . 299.12

What Shall We Educate For?
An Inquiry into Fundamentals.

1926 (Apr.) in "Harper's Monthly Magazine",
    vol. 152, p. 586-597 . . . . 300.01
    1936 in "Modern Reader",
        Boston: Heath, p. 473-489 . . . . . . 300.02

Capitalism or What?

1926 (May) in "Banker's Magazine",
    vol. 112, p. 679-680, 725, 727 . . . . . . 301.00

Relativity and Religion.
Review of Whitehead's
"Science and the Modern World".

1926 (May 29) in "Nation and Athenaeum",
    vol. 39, p. 206-207 . . . . 302.00

Review of N. Bukharin's
"Historical Materialism"

1926 (Aug. 20) in "New Leader",
    vol. 13, no. 45, p. 3-5 . . . . 303.00

Is Science Superstitious?

A review of Burtt's
"The Metaphysical Foundation of Modern Physics"
and Whitehead's "Science and the Modern World"

1926 (Sept.) in "Dial", vol. 81, p. 179-186 . . 304.01
    1927 in "Rationalist Annual" 304.02
    1928 in "Sceptical Essays": III (BN 331) . 304.03
    1941 in "Let the People Think" (BN 464) . . 304.04
    1947 Girard, Kansas: Haldeman-Julius Publ. 304.05
    1958 in "The Will to Doubt" (BN 638) . . . 304.06

```
T r a n s l a t i o n s
Chinesisch .... 1932 in BN 331.16 . . . . .   304.07
Deutsch ....... 1930 in BN 331.19 . . . . .   304.08
Französisch ... 1933 in BN 331.23 . . . . .   304.09
Italienisch ... 1953 in BN 331.25 . . . . .   304.10
Japanisch ..... 1963 in BN 331.29 . . . . .   304.11
Polnisch ...... 1937 in BN 331.33 . . . . .   304.12
Portugiesisch . 1955 in BN 331.35 . . . . .   304.13
Schwedisch .... 1950 in BN 331.36 . . . . .   304.14
Spanisch ...... 1956 in BN 331.39 = 615 . .   304.15
```

The Harm That Good Men Do?

```
1926 (Oct.) in "Harper's Monthly Magazine",
     vol. 153, p. 529-534 . . . . . . . . . . .   305.01
     1928 in "Sceptical Essays": IX (BN 331) . .   305.02
     1929 in "College Readings in Contemporary
     Thought", p. 398-406 . . . . . . . . .   305.03
```

```
     T r a n s l a t i o n s
Chinesisch .... 1932 in BN 331.16 . . . . .   305.04
Deutsch ....... 1930 in BN 331.19 . . . . .   305.05
Französisch ... 1933 in BN 331.23 . . . . .   305.06
Italienisch ... 1953 in BN 331.25 . . . . .   305.07
Japanisch ..... 1963 in BN 331.29 . . . . .   305.08
Polnisch ...... 1937 in BN 331.33 . . . . .   305.09
Portugiesisch . 1955 in BN 331.35 . . . . .   305.10
Schwedisch .... 1950 in BN 331.36 . . . . .   305.11
Spanisch ...... 1956 in BN 331.39 = 615 ...   305.12
```

Behaviourism: Its Effect on Ordinary Mortals
Should It Become a Graze

```
1926 (Dec.) in "Century", vol. 113, p. 148-153 .   306.00
```

Perception

```
1926 Lecture to British Institute of Philosophy,
     in "Journal of Philosophical Studies"
     vol. 1, p. 78-86 . . . . . . . . . . . . .   307.00
```

ON EDUCATION ESPECIALLY IN EARLY CHILDHOOD

```
1926 London: Allen & Unwin..254.pp. . . . . . . .   308.01
     Under the title
     "Education and the Good Life"
     New York: Boni & Liveright. 319 pp. . . . .   308.02
     New York: Avon Book Division, Hearst Corp.   308.03
     C o n t e n t s
     Introduction
     Part I: Education and the Good Life.
         I. Postulates of Modern Educational Theory
         II. The Aims of Education.
     Part II: Education of Character.
         III. The Fearst Year.  IV.Fear. V. Play and
     Fancy. VI.Constructiveness. VII.Selfish-
     ness and Property.   VIII. Truthfulness.
```

IX. Punishment. X. Importance of Other
Children. XI. Affection and Sympathy.
XII. Sex Education. XIII. The Nursery
School.
Part III: Intellectual Education.
XIV. General Principles. XV. The School
Curriculum Before Fourteen. XVI. Late
School Years. XVII. Day Schools and
Boarding Schools. XVIII. The University.
XIX. Conclusion.

C o m m e n t a r y
Russell's main interest for many years was
concentrated on education. The unorthodox
school set up by himself and Dora Russell in
1927 attracted a good deal of newspaper pub-
licity, which magnified the trivial and ob-
scured the important. Probably the leading
spirit in setting up the school was Dora
Russell, but Russell himself became absorbed
in the study of child behaviour. Russells
books on education, "On Education Especially
Early Childhood" (1926) and "Education and
the Social Order" (1932), still have an impact and interest today. Though some of his
views are now accepted as a matter of course,
other reforms he suggested have still to be
carried out.

K o m m e n t a r
Russell's Hauptinteresse konzentrierte sich
für viele Jahre auf die Erziehung. Die Son-
derschule, die er und Dora Russell 1927 grün-
deten, übten eine große Anziehungskraft auf
die Zeitungsschreiber aus, die das Belanglose
in großer Aufmachung brachten und das Wesent-
liche verwischten. Wahrscheinlich war Dora
Russell der treibende Geist bei der Gründung
der Schule Russell selbst aber versenkte sich
immer mehr in das Studium des kindlichen Verhaltens. Russell's Bücher über Erziehung, "On
Education Especially Early Childhood" (1926)
und "Education and the Social Order" (1932),
sind auch heute noch eindrucksvoll und interessant. Obwohl einige seiner Auffassungen
jetzt für selbstverständlich gelten, müssen
andere von ihm vorgeschlagene Reformen noch
verwirklicht werden.

R e p r i n t s
1927 Excerpt:
   "The Aims of Education" (I:II)
   in "Selected Papers of Bertrand Russell"
   (BN 317) 308.04
1930 London: Allen & Unwin 308.05
1931 New York: Boni & Liveright 308.06

1931 Excerpt:
    "Constructiveness" (II:VI)
    in "Book of Essays"
    New York: Heath, p. 318-325 . . . . . 308.07
1933 London: Allen & Unwin 308.08
1938 Excerpt:
    "Aims of Education" (I:II)
    in "Toward Today: A Collection of Eng-
    lish and American Essays"
    New York: Scott, p. 189-202 . . . . . 308.09
1948 London: Allen & Unwin 308.10
1951 "   : "   " " 308.11
1954 New York: Liveright Publishing Corp. . 308.12
1957 London: Allen & Unwin 308.13
1960 "   : "   " " 308.14
1961 Excerpts:
    "Education of Character" (II:III-XIII)
    New York: Philosophical Library . . . 308.15
1961 Excerpt:
    "The Aims of Education (I:II)
    in "The Basic Writings of B. Russell":
    X/46 (BN 659) 308.16
1964 London: Allen & Unwin 308.17
1970 New York: Liveright 308.18
1974 London: Allen & Unwin 308.19
1976 "   : "   " " 308.20

T r a n s l a t i o n s
Chinesisch:
    "Luosu jiaoyu lun"
    1931 Shanghai 308.21
    "Ertong jiaoyu yuanli"
    1933 Shanghai 308.22
Deutsch:
    "Ewige Ziele der Erziehung
    unter besonderer Berücksichtigung
    der ersten Kinderjahre"
    Ü.: F. Schnabel
    1928 Heidelberg: N. Kampmann. 242 S. . 308.23
    I n h a l t
    Teil I: Erziehungsideale.
      1. Forderungen der modernen Erzie-
    hungslehre. 2. Die Ziele der Er-
    ziehung.
    Teil II: Charakterbildung.
      3. Das erste Jahr. 4. Angst. 5.
    Spiel und Phantasie. 6. Der posi-
    tive Schaffensdrang. 7. Selbstsucht
    und Eigentum. 8. Wahrhaftigkeit.
    9. Die Bestrafung des Kindes. 10.
    Die Bedeutung anderer Kinder. 11.
    Zueignung und Mitgefühl. 12. Das
    sexuelle Problem in der Erziehung.
    13. Die Kleinkinderschule.

Teil III: Die Erziehung des Intellekts.
  14. Allgemeine Grundsätze. 15. Der
  Lehrplan bis zum vierzehnten Lebens-
  jahr. 16. Die letzten Schuljahre.
  17. Tagesschulen und Internate. 18.
  Die Universität. 19. Schlußbetrach-
  tung.
"Erziehung
vornehmlich in frühester Kindheit"
Ü.: Georg Govert
1948 Düsseldorf, Frankfurt: Meridian . 308.24
Auszüge:
"Die Ziele der Erziehung" (II)
"Liebe und Sympathie" (XI)
1974 in BN 707/II:3 . . . . 308.25
Auszüge:
"Sexuelle Erziehung" (XII
"Furchtlose Freiheit"(XIX: Conclusion)
1975 in BN 710/I 308.26
Ind./Bengali:
  "Siksha - prasanga"
  Tr.: Amalendu Das Cupta
  1954 Kalkutta: Prachi Prakashan . . . 308.27
  Tr.: Narayan Chandra Chanda
  1955 Kalkutta: Kalikata Pustakalaya . 308.28
  1965 "   : "   "   . 308.29
Ind./Gujarati:
  "Kelavani vicar"
  Tr.: Mulšankar Bhatt
  1966 Aliabada: Bhashantar Nidhi . . . 308.30
Ind./Marathi:
  "Sikṣaṇ vicar"
  Tr.: B. R. Khānvilkar
  1963 Poona: the translator 308.31
Italienisch:
  "L'Educazione Dei Nostri Figli"
  Tr.: Tommaso Fiore
  1934 Bari: Laterza 308.32
Japanisch:
  "Kyôiku-ron"
  Tr.: Hidehiko Hori
  1953 Tokio: Kawade shobô 308.33
  Tr.: Ikuo Uozu
  1959 Tokio: Misuzu-Shobo 308.34
  Tr.: Hori Hidehiko
  1971: Kadokawa shoten 308.35
Koreanisch:
  "Gyoyukhak"
  Tr.: Minjung Sugwan
  1958 Seoul: Lim Han Yeong 308.36
Polnisch:
  "O wychowaniu, ze specjalnem unuzgled-
  nieniem wczesnego dziecinstwa"
  Tr.: Janina Hosiassonowna
  1932 Warschau: Nasza Ksiegarna 308.37

Portugiesisch:
"Educacão e vida perfeita"
Tr.: Monteiro Lobato
1956 Sao Paulo: Ed. Nacional 308.38
"Da educacão, especialmente
da primeira infância"
Tr.: Monteiro Lobato
1969 Sao Paulo: Ed. Nacional (4th ed.) 308.39
Schwedisch:
"Uppfostran för Livet"
1933 Stockholm: Natur och Kultur . . . 308.40
1951 "   : "   "   "   . . . 308.41
Spanisch:
"Ensayos sobre educación,
especialmente en los años infantiles"
Tr.: Julio Huici
1967 Madrid: Espasa Calpe 308.42
Türkisch:
"Terbiyevîye dair"
Tr.: Hâmit Dereli
1964 Ankara: Basimevi 308.43

British Folly in China

1927 (Mar. 2) in "Nation", vol. 124, p. 227 - 228 309.00

The New Life That Is America's

1927 (May 22) in "New York Times", Sec. 4, p.1-2 310.00

The Training of Young Children

1927 (Aug.) in "Harper's Monthly Magazine",
vol. 155, p. 313-319 . . . . 311.01
T r a n s l a t i o n s
Deutsch:
"Die Erziehung junger Kinder"
1975 in BN 710/II 311.02

Things That Have Mouled Me

1927 (Sept.) in "Dial", vol. 83, p. 181-186 . . 312.00

Education Without Sex-Taboos

1927 (Nov. 16) in "The New Republic",
vol. 52, p. 346-348 . . . . 313.00

WHY I AM NOT A CHRISTIAN

1927 London: Watts & Co. 31 pp. 314.01
(Lecture delivered on March 6, 1927 at Bat-
tersea Town Hall under the auspices of South
London Branch of the National Secular Society)
I n h a l t
What is a Christian? The Existence of God.
The First Cause Argument.   The Natural Law
Argument.   The Argument from Design. The

Moral Argument for Deity.   The Argument for
the Remedying of Injustice.   The Character
of Christ.   Defect in Christ's Teaching.
The Moral Problem.   The Emotional Factor.
How the Churches Have Retarded Progress.
Fear the Foundation of Religion.   What We
Must Do.

R e p r i n t s
1927 in "Truth Seeker", p. 7-31 . . . . . .   314.02
1927 in pamphlet form by American Association
    for the Advancement of Atheism.   4 pp.   314.03
1928 London: Watts & Co. 314.04
1929 Girard, Kansas: Haldeman-Julius Publ.   314.05
1931 London: Watts & Co. 314.06
1936 "   : "   " " 314.07
1940 New York: Freethought Press Association   314.08
1945 London: Watts & Co. 314.09
1957 in "Why I Am Not a Christian and Other
    Essays" (BN 625) 314.10
1961 in "The Basic Writings of B. Russell":
    XV/63 (BN 659) 314.11
1970 London: National Secular Society . . .   314.12

T r a n s l a t i o n s
Dänisch . . . . 1966 in BN 625.11 . . . . .   314.13
Deutsch:
    "Warum ich kein Christ bin"
    Ü.: Anny Farchy
    1932 Dresden: Nestler. 32 S. 314.14
Deutsch . . . . 1963 in BN 625.12 . . . . .   314.15
    I n h a l t
    Was ist ein Christ? Die Existenz Got-
    tes. Der Beweis einer ersten Ursache.
    Der Beweis durch das Naturgesetz.   Der
    teleologische Gottesbeweis. Die mora-
    lischen Gottesbeweise.   Das Argument
    der ausgleichenden Gerechtigkeit. Der
    Charakter Christi. Mängel an der Lehre
    Christi.   Das moralische Problem. Der
    gefühlsmäßige Moment. Wie die Kirchen
    den Fortschritt verzögert haben. Angst
    als Grundlage der Religion.   Was wir
    tun müssen.
Finnisch:
    "Miksi vapaa-ajattelija
    ei voi olla kristity"
    1957 Helsinki: Vapaa-ajattelijani litto   314.16
Französisch ... 1960 in BN 625.16 . . . . .   314.17
Italienisch ... 1960 in BN 625.19 . . . . .   314.18
Japanisch ..... 1959 in BN 625.21 . . . . .   314.19
Koreanisch .... 1960 in BN 625.23 . . . . .   314.20
Niederländisch 1966 in BN 625.26 . . . . .   314.21

NL/Afrikaans:
"Waarom ek geen Christen is nie"
1960 Johannesburg: Rasionalistiese
Verenigung von Suid-Afrika 314.22
Persisch . . . . . . 1970 in BN 625.28 . . . . . . 314.23
Polnisch:
"Dlaczego nie jestem chrześcijaninem"
Tr.: Amelia Kurladzka
1958 Warschau: Ksiazka i Wiedza . . . 314.24
1959 "   : "   " "   . . . 314.25
1962 "   : "   " "   . . . 314.26
Portugiesisch . 1960 in BN 625.30 . . . . . 314.27
Russisch:
"Počemu ja ne hristianin"
Tr.: I. Z. Romanow
1958 Moskau: Izd-vo inostr. lit. . . . 314.28
Russ./Armenisch:
"Počemu ja ne khristianin"
1960 Erevan: Ajpetrat 314.29
Schwedisch . . . . 1958 in BN 625.32 . . . . . 314.30
Spanisch . . . . . . 1958 in BN 625.32 . . . . . 314.31
Tschechisch . . . 1961 in BN 625.35 . . . . . 314.32
Türkisch . . . . . . 1966 in BN 625.36 . . . . . 314.33
Ungarisch:
"Miért nem vagyok kresztény?"
Tr.: Gedeon Dienes
1960 Budapest: Kossuth Kiadó 314.34

THE ANALYSIS OF MATTER

1927 New York: Harcourt Brace & Co. VIII, 408 pp. 315.01
London: Kegan Paul, Trench, Trubner & Co. . 315.02
C o n t e n t s
Preface: I. The Nature of the Problem.
Part I: The Logical Analysis of Physics.
II. Pre-Relativity Physics. III. Elec-
trons and Protons. IV. The Theory of
Quanta. V. The Special Theory of Rela-
tivity. VI. The General Theory of Rela-
tivity. VII. The Method of Tensors. VIII.
Geodesics. IX. Invariants and their Physi-
cal Interpretation. X. Weyl's Theory.
XI. The Principle of Differential Law.
XII. Measurement. XIII. Matter and Space.
XIV. The Abstractness of Physics.
Part II: Physics and Perception.
XV. From Primitive Perception to Common
Sense. XVI. From Common Sense to Physics.
XVII. What is an Empirical Science? XVIII.
Our Knowledge of Particular Matters of
Fact. XIX. Data, Inferences, Hypotheses,
and Theories. XX. The Causal Theory of
Perception. XXI. Perception and Objec-
tivity. XXII. The Belief in General Laws.
XXIII. Substance. XXIV. Importance of

Structure in Scientific Inference. XXV.
Perception from the Standpoint of Physics.
XXVI. Non-Mental Analogues to Perception.
Part III: The Structure of the Physical World
XXVII. Particulars and Events. XXVIII.
The Construction of Points. XXIX. Space-
Time Orders. XXX. Causal Lines. XXXI.
Extrinsic Causal Laws. XXXII. Physical
and Perceptual Space-Time. XXXIII. Peri-
odicity and Qualitative Series. XXXIV.
Types of Physical Occurrences. XXXV.
Causality and Interval. XXXVI. The Gene-
sis of Space-Time. XXXVII. Physics and
Neutral Monism. XXXVIII. Summary and Con-
clusion. Index.

C o m m e n t a r y
Russell's mind was soon working on the philo-
sophical implications of Einstein's ideas.
"The ABC of Atoms" was published in 1923 and
"The ABC of Relativity" in 1925. Russell's
fuller philosophical study, "The Analysis of
Matter" was not published until 1927. In "The
Analysis of Matter", following the Theory of
Relativity, Russell described "events" as the
raw material out of which the logical con-
structions of both mind and matter were made.
Many of the new philosophical ideas they
reached their culmination 1948 in "Human
Knowledge".

K o m m e n t a r
Russell's Geist begann schnell mit den philosophischen Folgerungen von Einsteins Ideen
zu arbeiten. "The ABC of Atoms" wurde 1923
veröffentlicht und "The ABC of Relativity"
1925. Russell's umfassendere philosophische
Studie "The Analysis of Matter" erschien erst
1927. In "The Analysis of Matter" folgte Russell der Relativitätstheorie und beschrieb
"Ereignisse" als das Rohmaterial, aus dem die
logischen Konstruktionen sowohl des Geistes
wie der Materie geschaffen wurden. Viele der
darin enthaltenen neuen philosophischen Ideen
erreichten ihren Höhepunkt 1948 in "Human
Knowledge".

R e p r i n t s
1954 London: Allen & Unwin 315.03
1954 New York: Dover Publications 315.04
1959 London: Allen & Unwin 315.05
1961 Excerpt:
      "Physics and Neutral Monism" (XXXVII)
      in "The Basic Writings of B. Russell":
      XVI/65 (BN 659) 315.06

1965 Excerpt:
"What Is an Empirical Science?" (XVII)
in "On the Philosophy of Science": I/I
(BN 672) 315.07
1965 New York: Dover Publications 315.08
T r a n s l a t i o n s
Deutsch:
"Philosophie der Materie"
Ü.: Kurt Grelling
1929 Leipzig: Teubner. XI, 433 S. . . 315.09
1932 " : " 315.10
I n h a l t
Vorwort: I. Das Problem.
Teil I:
Die logische Zergliederung der Physik.
II. Die vorrelativistische Physik.
III. Elektronen und Protonen. IV.
Die Quantentheorie. V. Die speziel-
le Relativitätstheorie. VI. Die all-
gemeine Relativitätstheorie. VII.
Die Tensormethode. VIII. Geodäti-
sche Linien. IX. Invarianten und
ihre physikalische Bedeutung. X. Die
Weylsche Theorie. XI. Das Prinzip
der Differentialgesetze. XII. Vom
Messen. XIII. Materie u. Raum. XIV.
Die Abstrakheit der Physik.
Teil II:
Physik und Wahrnehmung.
XV. Von der ursprünglichen Wahrnehmung zum gemeinen Menschenverstand.
XVI. Vom gemeinen Menschenverstand
zur Physik. XVII. Was ist eine em-
pirische Wissenschaft? XVIII. Unsere Erkenntnis von Einzeltatsachen.
XIX. Daten, Schlüsse, Hypothesen und
Theorien. XX. Die kausale Theorie
der Wahrnehmung. XXI. Wahrnehmung
und Objektivität. XXII. Der Glaube
an allgemeine Gesetze. XXIII. Sub-
stanz. XXIV. Die Bedeutung der Struktur für das wissenschaftliche Schließen. XXV. Die Wahrnehmung, physika-
lisch betrachtet. XXVI. Nicht-psy-
chische Analoga der Wahrnehmung.
Teil III:
Die Struktur der physischen Welt.
XXVII. Elemente und Ereignisse.
XXVIII. Die Konstruktion von Punkten.
XXIX. Die Raum-Zeit-Ordnung. XXX.
Kausallinien. XXXI. Äußerliche Kau-
salgesetze. XXXII. Wahrnehmungsraum
und -zeit und die "Welt" der Physik.

XXXIII. Periodizität und qualitative
Reihen. XXXIV. Typen physikalischer
Vorgänge. XXXV. Kausalität und In-
tervall. XXXVI. Der Aufbau der "Welt!
XXXVII. Physik und neutraler Monis-
mus. XXXVIII. Zusammenfassung und
Schluß.
Französisch:
"L'Analyse de la matière"
Tr.: Philippe Deveaux
1965 Paris: Payot 315.11
Italienisch:
"L'analisi della materia"
Tr.: Luca Pavolini
1964 Mailand: Longanesi 315.12
Spanisch:
"Análisis de la materia"
Tr.: Eulogio Mellado
1969 Madrid: Taurus 315.13
1976 " : " 315.14

AN OUTLINE OF PHILOSOPHY

1927 London: Allen & Unwin. VI, 317 pp. 316.01
Under the title "Philosophy"
New York: W. W. Norton & Co. 307 pp. . . . 316.02
C o n t e n t s
I. Philosophic Doubts.
Part I: Man From Without.
II. Man and his Environment. III. The
Process of Learning in Animals and Infants
IV. Language. V. Perception Objectively
Regarded. VI. Memory Objectively Regarded.
VII. Inference as a Habit. VIII. Knowledge
Behaviouristically Considered.
Part II: The Physical World.
IX. The Structure of the Atom. X. Rela-
tivity. XI. Causal Laws in Physics. XII.
Physics and Perception. XIII. Physical
and Perceptual Space. XIV. Perception
and Physical Causal Laws. XV. The Nature
of Our Knowledge of Physics.
Part III: Man From Within.
XVI. Self-Observation. XVII. Images.
XVIII. Imagination and Memory. XIX. The
Introspective Analysis of Perception. XX.
Consciousness? XXI. Emotion, Desire, and
Will. XXII. Ethics.
Part IV: The Universe.
XXIII. Some Great Philosophies of the Past
XXIV. Truth and Falsehood. XXV. The Va-
lidity of Inference. XXVI. Events, Matter,
and Mind. XXVII. Man's Place in the Uni-
verse. Index.

R e p r i n t s
1949 London: Allen & Unwin 316.03
1951 "   : "   " " 316.04
1956 "   : "   " " 316.05
1960 New York: Meridian 316.06
1961 Cleveland: World Pub. Co. 316.07
1961 Excerpts:
    "Language" (IV)
    "Knowledge
    Behaviouristically Considered" (VIII)
    "The Validity of Inference" (XXV)
    in "The Basic Writings of B. Russell":
    III/9, VIII/39, IV/23 (BN 659) 316.08
1971 London: Allen & Unwin 316.09
1976 "   : "   " " 316.10
T r a n s l a t i o n s
Chinesisch:
    "Zhexue dagang"
    1948 Nanking 316.11
Deutsch:
    "Mensch und Welt"
    Ü.: Kurt Grelling
    1930 München: Drei Masken Verlag
       V, 343 S. 316.12
    I n h a l t
    (1) Philosophische Zweifel.
    Teil I: Der Mensch von außen gesehen.
       (2) Der Mensch und seine Umgebung.
       (3) Der Vorgang des Lernens bei Tie-
       ren und Kindern.   (4) Die Sprache.
       (5) Die Wahrnehmung in objektiver
       Betrachtung. (6) Das Gedächtnis in
       objektiver Betrachtung. (7) Schlie-
       ßen als Gewohnheit. (8) Das Wissen
       in behavioristischer Betrachtung.
    Teil II: Die physikalische Welt.
       (9) Der Bau des Atoms.   (10) Die Re-
       lativitätstheorie.   (11) Kausalge-
       setze in der Physik. (12) Physik und
       Wahrnehmung. (13) Der physikalische
       und der Wahrnehmungsraum. (14) Wahr-
       nehmung und physikalische Kausalge-
       setze. (15) Die Natur unserer phy-
       sikalischen Erkenntnis.
    Teil III: Der Mensch von Innen.
       (16) Selbst-Beobachtung. (17) Vor-
       stellungen. (18) Phantasie und Ge-
       dächtnis. (19) Die introspektive
       Analyse der Wahrnehmung.   (20) Be-
       wußtsein? (21) Emotionen, Begierde
       und Wille. (22) Ethik.
    Teil IV: Die Welt.
       (23) Einige große philosophische
       Systeme der Vergangenheit.   (24)

```
                  Wahrheit und Falschheit.  (25) Die
                  Gültigkeit des Schließens.  (26) Er-
                  eignisse, Materie und Geist.  (27)
                  Die Stellung des Menschen im Uni-
                  versum.
            Auszug:
            "Ethik" (XXII)
            1971 in BN 696 . . . . . . . . . . . .  316.13
      Italienisch:
            "Sintesi filosofica"
            Tr.: Aldo Visalberghi,
            Anke Visser 't Hooft Musacchio
            1966 Florenz: Nuova Italia . . . . . .  316.14
            1973 "      :  "       "     . . . . . .  316.15
      Japanisch:
            "Tetsugaku nyûmon"
            Tr.: Takashi Kakimura
            1953 Tokio: Shakai shisô kenkyûkai
                  shuppan-bu . . . . . . . . . . .  316.16
      Persisch:
            "Zaminehā-ye falsave"
            Tr.: Mohsen-e Amir
            1970 Teheran: Keyhān . . . . . . . . .  316.17
      Polnisch:
            "Zarys Filozifi"
            Tr.: Janina Hossiasson
            1939 Warschau: J. Przeworski . . . . .  316.18
      Portugiesisch:
            "Delineamentos da filosofia"
            Tr.: Brenno Silveira
            1954 Sao Paulo: Ed. Nacional . . . . .  316.19
            1956 "      "    :  "       "     . . . . .  316.20
            1969 Rio de Janeiro:
                  Civilizaçao brasileira . . . . .  316.21
      Schwedisch:
            "Den Nya Filosofien"
            Tr.: Alf Ahlberg
            .... Stockholm: Natur och Kultur . . .  316.22
      Spanisch:
            "Fundamentos de Filosofia"
            Tr.: R. Crespo y Crespo
            1935 Barcelona: Apolo . . . . . . . .  316.23
            1956 "         : José Janés . . . . . .  316.24
            (With Th. Mann's "Senōr y perro"
            and F. Mauriac's "La farisea":)
            1966 Barcelona: G. P. . . . . . . . .  316.25
            1972 "         : Plaza & Janés  . . . .  316.26
            1974 "         :  "       "  "     . . . .  316.27
```

Selected Papers of Bertrand Russell

Selected by and with a Special Introduction
by Bertrand Russell.

```
1927 New York: The Modern Library.  XIX, 390 pp.  317.01
1955 "     "    :  "       "         "      . . . . . . . .  317.02
```

C o n t e n t s

Effective Intolerance: Nothing More Encouraging
Than the Eminence of Mr. Bernard Shaw

1928 (Jan.) in "The Century", vol. 115, p. 316-325   318.00

Tortoise

1928 (Feb.) in "Forum", vol. 79, p. 262-263 . .   319.00

Bold Experiment in Education

1928 (Feb. 27) in "World Review", vol. 6, p. 53.   320.00

My Own View of Marriage

1928 (Mar. 7) in "The Outlook",
    vol. 148, p. 376-377 . . . .   321.00

How Will Science Change Morals?

1928 (Apr.) in "Menorah Journal",
    vol. 14, p. 312-329 . . . .   322.00

The New Philosophy of America

1928 (May) in "Fortnightly Review",
    vol. 129, p. 618-623 . . . .   323.00

Physics and Metaphysics

1928 (May 26) in "Saturday Review of Literature"
    vol. 4, p. 910-911 . . . .   324.00

Ostrich Code of Morals

1928 (July) in "Forum", vol. 80, p. 7-10 . . . .   325.00
(Part of a debate:
"Is Companionate Mariage Moral?")

School and the Very Young Child

1928 (July 11) in "The Outlook",
vol. 149, p. 418-420 . . . . 326.00

The Value of Scepticism

1928 (Oct.) in "Plain Talk", vol. 3, p. 423-430 327.01
    1928 in "Sceptical Essays": I (BN 331) . . 327.02
    1933 in "Fifty Modern English Writers"
        New York: Doubleday, p. 1276-1286 . . 327.03
    1941 in "Let the People Think" (BN 464) . . 327.04
    1947 Girard, Kansas: Haldeman-Julius Publ. 327.05
    1958 in "The Will to Doubt" (BN 638) . . . 327.06
    1972 in "Atheism" (BN 700) 327.07

    T r a n s l a t i o n s
    Chinesisch .... 1932 in BN 331.16 . . . . . 327.08
    Deutsch:
        "Der Wert des Skeptizismus"
        in "Neue Rundschau", Jahrg. 40, S. 1-13
        1929 Berlin 327.09
    Deutsch .... 1930 in BN 331.19 . . . . . 327.10
    Französisch ... 1933 in BN 331.23 . . . . . 327.11
    Italienisch ... 1953 in BN 331.25 . . . . . 327.12
    Japanisch ..... 1963 in BN 331.29 . . . . . 327.13
    Norwegisch .... 1947 in BN 331.32 = 519 . . 327.14
    Polnisch ...... 1937 in BN 331.33 . . . . . 327.15
    Portugiesisch . 1955 in BN 331.35 . . . . . 327.16
    Schwedisch .... 1950 in BN 331.36 . . . . . 327.17
    Spanisch ...... 1956 in BN 331.39 = 615 . . 327.18

Science and Education

1928 (Dec. 9) in "St.-Louis-Dispatch",
    50th Anniversary Number, p. 4-5 . . . . . . 328.01
    1930 in "The Drift of Civilization"
        New York: Simon & Schuster, p. 85-95 . 328.02
    1961 in "The Basic Writings of B. Russell":
        XVI/66 (BN 659) 328.03

Science

1928 in "Whither Mankind:
A Panorama of Modern Civilization"
New York, London, Toronto:
Longmans, Green & Co., p. 63-82 . . . . . . 329.00

Morris R. Cohen

1928 in "A Tribute to Professor Morris R. Cohen".
New York: "The Youth Who Sat At His Feet",
p. 46-49 . . . . 330.00

SCEPTICAL ESSAYS

1928 New York: W.W. Norton & Co. 256 pp. 331.01
     London: Allen & Unwin. 251 pp. 331.02
     C o n t e n t s
        I. Introduction:
           On the Value of Scepticism (1928/327)
       II. Dreams and Facts . . . . (1920/195)
      III. Is Science Superstitious? (1926/304)
       IV. Can Man Be Rational? . . . . (1923/262)
        V. Philosophy
           in the Twentieth Century (1924/278)
       VI. Machines and Emotions . . . . (1924/272)
      VII. Behaviourism and Values . . (1928/331)
     VIII. Eastern and
           Western Ideals of Happiness (1928/331)
       IX. The Harm that Good Men Do (1926/305)
        X. The Recrudescence
           of Puritanism . . . . (1923/259)
       XI. The Need
           for a Political Scepticism (1924/270)
      XII. Free Thought
           and Official Propaganda . . (1922/236)
     XIII. Freedom and Society . . . . . . (1926/299)
      XIV. Freedom versus
           Authority in Education . . . (1928/331)
       XV. Psychology and Politics . . (1924/271)
      XVI. The Danger of Creed Wars (1928/331)
     XVII. Some Prospects:
           Cheerful and Otherwise . . . (1928/331)
     R e p r i n t s
     1929 London: Allen & Unwin 331.03
     1931 "   : "   " " 331.04
     1931 New York: Norton 331.05
     1933 Excerpt:
          "Eastern and Western
          Ideals of Happiness" (VIII)
          in "Fifty Modern English Writers"
          New York: Doubleday, p. 1286-1293 . . 331.06
     1935 London: Allen & Unwin 331.07
     1948 "   : "   " " 331.08
     1956 "   : "   " " 331.09
     1960 "   : "   " " 331.10
     1961 Toronto: Nelson 331.11
     1961 Excerpt:
          "Eastern and Western
          Ideals of Happiness" (VIII)
          in "The Basic Writings of B. Russell":
          XIV/60 (BN 659) 331.12
     1962 Excerpts under the title
          "Essays in Scepticism"
          New York: Philosophical Library. 90 pp. 331.13
     1963 New York: W. W. Norton 331.14
     1977 London: Allen & Unwin 331.15

Translations
Chinesisch:
    "Huaiyi lunji"

Deutsch:
    Auszug:
    "Der Wert des Skeptizismus" (I)
    in "Neue Rundschau", Jahrg. 40, S. 1-13
    Auszug:
    "Psychologie und Politik" (XV)
    in "Neue Rundschau", Jg. 41, p. 600-610
    "Wissen und Wahn. Skeptische Essays."
    Tr.: Karl Wolfskehl
    "Skepsis"
    Ü.: R. Gillischewski
Inhalt
    I. Einführung:
      Über den Wert des Skeptizismus.
    II. Traum und Wirklichkeit.
    III. Ist die Wissenschaft abergläu-
       bisch?
    IV. Können die Menschen rational sein?
    V. Die Philosophie des zwanzigsten
      Jahrhunderts.
    VI. Maschinen und Gefühle.
    VII. Behaviorismus und Werte.
    VIII. Östliche und westliche
       Glücksideale.
    IX. Vom Schaden,
      den die guten Menschen anrichten.
    X. Der Widerspruch des Puritanismus.
    XI. Die Notwendigkeit des politischen
      Skeptizismus.
    XII. Freies Denken und offizielle Pro-
      paganda.
    XIII. Freiheit und Gesellschaft.
    XIV. Freiheit
      oder Autorität in der Erziehung.
    XV. Psychologie und Politik.
    XVI. Die Gefahr von Glaubenskriegen.
    XVII. Einige Ausblicke: erfreuliche und
      unerfreuliche.
    Auszug:
    "Freiheit oder Autorität
    in der Erziehung" (XIV)
Französisch:
    "Essais Sceptiques"

Italienisch:
    "Saggi scettici"
    Tr.: Donato Barbone
    1953 Bari: Laterza 331.25
    Tr.: Sergio Grignone
    1968 Mailand: Longanesi 331.26
    1968 in BN 686 . . . . 331.27
Japanisch:
    Excerpts
    1959 in BN 646 . . . . 331.28
    "Kaigi ronshû"
    Tr.: Takshi Tômiya
    1963 Tokio: Misu zu shobo 331.29
    "Kaigiron"
    Tr.: Kakimura Takashi
    1965 Tokio: Kadokawa shoten 331.30
    "Kaigi-ron"
    (with a writing of W. S. Churchill,
    in 'Nobel-shô bungaku zenshû' 22)
    1972 Tokio: Shufu no tomo sha. 331.31
Norwegisch:
    Excerpts:
    "Verdien av sunn skepsis" (I)
    "Opprøret mot fornuften" (IV)
    "Den nye puritanismen" (X)
    "Tankens frihet
    og statens propaganda" (XII)
    "Friheten og samfunet" (XIII)
    "Fare for kommende troskriger?" (XVI)
    1947 in BN 519 . . . . 331.32
Polnisch:
    "Szkice Sceptyczne"
    Tr.: Amelia Kurlandzka
    1937 Warschau: Roj 331.33
    1957 Warschau: Ksiazka i Wiedza . . . 331.34
Portugiesisch:
    "Ensaios cépticos"
    Tr.: Wilson Velloso
    1955 Sao Paulo: Ed. Nacional 331.35
Schwedisch:
    "Skeptiska essäer"
    Tr.: A. Byttner
    1950 Stockholm: Natur och Kultur . . . 331.36
Spanisch:
    Excerpts under the title
    "Ciencia, filosofía y política"
    Tr.: Pereyra
    1954 Madrid: Aguilar. 126 pp. 331.37
    1957 " : " 126 pp. 331.38
    1968 " : " 126 pp. 331.39
    1956 " : " ,
        in "Obras escogidas" (BN 615) . . 331.40

Three Ways to the World

1929 in vol. 12 of the Series: "Man and His World"
under the title "The World Man Lives In".
New York: D. Van Nostrand Co., p. 11-21. . . . 332.00
(An informal talk before the Contemporary
Thought Class at Northwestern University,
Chicago, Illinois, 1924)

On the Evils Due to Fear

1929 in "If I Could Preach Just Once",
New York, London: Harpers & Brothers,
p. 218-230 . . . . 333.01
Under the title
"If I Had Only One Sermon to Preach"
1929 England, Laymen Sermons 333.02
1932 New York, London: Harpers & Brothers . 333.03

Are Insects Intelligent?

Introduction to Major R. W. G. Hingston's
"Instinct and Intelligence"

1929 New York: Macmillan, p. VII-XIII 334.00

On Catholic and Protestant Sceptics

1929 (Jan.) in "Dial", vol. 86, p. 43-49 . . . . 335.01
1957 in "Why I Am Not a Christian and Other
Essays" (BN 625) 335.02

    T r a n s l a t i o n s
Dänisch . . . . . . 1966 in BN 625.11 . . . . . 335.03
Deutsch . . . . . . 1963 in BN 625.12 . . . . . 335.04
Italienisch . . . 1960 in BN 625.19 . . . . . 335.05
Japanisch . . . . 1959 in BN 625.21 . . . . . 335.06
Koreanisch . . . . 1960 in BN 625.23 . . . . . 335.07
Niederländisch 1966 in BN 625.26 . . . . . 335.08
Persisch . . . . . . 1970 in BN 625.28 . . . . . 335.09
Portugiesisch . 1960 in BN 625.30 . . . . . 335.10
Schwedisch . . . . 1958 in BN 625.32 . . . . . 335.11
Spanisch . . . . . . 1958 in BN 625.33 . . . . . 335.12
Türkisch . . . . . . 1966 in BN 625.36 . . . . . 335.13

Review of J. H. Denison's
"Emotion as the Basis of Civilization"

1929 (Jan. 23) in "Nation" (London),
vol. 128, p. 108 . . . . 336.00

Physics and Theology

Review of A. S. Eddington's
"The Nature of the Physical World"

1929 (Feb. 20) in "Nation" (London),
vol. 128, p. 232 . . . . 337.00

Disenchantment

Review of Josef Wood Krutch's
"The Modern Temper"

1929 (Apr. 10) in "Nation" (London),
    vol. 128, p. 428 . . . . 338.00

The Twilight of Science:
Is the Universe Running Down?

1929 (July) in "Century", vol. 118, p. 311-315 . 339.00

What Is Western Civilization?

1929 (July) in "Scientia", vol. 46, p. 35-41 . . 340.01
    T r a n s l a t i o n s
    Französisch:
      Tr.: H. de Varigny
      1929 (July) in "Scientia", Suppl.,
      vol. 46, p. 21-26 . . . . 340.02

How I Came by My Creed

1929 (Sept.) in "The Realist",
    vol. 1. no. 6, p. 14-21 . . . . 341.00

What I Believe

(Not identical with BN 293/1925 and BN 364/1931)

1929 (Sept.) in "Forum", vol. 82, p. 129-134 . . 342.01
    1931 in "Living Philosophies"
      New York: Simon & Schuster, p. 9-19 . 342.02

Bertrand Russell on Religion (Anonymous)

1929 (Oct.) in "The World Tomorrow",
    vol. 12, p. 391 . . . . 343.00

Idealism for Children

1929 (Dec. 14) in "Saturday Review of Literature"
    vol. 6, p. 575 . . . . 344.00

Opinion About the Sacco-Vanzetti Case

1929 in "Lantern", vol. II, p. 11 . . . . 345.00

A Liberal View of Divorce

1929 Girard, Kansas: Haldeman-Julius Publ. . . . 346.00

MARRIAGE AND MORALS

1929 New York: Liveright. 320 pp. 347.01
    London: Allen & Unwin. 254 pp. 347.02
    Garden City, N.Y.: Garden City Pub. 320 pp. 347.03
    C o n t e n t s
    I. Why a Sexual Ethic is Necessary. II. Where
    Fatherhood is Unknown. III. The Dominion

of the Father. IV. Phallic Worship, Asceticism and Sin. V. Christian Ethics. VI. Romantic Love. VII. The Liberation of Women. VIII. The Taboo on Sex Knowledge. IX. The Place of Love in Human Life. X. Marriage. XI. Prostitution. XII. Trial Marriage. XIII. The Family at the Present Day. XIV. The Family in Individual Psychology. XV. The Family and the State. XVI. Divorce. XVII. Population. XVIII. Eugenics. XIX. Sex and Individual Well-Being. XX. The Place of Sex Among Human Values. XXI. Conclusion.

C o m m e n t a r y
Russells writings on sex relations and "Female Emancipation" form only one small segment of his work, and one at the opposite extreme to his greatest achievements in thought. But nothing he wrote attracted more attention among the general public, or had more immediate influence. More than anyone else, he changed the outlook on sex morality of a whole new generation; and during his lifetime he saw the cause of Women's Rights, once regarded as a crank's crusade, end up as an established part of the laws and custons of the land.

K o m m e n t a r
Russell's Veröffentlichungen über die Beziehung der Geschlechter und über die Emanzipation der Frau bilden nur einen kleinen Ausschnitt seines Werkes, dazu einen, der seinen großartigsten gedanklichen Leistungen als entgegengerichtetes Extrem gegenüber steht. Nichts aber unter seinen Schriften erregte im großen Publikum mehr Aufmerksamkeit, nichts hatte stärkeren unmittelbaren Einfluß. Für eine ganze neue Generation änderte er die Einstellung zur sexuellen Moral einschneidender als irgend jemand; und er erlebte es, daß die Sache der Frauenrechte, einst als Kreuzzug eines Sonderlings betrachtet, zur gesetzlich festgelegten Ordnung des Landes wurde.

R e p r i n t s
1930 Excerpt:
     "Christian Ethics" (V)
     in "Twenty-Four Views of Marriage"
     from the Presbyterian General Assembly's
     Commission of Marriage, Diorce and Re-
     marriage. Ed. by C. A. Spaulding.
     New York: Macmillan, p. 54-67 . . . .   347.04
1938 Garden City, N. Y.: The Sun Dial Press   347.05
1942 Garden City, N.Y.: Sun Dial Center Books 347.06
1951 London: Allen & Unwin 347.07
1957 New York: Liveright 347.08

```
1961 Londen: Allen & Unwin  . . . . . . . .   347.09
1961 Excerpt:
     "The Place of Sex Among Human Values"(XX)
     in "The Basic Writings of B. Russell":
     IX/41 (BN 659) . . . . . . . . . . . .   347.10
1963 New York: Bantam Books . . . . . . . .   347.11
1970 New York: Liveright  . . . . . . . . .   347.12
1972 London: Allen & Unwin  . . . . . . . .   347.13
1976 "     : "      " "    . . . . . . . .   347.14
```

T r a n s l a t i o n s
Arabisch:
    "Al Zawāg Wa Al Al Akhlāg"
    Tr.: 'Abd El 'Azīz Ibrahīm Famī
    1958 Kairo: Al Sharikah Al 'Arabiyyah
        Lil Tebā'ah wa Al Nashr 347.15
Birmanisch (Burma):
    "Ain-htaung hmu hnint lu-kyint wut"
    Tr.: San Tint (Shan Pye)
    1968 Rangun:
        Ma Khin Tint Sarpay (2nd ed.) . .   347.16
Chinesisch:
    "Hunyin geming"
    1930 Shanghai 347.17
    "Hunyin yu daode"
    1935 Shanghai 347.18
    "Jiehun yu daode"
    1936 Shanghai 347.19
Deutsch:
    "Ehe und Moral"
    Ü.: Magda Kahn
    1930 München: Drei Masken Verlag . . .   347.20
    I n h a l t
    1. Einleitung. 2. Mutterrechtliche Ver-
    bände. 3. System der Vaterherrschaft.
    4. Phalluskult, Asketentum und Sünden-
    begriff. 5. Die christliche Ethik. 6.
    Die romantische Liebe. 7. Die Befrei-
    ung der Frauen. 8. Der Verruf der se-
    xuellen Aufklärung. 9. Die Bedeutung
    der Liebe im menschlichen Leben. 10.
    Die Ehe. 11. Die Prostitution. 12. Die
    Probeehe. 13. Die Familie von heute.
    14. Individuum und Familie. 15. Familie
    und Staat. 16. Die Ehescheidung. 17.
    Die Bevölkerungsfrage. 18. Eugenik.
    19. Geschlechtsleben und induviduelles
    Wohlbefinden. 20. Der Rang der Liebe
    unter den menschlichen Werten. 21. Zu-
    sammenfassung.
    Auszug:
    "Familie und Ehe"
    in "Neue Rundschau", Jg.42, p. 512-525   347.21
    "Ehe und Moral", Ü.: Krebs
    1951 Zürich: Europa Verlag 347.22
        Stuttgart: Kohlhammer 347.23

Finnisch:
    "Avioliitto ja moraali"
    Tr.: J. A. Hollo
    1951 Jyväskylä: K. J. Gummerus 347.24
Französisch:
    "Le mariage et la morale"
    Tr.: Gabriel Beauroy
    1970 Paris: R. Laffont 347.25
Griechisch:
    "Ho gamos kai he ethike"
    1934 Athen 347.26
    "Gamos kai ethike"
    Tr.: Giannes Duriotes
    1962 Athen: Arsenides 347.27
Hebräisch:
    "ha-Nesuin veha-musar"
    1930 Tel-Aviv 347.28
Italienisch:
    "Matrimonio E Morale"
    Tr.: G. Tornabuoni
    1949 Mailand 347.29
    1961 "   : Longanesi 347.30
    1966 "   : " 347.31
Japanisch:
    "Kekkon to dôtoku"
    Tr.: Teruhiko Egami
    1955 Tokio:
        Shakaishisô Kenkyûkai Shuppanbu . 347.32
    "Ai to sei no ichi"
    Tr.: Tôshi Manzawa, Giich Ôuchi
    1956 Tokio: Kawade shobô 347.33
    "Kekkon ron" (= Russell Chosakushu. 8)
    Tr.: Hiroyuki Goto
    1959 Tokio: Misuzu-Shobo 347.34
    Tr.: Takashi Kakimura
    1963 Tokio: Kadokawa Shoten 347.35
Koreanisch:
    "Gyeolhon gwa dodeog"
    Tr.: Gim Yeong-cheol
    1960 Seoul: Yangmunsa 347.36
    1966 "   : " 347.37
Niederländisch:
    "Hedendaagse huwelijksmoraal"
    Tr.: Hans de Vries
    1957 's-Gravenhage: Zuid-Holl. U. M. . 347.38
Persisch:
    "Zanāšu'i o axlāq"
    Tr.: Hossein Montazam
    1958 Teheran: Našr-e Andiše 347.39
    1962 "   : " 347.40
Polnisch:
    "Malzen stne i moralnoscz"
    Tr.: Helena Bolz
    1931 Warschau: Roj 347.41

Portugiesisch:
"O casamente e a moral"
Tr.: Wilson Velloso
1955 Sao Paulo: Ed. Nacional 347.42
1966 "   "   : "   "   (3rd ed.) 347.43
Schwedisch:
"Äktenskap och moral"
Tr.: Alf Ahlberg
1965 Stockholm: Natur och Kultur
      (4th ed.) 347.44
Spanisch:
"Matrimonio moral"
Tr.: León Rozitchner
1965 Buenos Aires:
      Siglo Veinte (2nd ed.) 347.45
Türkisch:
"Evlilik ve ahlâk"
Tr.: Ender Gürol
1963 Istanbul: Varlik Yayinevi 347.46
1967 "   : "   " 347.47
1971 "   : "   " 347.48

China's Philosophy of Happiness

1930 (Feb.) in "The Thinker", p. 16-23 . . . . . 348.00

Homogeneous America

1930 (Feb. 19) in "The Outlook and Independent",
     vol. 154, p. 285-287, 318 . . . . 349.00

Why Is Modern Youth Cynical

1930 (May) in "Harper's Monthly Magazine",
     vol. 160, p. 720-724 . . . . 350.00

Are Parents Bad for Children?

1930 (May) in "Parents' Magazine", vol.5, p.18-19 351.01
1930 (June) Excerpts in "Review of Reviews"
     vol. 81, p. 62-63 . . . . 351.02

Heads or Tails

1930 (Aug.) in "The Atlantic Monthly",
     vol. 146, p. 163-170 . . . . 352.00

Do Men Want Children?

1930 (Oct.) in "Parents' Magazine", vol.5, p.14-15 353.00

Thirty Years from Now

1930 (Oct.) in "Virginia Quarterly Review",
     vol. 6, p. 575-585 . . . . 354.00

Religion and Happiness

1930 (Nov. 15) in "Spectator", vol.145, p.714-715 355.00

Introduction to
"The New Generation: The Intimate Problems
of Modern Parents and Children"

1930 New York: The Macaulay Co., p. 17-24 . . .   356.01
    1957 under the title
        "The New Generation"
        in "Why I Am Not a Christian and Other
        Essays" (BN 625) 356.02

    T r a n s l a t i o n s
    Dänisch .... 1966 in BN 625.11 . . . . .   356.03
    Deutsch .... 1963 in BN 625.12 . . . . .   356.04
    Italienisch ... 1960 in BN 625.19 . . . . .   356.05
    Japanisch ..... 1959 in BN 625.21 . . . . .   356.06
    Koreanisch .... 1960 in BN 625.23 . . . . .   356.07
    Niederländisch 1966 in BN 625.26 . . . . .   356.08
    Persisch ...... 1970 in BN 625.28 . . . . .   356.09
    Portugiesisch . 1960 in BN 625.30 . . . . .   356.10
    Schwedisch .... 1958 in BN 625.32 . . . . .   336.11
    Spanisch ...... 1958 in BN 625.33 . . . . .   336.12
    Türkisch ...... 1966 in BN 625.36 . . . . .   336.13

Has Religion Made Useful Contributuion
to Civilization? An Examination and a Criticism.

1930 London: Watts & Co. 30 pp. 357.01
    194- Girard, Kansas: Haldeman-Julius Publ.   357.02
    1957 in "Why I Am Not a Christian and Other
        Essays" (BN 625) 357.03

    T r a n s l a t i o n s
    Dänisch .... 1966 in BN 625.11 . . . . .   357.04
    Deutsch .... 1963 in BN 625.12 . . . . .   357.05
    Französisch ... 1960 in BN 625.16 . . . . .   357.06
    Italienisch ... 1960 in BN 625.19 . . . . .   357.07
    Japanisch ..... 1959 in BN 625.21 . . . . .   357.08
    Koreanisch .... 1960 in BN 625.23 . . . . .   357.09
    Niederländisch 1966 in BN 625.26 . . . . .   357.10
    Persisch ...... 1970 in BN 625.28 . . . . .   357.11
    Portugiesisch . 1960 in BN 625.30 . . . . .   357.12
    Schwedisch .... 1958 in BN 625.32 . . . . .   357.13
    Spanisch ...... 1958 in BN 625.33 . . . . .   357.14
    Türkisch ...... 1966 in BN 625.36 . . . . .   357.15

Divorce by Mutual Consent

1930 in "Divorce"
    New York: The John Day Co., p. 11-18 . . .   358.01
    1930 under the title
        "Divorce as I See It"
        London: Douglas 358.02

Is Modern Marriage a Failure?

Debate between B. Russell and John C. Powys

1930 New York City: "The Discussion Guild". 60pp.   359.00
    Introduction: Heywood Broun

1930

Politics and Theology

1930 in "Political Quarterly", vol. 1, p. 179-185   360.00

Mental Health and the School — A Teacher's View

1930 in "The Healthy-Minded Child"
   New York: Goward-McCann, p. 77-88 . . . . . 361.00

Preface to Jean Nicod's
"Foundations of Geometry and Induction"

1930 New York: Harcourt Brace & Co. 362.01
   London: Kegan Paul (International Library of
   Psychology, Philosophy, and Scientific Method) 362.02
   1961 in J. Nicod's "Le Problème logique de
      l'inducation",
      Paris: Presses Universitaires de France 362.03

THE CONQUEST OF HAPPINESS

1930 New York: Liveright. 249 pp. 363.01
   London: Allen & Unwin. 252 pp. 363.02
   New York: The Book League of America. 240 pp. 363.03
   C o n t e n t s
   Preface.
   Part I: Causes of Unhappiness.
     I. What Makes People Unhappy. II. Byronic
     Unhappiness. III. Competition. IV. Bore-
     dom and Excitement. V. Fatigue. VI. Envy.
     VII. The Sense of Sin. VIII. Persecution
     Mania. IX. Fear of Public Opinion.
   Part II: Causes of Happiness.
     X. Is Happiness Still Possible? XI. Zest.
     XII. Affection. XIII. The Family. XIV.
     Work. XV. Impersonal Interests. XVI. Ef-
     fort and Resignation. XVII. The Happy Man
     (Not identical with "The Happy Man" in
     BN 582/XX).

   C o m m e n t a r y
   Russell urged people to escape from self-
   preoccupation by the contemplation of greater
   things. The following, for instance, was very
   useful and plain advice he gave in "The Conquest of Happiness" to those who cannot stop
   worrying: "When some misfortune threatens,
   consider seriously and deliberately what is
   the very worst that could happen. Having
   looked this possible misfortune in the face,
   give yourself sound reasons for hinking that
   after all it would be no such very terrible
   disaster. Such reasons always exist, since
   at the worst nothing that happens to oneself
   has any cosmic importance."

   K o m m e n t a r
   Russell regte die Leute an, aus der Beschäf-

tigung mit sich selbst durch die Betrachtung
größerer Gegenstände auszubrechen. Denen, die
mit ihren Sorgen nicht fertig werden können,
gab er zum Beispiel in"The Conquest of Happiness" den ebenso nützlichen wie einfachen
Rat: "Droht ein Unglück, so überlegen Sie sich
ernsthaft und gründlich, was im allerschlimm-
sten Falle geschehen könnte. Haben Sie dieses mögliche Unglück recht betrachtet, so su-
chen Sie vernünftige Gründe für den Gedanken,
daß es schließlich wohl doch nicht ein so
furchtbares Unheil sein würde. Solche Gründe
gibt es immer, denn auch das Schlimmste, das
uns zustößt, hat für die Welt keine Bedeutung."

R e p r i n t s
1933 New York: Doubleday. Garden City Publ.   363.04
1951 "   "   : New American Library 363.05
1956 London: Allen & Unwin 363.06
1958 New York: Liveright 363.07
1968 "   "   : Bantam Books 363.08
1971 "   "   : Liveright 363.09
1975 London: Allen & Unwin 363.10
1977 "   : "   " " 363.11

T r a n s l a t i o n s
Arabisch:
        "Kayf taksab al-sa'adat"
        Tr.: Munir Ba'albaki
        1951 Beirut: Dal al-'Ilm Lil-Malayin . 363.12
        "Al-Sa'ādah wa al-insān al-'Asrī"
        Tr.: Nazmī Lūqā
        1967 Kairo: Al-Dār al-Qawmīyah 363.13
Chinesisch:
        "Kuaile de xinli"
        1932 Shanghai 363.14
Dänisch:
        "Lykkens erobring"
        Tr.: Jesper Ewald
        1950 Kopenhagen: Martin 363.15
        1962 "   : Spektrum 363.16
Deutsch:
        "Schlüssell zum Glück"
        Ü.: Magda Kahn
        1932 München: Drei Masken Verlag . . .   363.17
        "Eroberung des Glücks"
        1951 Darmstadt, Baden-Baden, Genf:
             J. A. Holle 363.18
        I n h a l t
        Vorwort.
        Teil I: Ursachen des Unglücks
           1. Was macht den Menschen unglück-
           lich? 2. Byron'scher Weltschmerz
           3. Der Geist der Konkurrenz. 4. Lan-
           geweile und Anregung. 5. Müdigkeit.

6. Neid. 7. Schuldgefühle. 8. Ver-
folgungswahn. 9. Was wird die Welt
dazu sagen?
Teil II: Ursachen des Glücks.
10. Können wir noch glücklich sein?
11. Lebensbejahung. 12. Zuneigung.
13. Familie und Ehe. 14. Arbeit.
15. Der Wert "unpersönlicher Interessen". 16. Streben und Entsagung.
17. Der glückliche Mensch.
Finnisch:
"Onnen valloittaminen"
Tr.: J. A. Hollo
1952 Jyväskylä: K. J. Gumerus 363.19
1953 "   : "   "   " 363.20
1970 "   : "   "   " 363.21
Französisch:
"La conquête du bonheur"
Tr.: N. Rabinot
1949 Paris: Payot 363.22
1951 "   : " 363.23
1962 "   : " 363.24
Hebräisch:
"Kibush ha-osher"
Tr.: Hedva Rothem
1954 Jerusalem: Ahiassaf 363.25
1966 "   : " 363.26
Ind./Assamese:
"Sukhar sandhan"
Tr.: Suren Chaudhuri
1964 Gauhati: Prakašan Parshad 363.27
Ind./Bengali:
"Sukher sandhane"
Tr.: Parimal Gosvami
1960 Kalkutta: Bengal Publishers . . . 363.28
Ind./Bengali:
"Sukh"
Tr.: Mutahar Hussain Choudhry
1968 Dakka: Bengali Akademiy 363.29
Ind./Gujarati:
"Sukhani siddhi"
Tr.: Vinodini Nilkanth
1969 Bhavnagar: Translation Trust . . 363.30
Ind./Kannada:
"Sukha sadhane"
Tr.: H. Yoganarasimhan
1966 Mysore: Kavyalaya 363.31
Ind./Malayalam:
"Saukhy abhijayam"
Tr.: P. Damodaran Pilla
1963 New Delhi: National Book Trust . 363.32
Ind./Marathi:
"Sukha-sādhanā"
Tr.: B. R. Khanvilkar
1964 Urulikanchan: B. R. Khanvilkar . 363.33

Ind./Tamil:
    "Inpathin verti"
    Tr.: Vairana Pillai
    1969 Madras: Kalaimagal 363.34
Italienisch:
    "Conquista della felicità"
    Tr.: G. Pozzo Galeazzi
    1947 Mailand: Langanesi 363.35
Japanisch:
    "Kôfuku ron"
    Tr.: Hidehiko Hori
    1952 Tokio: Kadokawa shoten 363.36
    Tr.: Yuzuru Katagiri
    1959 Tokio: Misuzu-shobo
        (Russell Chosaku-shu 6) 363.37
    Tr.: Hidehiko Hori
    1970 Tokio: Kadokawa shoten 363.38
    Tr.: Hidaka Kazuteru
    1972 Tokio: Kôdansha 363.39
Koreanisch:
    "Haengbogeui jogeon"
    Tr.: Yang Byeong Tag, Jeong Bong Hwa
    1970 Seoul: Daeyang-Seojeog 363.40
    "Haengbogron"
    Tr.: Kim Byeong Ho
    1971 Seoul: Jibmun 363.41
    "Haengbogeui jeongbog"
    Tr.: Kim Byeong Ho
    1973 Seoul: Jibmundang 363.42
Niederländisch:
    "Verover uw geluk"
    Tr.: W. A. Fick-Lugten
    1950 's-Graveland: De Driehoek 363.43
    1958 Amsterdam: Meulenhoff (9th ed.) .   363.44
Norwegisch:
    "Menneskelykke"
    Tr.: Lotte Holmboe
    1948 Oslo: Tanum 363.45
Persisch:
    "Shahrahe koshbakhti"
    Tr.: Vahid Mazandarani
    1973 Teheran: Amir Kabir 363.46
Polnisch:
    "Podboj Szczescia"
    Tr.: Antonio Panski
    1933 Warschau: Roj 363.47
Portugiesisch:
    "A conquista da felicidade"
    Tr.: José Antonio Machado
    1952 Lissabon: Guimaraes 363.48
    1957 "   : " 363.49
    1966 "   : " 363.50
    Tr.: Breno Silveira
    1956 Sao Paulo: Ed. Nacional 363.51
    1966 "   "   : "   " 363.52

1930/1931

Schwedisch:
"Hur nutismänniskan blir lycklig"
Tr.: Alf Ahlberg
1951 Stockholm: Natur och Kultur
(3rd ed.) 363.53
Serbokroatisch:
"Osvajanje sreće"
Tr.: Ljuba Popović
1964 Subotica, Belgrad: Minerva . . . 363.54
Spanisch:
"La conquista de la felicidad"
Tr.: Julio Huici
1931 Madrid: Espasa-Calpe 363.55
1976 "   : "   "   (10th ed.) . 363.56
Türkisch:
"Saadet yolu"
Tr.: Nurettin Özyürek
1963 Istanbul: Varlik Yayinevi 363.57
1966 "   : "   " 363.58
1970 "   : "   " 363.59

What I Believe

(Not identical with BN 293/1925 and BN 342/1929)

1931 (Apr. 29) in "Nation", vol. 132, p. 469-471 364.01
1940 (Mar. 30) in "Nation",
vol. 150, p. 412-414 . . . . 364.02

Free Speech in Childhood

1931 (May 30, June 13, 27)
in "New Statesman and Nation"
vol. 1, p. 486-488; 575, 643 . . . . 365.01
(The last two are in the forms of letters as
answer to letters of readers.)
Translations
Deutsch:
"Freie Rede in der Kindheit"
1974 in BN 707/III 365.02
1975 in BN 710/II 365.03

Modern Tendencies in Education

1931 (June 13) in "Spectator", vol.146, p.926-927 366.01
Translations
Deutsch:
"Moderne Tendenzen in der Erziehung"
1974 in BN 707/III 366.02

Free Speech in Childhood

1931 (July 1) in "Nation", vol. 133, p. 12-13 . 367.00

Nice People

1931 (July) in "Harper's Monthly Magazine"
vol. 163, p. 226-230 . . . . 368.01

1957 in "Why I Am Not a Christian and Other
    Essays" (BN 625) 368.02
T r a n s l a t i o n s
Dänisch . . . . 1966 in BN 625.11 . . . . . 368.03
Deutsch . . . . 1963 in BN 625.12 . . . . . 368.04
Italienisch . . . 1960 in BN 625.19 . . . . . 368.05
Japanisch . . . . . 1959 in BN 625.21 . . . . . 368.06
Koreanisch . . . . 1960 in BN 625.23 . . . . . 368.07
Niederländisch 1966 in BN 625.26 . . . . . 368.08
Persisch . . . . . . 1970 in BN 625.28 . . . . . 368.09
Portugiesisch . 1960 in BN 625.30 . . . . . 368.10
Schwedisch . . . . 1958 in BN 625.32 . . . . . 368.11
Spanisch . . . . . . 1958 in BN 625.33 . . . . . 368.12
Türkisch . . . . . . 1966 in BN 625.36 . . . . . 368.13

In Our School

1931 (Sept. 9) in "The New Republik",
    vol. 68, p. 92-94 . . . . 369.01
    T r a n s l a t i o n s
    Deutsch:
        "In unserer Schule"
        1974 in BN 707/III 369.02
        1975 in BN 710/II 369.03

Review of E. P. Ramsey's
"Foundations
of Mathematics and other Logical Essays"

1931 (Oct.) in "Mind", vol. 40, p. 476-482 . . . 370.01
    1932 in "Philosophy", vol. 7, p. 84-86 . . 370.02

Shall the Home be Abolished?

(Bertrand Russell / Sherwood Anderson Debate)

1931 (Nov. 28) in "Literary Digest",
    vol. 111, p. 25-36 . . . . 371.00

THE SCIENTIFIC OUTLOOK

1931 New York: W. W. Norton & Co. X, 277 pp. . . 372.01
    London: Allen & Unwin 372.02
    Toronto: McLeod 372.03
    New York: Free Press 372.04
    C o n t e n t s
    Introduction
    Part I: Scientific Knowledge.
        I. Examples of Scientific Method. II.
        Characteristics of Scientific Method.
        III. Limitations of Scientific Method.
        IV. Scientific Metaphysics. V. Science
        and Religion.
    Part II: Scientific Technique.
        VI. Beginnings of Scientific Technique.
        VII. Technique in Inanimate Matter. VIII.

Technique in Biology.   IX. Technique in
Physiology. X. Technique in Psychology.
XI. Technique in Society.
Part III: The Scientific Society.
    XII. Artificially Greated Societies. XIII.
    The Individual and the Whole. XIV. Sci-
    entific Government.   XV. Education in a
    Scientific Society. XVI. Scientific Re-
    production. XVII. Science and Values.

R e p r i n t s
1934 London: Allen & Unwin 372.05
1935 Excerpt:
    "Science and Values" (XVII)
    in "Leadership in a Changing World"
    New York: Harper, p. 278-284 . . . . . 372.06
1947 Glencoe, Ill.: Free Press 372.07
1949 London: Allen & Unwin 372.08
1954 "   : "   " " 372.09
1961 Excerpt:
    "Limitations of Scientific Method" (III)
    in "The Basic Writings of B. Russell":
    XVI/67 (BN 659) 372.10
1962 London: Allen & Unwin 372.11
1962 New York: W. W. Norton & Co. 372.12

T r a n s l a t i o n s
Chinesisch:
    "Kexueguan"
    1935 Shanghai 372.13
Deutsch:
    "Das naturwissenschaftliche Zeitalter"
    Ü.: Erwin Heinzel
    1953 Stuttgart, Wien: Humboldt Verlag 372.14
    I n h a l t
    Einleitung
    Teil I: Naturwissenschaftl. Erkenntnis.
        I. Die naturwissenschaftliche Metho-
        de in der Hand großer Forscher. II.
        Das Wesen der naturwissenschaftli-
        chen Methode.   III. Die Grenzen der
        naturwissenschaftlichen Methode. IV.
        Naturwissenschaftliche Metaphysik .
        V. Naturwissenschaften und Religion.
    Teil II: Naturwissenschaftl. Technik.
        VI. Die Anfänge der naturwissen-
        schaftlichen Technik. VII. Die Tech-
        nik in der unbeseelten Natur. VIII.
        Die Technik in der Biologie. IX. Die
        Technik in der Physiologie. X. Die
        Technik in der Psychologie. XI. Die
        Technik im sozialen Leben.
    Teil III: Die wissenschaftl. Gesellschaft
        XII. Künstlich geschaffene Gesell-
        schaften. XIII. Individuum und Ge-
        meinschaft. XIV. Wissenschaftliche

Regierung. XV. Die Erziehung in ei-
ner wissenschaftlichen Gesellschaft.
XVI. Wissenschaftliche Fortpflanzung
XVII. Die Wissenschaft und das Reich
der Werte.
Auszüge:
"Die wissenschaftliche
Gesellschaft" (III: XII-XVII)
1962 Essen-Bredeney: Gemeinnützige Ver-
waltungs-Gesellsch. für Wissenschafts-
pflege = Forschung und Wirtschaft, Part-
ner im Fortschritt. Jahrg. 11/1 . . .   372.15
Französisch:
"L'esprit scientifique et la science
dans le monde moderne.
Tr.: S. Jankelevitch
1947 Paris: Janin 372.16
Griechisch:
"Ē epistemē kai o anthrōpos"
Tr.: Giannes Dyriōtes
1963 Athen: Arsenidēs 372.17
Ind./Hindi:
"Vaijanik paridrishti"
Tr.: Gangaratan Pandey
1967 Delhi: Rajkamal Prakas 372.18
Italienisch:
"Panorama Scientifico"
Tr.: A. G. Loliva
1934 Bari: Laterza 372.19
Polnisch:
"Poglady i Widoki Nauki Wspolcznej"
Tr.: Jan Krassowski
1934 Warschau: J. Przenorski 372.20
1936   "   : "   " 372.21
1938   "   : "   " 372.22
Portugiesisch:
"A perspektiva cientifica"
Tr.: João Batista Ramos
1956 Sao Paulo: Ed. Nacional 372.23
Tr.: J. S. da Camargo Pereira
1962 Sao Paulo: Ed. Nacional 372.24
1969   "   "   : "   " 372.25
Spanisch:
"Perspectiva científica"
Tr.: G. Sans Huelin
1969 Barcelona: Ariel 372.26
1971   "   : " 372.27
Türkisch:
"Bilimden beklediğimiz"
Tr.: Avni Yakalioğlu
1962 Istanbul: Varlik Yayinevi 372.28
1969   "   : "   " 372.29

On the Meaning of Life

1932 in "On the Meaning of Life", ed. by W.Durant
New York: Ray Long & Richard R.Smith, p. 106.   373.00
(Letter of June 20, 1931 in response to in-
quiry on the subject)

Reformulation of the Nature of Mind

Contributed to Charles W. Morris
"Six Theories of Mind"

1932 University of Chicago Press, p. 135-138 . .   374.00

Review of R. Weiss's
"Principles of Mathematics"

1932 (Jan.) in "Monist", vol. 42, p. 112-154 . .   375.00

In Praise of Idleness

1932 (Oct.) in "Review of Reviews",
    vol. 82, p. 48-54 . . . .   376.01
    1932 (Oct.) in "Harper's Monthly Magazine",
    p. 552-559 . . . .   376.02
    1933 in "Contemporary Opinion", p. 519-530
    Boston: Houghton 376.03
    1935 in "Essays of Today", p. 499-512
    New York: Macmillan 376.04
    1935 in "In Praise of Idleness": I (BN 401)   376.05

Translations
Deutsch .... 1957 in BN 401.16 + 1971/696   376.06
Italienisch ... 1963 in BN 401.24 . . . . .   376.07
Japanisch ..... 1958 in BN 401.26 . . . . .   376.08
Norwegisch .... 1947 in BN 401.27 = 519 . .   376.09
Persisch ...... 1970 in BN 401.28 . . . . .   376.10
Polnisch ...... 1937 in BN 401.29 . . . . .   376.11
Portugiesisch . 1957 in BN 401.30 . . . . .   376.12
Schwedisch .... 1937 in BN 401.31 . . . . .   376.13
Spanisch ...... 1953 in BN 401.32 = 615 . .   376.14
Türkisch ...... 1969 in BN 401.34 . . . . .   376.15

How Science Has Changed Society

1932 in "Listener", vol. 7, p. 39-40, 42 . . . .   377.00

EDUCATION AND THE SOCIAL ORDER

1932 London: Allen & Unwin. 254 pp. 378.01
Under the title:
"Education and the Modern World"
New York: W. W. Norton & Co. 245 pp. . . .   378.02
Toronto: McLeod 378.03
Contents
I. The Individual Versus the Citizen. II. The
Negative Theory of Education. III. Education
and Heredity.   IV. Emotion and Discipline.

C o m m e n t a r y

Russell's educational ideas continually fluctuated between theories derived from modern psychologists, and good sense which he provided himself. He suggested for instance that the children should be picked out for University educations at the age of twelve, with not further competitive examinations. But this system was soon attacked among other things on the grounds that, in the interests of equalitarianism, all Children should be mixed up in huge "comprehensive schools". To this sort of argument, Russell had given a devastating reply. He wrote in his "Education and the Social Order": "A great deal of needless pain and friction would be saved to clever children of they were not compelled to associate intimately with stupid contemporaries. .... No one, in later life, associates with all and sundry". Russell's books on education, "On Education Especially Early Childhood" (1926) and "Education and the Social Order" (1932), still have an impact and an interest today. Though some of his views are now accepted as a matter of course, other reforms he suggested have still to be carried out.

K o m m e n t a r

Russell's Ideen über Erziehung bewegten sich ständig zwischen den Theorien moderner Psychologen und dem gesunden Menschenverstand, den er selbst lieferte. Er schlug zum Beispiel vor, die Kinder sollten mit zwölf Jahren für die Hochschulausbildung ausgesucht werden, ohne spätere Ausscheidungsprüfungen. Dieses System wurde jedoch bald angegriffen unter anderem mit der Begründung, im Interesse der Gleichmachung sollten alle Kinder in großen "verständnisvollen Schulen" miteinander vermischt werden. Auf diese Art der Beweisführung hatte Russell eine niederschmetternde Antwort gegeben. In "Education and the Social Order" schrieb er: "Eine Menge von unnützem Leid und Reibereien könnte klugen Kindern erspart werden, wenn sie nicht dazu

gezwungen würden, in engster Gemeinschaft mit
dummen Zeitgenossen zu leben. .... Im späteren Leben läßt sich niemand mit all und jedem
ein." Russell's Bücher über Erziehung, "On
Education Especially Early Childhood" (1926)
und "Education and the Social Order" (1932),
sind auch heute noch eindrucksvoll und interessant. Obwohl einige seiner Auffassungen
jetzt für selbstverständlich gelten, müssen
andere von ihm vorgeschlagene Reformen noch
verwirklicht werden.

R e p r i n t s
1938 London: Allen & Unwin 378.04
1961 "   : "   " " 378.05
1961 Excerpts:
    "Emotion and Discipline" (IV),
    "The Reconciliation
    of Individuality and Citizenship"(XVI)
    in "The Basic Writings of B. Russell":
    X/47, XI/49 (BN 659) 378.06
1967 London: Allen & Unwin 378.07
1970 "   : "   " " 378.08
1977 "   : "   " " 378.09

T r a n s l a t i o n s
Chinesisch:
    "Jiaoyu yu qunzhi"
    1934 Shanghai 378.10
Deutsch:
    "Erziehung und Gesellschaft"
    in "Erziehung ohne Dogma" (BN 707)
    Ü.: Ilse Krewinkel
    1974 München: Nymphenburger Verlags-
         handlung, p. 7-168 . . . . 378.11
    I n h a l t
    1. Individuum contra Bürger. 2. Die Ne-
    gativtheorie der Erziehung. 3. Erzie-
    hung und Vererbung. 4. Emotion und Dis-
    ziplin. 5. Elternhaus contra Schule.
    6. Aristokraten, Demokraten und Büro-
    kraten. 7. Die Masse in der Erziehung.
    8. Religion in der Erziehung. 9. Sex
    in der Erziehung. 10. Patriotismus in
    der Erziehung. 11. Klassengefühl in der
    Erziehung. 12. Konkurrenz in der Er-
    ziehung. 13. Erziehung unter dem Kom-
    munismus. 14. Erziehung und Volkswirt-
    schaft. 15. Propaganda in der Erziehung.
    16. Versöhnung von Individualität und
    Bürgerdasein.
    Auszüge:
    "Bürgerbewußtsein
    oder Individualität" (I)
    "Die emotionale Umwelt des Kindes" (IV)

"Erziehung zu Nationalismus
und Militarismus" (X)
"Destruktion oder Kooperation?" (XVI)
1975 in BN 710 . . . .   378.12
Ind./Hindi:
"Siksa aur samaj vyavastha"
Tr.: Rajendrasimha Bhandari
1968 Delhi: Rajkamal 378.13
Ind./Urdu:
"Nizam-i-mu'ashara our ta'lim"
Tr.: Abdul Majid Salik, G. Aziz
1955 Lahore:
   Board for the Advancement of
   Literature 378.14
1962 2nd ed. 378.15
Italienisch:
"L'educazione e l'ordinamento sociale"
1951 Florenz: La Nuova Italia 378.16
1962 "   : "   "   " 378.17
Japanisch:
"Kyôiku to shakai taisei"
Tr.: Shôzô Suzuki
1959 Tokio: Meiji tosho shuppan . . .   378.18
Niederländisch:
"Opvoeding en de Moderne Samenleving"
Tr.: W. Phielix
1938 Den Dolder: de Driehoek 378.19
Polnisch:
Excerpts:
"Negatywna teoria wychowania" (II)
"Wychowanie a religia" (VIII)
"Zagadnienia seksualne
w wychowaniu" (IX)
1958 Warschau: Iskry. 93 pp. 378.20
Portugiesisch:
"Educação e ordem social"
Tr.: Leonidas Gontijo de Carvalho
1956 Sao Paulo: Ed. Nacional 378.21
Spanisch:
"La educación y el mundo moderno"
Tr.: Marcello Chéret
1964 Buenos Aires: Fabril 378.22
Türkisch:
"Eğitim ve toplum düzeni"
Tr.: Nail Bezel
1969 Istanbul: Varlik Yayinevi 378.23

The Modern Midas

1933 (Feb.) in "Harper's Monthly Magazine"
vol. 166, p. 327-334 . . . .   379.01
1935 in "In Praise of Idleness": IV (BN 401) 379.02

Translations
Deutsch . . . . 1957 in BN 401.16 . . . . .   379.03
Italienisch . . . 1963 in BN 401.24 . . . . .   379.04

```
Japanisch ..... 1958 in BN 401.26 . . . . .   379.05
Persisch ...... 1970 in BN 401.28 . . . . .   379.06
Polnisch ...... 1937 in BN 401.29 . . . . .   379.07
Portugiesisch . 1957 in BN 401.30 . . . . .   379.08
Schwedisch .... 1937 in BN 401.31 . . . . .   379.09
Spanisch ...... 1953 in BN 401.32 = 615 . .   379.10
Türkisch ...... 1969 in BN 401.34 . . . . .   379.11
```

The Essence of Law

1933 (Dec. 28) in "New York American", p. 15 . .   380.00

Scientific Society

1933 in "Science in the Changing World"
New York: Appleton-Century, p. 201-208   . .   381.00

Is Euthanasia Justifiable?

1934 (Jan. 1) in "New York American", p. 21   . .   382.00

Pioneer Ethics

1934 (Mar. 19) in "New York American", p. 15   . .   383.00

The Technique for Politicians

1934 (Mar.) in "Esquire", vol. I, p. 26, 133 . .   384.00

Education and Civilization

1934 (May 5) in "New Statesman and Nation",
vol. 7, p. 666-668 . . . .   385.01
1935 under the title
"Education and Discipline"
in "In Praise of Idleness": XII (BN401)   385.02

```
T r a n s l a t i o n s
Deutsch ....... 1957 in BN 401.16 . . . . .   385.03
Italienisch ... 1963 in BN 401.24 . . . . .   385.04
Japanisch ..... 1958 in BN 401.26 . . . . .   385.05
Persisch ...... 1970 in BN 401.28 . . . . .   385.06
Polnisch ...... 1937 in BN 401.29 . . . . .   385.07
Portugiesisch . 1957 in BN 401.30 . . . . .   385.08
Schwedisch .... 1937 in BN 401.31 . . . . .   385.09
Spanisch ...... 1953 in BN 401.32 = 615 . .   385.10
Türkisch ...... 1969 in BN 401.34 . . . . .   385.11
```

The Sphere of Liberty

1934 (July) in "Esquire", vol. II, p. 29 . . . .   386.00

Science's Goal

1934 (July 27) in "New York American", p. 19 . .   387.00

Contemplation

1934 (Oct. 26) in "New York American", p. 23 . .   388.00

The Limitations of Self-Help

1934 (Oct.) in "Esquire", vol. II, p. 27 . . . .   389.00

Men Versus Insects

1934 (Dec.) in "Scribner's Magazine",
      vol. 96, p. 380 . . . .   390.01
      1935 in "In Praise of Idleness": XI (BN 401)   390.02
      1941 in "Let the People Think" (BN 464) . .   390.03
      1958 in "The Will to Doubt" (BN 638) . . .   390.04

      T r a n s l a t i o n s
      Deutsch .... 1957 in BN 401.16 . . . . .   390.05
      Italienisch ... 1963 in BN 401.24 . . . . .   390.06
      Japanisch ..... 1958 in BN 401.26 . . . . .   390.07
      Persisch ..... 1970 in BN 401.28 . . . . .   390.08
      Polnisch ...... 1937 in BN 401.29 . . . . .   390.09
      Portugiesisch . 1957 in BN 401.30 . . . . .   390.10
      Schwedisch .... 1937 in BN 401.31 . . . . .   390.11
      Spanisch ...... 1953 in BN 401.32 = 615 . .   390.12
      Türkisch ...... 1969 in BN 401.34 . . . . .   390.13

Why I Am Not a Communist

1934 in "The Meaning of Marx: A Symposium"
      New York: Farrar & Rinehart, p. 83-85 . . .   391.01
      1934 (Apr.) in "Modern Monthly",
         vol. VIII, p. 133-134 . . . .   391.02
      1956 in "Portraits from Memory" (BN 617) .   391.03
      1961 in "The Basic Writings of B. Russell":
         XI/52 (BN 659) 391.04

      T r a n s l a t i o n s
      Chinesisch .... 1967 in BN 617.07 . . . . .   391.05
      Finnisch ...... 1957 in BN 617.09 . . . . .   391.06
      Italienisch ... 1958 in BN 617.10 . . . . .   391.07
      Japanisch ..... 1959 in BN 617.12 . . . . .   391.08
      Portugiesisch . 1958 in BN 617.14 . . . . .   391.09
      Schwedisch .... 1956 in BN 617.15 . . . . .   391.10
      Spanisch ...... 1960 in BN 617.16 . . . . .   391.11

Thomas Paine

1934 in "Great Democrats".
      London: Nicholson, p. 527-538 . . . .   392.01
      1957 under the title
            "The Fate of Thomas Paine"
            in "Why I Am Not a Christian and Other
            Essays" (BN 625) 392.02

      T r a n s l a t i o n s
      Dänisch .... 1966 in BN 625.11 . . . . .   392.03
      Deutsch .... 1963 in BN 625.12 . . . . .   392.04
      Italienisch ... 1960 in BN 625.19 . . . . .   392.05
      Japanisch ..... 1959 in BN 625.21 . . . . .   392.06
      Koreanisch .... 1960 in BN 625.23 . . . . .   392.07
      Niederländisch 1966 in BN 625.26 . . . . .   392.08

```
Persisch ...... 1970 in BN 625.28 ......  392.09
Portugiesisch . 1960 in BN 625.30 ......  392.10
Schwedisch .... 1958 in BN 625.32 ......  392.11
Spanisch ...... 1958 in BN 625.33 ......  392.12
Türkisch ...... 1966 in BN 625.36 ......  392.13
```

Marriage and Children

```
1934 in "Modern English Readings",
     New York: Farrar, p. 241-248 ........  393.00
```

Dora Russell: "Beacon Hill"

```
1934 in "The Modern Schools Handbook".
     Ed. by Trevor Blewitt
     London: Collanz ..............  394.01
     T r a n s l a t i o n s
     Deutsch:
         "Beacon Hill"
         1974 in BN 707/III:4 ..........  394.02
         1975 in BN 710/Anhang ........  394.03
```

FREEDOM AND ORGANIZATION 1814-1914

```
1934 London: Allen & Unwin. 528 pp. .......  395.01
     Under the title
     "Freedom versus Organization 1812-1914"
     New York: W. W. Norton & Co. VIII, 477 pp. .  395.02
     Toronto: McLeod ..............  395.03
     C o n t e n t s
     Preface.
```
Part I: The Principles of Legitimacy.
    I. Napoleon's Successors.   II. The Congress of Vienna.   III. The Holy Alliance.
    IV. The Twilight of Metternich.
Part II: The March of Mind.
    A: The Social Background.
    V. The Aristocracy.   VI. Country Life.
    VII. Industrialism.
    B: The Philosophical Radicals.
    VIII. Malthus.   IX. Bentham.   X. James
    Mill.   XI. Ricardo.   XII. The Benthamite
    Doctrine.   XIII. Democracy in England.
    XIV. Free Trade.
    C: Socialism.
    XV. Owen and Early Socialism.   XVI. Early
    Trade Unionism.   XVII. Marx and Engels.
    XVIII. Dialectical Materialism.   XIX. The
    Theory of Surplus Value.   XX. The Politics
    of Marxism.
Part III: Democracy and Plutocracy in America
    A: Democracy in America.
    XXI. Jeffersonian Democracy.   XXII. The
    Settlement of the West.   XXIII. Jacksonian
    Democracy.   XXIV. Slavery and Disunion.
    XXV. Lincoln and National Unity.

C o m m e n t a r y
Much of Russell's work was devoted to a sys-
tematic study of the causes of historical development. Ever since 1896, he had always
rejected the oversimplification of the Mar-
xist attempts to explain everything in terms
of economic forces. If human history was not
governed solely or dominantly by economics,
what were the causal factors at work? To answer this question, Russell wrote "Freedom
and Organization; 1814-1914", a historical
study which remains one of the most valuable and readable of his non-philosophical
books. His scobe embraced both Europe and
America. Historical events, he said, resulted from a complicated tangle of causes,
grouped under three headings: economic techniques, political theories, and important in-
dividuals. Illustrating his thesis, he described doctrines such as Nationalism, Philosophical Radicalism, Marxism, and American
democracy; and he gave vivid sketches of the
personalities and work.

K o m m e n t a r
Einen großen Teil seiner Arbeit widmete Russell dem systematischen Studium der ursäch-
lichen Zusammenhänge in der geschichtlichen
Entwicklung. Schon seit 1896 hatte er stets
die Vereinfachungssucht der Marxistischen Bestrebungen abgelehnt, die alles durch wirtschaftliche Kräfte bedingt erklären wollte.
Wurde aber die menschliche Geschichte nicht
ausschließlich oder vorherrschend von wirtschaftlichen Beweggründen beherrscht, welche
treibenden Kräfte waren dann am Werk? Um diese
Frage zu beantworten, schrieb Russell "Freedom and Organization; 1814-1914", eine historische Studie, die auch heute noch eines seiner wertvollsten und lesbarsten nichtphilo-
sophischen Bücher ist. Sein Thema umfaßte
Europa und Amerika. Historische Ereignisse,
so sagte er, seien das Ergebnis eines kom-
plizierten Zusammenwirkens von Ursachen, die
sich in drei Hauptrichtungen gruppieren

lassen: Wirtschaftswissenschaft, politische
Theorien, bedeutende Einzelmenschen. Zur Beleuchtung seiner Behauptung schilderte er
verschiedene Doktrinen, wie Nationalismus,
philosophischen Radikalismus, Marxismus, amerikanische Demokratie. Dazu gab er lebhafte
Skizzen einzelner Persönlichkeiten und ihrer
Werke.

R e p r i n t s
1936 London: Allen & Unwin . . . . · 395.04
1949 "   : "   " " 395.05
1952 "   : "   " " 395.06
1961 Excerpts:
    "Dialectical Materialism" (XVIII)
    "The Theory of Surplus Value" (XIX)
    in "The Basic Writings of B. Russell":
    XII/54, 55 (BN 659) 395.07
1962 New York: W. W. Norton 395.08
1964 London: Allen & Unwin 395.09
1965 under the title "Legitimacy versus
    Industrialism, 1841-1848" (Part I + II
    of "Freedom and Organization"). 236 pp.
    London: Allen & Unwin (Unwin Books 57). 395.10
1965 under the title "Freedom versus Or-
    ganization, 1776-1914" (Part III + IV
    of "Freedom and Organization"). 247 pp.
    London: Allen & Unwin (Unwin Books 58). 395.11

T r a n s l a t i o n s
Chinesisch:
    "Ziyou yu zuzhi"
    1936 Shanghai 395.12
Deutsch:
    "Freiheit und Organisation. 1814-1914"
    Ü.: Alfred Faber
    1948 Berlin: Cornelsen. 548 S. 395.13
    I n h a l t
    Vorwort
    Teil I: Das Prinzip der Legitimität.
        I. Napoleons Nachfolger. II. Der
        Wiener Kongress. III. Die Heilige
        Allianz. IV. Metternichs sinkender
        Stern.
    Teil II: Der geistige Fortschritt.
        A: Der soziale Hintergrund.
        V. Die Aristokratie. VI. Das Leben
        auf dem Lande. VII. Das industri-
        elle Leben.
        B: Die Philosophischen Radikalen.
        VIII. Malthus. IX. Bentham. X. James
        Mill. XI. Ricardo. XII. Die Ben-
        tham-Doktrin. XIII. Die Demokratie
        in England. XIV. Der Freihandel.

C: Sozialismus
XV. Owen und der frühe britische So-
zialismus. XVI. Erste Gewerkschafts-
bestrebungen. XVII. Marx und Engels.
XVIII. Der dialektische Materialis-
mus. XIX. Die Theorie vom Mehrwert.
XX. Die Politik des Marxismus.
Teil III: Demokratie und Plutokratie
in Amerika.
A: Demokratie in Amerika.
XXI. Jefferson's Demokratie. XXII.
Die Besiedlung des Westens. XXIII.
Jacksons Demokratie. XXIV. Sklave-
rei und Zwietracht. XXV. Lincoln
und die nationale Einheit.
B: Wettbewerb und Monopolwesen
in Amerika.
XXVI. Der Kapitalismus im Konkurrenz-
kampf. XXVII. Die Entwicklung zum
Monopolwesen.
Teil IV: Nationalismus und Imperialismus
XXVIII. Das Nationalitätsprinzip.
XXIX. Bismarck und die deutsche Ein-
heit. XXX. Die wirtschaftliche Ent-
wicklung des deutschen Kaiserreiches.
XXXI. Imperialismus. XXXII. Die
Herren Europas. Bibliographie.
Französisch:
"Histoire des idées au XIXe siècle:
liberté et organisation"
Tr.: A. M. Petitjean
1938 Paris: Gallimard 395.14
1950 " : " 395.15
Italienisch:
"Storia delle idee del secolo XIX"
Tr.: Clara Maturi Egidi
1950 Turin: Einaudi 395.16
1963 Mailand: Mondadori 395.17
1968 " : " 395.18
Japanisch:
"Jiyû to soshiki"
Tr.: Kazuo Obuchi, Yoshiyuki Tsurumi
1959 Tokio: Misuzu shobô. 2 vols. . . 395.19
Polnisch:
"Wiek Dziewietnasty"
Tr.: Antoni Panski
1936 Warschau: Roj. 2.vols. 395.20
Portugiesisch:
"Liberdade e organização"
Tr.: Brenno Silveira
1959 Sao Paulo: Ed. Nacional. 2 vols. 395.21
Spanisch:
"Liberdad y Organización, 1814 - 1914."
Tr.: León Felipe
1936 Madrid: Espasa-Calpe 395.22
1970 " : " " 395.23

Tschechisch:
"Svoboda a Organisage 1814-1914"
Tr.: Jaroslav Kriz
1948 Prag: Denické nakaladatelstoi . . 395.24
Türkisch:
Excerpt:
"Sosyalizm" (II/C)
Tr.: Murat Belge
1965 Istanbul: De Yayinevi. 95 pp. . . . 395.25
1966 "   : " " 395.26
Ungarisch:
"Egye Vszazad Elettörtenete,1814-1914"
Tr.: Anna Feiler Wertheimsteinne
1936 Budapest: Revai. 2 vols. 395.27

The Revolt Against Reason

1935 (Jan.) in "Political Quarterly",
vol. 6, p. 1-19 . . . . 396.01
1935 (Feb.) in "The Atlantic Monthly",
vol. 155, p. 222-232 . . . . 396.02
1935 under the title
"The Ancestry of Fascism"
in "In Praise of Idleness": V (BN 401) 396.03
1941 in "Let the People Think" (BN 464) . . 396.04
1958 in "The Will to Doubt" (BN 638) . . . 396.05

Translations
Deutsch . . . . 1957 in BN 401.16 + 1971/696 396.06
Italienisch . . . 1963 in BN 401.24 . . . . . 396.07
Japanisch . . . . . 1958 in BN 401.26 . . . . . 396.08
Persisch . . . . . . 1970 in BN 401.28 . . . . . 396.09
Polnisch . . . . . . 1937 in BN 401.29 . . . . . 396.10
Portugiesisch . 1957 in BN 401.30 . . . . . 396.11
Schwedisch . . . . 1937 in BN 401.31 . . . . . 396.12
Spanisch . . . . . . 1953 in BN 401.32 = 615 . . 396.13
Türkisch . . . . . . 1969 in BN 401.34 . . . . . 396.14

England's Duty to India

1935 (Feb.) in "Asia", vol. 35, p. 68-70 . . . . 397.00

A Weekly Diary

1935 (May 25 - June 22)
in "New Statesman and Nation",
p. 742-743, 798-799, 854-855, 886-887, 918-919 398.00

Review of A. S. Eddington's
"New Pathways in Science"

1935 in "Time & Tide",
vol. 16. p. 550-551 . . . . 399.00

RELIGION AND SCIENCE

C o n t e n t s
I. Grounds of Conflict. II. The Copernican
Revolution. III. Revolution. IV. Demono-
logy and Medicine. V. Soul and Body. VI.
Determinism. VII. Mysticism. VIII. Cosmic
Purpose. IX. Science and Ethics. X. Con-
clusion. Index.

C o m m e n t a r y
Russell's writings often refer to the insig-
nificance of man in comparison with the Universe. He carried the same point of view a
bit further - I think too far - in his "Religion and Science". He wrote: "If it is the
purpose of the Cosmos to evolve mind, we
should regard it as rather incompetent in
having produced so little in such a long
time. .... It may seem odd that life should
occur by accident, but in such a large universe accidents will happen." There may be
good reasons for denying cosmic purpose and
belittling the importance of human life, but
I do not think this a good one. Frank Ramsey
once wrote that "I don't feel the least humble
before the vastness of the heavens. The stars
may be large, but they cannot think or love;
and these are qualities which impress me far
more than size does." I agree, at least in
part, with Ramsey's point of view; and I think
that Russell would really agree in part too.
(His considered view on two ways of looking
at man and the universe can be found at the
beginning of Part III of "Human Knowledge".)

K o m m e n t a r
Russell's Schriften weisen oft auf die geringe
Bedeutung des Menschen im Vergleich zum Universum hin. Denselben Gesichtspunkt verfolgte
er in "Religion and Science" noch weiter -
mir scheint, zu weit. Er schrieb: "Wenn es
der Zweck des Kosmos ist, den Geist zu ent-
wickeln, so müssen wir ihn als nicht sehr be-
fähigt dazu betrachten, da er in so langer
Zeit erst so wenig hervorgebracht hat. ... Es
mag seltsam erscheinen, daß das Leben zu-
fällig entstanden ist, doch in einem so riesigen Universum werden stets Zufälle vorkom-
men." Es mag vielleicht gute Gründe geben,
den Sinn des Kosmos zu leugnen und die

Bedeutung des menschlichen Lebens zu verklei-
nern; ich glaube aber nicht, daß dies ein guter Grund ist. Frank Ramsey schrieb einmal:
"Ich fühle mich nicht im geringsten demütig
vor der Unermeßlichkeit des Himmels. Die Ge-
stirne mögen riesig sein, aber sie können
nicht denken und nicht lieben; und diese Fä-
higkeiten beeindrucken mich weit mehr als
bloße Größe." Zum Teil wenigstens pflichte
ich Ramseys Auffassung bei; und ich glaube
sogar, daß auch Russell in einigem zustimmen
würde. (Im Anfang des III. Teiles von "Human
Knowledge" legte er dar, wie man den Menschen
und das Universum auf zwei verschiedene Arten betrachten kann.)

R e p r i n t s
1947 London,	New York:	Oxford	Univ.	Press	400.05
1949 "	, " " :	"	"	"	400.06
1953 "	.... :	"	"	"	400.07
1956 "	, " " :	"	"	"	400.08
1961	" " :	"	"	"	400.09
1970 "	, " " :	"	"	"	400.10
1975 "	.... :	"	"	"	400.11

T r a n s l a t i o n s
Französisch:
    "Science et religion"
    1958 Paris: Gallimard 400.12
    1971 Paris: Gallimard 400.13
Italienisch:
    "Religione e scienza"
    Tr.: P. Vitorelli
    1951 Florenz: La nuova Italia 400.14
    "Scienza e religione"
    1974 Mailand: Longanesi 400.15
Japanisch:
    "Shûkyo to kagaku"
    Tr.: Gen'ichirô Tsuda
    1956 Tokio: Gengen-sha 400.16
    1965 Tokio: Arechi shuppansha 400.17
Niederländisch:
    "Godsdienst en Wetenshap"
    Tr.: J. Aalbers
    1948 Rotterdam: Av. Douker 400.18
    "Religie en de wetenschap"
    Tr.: J. Aalbers
    1968 Meppel: Boom 400.19
Schwedisch:
    "Religion och Vetenskap"
    Tr.: Ake Malmström
    1937 Stockholm: Natur och Kultur . . . 400.20
Spanisch:
    "Religión y cienca"
    1951 Mexiko: Fondo de Cultura Económica 400.21
    1956 " : " " " " 400.22

1935

Türkisch:
  "Din ile bilim"
  1963 Istanbul: Baha Matbaasi 400.23
  "Bilim ve din"
  Tr.: Hilmi Yavuz
  1972 Istanbul: Varlik Yayinevi 400.24
  "Din ve bilim"
  Tr.: Aksit Göktürk
  1972 Ankara: Bilgi Yayinevi 400.25

IN PRAISE OF IDLENESS AND OTHER ESSAYS

1935 New York: W. W. Norton & Co. VIII, 270 pp. . 401.01
  London: Allen & Unwin. 231 pp. 401.02
  Toronto: McLeod 401.03
  C o n t e n t s
    I. In Praise of Idleness .... (1932/376)
    II. "Useless" Knowledge ...... (1935/401)
    III. Architecture
       and Social Questions ..... (1935/401)
    IV. The Modern Midas .... (1933/379)
    V. The Ancestry of Fascism .. (1935/396)
    VI. Scylla and Charybdis,
       or Communism and Fascism . (1935/401)
    VII. The Case for Socialism ... (1935/401)
    VIII. Western Civilization ..... (1935/401)
    IX. On Youthful Cynicism ..... (1935/401)
    X. Modern Homogeneity .... (1935/401)
    XI. Men Versus Insects .... (1934/390)
    XII. Education and Discipline . (1934/385)
    XIII. Stoicism and Mental Health (1935/401)
    XIV. On Comets .... (1935/401)
    XV. What Is the Soul? .... (1935/401)

  R e p r i n t s
  1941 Excerpts:
    II. / V. / IX. / X. / XI. / XIII. / XIV./XV.
    in "Let the People Think" (BN 464) . . 401.04
  1942 London: Allen & Unwin 401.05
  1947 Excerpts:
    "The Ancestry of Fascism" (V)
    "What is the Soul? (XV)
    Girard, Kansas: Haldeman-Julius Publ. 401.06
  1948 London: Allen & Unwin 401.07
  1954 "   : "   " " 401.08
  1958 "   : "   " " 401.09
  1958 Excerpts:
    II. / V. / IX. / X. / XI. / XIII. / XIV./XV.
    in "The Will to Doubt" (BN 638) . . . 401.10
  1960 London: Allen & Unwin 401.11
  1960 New York: Barnes & Noble 401.12
  1962 "   "   : "   " " 401.13
  1972 "   "   : Simon & Schuster 401.14
  1976 London: Allen & Unwin 401.15

- 140 -

T r a n s l a t i o n s
Deutsch:
  "Lob des Müßiggangs"
  Ü.: Elisabeth Fischer-Wernecke
  1957 Hamburg, Wien: Zsolnay. 257 S. . 401.16
  1962 "   , "   : " 401.17
  1970 Zürich: Coron 401.18
  1972 Hamburg, Wien: Zsolnay 401.19
  I n h a l t
    I. Lob des Müßiggangs.
    II. "Unnützes" Wissen.
    III. Architektur und soziale Fragen.
    IV. Der moderne Midas.
    V. Die geistigen Väter des Faschismus
    VI. Scylla und Charybdis
        oder Kommunismus und Faschismus.
    VII. Was für den Sozialismus spricht.
    VIII. Die abendländische Zivilisation.
    IX. Über den Zynismus der Jugend.
    X. Moderne Gleichförmigkeit.
    XI. Menschen contra Insekten.
    XII. Erziehung und Disziplin.
    XIII. Stoizismus u. geistige Gesundheit.
    XIV. Über Kometen
    XV. Was ist Seele?
  Auszüge:
  "Lob des Müßiggangs" (I)
  "Die geistigen Väter d. Faschismus" (V)
  "Was für den Sozialismus spricht" (VII)
  1971 in BN 696 . . . .   401.20
  Auszug:
  "Scylla und Charybdis
  oder Kommunismus und Faschismus" (VI)
  1972 in BN 703/IV:10 . . . .   401.21
  Auszug:
  "Erziehung und Disziplin" (XII)
  1974 in BN 707/II:6 . . . .   401.22
  1975 in BN 710/II 401.23
Italienisch:
  "Elogio dell'ozio"
  Tr.: Elisa Marpicati
  1963 Mailand: Longanesi 401.24
  1974 "   : " 401.25
Japanisch:
  "Taida eno sanka"
  Tr.: Hidehiko Hori, Takashi Kakimura
  1958 Tokio: Kadokawa Shoten 401.26
Norwegisch:
  Auszüge:
  "Til lediggangens lov" (I)
  "Scylla og Charybdis" (VI)
  1947 in BN 519 . . . .   401.27
Persisch:
  "Dar setāyesh-e Farāghat"
  1970 Teheran: Andisheh 401.28

Polnisch:
      "Puchwala Prozniactwa"
      Tr.: Antoni Panski
      1937 Warschau: Roj 401.29
Portugiesisch:
      "O elogio do lazer"
      Tr.: Luiz Ribeiro de Sena
      1957 Sao Paulo: Ed. Nacional 401.30
Schwedisch:
      "Till Lättjans Lov"
      Tr.: Alf Ahlberg
      1937 Stockholm: Natur och Kultur . . . 401.31
Spanisch:
      "Elogio de la ociosidad y otros ensayos"
      Tr.: Juan Novella Domingo
      1953 Madrid: Aguilar 401.32
      1956 in BN 615 . . . . 401.33
Türkisch:
      "Aylakiǧa övgü"
      Tr.: Mete Ergin
      1969 Istanbul: Altin Kitaplar Yayinevi 401.34

Determinism and Physics

The 18th Earl Grey Memorial Lecture delivired at
King's Hall, Armstrong College, Newcastle-upon-
Tyne, Jan. 14. 1936.

1936 Newcastle-upon-Tyne (England):
      The Librarian, Armstrong College. 18 pp. . 402.01
      1936 (Mar.) Durham (England): Proceedings of
      the University of Durham Philosophical
      Society, vol.9, part 4, p. 228-245 . . 402.02

Why Radicals Are Unpopular

1936 (Mar.) in "Common Sense", vol. 5, p. 13-15 403.00

Our Sexual Ethics

1936 (May) in "The American Mercury",
      vol. 38, p. 36-41 . . . . 404.01
      1957 in "Why I Am Not a Christian and Other
      Essays" (BN 625) 404.02

      T r a n s l a t i o n s
      Dänisch . . . . 1966 in BN 625.11 . . . . . 404.03
      Deutsch . . . . 1963 in BN 625.12 . . . . . 404.04
      Italienisch . . . 1960 in BN 625.19 . . . . . 404.05
      Japanisch . . . . . 1959 in BN 625.21 . . . . . 404.06
      Koreanisch . . . . 1960 in BN 625.23 . . . . . 404.07
      Niederländisch 1966 in BN 625.26 . . . . . 404.08
      Persisch . . . . . . 1970 in BN 625.28 . . . . . 404.09
      Portugiesisch . 1960 in BN 625.30 . . . . . 404.10
      Schwedisch . . . . 1958 in BN 625.32 . . . . . 404.11
      Spanisch . . . . . . 1958 in BN 625.33 . . . . . 404.12
      Türkisch . . . . . . 1966 in BN 625.36 . . . . . 404.13

British Foreign Policy
1936 (July 18) in "New Statesman and Nation",
    vol. 12, p. 82 . . . .   405.00

Auto-Obituary
The Last Survivor of a Dead Epoch
1936 (Aug. 12) in "Listener", Publication of the
    British Broadcasting Corporation (BBC),
    vol. 16, p. 289 . . . .   406.01

      C o m e n t a r y
          Russell supplied the following foot-note
        to his "Auto-Obituary. The Last Survivor
        of a Dead Epoch":
"This obituary will (or will not) be published
in 'The Times' for June 1, 1962, on the occasion of my lamented but belated death. It was
printed prophetically in 'The Listener' in
1937" (this is an error of Russell: it was
August 12, 1936). - Russell therefore does
not seem to have expected that the would reach
his 90th year of life. In fact, he completed
his 97th year of life on 18th May 1969 and
died on 2nd Februar 1970.

      K o m m e n t a r
          Russell hat seinen "Selbst-Nachruf. Der
        letzte Überlebende einer toten Epoche."
        mit folgender Fußnote versehen:
"Dieser Nachruf wird in der 'Times' vom 1. Juni
1962 anläßlich meines betrauerten, aber ver-
späteten Hinscheidens veröffentlicht werden
(oder auch nicht). Er wurde in vorausschau-
ender Weise 1937 in 'The Listener' abge-
druckt" (dies ist ein Irrtum von Russell:
es war der 12. August 1936). - Russell rech-
nete demnach, daß er das 90. Lebensjahr nicht
erreichen würde. In Wirklichkeit vollendete
er am 18. Mai 1969 sein 97. Lebensjahr und
starb am 2. Februar 1970.

      R e p r i n t s
      1941 in "Coronet", vol. 10, p. 36-38 .... .   406.02
      1950 in "Unpopular Essays": XII (BN 567) .   406.03
      1970 (Feb. 12) in "Listener" in "Bertrand
          Russell", an article by Gilbert Ryle.   406.04
      1970 (May) in "Bertrand Russell - 1872-1970"
          Nottingham: B. Russell Peace Foundation
          (The Spokesman) 406.05
      1972 in "The Collected Stories" (BN 701) .   406.06

      T r a n s l a t i o n s
      Chinesisch .... 1970 in BN 567.13 . . . . .   406.07
      Dänisch .... 1950 in BN 567.14 . . . . .   406.08
      Deutsch .... 1951 in BN 567.15 . . . . .   406.09

```
Finnisch ...... 1950 in BN 567.20 . . . . .  406.10
Italienisch ... 1963 in BN 567.23 . . . . .  406.11
Japanisch ..... 1958 in BN 567.24 . . . . .  406.12
Koreanisch .... 1958 in BN 567.25 . . . . .  406.13
Portugiesisch . 1954 in BN 567.27 . . . . .  406.14
Schwedisch .... 1950 in BN 567.28 . . . . .  406.15
Spanisch .,,... 1952 in BN 567.30 . . . . .  406.16
Sp./Catalanisch 1965 in BN 567.31 . . . . .  406.17
```

Spanish Conspiracy

1936 (Aug. 15) in "New Statesman and Nation",
    vol. 12, p. 218 . . . . 407.00

Review of John Laird's
"Recent Philosophy"

1936 (Oct. 14) in "Listener", supp., p. 3 . . . 408.00

Far Eastern Imperialism

A review of Freda Utley's "Japan's Feet of Clay"

1936 (Nov. 7) in "New Statesman and Nation",
    vol. 12, p. 736 . . . . 409.00

On Order in Time

1936 in "Proceedings
    of the Cambridge Philosophical Society",
    vol. 32, p. 216-228 . . . . 410.01
    1956 in "Logic and Knowledge" (BN 616) . . 410.02

    Translations
    Italienisch ... 1961 in BN 616.08 . . . . . 410.03
    Portugiesisch . 1974 in BN 616.09 . . . . . 410.04
    Spanisch ...... 1966 in BN 616.10 . . . . . 410.05

The Congress of Scientific Philosophy

1936 "Actes du congres international
    de philosophie scientifique", vol.I, p.10-11
    Paris: Herman & Cie. 411.00

Review of A. J. Ayer's
"Language, Truth and Logic"

1936 in "London Mercury", vol. 33, p. 541-543 . 412.01
    1947 in "Horizon", vol. 15, p. 71.72 . . . 412.02

The Limits of Empiricism

1936 in "Proceedings of the Aristotelian Society"
    vol, 36, p. 131-150 . . . . 413.00

Do We Survive Death?

1936 in "The Mysteries of Life and Death"
    London: Hutchinson (see also BN 618) . . . 414.01
    1957 in "Why I Am Not a Christian and Other
        Essays" (BN 625) 414.02
```
```

T r a n s l a t i o n s

WHICH WAY TO PEACE?

1936 London: Michael Joseph. 224 pp. 415.01
Canada: S. J. R. Saunders 415.02
C o n t e n t s
I. The Imminent Danger of War. II. The Na-
ture of the Next War. III. Isolationism.
IV. Collective Security. V. Alliances. VI.
The Policy of Expedients. VII. Wars of Prin-
ciple. VIII. Pacifism as a National Policy.
IX. Some Warlike Fallacies. X. Conditions
for Permanent Peace. XI. Peace and Current
Politics. XII. Individual Pacifism.

C o m m e n t a r y
It is somewhat unfair to Russells reputation,
though easily understandable, that books like
"Freedom and Organization" (1934) and "Power"
(1938) attracted less public attention than
"Which Way to Peace?" (1936) and his pacifist
propaganda during the same years. It is fair
to add that "Which Way to Peace?", considered
as a book in which the main conclusion was
wrong, included an extraordinary number of
points which were right. Perhaps, in retrospect, one of the most interesting passages
in the book is where Russell noted: "of all
the danger points of Europe Poland is now
perhaps the most exposed. ..... There is no
impossibility in an alliance between Germany
and Russia, leading to a new partition ..."
It is now ancient history to recall how the
Soviet-German Pact of 1939 preluded the in-
vasion of Poland, and how this started the
Second World War. Russell's forecast was an
extraordinary one to have made as early as
1936.

K o m m e n t a r
Es ist zwar leicht verständlich, aber für
Russell's Ruf etwas beeinträchtigend, daß
Bücher, wie "Freedom and Organization" (1934)
und "Power" (1938) die Aufmerksamkeit des

großen Publikums weniger auf sich zogen als
"Which Way to Peace?" (1936) und seine pazifistische Propaganda in den gleichen Jahren.
Eins ist gerechter Weise hinzuzufügen: war
"Which Way to Peace?" auch ein Buch mit ver-
kehrtem Hauptergebnis, so enthielt es doch
eine außerordentliche Anzahl richtiger Punkte. Im Rückblick ist vielleicht eine der in-
teressantesten Stellen in diesem Buch Russell's Bemerkung: "Von allen Gefahrenzonen
Europas ist Polen jetzt vielleicht am stärk-
sten exponiert. .. Es ist nicht ausgeschlos-
sen, daß Deutschland und Rußland sich zu einem Bündnis zusammenfinden, das zu einer neu-
en Teilung führt ...." Jetzt ist es Weltge-
schichte, wenn man daran erinnert, daß der
sowjetisch-deutsche Pakt 1939 dem Einfall in
Polen vorausging und daß dieser Einfall den
Zweiten Weltkrieg auslöste. Es war ganz au-
ßerordentlich, daß Russell die Voraussage
schon 1936 gemacht hatte.

R e p r i n t
1936 Excerpt:
    "Individual Pacifism" (XII)
    New York:
    Fellowship of Reconciliation. 12 pp. . 415.03

T r a n s l a t i o n s
Polnisch:
    "Droga do Pokoju"
    Tr.: Antoni Panski
    1937 Warschau: Roj 415.04
Schwedisch:
    "Vägen till Freden"
    Tr.: Carl-Frederik Palmstierna
    1938 Stockholm: Bonnier 415.05

Which Way to Peace

1936 (Nov. 28) in "New Statesman and Nation",
    vol. 12, p. 847 (Letter to the editor) . . 416.00

On Being Modern-Minded

1937 (Jan. 9) in "Nation", vol. 144, p. 47-48 . 417.00

Philosophy's Ulterior Motives

1937 (Feb.) in "The Atlantic Monthly",
    vol. 159, p. 149-155 . . . . 418.01
    1950 in "Unpopular Essays": IV (BN 567) . . 418.02

T r a n s l a t i o n s
Chinesisch .... 1970 in BN 567.13 . . . . . 418.03
Dänisch .... 1950 in BN 567.14 . . . . . 418.04
Deutsch .... 1951 in BN 567.15 . . . . . 418.05

```
Finnisch ......  1950 in BN 567.20 . . . . .  418.06
Italienisch ...  1963 in BN 567.23 . . . . .  418.07
Japanisch .....  1958 in BN 567.24 . . . . .  418.08
Koreanisch ....  1958 in BN 567.25 . . . . .  418.09
Portugiesisch .  1954 in BN 567.27 . . . . .  418.10
Schwedisch ....  1950 in BN 567.28 . . . . .  418.11
Spanisch ......  1952 in BN 567.30 . . . . .  418.12
Sp./Catalanisch 1965 in BN 567.31 . . . . .  418.13
```

Power - Ancient and Modern

1937 (Apr.) in "Political Quarterly",
  vol. 8, p. 155-164 . . . . 419.00

The Future of Democracy

1937 (May 5) in "The New Republic",
  vol. 80, p. 381-382 . . . . 420.00

Man's Diary in Sticks and Stones

1937 (June) in "Rotarian", vol. 50, p. 15-16 . . 421.00

The Superior Virtue of the Oppressed

1937 (June 26) in "Nation", vol. 144, p. 731-732 422.01
  1950 in "Unpopular Essays": V (BN 567) . . . 422.02

```
     T r a n s l a t i o n
Chinesisch ....  1970 in BN 567.13 . . . . .  422.03
Dänisch .......  1950 in BN 567.14 . . . . .  422.04
Deutsch .......  1951 in BN 567.15 . . . . .  422.05
Finnisch ......  1950 in BN 567.20 . . . . .  422.06
Italienisch ...  1963 in BN 567.23 . . . . .  422.07
Japanisch .....  1958 in BN 567.24 . . . . .  422.08
Koreanisch ....  1958 in BN 567.25 . . . . .  422.09
Portugiesisch .  1954 in BN 567.27 . . . . .  422.10
Schwedisch ....  1950 in BN 567.28 . . . . .  422.11
Spanisch ......  1952 in BN 567.30 . . . . .  422.12
Sp./Catalanisch 1965 in BN 567.31 . . . . .  422.13
```

On Verification

1937 (Nov. 8) Presidential Adress,
  in "Proceedings Aristotelian Society",
  vol. 38, p. 1-20 . . . . 423.00

Two Prophets

A Review of R. Osborn's "Freud and Marx".

1937 in "New Statesman and Nation", vol. 13, p. 416 424.00

Plato in Modern Dress

1937 in "New Statesman and Nation",
  vol. 13, p. 850 . . . . 425.00

THE AMBERLEY PAPERS

The Letters and Diaries of B. Russell's Parents,
edited by Bertrand Russell and Patricia Russell.

1937 New York: W. W. Norton. 2vols., 552, 581 pp.   426.01
    Toronto: Longmans 426.02
    London: Hogarth 426.03
    C o n t e n t s
    Vol. I
      Genealogical Tables. Preface.
      I. The Stanleys of Alderley. II. The Rus-
      sells. III. Kate Stanley's Childhood and
      Youth. IV. Amberley's Early Boyhood. V.
      Harrow. VI. Edinburgh, Cambridge, and
      Travels. VII. Courtship. VIII. Marriage
      to End of 1865. IX. 1866. Index.
    Vol. II
      X. Parliament and America, 1867 and 1868.
      XI. The South Devon Election. XII. 1869.
      XIII. 1870. XIV. 1871. XV. Can War Be
      Abolished? XVI. Family Controversies.
      XVII. 1872. XVIII. 1873-1874. XIX. The
      Death of Kate, Rachel, and Amberley.
      Index.

    R e p r i n t s
    1940 London: Hogarth 426.04
      Under the title
      "The Amberley Papers:
      Bertrand Russell's Family Background."
    1966 London: Allen & Unwin 426.05
      New York: Simon & Schuster 426.06

Aristocratic Rebels: Byron and the Modern World

1938 (Feb. 12) in "Saturday Review of Literature"
    vol. 17, p. 3-4 (see also BN 447) 427.00

Taming Economic Power

Radio Discussion with T. V. Smith and P. Douglas.
The University of Chicago Round Table, Nov. 15,
1938, Red Network of the National Broadcasting
Company.

1938 printed in pamphlet, The University of Chicago
    Round Table, University of Chicago.
    Chicago, Illinois. 428.00

On the Importance of Logical Form

1938 in "Encyclopaedia and Unified Science"; In-
    ternational Encyclopaedia of Unified Science.
    University of Chicago, vol. I, p. 39-41 . .   429.00

Science and Social Institutions

1938 in "Dare We Look Ahead?"
New York: Macmillan, p. 9-29 . . . . 430.01
London: Allen & Unwin 430.02

The Relevance of Psychology to Logic

1938 in "Proceedings Aristotelian Society",
vol. 17, p. 42-53 . . . . 431.00

My Religious Reminiscences

1938 in "The Rationalist Annual",
55th Year of Publication, p. 3-8,
published by C. A. Watts & Co. 432.01
1961 in "The Basic Writings of B. Russell":
I/1 (BN 659) 432.02

Happiness

1938 in "What Is Happines?"
London: Bodley Head 433.01
1939 New York: Kinsey 433.02
1939 Toronto: Nelson, p. 55-65 . . . . . . 433.03

Review of H. Levy's
"A Philosophy for a Modern Man"

1938 in "New Statesman and Nation",
vol. 15, p. 252-254 . . . . 434.00

Philosophy and Common Sense

1938 in "New Statesman and Nation",
vol. 15, p. 365 . . . . 435.00

POWER: A NEW SOCIAL ANALYSIS

1938 New York: W. W. Norton & Co. 315 pp. . . . 436.01
London: Allen & Unwin. 328 pp. 436.02
Toronto: McLeod 436.03
C o n t e n t s
I. The Impulse to Power. II. Leaders and
Followers. III. The Forms of Power. IV.
Priestly Power. V. Kingly Power. VI. Naked
Power. VII. Revolutionary Power. VIII. Eco-
nomic Power. IX. Power over Opinion. X.
Sources of Power. XI. The Biology of Organi-
zations. XII. Powers and Forms of Govern-
ments. XIII. Organizations and the Indi-
vidual. XIV. Competition. XV. Power and
Moral Codes. XVI. Power Philosophies. XVII.
The Ethics of Power. XVIII. The Taming of
Power. Index.
C o m m e n t a r y
Russell published his book "Power" in 1938,
devoted to the thesis that "Love of power is

the chief motive producing the changes which
social science has to study". Russell argued
that economic needs were finite and could
therefore be satisfied; but the craving for
power had no limits. He stressed that socialism had to be safeguarded by a more thor-
ough-going democracy than any known before,
including special measures to safeguard lib-
erties; otherwise the result might be "a new
tyranny at once economic and political, more
drastic and more terrible than any previously
known". He said that "To suppose that irre-
sponsible power, just because it is called
Socialist or Communist, will be freed mirac-
ulously from the bad qualities of all ar-
bitrary power in the past, is mere childish
nursery psychology". This problem of "the
taming of power" was one which Russell always recognized, and to which he continually
returned.

K o m m e n t a r
Russell veröffentlichte sein Buch "Power"
1938; er vertrat darin die These, daß "Macht-
liebe den Hauptantrieb für die Veränderungen
bildet, die die Sozialwissenschaft zu ergrün-
den hat". Als Beweis führte Russell an, wirtschaftliche Bedürfnisse sind begrenzt und
können darum befriedigt werden; der Macht-
hunger aber ist grenzenlos. Er unterstrich
immer wieder, daß der Sozialismus durch vollständige Demokratie gesichert werden müsse,
vollständiger als jede bisher bekannte; auch
besondere Maßnahmen zum Schutz der Freiheit
gehörten dazu. Ließe man das außer acht, so
könnte das Resultat "eine gleichzeitig wirtschaftliche und politische neue Tyrannei
sein, gewalttätiger und schrecklicher als
jede früher erfahrene". Er sagte: "Die Annahme, daß unverantwortliche Macht, einfach
weil sie sozialistisch oder kommunistisch
heißt, auf rätselhafte Weise von den verderb-
lichen Eigenschaften jeder früheren willkür-
lichen Macht frei sein sollte, ist nichts als
unreife Kinderstuben-Psychologie." Dieses
Problem der "Zähmung der Macht" erkannte Russell stets an, und er kam dauernd wieder darauf zurück.

R e p r i n t s
1938 Excerpt:
    "Power over Opinion" (IX)
    in "Saturday Review of Literature",
    Aug. 13, p. 13-14 . . . . 436.04

```
1938 Excerpt:
     "The Taming of Power" (XVIII)
     in "The Atlantic Monthly",
     Oct., vol. 162, p. 439-449 . . . . . .   436.05
1939 London: Allen & Unwin . . . . . . . . .  436.06
1946  "     : "      " "     . . . . . . . .  436.07
1948 Excerpt:
     "The Taming of Power" (XVIII)
     in "Opinions and Attitudes in the Twen-
     tieth Century", 4th ed.,
     New York: Ronald Press, p. 447-464 . .   436.08
1957 London: Allen & Unwin . . . . . . . . .  436.09
1960  "     : "      " "     . . . . . . . .  436.10
1960 Toronto: Nelson . . . . . . . . . . .    436.11
1961 Excerpt:
     "The Taming of Power" (XVIII)
     in "The Basic Writings of B. Russell":
     XVII/71 (BN 659) . . . . . . . . . . .   436.12
1962 London: Allen & Unwin . . . . . . . .    436.13
1962 New York: Barnes & Noble . . . . . . .   436.14
1969  "     "  : W. W. Norton . . . . . . .   436.15
1975 London: Allen & Unwin . . . . . . . .    436.16
```

T r a n s l a t i o n s
Arabisch:

```
     "Al-Quwwah"
     Tr.: 'Abd al-Karīm Aḥmad,
          Murāja'at 'ali Ādham.
     1959 Kairo: Maktabit al-Anglo
          al-Misriyyah. 238 pp. . . . . . .   436.17
```

Chinesisch:

```
     "Quanli"
     1941 . . . . . . . . . . . . . . . . .   436.18
     1943 Tshunking . . . . . . . . . . . .   436.19
     "Ch'üan Li Lun"
     Tr.: Hsu-hsüan T-u
     1958 Taipeh: Chêng Chung Book Co. . .    436.20
```

Deutsch:

```
     "Macht. Eine sozialkritische Studie."
     Ü.: Stephan Hermlin
     1947 Zürich: Europa Verlag. 264 S. . .   436.21
     1973  "     : "        "    . . . . .    436.22
```

I n h a l t
1. Der Trieb zur Macht. 2. Führer und
Geführte. 3. Die Formen der Macht. 4.
Priesterliche Macht. 5. Königliche
Macht. 6. Nackte Gewalt. 7. Revolutionäre Macht. 8. Wirtschaftliche
Macht. 9. Macht über die Meinung.
10. Der Glaube als Ursprung der Macht.
11. Die Biologie der Organisationen.
12. Regierungsmacht und ihre Formen.
13. Organisationen und das Individuum.

14. Wettbewerb. 15. Macht und morali-
sche Prinzipien. 16. Machtphilosophie.
17. Die Ethik der Macht. 18. Die Zäh-
mung der Macht. Register.
Auszug:
"Die Zähmung der Macht" (XVIII)
1972 in BN 703/IV:11 . . . . 436.23
Hebräisch:
"Shilton"
Tr.: Naftali Golan
1953 Tel Aviv: Amoved 436.24
Ind./Gujarati:
"Satta"
Tr.: Yašavant Šukla
1970 Bhavnagar: Bhashantar nidhi . . . 436.25
Italienisch:
"Il potere"
Tr.: Lionello Torossi
1954 Mailand: Bocca 436.26
1967 " : Feltrinelli 436.27
Japanisch:
"Kenryoku"
Tr.: Takashi Tomiya
1951 Tokio: Misuzu shobô 436.28
1959 " : " " 436.29
Koreanisch:
"Jeong'chi gweon'ryeog'ron"
Tr.: Lee Geug-chan
1958 Seoul: Eul'yu'mun'hwa'sa 436.30
Norwegisch:
"Makt"
Tr.: Fridtjof Voss
1950 Stavanger: Stabenfeldt 436.31
Portugiesisch:
"O poder"
Tr.: Rubens Gomes de Sonza
1941 Sao Paulo: Livraria Martins . . . 436.32
Tr.: Breno Silveira
1957 Sao Paulo: Ed. Nacional 436.33
Schwedisch:
"Makt"
Tr.: Paul Gerner
1939 Stockholm: Natur och Kultur . . . 436.34
Spanisch:
"El poder"
Tr.: L. Echavarri
1939 Buenos Aires: Losoda 436.35
1960 " " : " , 4th ed. . . 436.36
Türkisch:
"Iktidar"
Tr.: Mete Ergin
1967 Istanbul: Altin Kitaplar Yayinevi 436.37

Role of the Intellectual in the Modern World
1939 (Jan.) in "American Journal of Sociology",
vol. 44, p. 491-498 . . . . 437.00

Munich Rather than War

1939 (Feb. 11) in "Nation", vol. 148, p. 173-175   438.00

The Case for United States Neutrality -
If War Comes, Shall We Participate or Be Neutral?
A Symposium.

1939 (Mar.) in "Common Sense", vol. 8, p. 8-9 . 439.00

Education for Democracy

1939 (Apr.) in "Elementary School Journal",
  vol. 39, p. 564-567 . . . .   440.01
  1939 (Apr.) in "Bulletin of the Department
  of Secondary School Principals of the
  National Education Association",
  vol. 28, p. 97-98 . . . .   440.02

Can Power Be Humanized?

1939 (Oct.) in "Forum", vol. 102, p. 184-185 . . 441.00

Living Philosophy, Revised.

1939 in "I Believe: The Personal Philosophies of
  Certain Eminent Men and Women of Our Time".
  New York: Simon & Schuster, p. 409-412 . . 442.00

Dewey's New Logic

1939 in "The Philosophy of John Dewey"
  Evanston, Chicago: Northwestern University;
  New York: Tudor Publishing Co., p. 135 - 156 443.01
  1961 in "The Basic Writings of B. Russell":
  IV/24 (BN 659) 443.02

Democracy and Economics

1939 in "Calling America:
  The Chalenge to Democracy Reaches Over Here".
  New York, London: Harper & Brothers, p. 76-78 444.00

Is Security Increasing?

Radio Discussion with A. Hart and M. H. C. Laves.
The University of Chicago Round Table, Jan. 15,
1939. Red Network of the National Broadcasting Co.

1939 printed in pamphlet, The University of Chicago
  Round Table, University of Chicago.
  Chicago, Illinois. 445.00

My Philosophy

1939 in "I Believe"
  New York: Simon & Schuster, p. 409-412
  (Erroneous repetition of BN 442.00) 446.00

Byron and the Modern World

1940 (Jan.) in "Journal of the History of Ideas"
    vol. 1, p. 24-37 (see also BN 427) 447.00

Toward World Federation - Too Optimistic

1940 (Mar.) in "Asia", vol. 40, p. 126-127 . . . 448.00

Letter on "The Bertrand Russell Case

1940 (Apr. 26) in "New York Times". 449.01
    1941 in part in "The Bertrand Russell Case"
    ed. by John Dewey and Horace M. Kallen.
    New York: Viking Press 449.02
    In "Behind the Bertrand Russell Case",
    by Horace M. Kallen, p. 29 . . . . . . 449.03
    (See also in BN 625:
    "How B. Russell Was Prevented from Teaching
    at The College of the City of New York"
    by P. Edwards)

Freedom and the Colleges

("On Freedom in Time of Stress".
New York Regional Progressive Conference, 1940 .
See also BN 467)

1940 (May) in "The American Mercury",
    vol. 50, p. 24-33 . . . . 450.01
    1957 in "Why I Am Not a Christian and Other
    Essays" (BN 625) 450.02

    T r a n s l a t i o n s
    Dänisch . . . . 1966 in BN 625.11 . . . . . 450.03
    Deutsch . . . . 1963 in BN 625.12 . . . . . 450.04
    Italienisch . . . 1960 in BN 625.19 . . . . . 450.05
    Japanisch . . . . . 1959 in BN 625.21 . . . . . 450.06
    Koreanisch . . . . 1960 in BN 625.23 . . . . . 450.07
    Niederländisch 1966 in BN 625.26 . . . . . 450.08
    Persisch . . . . . . 1970 in BN 625.28 . . . . . 450.09
    Portugiesisch . 1960 in BN 625.30 . . . . . 450.10
    Schwedisch . . . . 1958 in BN 625.32 . . . . . 450.11
    Spanisch . . . . . . 1958 in BN 625.33 . . . . . 450.12
    Türkisch . . . . . . 1966 in BN 625.36 . . . . . 450.13

Do I Preach Adultery?

1940 (May 18) in "Liberty",
    vol. 17, no. 20, p. 57-59 . . . . 451.00

The Functions of a Teacher

1940 (June) in "Harper's Magazine",
    vol. 181, p. 11-16 . . . . 452.01
    1950 in "Unpopular Essays": VIII (BN 567) 452.02
    1961 in "The Basic Writings of B. Russell":
    X/48 (BN 659) 452.03

```
T r a n s l a t i o n s
Chinesisch ....  1970 in BN 567.13 . . . . .  452.04
Dänisch .......  1950 in BN 567.14 . . . . .  452.05
Deutsch .......  1951 in BN 567.15 . . . . .  452.06
Finnisch ......  1950 in BN 567.20 . . . . .  452.07
Italienisch ...  1963 in BN 567.23 . . . . .  452.08
Japanisch .....  1958 in BN 567.24 . . . . .  452.09
Koreanisch ....  1958 in BN 567.25 . . . . .  452.10
Portugiesisch .  1954 in BN 567.27 . . . . .  452.11
Schwedisch ....  1950 in BN 567.28 . . . . .  452.12
Spanisch ......  1952 in BN 567.30 . . . . .  452.13
Sp./Catalanisch 1965 in BN 567.31 . . . . .  452.14
```

Freedom and Government

1940 in "Freedom: Its Meaning",
New York: Harcourt, Brace & Co., p. 249-264   453.00

The Philosophy of Santayana

1940 in "The Philosophy of George Santayana",
Evanston, Chicago:
Northwestern University, p. 453-474 . . . .   454.00

AN INQUIRY INTO MEANING AND TRUTH

1940 New York: W. W. Norton. 445 pp. 455.01
London: Allen & Unwin. 352 pp. 455.02
C o n t e n t s
Preface.   Introduction.
I. What is a Word?   II. Sentences, Syntax,
and Parts of Speech.   III. Sentences Describing Experiences.   IV. The Object-Lan-
guage.   V. Logical Words.   VI. Proper Names.
VII. Egocentric Particulars.   VIII. Perception and Knowledge.   IX. Epistemological
Premisses.   X. Basic Propositions.   XI. Fac-
tual Premisses.   XII. An Analysis of Problems
Concerning Propositions.   XIII. The Significance of Sentences: A. General. B. Psychological Analysis of Significance.   C. Syntax and Significance.   XIV. Language as Expression.   XV. What Sentences "Indicate".
XVI. Truth and Falsehood: Preliminary Discussion.   XVII. Truth and Experience.   XVIII.
General Beliefs.   XIX. Extensionality and
Atomicity.   XX. The Law of Excluded Middle.
XXI. Truth and Verification.   XXII. Significance and Verifiability.   XXIII. Warranted
Assertibility.   XXIV. Analysis.   XXV. Language and Metaphysics.   Index.

R e p r i n t s
1943 London: Allen & Unwin 455.03
1951 "   : "   " " 455.04
1956 "   : "   " " 455.05

1961 Excerpts:
   "Sentences, Syntax,
   and Parts of Speech" (II)
   "Epistemological Premisses" (IX)
   "Language and Metaphysics" (XXV)
   in "The Basic Writings of B. Russell":
   III/10, V/28, VI/30 (BN 659) 455.06
1962 Harmondsworth: Penguin Books 455.07
1967 London: Allen & Unwin 455.08
1973 Harmondsworth: Penguin Books 455.09
1977 London: Allen & Unwin 455.10

T r a n s l a t i o n s
Französisch:
   "Signification et vérité"
   Tr.: Pierre Devaux
   1959 Paris: Flammarion 455.11
Italienisch:
   "Significato e verità"
   Tr.: Luca Pavolini
   1963 Mailand: Longanesi 455.12
Japanisch:
   "Imi to shingisei,
   Gengo tetsugakutegi kenkyû"
   Tr.: Môri Yoshinobu
   1973 Tokio: Bunka Hyôron shuppan . . . 455.13
Spanisch:
   "Investigación sobre
   el significado y la verdad"
   .... Buenos Aires: Ateneo 455.14

Dr. Russell Denies Pacifism

1941 (Jan. 27) Letter in "New York Times" . . . 456.00

Long Time Advocate of Peace Approves Present War

1941 (Feb. 16) Letter in "New York Times" . . . 457.00

Blueprint for an Enduring Peace

1941 (June) in "American Mercury",
   vol. 52, p. 66-676 . . . . 458.00

Speaking of Liberty

Dialogue with Rex Stout, broadcast WEAF and Red
Network, July 1941.

1941 Mimeographed copy, prepared by Council for
   Democracy, New York, no. 15 . . . . 459.00

Bertrand Russell Urges Creation
of World Federation Controlling All Armaments

1941 (Sept. 27) in "The New Leader",
   vol. 24, p. 4 . . . . 460.00

A Philosophy for You in These Times

1941 (Oct.) in "The Reader's Digest",
vol. 93, p. 5-7 . . . . 461.00

Hegel's Philosophy of History

Dialogue with Huntington Cairns, Allen Tate and
Mark Van Doren. Columbia Broadcasting System.

1941 printed in "Invitation to Learning".
New York: Random House, p. 410-422 . . . . 462.01
1941 Canada: Macmillan Company. 462.02
1942 . . . . Home Library 462.03

God Is Not a Mathematician

1941 in "New Worlds in Science",
edited by H. Ward, McBride. 463.01
1944 Popular Edition 463.02

Let the People Think

A Selection of Essays.

1941 London: Watts & Co. 116 pp. 464.01
1961 London: Rationalist Press Assoc. . . . 464.02
C o n t e n t s
On the Value of Scepticism . . . . . (1928/327)
Can Man Be Rational? . . . . (1923/262)
Free Thought
and Official Propaganda . . . . . (1922/236)
Is Science Superstitious? . . . . . . (1926/304)
Stoicism and Mental Health . . . . . (1935/401)
The Ancestry of Fascism . . . . (1935/396)
"Useless" Knowledge . . . . (1935/401)
On Youthful Cynicism . . . . (1935/401)
Modern Homogeneity . . . . (1935/401)
Men Versus Insects . . . . (1934/390)
What Is the Soul? . . . . (1935/401)
On Comets . . . . (1935/401)
(Same contents as in "The Will to
Doubt", 1958/638)

To End the Deadlock in India

1942 (June) in "Asia", vol. 42, p. 338-340 . . . 465.00

Proposals for an International University

1942 (July) in "Fortnightly", vol. 158, p. 8-16 466.00

Freedom in a Time of Stress

1942 (Sept.) in "Rotarian", vol. 61, p. 23-24 . 467.00
(See also BN 450)

Indian Situation

1942 (Sept. 5) in "Nation", vol. 155, p. 200 . . 468.00

What about India?

Adress and Discussion with others.
The American Forum of the Air, Oct. 11, 1942.

1942 printed Washington, D.C.: Ransdell, p. 7-13   469.00

Descartes' "Discourse on Method"

Dialogue with Jacques Barzun and Mark Van Doren.
(CBSprogram "Invitation to Learning")

1942 in "New Invitation to Learning",
New York: Random House, p. 93-104 . . . . .   470.00

Spinoza's Ethics

Dialogue with Scott Buchanan and Mark Van Doren.
(CBSprogram "Invitation to Learning")

1942 in "New Invitation to Learning",
New York: Random House, p. 107-118 . . . .   471.00

Carroll's "Alice in Wonderland"

Dialogue with Katherine A. Porter and Mark Van Doren.
(CBSprogram "Invitation to Learning")

1942 in "New Invitation to Learning",
New York: Random House, p. 208-220 . . . .   472.00

Non-Materialistic Naturalism

1942 in "Kenyon Review", vol. 4, p. 361-365 . .   473.00

How to Become a Philosopher:
The Art of Rational Conjecture.

1942 Girard, Kansas: Haldeman-Julius Publ.,
The "How-To" Series, vol. 7, p. 5-16 . . .   474.01
1968 in BN 685 . . . .   474.02

How to Become a Logieian:
The Art of Drawing Inferences.

1942 Girard, Kansas: Haldeman-Julius Publ.,
The "How-To" Series, vol. 8, p.16-27 . . .   475.01
1968 in BN 685 . . . .   475.02

How to Become a Mathematician:
The Art of Reckoning.

1942 Girard, Kansas: Haldeman-Julius Publ.,
The "How-To" Series, vol. 9, p.28-40 . . .   476.01
1968 in BN 685 . . . .   476.02

The International Significance
of the Indian Problem (With Patricia Russell)

1943 (Jan.) in "FreeWorld", vol. 5, p. 63-69 . .   477.01

1945 under the title
"India Looms Up"
in "Treasury for the Free World"
New York: Arco Publishing Co., p. 74-77   477.02

Some Problems of the Post-War World

1943 (Mar.) in "Free World", vol. 5, p. 297-301   478.01
1945 under the title
"Problems We Will Face"
in "Treasury for the Free World"
New York: Arco Publishing Co., p. 31-44   478.02

What Shall We Do With Germany?

1943 (May 29) in "Saturday Review of Literature",
vol. 26, p. 8 . . . .   479.00

Zionism and the Peace Settlement

1943 (June 11) in "New Palestine", vol. 33, p. 5-7   480.01
1943 in "Palestine - Jewish Commonwealth in
Our Times". Washington, D.C.: Zionist
Organization of America. 480.02

Education in America

1943 (June) in "Common Sense Magazine" (New Jersey)   481.01
See also: "Bertrand Russell's America". His
transatlantic travels and writings. A documented account by Barry Feinberg and Roland
Kasrils. Vol. I: 1896-1945 (BN 704)
1973 London: Allen & Unwin, p. 299-307 . .   481.02

Education After the War

1943 (Aug.) in "American Mercury",
vol. 78, p. 194-203 . . . .   482.00

Our World after the War:
A Plan for International Action.

1943 (Nov. 27) in "The New Leader",
vol. 26, p. 5, 7. . . . .   483.01
C o n t e n t s
I. The International Authority. II. Territorial Questions. III. The Treatment of Germany.   IV. Self-Government in Weaker Coun-
tries. V. Relations of the Great Powers.

R e p r i n t
1943 (Dec. 4) Excerpt:
"Territorial Questions" (II)
under the title
"Britain's Shrunken Economy Makes Her
Dependent on U. S."
in "The New Leader", vol. 26, p. 5 . .   483.02

Citizenship in a Great State

1943 (Dec.) in "Fortune", vol. 28,
    p. 167, 168, 170, 172, 175, 176, 178, 180, 182,
    and 185. . . . .   484.00

How to Read and Understand History:
The Past as the Key to the Future.

1943 Girard, Kansas: Haldeman-Julius Publications   485.01
    1957 in "Understanding History" (BN 624) .   485.02
    T r a n s l a t i o n s
    Persisch . . . . . . 1963 in BN 624.02 . . . . .   485.03

An Outline of Intellectual Rubbish:
A Hilarious Catalogue
of Organized and Individual Stupidity

1943 Girard, Kansas: Haldeman-Julius Publications   486.01
    1950 in "Unpopular Essays": VII (BN 567) .   486.02
    1961 in "The Basic Writings of B. Russell":
      II/7 (BN 659) 486.03
    1972 in "Atheism" (BN 700) 486.04

    T r a n s l a t i o n s
    Chinesisch . . . . 1970 in BN 567.13 . . . . .   486.05
    Dänisch . . . . 1950 in BN 567.14 . . . . .   486.06
    Deutsch . . . . 1951 in BN 567.15 . . . . .   486.07
                  (u.d.T. "Zur Genealogie
                   des Unsinns": BN 567:7)
    Finnisch . . . . . . 1950 in BN 567.20 . . . . .   486.08
    Italienisch . . . 1963 in BN 567.23 . . . . .   486.09
    Japanisch . . . . . 1958 in BN 567.24 . . . . .   486.10
    Koreanisch . . . . 1958 in BN 567.25 . . . . .   486.11
    Portugiesisch . 1954 in BN 567.27 . . . . .   486.12
    Schwedisch . . . . 1950 in BN 567.28 . . . . .   486.13
    Spanisch . . . . . . 1952 in BN 567.30 . . . . .   486.14
    Sp./Catalanisch 1965 in BN 567.31 . . . . .   486.15

Future of Pacifism

1944 (Jan.) in "American Scholar", vol. 13, p. 7-13   487.00

Cooperate with Soviet Russia

1944 (Feb. 5) in "The New Leader", vol. 27, p. 8   488.00

Western Hegemony in Post-War Asia

1944 (Feb. 26) in "The New Leader", vol. 27, p. 7   489.00

Victors and Vanquished

1944 (Mar. 18) in "The New Leader", vol. 27, p. 9
    21st Anniversary Number 490.00

Progressive Education

1944 (Apr. 22) in "New Statesman and Nation",
    vol. 27, p. 274 . . . .   491.00

Can Americans and Britains Be Friends?

1944 (June 3) in "The Saturday Evening Post",
    vol. 216, p. 14-15, 57-59 . . . . 492.00

Education in International Understanding

1944 (June) in "Tomorrow", vol. III, p. 19-21 . 493.00

Four Power Alliance: Step to Peace

1944 (Aug. 12) in "The New Leader", vol. 27, p. 9 494.00

My Mental Development

1944 in P. A. Schilpp (ed.): "The Philosophy of
    Bertrand Russell", p. 1-17.
    Evanston, Chicago: Northwestern University. 495.01
    1951 La Salle, Ill.: Open Court 495.02
    1961 in "The Basic Writings of B. Russell":
        I/2 (BN 659) 495.03
    1971 La Salle, Ill.: Open Court 495.04

Reply to Criticism

B. R.'s Rejoinder to his expositors and critics.

1944 in P. A. Schilpp (ed.): "The Philosophy of
    Bertrand Russell", 681-741.
    Evanston, Chicago: Northwestern University. 496.01
    1951 La Salle, Ill.: Open Court 496.02
    1971 " " , " : "   " 496.03
    T r a n s l a t i o n s
    Deutsch:
        Auszüge u. d. T.
        "Über den Gegenstand der Physik"
        "Über die Verbindlichkeit
        ethischer Urteile"
        1971 in BN 696 . . . . 496.04

The Value of Free Thought:
How to Become a Truth-Seeker
and Break the Chains of Mental Slavery

1944 (Aug.) in "The American Freeman",
    Girard, Kansas: Haldeman-Julius Publ. p.1-4 497.01
    1944 Girard, Kansas: Haldeman-Julius Publ.
    (Big Blue Book) 497.02
    1957 in "Understanding History" (BN 624) . 497.03
    1972 in "Atheism" (BN 700) 497.04
    T r a n s l a t i o n s
    Persisch . . . . . . 1963 in BN 624.02 . . . . . 497.05

American and British Nationalism

1945 (Jan.) in "Horizon" (British). 498.00

How to Avoid the Atomic War

1945 (Oct.) in "Common Sense", vol. 14, p. 3-5 . 499.00

Food Parcels Still Needed

1945 (Nov. 3) Letter on editorial page
in "New York Times",signed also by the Bishop
of Chichester and Victor Collancz 500.00

Conversations With Bertrand Russell

Conversations with Romain Rolland, Mahatma Gandhi,
Bertrand Russell, Rabindranath Tagore,
Sri Aurobindo by Dilip Kumar Roy.
Introduction by S. Radhakrishnan.

1945 in "Among the Great",
Bombay: N. M. Tripathi. XX, 330 pp. 501.00

Speech on Atomic Weapons and Atomic Warfare

1945 (Nov. 28) Official Record (Protokoll),
House of Lords (Oberhaus), vol. 138, no. 30.   502.01
1961 in "Has Man a Future?" (Excerpt from
2: "The Atom Bomb") BN 661. . . . . .   502.02

    T r a n s l a t i o n s
    Deutsch:
      "Rede über Atomwaffen und atomare Kriegs-
      führung" im Oberhaus am 28. Nov. 1945.
      Auszug aus II: "Die Atembombe"
      1963 in BN 661.14 . . . .   502.03
      1972 in BN 703/V:12 . . . .   502.04

Logical Positivism

1945 in "Polemic", no. 1, p. 6-13   503.01
    1956 in "Logic and Knowledge" (BN 616) . .   503.02

    T r a n s l a t i o n s
    Italienisch ... 1961 in BN 616.08 . . . . .   503.03
    Portugiesisch . 1974 in BN 616.09 . . . . .   503.04
    Spanisch . . . . . . 1966 in BN 616.10 . . . . .   503.05

A HISTORY OF WESTERN PHILOSOPHY:
Its connection with Political and Social Circumstances from the Earliest Times to the Present Day.

1945 New York: Simon & Schuster. XXIII, 895 pp. .   504.01
1946 London: Allen & Unwin. 916 pp. 504.02
1946 Toronto: Nelson 504.03
    C o n t e n t s
    B o o k   O n e :
      Ancient Philosophy.
    Part I: The Pre-Socratics.
      I. The Rise of Greek Civilization. II.
      The Milesian School. III. Pythagoras.
      IV. Heraclitus. V. Parmenides. VI. Em-
      pedocles. VII. Athens in Relation to Cul-
      ture. VIII. Anaxagoras. IX. The Atomists.
      X. Protagoras.

XXIII. Byron. XXIV. Schopenhauer. XXV.
Nietzsche. XXVI. The Utilitarians. XXVII.
Karl Marx. XXVIII. Bergson. XXIX. William James. XXX. John Dewey. XXXI. The
Philosophy of Logical Analysis.

C o m m e n t a r y
Even in his desperate position, pressed for
money and isolated in a foreign country.(America), Russell's spirit remained unbroken ...
for a book, which he proceeded to make out
of his Barnes Foundation lectures. This book,
a masterpiece to emerge under such turbulent
and unhappy circumstances, was published as
"A History of Western Philosophy", with the
subtitle "and its connection with political
and social circumstances". The book was the
first of its kind ever written by a philosopher who was himself in the first rank; it
was also one of the very rare attempts to
write a comprehensive history based on a conscientious reading or re-reading at first hand
of the philosophers discussed. A book of such
massive proportions was bound to contain a
few slips. In view of the subtitle, one might
have expected his "History of Western Philosophy" to be centred on the relation between the
views of philosophers and the times in which
they lived. In fact, though he had many illuminating comments about philosophers and
their times, he did not really write the book
he set out to write; and with some philosophers he forgot to discuss their surrounding
circumstances altogether. What Russell did
succeed in writing was the most illuminating
history of philosophy which has ever been
brought together in one volume. And its weaknesses as a book increased its virtues as a
history: his summaries and criticisms of different philosophies would have suffered if,
in the interests of artistic unity, he had
tried to turn them into neat exemplifications
of some theory. His critics used to argue that
analysis means falsification; it is more often
the case that unify means falsification.
A l b e r t   E i n s t e i n
on B. Russell's "History of Western Philosophy": "... makes delightful reading. I am not
sure if the delightful freshness and originality of this great thinker or his empathic
sensitivity for distant ages and foreign mentalities deserve a greater share of admiration. I consider it fortunate that our generation which is so dry and, at the same time,

so brutal possesses such a wise, honest, brave
and yet humorous man. It is an educational
work in the highest sense which rises above
the disputes of parties and opinions."

K o m m e n t a r
Selbst in seiner verzweifelten Lage, in Geld-
bedrängnis und einsam in einem fremden Lande
(Amerika), blieb Russell's Geist ungebrochen
... für ein Buch, das er aus seinen Vorlesungen
an der Barnes Foundation aufzubauen begann.
Dieses Buch, ein Meisterwerk, wenn man be-
denkt, unter welchen verwirrenden und un-
glücklichen Verhältnissen es entstanden ist,
wurde als "A History of Western Philosophy"
veröffentlicht und trug den Untertitel: "und
ihre Zusammenhänge mit politischen und sozialen Verhältnissen". Das Buch war das erste
seiner Art, das je von einem Philosophen geschrieben wurde, der selbst zu den bedeutendsten seines Faches gehörte. Es war außerdem
einer der sehr seltenen Versuche, eine umfas-
sende Geschichte zu schreiben, die auf ge-
wissenhaftem Lesen und Wiederlesen der besprochenen Philosophen im Original basierte.
Ein Buch von so gewaltigen Ausmaßen mußte einige Ungenauigkeiten enthalten. Im Hinblick
auf den Untertitel hätte man erwarten sollen,
daß als roter Faden der "History of Western
Philosophy" die Beziehung zwischen den Auffassungen der Philosophen und den Zeiten, in
denen sie lebten, herausgearbeitet wäre. Aber
obwohl er viele sehr aufschlußreiche Ausführungen über Philosophen und ihre Zeiten brachte, schrieb er doch tatsächlich nicht eigentlich das Buch, das er hatte schreiben wollen;
bei einigen Philosophen vergaß er sogar ganz
und gar, etwas über ihre Lebensumstände zu
sagen. Gelungen aber war es Russell, die er-
leuchtendste Geschichte der Philosophie zu
schreiben, die je in einem Band zusammenge-
bracht wurde. Seine Schwächen als Buch er-
höhten seine Vorzüge als Geschichte: seine
Zusammenfassungen und kritischen Betrachtun-
gen verschiedener Philosophien würden gelit-
ten haben, wenn er im Interesse künstlerischer
Einheit versucht hätte, sie als saubere Bei-
spiele irgendeiner Theorie zurechtzurücken.
Seine Kritiker pflegten gegen ihn anzuführen,
daß Analyse Fälschung bedeutet; häufiger ist
aber der Fall, daß Vereinheitlichung Fälschung bedeutet.
A l b e r t   E i n s t e i n
über Russell's "History of Western Philosophy": ".... ist eine köstliche Lektüre. Ich

weiß nicht, ob man die köstliche Frische und
Originalität oder die Sensitivität der Ein-
fühlung in ferne Zeiten und fremde Mentalität
bei diesem großen Denker mehr bewundern soll.
Ich betrachte es als ein Glück, daß unsere
so trockene und zugleich brutale Generation
einen so weisen, ehrlichen, tapferen und dabei humorvollen Mann aufzuweisen hat. Es ist
ein im höchsten Sinne pädagogisches Werk, das
über dem Streite der Parteien und Meinungen
steht."

R e p r i n t s
1957 New York: Simon & Schuster 504.04
1959 "   "   : "   " " 504.05
1961 London: Allen & Unwin 504.06
1961 Excerpts:
     "Aristotle's Logic" (Book One: XXII)
     "Saint Thomas Aquinas" (Book Two: XIII)
     "Currents of Thought in the Nineteenth
     Century" (Book Three: XXI)
     "John Dewey" (Book Three: XXX)
     "The Philosophy
     of Logical Analysis" (Book Three: XXXI)
     in "The Basic Writings of B. Russell":
     VII/33, 34, 35, IV/25, VII/36 (BN 659) 504.07
1963 London: Allen & Unwin 504.08
1965 "   : "   " " 504.09
1968 "   : "   " " 504.10
1974 "   : "   " "   (Paperback) . 504.11
1975 "   : "   " "   "   . 504.12

T r a n s l a t i o n s
Arabisch:
     "Tārīkh al-falsafah al-gharbīyah"
     Tr.: Zāki Najīb Mahmūd
     1967/68 Kairo: Lajnat al-Ta'līf wa al-
             Tarjamah wa al'Nashr. 2 vols. . . 504.13
Chinesisch:
     "Hsi Fang Chê Hsioh Shih"
     Tr.: Chung Chien-huang
     1955 Taipeh: China Culture Publ.
          Foundation. 5 vols. 504.14
     "Xifang zhexue shi ji qi yu gong gudai
     dao xiandai de zhengzhi shehui
     qingkuang de lianxi"
     1963 Peking, vol. I, 1976 vol. II . .   504.15
Dänisch:
     "Venstens filosofi"
     Tr.: Elsa Gress
     1953 Kopenhagen: Munksgaard 504.16
     1962 "   : "   2 vols. .   504.17

Deutsch:
"Philosophie des Abendlandes.
Ihr Zusammenhang mit der
politischen und sozialen Entwicklung."
Ü.: ElisabethFischer-Wernecke und
    Ruth Gillischewski
1950 Zürich: Europa Verlag. 690 S. . .   504.18
1951 "   : " 504.19
1954 "   : " 504.20
1975 "   : "   . 886 S. . .   504.21
I n h a l t
Einführung
E r s t e s   B u c h :
    Die Philosophie der Antike.
Teil I: Die Vorsokratiker.
    1. Der Aufschwung der griechischen
Kultur.   2. Die milesische Schule.
3. Pythagoras. 4. Heraklit. 5. Par-
menides. 6. Empedokles. 7. Die kulturgeschichtliche Bedeutung Athens.
8. Anaxagoras.   9. Die Atomisten.
10. Protagoras.
Teil II: Sokrates, Plato, Aristoteles.
11. Sokrates. 12. Spartas Einfluß.
13. Der Ursprung der platonischen An-
schauungen. 14. Platos Utopie. 15.
Die Ideenlehre. 16. Platos Unsterb-
lichkeitslehre.   17. Platos Kosmo-
gonie. 18. Wahrnehmung und Erkenntnis bei Plato. 19. Die Metaphysik
des Aristoteles. 20. Die Ethik des
Aristoteles.   21. Die Politik des
Aristoteles. 22. Die Logik des Aristoteles. 23. Die Physik des Aristoteles. 24. Die Anfänge der griechischen Mathematik und Astronomie.
Teil III: Antike Philosophie
    nach Aristoteles.
25. Die hellenistische Welt. 26. Zyniker und Skeptiker.   27. Die Epi-
kureer. 28. Der Stoizismus. 29. Die
kulturgeschichtliche Bedeutung des
römischen Reiches. 30. Plotin.
Z w e i t e s   B u c h :
    Die katholische Philosophie.
    Einführung.
Teil I: Die Kirchenväter.
    1. Die religiöse Entwicklung der Ju-
den. 2. Das Christentum in den ersten vier Jahrhunderten. 3. Drei
Doctores Ecclesiae. 4. Die Philosophie und Theologie Augustins. 5. Das
5. und 6. Jahrhundert. 6. Benedikt
und Gregor der Große.

Teil II: Die Scholastiker.
  7. Das Papsttum im dunklen Zeitalter.
  8. Johannes Scotus. 9. Die Kirchen-
  reform im 11.Jahrhundert. 10. Moham-
  medanische Kultur und Philosophie.
  11. Das 12. Jahrhundert. 12. Das
  13. Jahrhundert. 13. Thomas von
  Aquino. 14. Franziskanische Scholastiker. 15. Der Verfall des Papst-
  tums.
D r i t t e s   B u c h :
  Die Philosophie der Neuzeit.
Teil I: Von der Renaissance bis Hume.
  1. Allgemeine Charakteristik, 2. Die
  italienische Renaissance, 3. Mac-
  chiavell. 4. Erasmus und Morus. 5.
  Reformation und Gegenreformation. 6.
  Der Aufschwung der Naturwissenschaf-
  ten. 7. Francis Bacon. 8. Hobbes'
  Leviathan. 9. Descartes. 10. Spinoza. 11. Leibniz. 12. Der philosophische Liberalismus. 13. Lockes
  Erkenntnistheorie. 14. Lockes politische Philosophie. 15. Lockes Einfluß. 16. Berkely. 17. Hume.
Teil II: Von Rousseau bis zur Gegenwart.
  18. Die romantische Bewegung. 19.
  Rousseau. 20. Kant. 21. Geistige
  Strömungen im 19. Jahrhundert. 22.
  Hegel. 23. Byron. 24. Schopenhau-
  er. 25. Nietzsche. 26. Die Utili-
  tarier. 27. Karl Marx. 28. Bergson.
  29. William James. 30. John Dewey.
  31. Die Philosophie der logischen
  Analyse.
Finnisch:
  "Länsimaisen Filosofian Historia"
  Tr.: J. A. Hollo
  1948 Helsinki: Söderström 504.22
  1967 "   : "   . 2 vols. . . 504.23
Französisch:
  "Histoire de la philosophie occidentale"
  Tr.: Hélène Kern
  1952 Paris: Gallimard 504.24
  1957 "   : " 504.25
Griechisch:
  "Istoria tēs dytikēs filosofias"
  Tr.: Aim Hourmouzios
  1970/71 Athen: Arsenidēs 504.26
Italienisch:
  "Storia della filosofia occidentale"
  Tr.: Luca Pavolini
  1948 Mailand: Longanesi. 3 vols. . . . 504.27
  1966 "   : "   . 4 vols. . . . 504.28

Japanisch:
    "Seiyô tetsugakushi"
    Tr.: Saburo Ichii
    1954/55 Tokio: Misuzu shobô. 2 vols. . 504.29
    1959 Tokio: Misuzu shobô. 3 vols. . . . 504.30
    1969 "   : "   " . 1 vol. 504.31
    1970 "   : "   " . 3 vols. . . 504.32
Koreanisch:
    "Seo'yang'cheol'hag'sa"
    Tr.: Jeong Seog-hae
    1959 Seoul: Lee Yong-seob 504.33
    Tr.: Choe Min Hong
    1973 Seoul: Jibmundang. 2 vols. . . . 504.34
Niederländisch:
    "Geschiedenis der Westerse filosofie"
    Tr.: Rob. Limburg
    1948 's-Gravenhage: Servire 504.35
    1948 Brüssel: Standard-Boekhandel . . 504.36
    1955 's-Gravenhage: Servire 504.37
    1955 Brüssel: Standard-Boekhandel . . 504.38
    1975 Wassenaar: Servire 504.39
Persisch:
    "Tārīkh-e falsafeh-ye gharb"
    Tr.: Najaf Daryābandarī
    1961 Teheran 504.40
Portugiesisch:
    "História da filosofia ocidental"
    Tr.: Brenno Silveira
    1957 Sao Paulo: Ed. Nacional. 3 vols. 504.41
    Tr.: Francisco Lopes Vieira de Almeida
    1967 Lissabon: Horizonte 504.42
Russisch:
    "Istorija zapadnoj filosofii"
    1959 Moskau: Isd-vo inostr. lit. . . . 504.43
Schwedisch:
    "Västerlandets filosofi"
    Tr.: Alf Ahlberg
    1957 Stockholm: Natur och Kultur. 3rd e. 504.44
Serbokroatisch:
    "Istorija zapadne filozofije"
    Tr.: Dušanka Obradović
    1962 Belgrad: Kosmos 504.45
Spanisch:
    "Historia de la filosofia occidental"
    Tr.: J. Gómez de la Sena, Antonio Dorta
    1947 Buenos Aires: Espasa-Calpe. 2 vols. 504.46
    1971 Madrid: Espasa-Calpe 504.47
    1973 in BN 706 (Tr.: Juan Martin Ruiz-
        Werner y Juan Garcia-Puente) . . 504.48
Sp./Catalanisch:
    "Historia social de la filosofia"
    Tr.: Jordi Sole-Tura
    1967 Barcelona: Edicions 62. 2 vols. . 504.49

Türkisch:
"Bati felsefesi tarihi"
Tr.: Muammer Sencer
1970 Istanbul: Kitapcilik Ticaret
    Limited Sirketi. 2 vols. 504.50
1972 Ankara: Bilgi Yayinevi. 2 vols. . 504.51

Should Russia Share in the Control of the Ruhr?

With Dr. Joad, Lord Vansittart and Prof. Cole.

1946 (Jan.) in "Free World", vol. 11, p. 55-56 . 505.00

The Problem of Universals

1946 in "Polemic", no. 2, p. 21-35 . . . . 506.00

The Atomic Bomb and the Prevention of War

1946 (July/Aug.) in "Polemic", no. 4, p. 15-22 . 507.00

Foreword to James Feibleman's
"An Introduction to Pierce's Philosophy"

1946 New York, London: Harper & Brothers,
    p. XV-XVI 508.01
1960 London: Allen & Unwin 508.02

Ideas That Have Helped Mankind

1946 Girard, Kansas: Haldeman-Julius Company . . 509.01
1950 in"Unpopular Essays": IX (BN 567) . . 509.02
1972 in "Atheism"   (BN 700) 509.03

    T r a n s l a t i o n s
    Chinesisch .... 1970 in BN 567.13 . . . . . 509.04
    Dänisch .... 1950 in BN 567.14 . . . . . 509.05
    Deutsch .... 1951 in BN 567.15 . . . . . 509.06
    Finnisch ...... 1950 in BN 567.20 . . . . . 509.07
    Italienisch ... 1963 in BN 567.23 . . . . . 509.08
    Japanisch ..... 1958 in BN 567.24 . . . . . 509.09
    Koreanisch .... 1958 in BN 567.25 . . . . . 509.10
    Portugiesisch . 1954 in BN 567.27 . . . . . 509.11
    Schwedisch .... 1950 in BN 567.28 . . . . . 509.12
    Spanisch ...... 1952 in BN 567.30 . . . . . 509.13
    Sp./Catalanisch 1965 in BN 567.31 . . . . . 509.14

Ideas That Have Harmed Mankind

1946 Girard, Kansas: Haldeman-Julius Company . . 510.01
1950 in "Unpopular Essays": X (BN 567) . . 510.02
1972 in "Atheism" (BN 700) 510.03

    T r a n s l a t i o n
    Chinesisch .... 1970 in BN 567.13 . . . . . 510.04
    Dänisch .... 1950 in BN 567.14 . . . . . 510.05
    Deutsch .... 1951 in BN 567.15 . . . . . 510.06
    Finnisch ...... 1950 in BN 567.20 . . . . . 510.07
    Italienisch ... 1963 in BN 567.23 . . . . . 510.08

```
Japanisch ..... 1958 in BN 567.24 . . . . .    510.09
Koreanisch .... 1958 in BN 567.25 . . . . .    510.10
Portugiesisch . 1954 in BN 567.27 . . . . .    510.11
Schwedisch .... 1950 in BN 567.28 . . . . .    510.12
Spanisch ...... 1952 in BN 567.30 . . . . .    510.13
Sp./Catalanisch 1965 in BN 567.31 . . . . .    510.14
```

Is Materialism Bankrupt?
<u>Mind and Matter In Modern Science.</u>

```
1946 in "Rationalist Annual" . . . . . . . . . .    511.01
1946 Girard, Kansas: Haldeman-Julius Co.  .    511.02
```

<u>Physics and Experience</u>

```
1946 London: Cambridge University Press.  26 pp.   512.01
     New York: Macmillan . . . . . . . . . . . .   512.02
     Toronto:  "     . . .. . . . . . . . . .      512.03
     1948 in "Human Knowledge": III:IV (BN 536)    512.04
     1965 in "On the Philosophy of Science"(BN 672)
```

```
     T r a n s l a t i o n s
     Deutsch:
       "Physik u. Erfahrung" in "Zeitschrift f.
       Philosophische Forschung" (1:445-464)
       1947 Schlehdorf am Kochelsee;Meisenheim   512.05
       1948 Zürich: Rascher & Cie . . . . . .     512.06
       1952  "     :  "        "  "   . . . . . . 512.07
     Deutsch ....... 1952 in BN 536.13 . . . . .  512.08
     Italienisch ... 1951 in BN 536.15 . . . . .  512.09
     Japanisch ..... 1960 in BN 536.17 . . . . .  512.10
     Niederländisch  1950 in BN 536.18 . . . . .  512.11
     Portugiesisch . 1958 in BN 536.19 . . . . .  512.12
     Russisch ...... 1957 in BN 536.20 . . . . .  512.13
     Serbokroatisch  1961 in BN 536.21 . . . . .  512.14
     Spanisch ...... 1950 in BN 536.22 . . . . .  512.15
     Türkisch ...... 1964 in BN 536.26 . . . . .  512.16
```

Preface to William K. Clifford's
<u>"The Common Sense of the Exact Sciences"</u>

```
1946 New York: Knopf . . . . . . . . . . . . . .    513.01
     1946 Toronto: Ryerson . . . . . . . . . . .     513.02
     1947 London: Sigma, p. V-X . . . . . . . .      513.03
     1955 New York: DoverPublications . . . . .      513.04
     1956 London: Mayflower Publ. Vision Press .     513.05
```

<u>Logical Analysis</u>

```
1947 (Apr. 3) in "Listener",
     Publication of the BBC, p. 500 . . . . . .     514.01
     1956 under the title
       "A Plea for Clear Thinking"
       in "Portraits from Memory" (BN 617)  .       514.02
     T r a n s l a t i o n s
     Chinesisch .... 1967 in BN 617.07 . . . . .    514.03
     Finnisch ...... 1957 in BN 617.09 . . . . .    514.04
```

```
Italienisch ...  1958 in BN 617.10 . . . . .  514.05
Japanisch .....  1959 in BN 617.12 . . . . .  514.06
Portugiesisch .  1958 in BN 617.14 . . . . .  514.07
Schwedisch ....  1956 in BN 617.15 . . . . .  514.08
Spanisch ......  1960 in BN 617.16 . . . . .  514.09
```

Still Time for Good Sense

1947 (Nov.) in " '47 The Magazine of the Year"
vol. 1. p. 56-63 . . . . 515.00

Philosophy and Politics

Fourth Annual Lecture of the National Book League
at Friends House, London, Oct. 23, 1946.

```
1947 London: Cambridge University Press,
     National Book League. 29 pp. . . . . . . . .  516.01
1950 in "Unpopular Essays": I (BN 567) . .  516.02
1960 as a terminal Essay
     in "Authority and the Individual"
     Boston: Beacon Press (BN 554.03) . . .  516.03
1961 in "The Basic Writings of B. Russell":
     XI/50 (BN 569) . . . . . . . . . . . .  516.04
```

```
     T r a n s l a t i o n s
     Arabisch:
        "Muthul 'ulyā siyaiyyal"
        Tr.: Fu'ād Kāmil 'abd-al 'azīz
        1962 Kairo: al-Dār al-Qawmiyyah  . . .  516.05
     Chinesisch ....  1970 in BN 567.13 . . . . .  516.06
     Dänisch .......  1950 in BN 567.14 . . . . .  516.07
     Deutsch .......  1951 in BN 567.15 . . . . .  516.08
     Finnisch ......  1950 in BN 567.20 . . . . .  516.09
     Italienisch ...  1963 in BN 567.23 . . . . .  516.10
     Japanisch .....  1958 in BN 567.24 . . . . .  516.11
     Koreanisch ....  1958 in BN 567.25 . . . . .  516.12
     Portugiesisch .  1954 in BN 567.27 . . . . .  516.13
     Schwedisch ....  1950 in BN 567.28 . . . . .  516.14
     Spanisch ......  1952 in BN 567.30 . . . . .  516.15
     Sp./Catalanisch 1965 in BN 567.31 . . . . .  516.16
```

The Faith of a Rationalist:
No Supernatural Reasons Needed to Make Men Kind

```
1947 (May 29) in "Listener", vol. 37, p. 826,828  517.01
1947 London: Barrie & Rockliff. 9 pp. . . . .  517.02
1947 Girard, Kansas: Haldeman-Julius Co. .  517.03
1972 in "Atheism" (BN 700) . . . . . . . .  517.04
```

Teaching Philosophy

1947 in "Univ. Quarterly",
vol. 1, p. 367 . . . . 518.00

Miscellany/Sammelband in Norwegisch
under the title
"Frihet og fornuft"

1947 Oslo: E. G. Mortensen. 188 pp. 519.00
    C o n t e n t s
    En fri manns tro
        (A Free Man's Worship .... 1903/036)
    Friheten og samfunnet
        (Freedom in Society .... 1926/299)
    Tankens frihet og statens
    propaganda
        (Free Thoght and Official
        Propaganda .... 1922/236)
    Scylla og Charybdis
        (Scylla and Charybdis .... 1935/401)
    Fare for kommende troskriger?
        (The Danger of Creed Wars .... 1928/331)
    Verdien af sunn skepsis
        (The Value of Scepticism ..... 1928/327)
    Opprøret mot fornuften
        (Can Man Be Rational? .... 1923/262)
    Vitenskapens plase i en fri
    oppdragelse
        (The Place of Science
        in a Liberal Education .... 1913/120)
    Den nye puritanismen
        (The Recrudescence of Puritanism 1923/259)
    Till lediggangens lov
        (In Praise of Idleness .... 1932/376)

Ideas and Beliefs of the Victorians

1948 (Feb. 5) in "Listener", vol. 39, p. 211-212   520.00

How to Achieve World Government

1948 (Mar. 6) in "The New Leader", vol. 31, p. 8   521.00

Whitehead and Principia Mathematica

1948 (Apr.) in "Mind", vol. 57, p. 137-138 . . .   522.00

Rewards of Philosophy

1948 (Mar. 18) in "Listener", vol. 39, p. 459 .   523.00

Toleration

1948 in "Listener", vol. 39, p. 695-697 . . . .   524.00

John Stuart Mill

1948 (May 13) in "Listener", vol. 39, p. 785 . .   525.00

Science as a Product of Western Europe

1948 (May 27) in "Listener", vol. 39, p. 865-866   526.00

Boredom or Doom in a Scientific World
1948 (Aug.) in "United Nations World",
vol. 2, p. 14-16 . . . . 527.00

The Way of the World
1948 (Sept.) in "World Review",
vol. 26, no. 9, p. 11-15 . . . . 528.00

World Government - By Force or Consent?
1948 (Sept. 4) in "The New Leader", vol. 31, p. 8 529.00

Why Fanaticism Brings Defeat
1948 in "Listener", vol. 40, p. 452-453 . . . . 530.01
1950 (Apr.) in "Science Digest",.
vol. 27, p. 34-35 . . . . 530.02

Review of John Bowle's
"The Unity of European History"
1948 (Oct. 7) in "Listener", vol. 40, p. 537 . . 531.00

The Outlook for Mankind
1948 in "Horizon", vol. 17, p. 238-246 . . . . . 532.00

A Turning-Point in My Life
1948 in "The Saturday Book", vol. 8.
London: Hutchinson, p. 142-146 . . . . . . 533.00

Answers to Questions
A Symposium on the Problems of the Modern World
presenting the Answers of H. M. Baner, B. Croce,
John Dos Passos, Bertrand Russell and others.

1948 in "Last Chance: Eleven Questions That Will
Decide Our Destiny". Ed. by Clara Urquhart.
Boston, Massachusetts: Beacon Press,
p. 73, 82-83, 92, 103, 112, 123, 133, 142, 151,
160, 168. . . . . 534.00

The Existence of God
A Discussion between Russell and Father Coplestan
(See also: "Proofs of the Existence of God" in "The
Philosophy of Leibniz": XV, BN 19)

1948 BBC 3rd program 535.01
1948 (autumn/Herbst) in "Humanitas" 535.02
1964 in "The Existence of God", ed. John Hick
New York 535.03
T r a n s l a t i o n s
Deutsch:
"Die Existenz Gottes"
1963 in BN 625.12 . . . . 535.04

Norwegisch:
"En samtale om Guds eksistens"
Tr.: Finn Jor
1958 Oslo: Capelen. 39 pp. 535.05

HUMAN KNOWLEDGE: ITS SCOPE AND LIMITS

1948 London: Allen & Unwin. 538 pp. 536.01
New York: Simon & Schuster. XVI, 524 pp. . . 536.02
Toronto: Nelson 536.03
C o n t e n t s
Part I: The World of Science.
   I. Individual and Social Knowledge. II.
   The Universe of Astronomy. III. The World
   of Physics.   IV. Biological Evolution. V.
   The Physiology of Sensation and Volition.
   VI. The Science of Mind.
Part II: Language.
   I. The Uses of Language.   II. Ostensive
   Definition. III. Proper Names. IV. Ego-
   centric Particulars. V. Suspended Reac-
   tions: Knowledge and Belief.   VI. Sen-
   tences. VII. External Reference of Ideas
   and Beliefs.   VIII. Truth: Elementary
   Forms. IX. Logical Words and Falsehood.
   X. General Knowledge. XI. Fact, Belief,
   Truth, and Knowledge.
Part III: Science and Perception.
   I. Knowledge of Facts and Knowledge of
   Laws. II. Solipsism. III. Common-sense
   Inference.   IV. Physics and Experience.
   (1946/512). V. Time in Experience. VI.
   Space in Psychology. VII. Mind and Matter.
Part IV: Scientific Concepts.
   I. Interpretation. II. Minimum Vocabu-
   laries.   III. Structure. IV. Structure
   and Minimum Vocabularies. V. Time, Public
   and Private. VI. Space in Classical Phys-
   ics. VII. Space-Time. VIII. The Princi-
   ple of Individuation.   IX. Causal Laws.
   X. Space-Time and Causality.
Part V: Probability.
   I. Kinds of Probability. II. The Calculus
   of Probability. III. The Finite-Frequency
   Interpretation. IV. The Mises and Reichen-
   bach Frequency Theory. V. Keynes's Theory
   of Probability. VI. Degrees of Credi-
   bility. VII. Probability and Induction.
Part VI: Postulates of Scientific Inference.
   I. Kinds of Knowledge. II. The Role of In-
   duction.   III. The Postulate of Natural
   Kinds or of Limited Variety. IV. Knowledge
   Transcending Experience. V. Causal Lines.
   VI. Structure and Causal Laws. VII. Inter-
   action. VIII. Analogy. IX. Summary of
   Postulates. X. The Limits of Empiricism.

C o m m e n t a r y
The fullest statement of his philosophical
conclusions was given in Russell's "Human
Knowledge: Its Scope and Limits", when he
was 76. It is one of the most important of
Russell's books, and a landmark in the history of philosophy. In "Human Knowledge" and
the books which led up to it, as in his work
on mathematical philosophy and the Theory of
Descriptions, Russell performed the supreme
philosophical task of questioning assumptions
previously taken for granted. Inference: The
justification for dissection in philosophy
remains the same as in anatomy. It increases
knowledge, even if it does not explain everything; and it focuses attention on what it
leaves unexplained.

K o m m e n t a r
Das vollständigste Gesamtbild seiner philosophischen Ergebnisse gab Russell in"Human
Knowledge: Its Scope and Limits", als er 76
Jahre alt war. Es ist eins der bedeutendsten
von Russell's Büchern und ein Markstein in
der Geschichte der Philosophie. In "Human
Knowledge" und in den vorausgehenden Büchern
vollbrachte Russell ebenso wie in seinem Werk
über die mathematische Philosophie und in der
Theorie der Beschreibungen die höchste philosophische Leistung, früher als selbstverständlich geltende Annahmen in Frage zu stellen. Folgerung: Die Rechtfertigung des Sezie-
rens bleibt für die Philosophie die gleiche
wie für die Anatomie. Es vermehrt das Wissen,
auch wenn es nicht alles erklärt, und konzen-
triert die Aufmerksamkeit auf ungeklärte Fragen.

R e p r i n t s
1951 London: Allen & Unwin 536.04
1961 "   : "   " " 536.05
1961 Excerpt:
     "The Uses of Language" (II:I)
     in "The Basic Writings of B. Russell":
     III/11 (BN 659) 536.06
1962 New York: Simon & Schuster 536.07
1965 Excerpts:
     "Physics and Experience" (III:IV)
     "Interpretation" (IV:I)
     "Minimum Vocabularies" (IV:II)
     "Structure"(IV:III)
     "Time, Public and Private" (IV:V)
     "Space in Classical Physics" (IV:VI)
     "Space-Time" (IV:VII)
     "Space-Time and Causality" (IV:X)

in "On the Philosophy of Science"(BN 672)
(III:III in BN 672 = IV:V,VI in BN 536)   536.08
1967 New York: Simon & Schuster 536.09
1967 London: Allen & Unwin 536.10
1976 "   : Allen & Unwin 536.11
1976 New York: Simon & Schuster 536.12
T r a n s l a t i o n s
Deutsch:
   "Das menschliche Wissen"
   Tr.: Werner Bloch
   1952 Zürich, Genf, Darmstadt (Holle) .   536.13
      1958 Berlin: Darmstadt, Wien:
      Deutsche Buchgemeinschaft. 500 S.   536.14
   I n h a l t
   Teil I: Die Welt der Wissenschaft.
      I. Individuelle und allgemeine Er-
      kenntnis. II. Das Weltall der Astro-
      nomie. III. Die Welt der Physik.
      IV. Biologische Entwicklung. V. Die
      Physiologie der Empfindungen und
      Wollungen. VI. Die Wissenschaft vom
      Seelischen.
   Teil II: Die Sprache.
      I. Der Gebrauch der Sprache. II. Hin-
      weisdefinitionen. III. Eigennamen.
      IV. Egozentrische Partikel. V. Ver-
      zögerte Handlungen: Erkenntnis und
      Glaube. VI. Sätze. VII. Bezogenheit
      von Vorstellungen und Glauben. VIII.
      Wahrheit: Elementare Formen. IX. Lo-
      gische Wörter und Falschheit. X. All-
      gemeine Erkenntnis. XI. Tatsache,
      Glaube, Wahrheit und Erkenntnis.
   Teil III: Wissenschaft und Wahrnehmung.
      I. Erkenntnis von Tatsachen und Er-
      kenntnis von Gesetzen. II. Solip-
      sismus. III. Wahrscheinlichkeits-
      schlüsse des gesunden Menschenver-
      standes. IV. Physik und Erfahrung.
      V. Die Zeit in der Erfahrung. VI.
      Der Raum in der Psychologie. VII.
      Seele und Körper.
   Teil IV: Wissenschaftliche Begriffe.
      I. Deutung. II. Mindestwortschätze.
      III. Struktur. IV. Struktur und Min-
      destwortschätze. V. Die öffentliche
      und die private Zeit. VI. Der Raum
      in der klassischen Physik. VII. Die
      Raum-Zeit-Welt. VIII. Das Individu-
      ationsprinzip. IX. Kausalgesetze.
      X. Die Raum-Zeit-Welt und die Kausa-
      lität.

Teil V: Wahrscheinlichkeit.
   I. Arten der Wahrscheinlichkeit. II.
Die mathematische Wahrscheinlichkeit.
III. Die Deutung auf Grund endlicher
Häufigkeit.   IV. Die Häufigkeits-
theorie von Mises und Reichenbach.
V. Keynes' Wahrscheinlichkeitstheo-
rie. VI. Grade der Glaubwürdigkeit.
VII. Wahrscheinlichkeit und Induk-
tion.
Teil VI: Postulate
des wissenschaftlichen Schließens.
   I. Formen der Erkenntnis. II. Die
Rolle der Induktion. III. Das Postu-
lat der natürlichen Arten oder der be-
grenzten Manigfaltigkeit. IV.Wissen,
das die Erfahrung überschreitet. V.
Kausallinien. VI. Struktur und Kau-
salgesetze. VII. Wechselwirkung.
VIII. Analogie.   IX. Systematische
Aufstellung von Postulaten. X. Die
Grenzen des Empirismus.

Italienisch:
   "La conoscenza umana"
   Tr.: Camillo Pellizzi.
   1951 Mailand: Longanesi 536.15
   1963 "   : " 536.16
Japanisch:
   "Ningen no shishiki"
   Tr.: Yasuo Shizume
   1960 Tokio: Misuzu Shohe. 2 vols. . . 536.17
Niederländisch:
   "De menselijke Kennis"
   1950 Amsterdam, Antwerpen:
        De Nederlandsche Boekhandel . . . 536.18
Portugiesisch:
   "O conhecimento humano"
   Tr.: Leonidas Contijo de Carvalho,
   revista por Carlos Prôsperi
   1958 Sao Paulo: Ed. Nacional 536.19
Russisch:
   "Čelovečeskoe poznanie"
   Tr.: N. V. Vorob'er
   1957 Moskau: Izd. inostr. lit. 536.20
Serbokroatisch:
   "Ljudsko znanje"
   Tr.: Jovan Christič
   1961 Belgrad: Nolit 536.21
Spanisch:
   "El conocimiento humano"
   Tr.: Antonio Tovar
   1950 Madrid: Revista de Occidente . . 536.22
   1959 Madrid: Taurus 536.23
   1964 "   : " 536.24

Tschechisch:
    Excerpts:
    "Jazyk" (II:II-X)
    "Vědecké pojmy" (IV:I-III)
    1967 in BN 680: C/8:I-III 536.25
Türkisch:
    "Insanligen Geleceği"
    Tr.: Memduh Balban
    1964 Istanbul: Atac Kitabevi 536.26
    Tr.: Ismail Hakki Öğuz
    1965 Ankara: Ajans Türk Matbaasi . . . 536.27

Atomic Energy and the Problems of Europe

Adress given at the Westminster School, 20.Nov.1948

1949 (Jan.) in "Nineteenth Century and After",
    vol. 145, p. 39-43 . . . . 537.00

The Atom Bomb and the Problems of Europe

1949 (Feb. 12) in "The New Leader", vol. 32, p. 6 538.00

Einstein and the Theory of Relativity

1949 (Mar. 17) in "Listener", vol. 41, p.452-453 539.00

Unity of Western Culture

1949 (Apr.) in "World Review", no. 2, p. 5-8 . . 540.00

Reply to Inquiry: Should U. N. Meetings
Open With Prayer or Meditation?

1949 (Aug.) in "U. N. World", vol. 3, p. 13 . . . 541.00

Ten Years Since the War Began

1949 (Sept. 3) in "The New Leader", vol. 32, p. 6 542.00

On Russian Science

1949 (Sept. 7) in "The Evening Standard" (England) 543.00

A Guide For Living in the Atomic Age

1949 (Nov.) in "U. N. World", vol. 3, p. 33-36 . 544.00

Exceptional Man

1949 (Nov.) in "Atlantic Monthly",
    vol. 184, p. 52-56 . . . . 545.00

William of Occam

1949 (Dec. 1) in "Listener", vol. 42, p. 949-951 546.00

Americans are ...
"The Impact of America Upon European Culture."

1949 (Dec. 8) in "Listener" 547.01
    1950 (Feb.) in "Vogue, p. 164, 210, 211 . . . 547.02

The High Cost of Survival

1949 (Dec. 18) in "This Week"
(New York Herald Tribune), p. 5, 12. . . . 548.00

Values in the Atomic Age

The Sir Halley Stewart Lectures for 1948.

1949 London: Allen & Unwin, p. 81-104 . . . . . 549.00

Postulates of Scientific Inference

1949 in "Proceedings of the Tenth International
Congress of Philosophy (11.8. - 18.8.1948)".
Amsterdam: North-Holland Publishing, p. 33-41   550.00

L'individu et l'état moderne

1949 in "Bulletin de la Société Française de Philosophie"(43/80-100).
Paris 551.00

Sammanhalling och Styrelse
(Social Harmony and Government)

1949 in "Samtid och Frantid" (2/78-84) 552.00

Am I an Atheist or an Agnostic?

A plea for tolerance in the face of new dogmas,
and a variety of short articles by E. A. McDonald
and others.(see also BN 596).

1949 Girard, Kansas: Haldeman-Julius Publ. . . .   553.01
     1972 in "Atheism" (BN 700) 553.02

AUTHORITY AND THE INDIVIDUAL

1949 London: Allen & Unwin. 123 pp. 554.01
     New York: Simon & Schuster 554.02
     C o n t e n t s
     I. Social Cohesion and Human Nature. II. So-
     cial Cohesion and Government. III. The Role
     of Individuality. IV. The Conflict of Tech-
     nique and Human Nature. V. Control and Ini-
     tiative: Their Respective Spheres. VI. In-
     dividual and Social Ethics.
     Printed in "The Listener":
     I/30.12.1948, II/6.1.1949, III/13.1.1949,
     IV/20.1.1949, V/27.1.1949, IV / 3.2.1949.

     C o m m e n t a r y
     During all this period Russell's eminence in
     British life was rising steadily. In the win-
     ter of 1948 he had been invited to give the
     first BBC "Reith Lectures", on "Authority and
     the Individual". In these he supported the
     Labour Party's nationalization of key indus-
     tries, but on the whole was more concerned to

defend the individual against authority. He
said that the powers of a World Government
should be limited to those essential for e-
liminating war; that national Governments
should leave as many powers as possible to
regional authorities;and so on down the scale.
He praised experiments in industrial democracy like the Lewis Partnership.

K o m m e n t a r
Während dieser ganzen Zeit stieg Russell's
Bedeutung für das englische Leben immer weiter. Im Winter 1948 war er aufgefordert worden, die ersten BBC "Reith Lectures" zu halten, über "Authority and the Individual".
Darin unterstützte er die von der Labour Party
verlangte Nationalisierung der Schlüsselin-
dustrien, aber im ganzen lag ihm doch mehr
daran, das Individuum gegen die Autorität zu
verteidigen. Er erklärte, die Machtbefugnisse
einer Weltregierung sollten auf solche beschränkt werden, die für die Ausschaltung eines Krieges wesentlich sind; nationale Regie-
rungen sollten den regionalen Autoritäten so-
viel wie möglich Macht überlassen, und so müßte es sich weiter nach unten fortsetzen. Er
äußerte sich anerkennend über demokratische
Versuche in der Industrie wie die Lewis Partnership (Teilhaberschaft).

R e p r i n t s
1960 Boston: Beacon Press
     (with a terminal Essay: "Philosophy and
     Politics" - BN 516.03) 554.03
1961 Excerpt:
     "Individual and Social Ethics" (VI)
     in "The Basic Writings of B. Russell":
     IX/42 (BN 659) 554.04
1965 London: Allen & Unwin 554.05
1968 New York: AMS Press 554.06
1977 London: Allen & Unwin (Paperback) .. 554.07
T r a n s l a t i o n s
Arabisch:
     "Al Sultan Wal Fard"
     Tr.: Mohammad Bakīr Khalīl
     1958 Kairo: Dār El Ma'āref 554.08
Dänisch:
     "Samfundets magt og individets frihet"
     Tr.: Carl Gad
     1949 Kopenhagen: Schultz 554.09
Deutsch:
     "Macht und Persönlichkeit"
     Ü.: Karl König, Angelika Hübscher-Knote
     1949 Stuttgart: Kohlhammer 554.10
     1951 Zürich: Europa Verlag 554.11
     1967 Stuttgart: Kohlhammer 554.12

I n h a l t
I. Gemeinschaft und Individualität. II.
Gemeinschaft und Führung. III. Die Rolle
der Persönlichkeit. IV. Der Mensch und
die Technik. V. Zwang und Freiheit.
VI. Individualethik und Sozialethik.
Finnisch:
  "Yksilön vapaus ja sen rajoitukset"
  Tr.: J. A. Hollo
  1949 Helsinki, Porvoo: W. Söderström . 554.13
Hebräisch:
  "ha-Samkhut veha-yahid"
  1967 (?) Tel Aviv. 89 pp. 554.14
Ind./Hindi:
  "Satta aura vyakti"
  Tr.: Mohan Lal
  1952 Delhi: Ranjit printers and publ. 554.15
Ind./Marathi:
  "Sasansamstha ani vyakti"
  Tr.: Suma Devedatta Dabhol-kar
  1967 Poona: Samaj prabodhan samstha . . 554.16
Indonesisch:
  "Kekuasan dan individu"
  Tr.: Kamaruzzaman
  1953 Djakarta: Jajasan Pembanguanan . . 554.17
Italienisch:
  "Autorità ed individuo"
  Tr.: C. Pellizzi
  1949 Mailand: Longanesi 554.18
  1970 "   : " 554.19
Japanisch:
  Excerpts:
  1959 in BN 646 . . . . 554.20
Koreanisch:
  "Gweon'wi wa gae'in"
  Tr.: Lee Geug-chan
  1958 Seoul: Sin'yang'sa 554.21
Niederländisch:
  "Gezag en enkeling"
  1949 Antwerpen: De Nederl. Boekhandel. 554.22
Norwegisch:
  "Staten og individet"
  Tr.: Leiv Frodesen
  1950 Oslo: Mortensen 554.23
Portugiesisch:
  "A autoridade e o individuo"
  Tr.: Agenor Soarres Santos
  1956 Sao Paulo: Ed. Nacional 554.24
Schwedisch:
  "Samhället och individuen"
  Tr.: Andres Byttner
  1949 Stockholm: Natur och Kultur . . . 554.25

1949/1950

Spanisch:
"Autoridade es individuo"
Tr.: Margareta Villegas de Robles . .
1950 Mexico, Buenos Aires:
Fondo de Cultura económica . . . 554.26
1961 Mexico, Buenos Aires: " . . . 554.27
1967 "   , "   "   : "   . . . 554.28

Is a Third World War Inevitable?

1950 (Mar.) in "U. N. Word", vol. IV, p. 11-13 . 555.00

The Science To Save Us From Science

1950 (Mar. 19) in"New York Times Magazine",p.9,31-33 556.00

Came the Revolution

1950 (Mar. 25) in "Saturday Review of Literature",
vol. 33, p. 9, 10, 36, 37 . . . . 557.00

Can We Afford To Keep Open Minds?

1950 (June 11) in "New York Times Magazine",
p. 9, 37, 39 . . . . 558.00

If We Are to Survive This Dark Time.

1950 (Sept. 3) in "New York Times Magazine",
p. 5, 7, 18 . . . . 559.01
1961 in "The Basic Writings of B. Russell":
XVII/72 (BN 659) 559.02

Little Wisdom in the World Today

1950 (Oct. 5) in "Glasgow Herald", p. 4 . . . . 560.00

The Kind of Fear We Sorely Need

1950 (Oct. 29) in "New York Times Magazine",
p. 9, 52-55 . . . . 561.00

Comments on J. Z. Young's
"Doubt and Certainty in Science"

1950 (Dec. 24) in London "Observer", p. 4 . . . 562.00

To Replace Our Fears With Hope

1950 (Dec. 31) in "New York Times Magazine",
p. 5, 23, 25 . . . . 563.00

Autobiographical Remarks

1950 in Milton Schulman "How to Be a Celebrity"
London: Reinhardt & Evans, p. 189-199 . . . 564.00

Le principe d'individuation

1950 in "Revue de Métaphysique et de Morale",
Paris, (55/1-15) 565.00

Politically Important Desires

1950 (Dec. 10) The Nobel Prize Acceptance Speech
Stockholm 566.01
  1951 in "Les Prix Nobel en 1950"
     Stockholm: Nobelfoundation 566.02
  1954 in "Human Society in Ethics and Politics"
     Part Two: II (BN 609) 566.03
  1961 in "The Basic Writings of B. Russell":
     XI/51 (BN 659) 566.04
  1969 in "Nobellectures. Literature 1901-1967"
     Amsterdam: Elsevier, p. 452-463 . . . 566.05

T r a n s l a t i o n s
Deutsch . . . . 1956 in BN 609.09 . . . . . 566.06
Finnisch . . . . . . 1955 in BN 609.11 . . . . . 566.07
Koreanisch . . . . 1958 in BN 609.12 . . . . . 566.08
Persisch . . . . . . 1970 in BN 609.13 . . . . . 566.09
Portugiesisch . 1956 in BN 609.15 . . . . . 566.10
Schwedisch . . . . 1957 in BN 609.16 . . . . . 566.11
Spanisch . . . . . . 1957 in BN 609.17 . . . . . 566.12

UNPOPULAR ESSAYS

1950 London: Allen & Unwin 567.01
  New York: Simon & Schuster 567.02
C o n t e n t s
    I. Philosophy and Politics ... (1947/516)
   II. Philosophy for Laymen ..... (1950/567)
  III. The Future of Mankind ..... (1950/567)
  IV. Philosophy's Ulterior Motives (1937/418)
    V. The Superior Virtue
       of the Oppressed .... (1937/422)
  VI. On Being Modern Minded .... (1950/567)
 VII. An Outline
       of Intellectual Rubbish ... (1943/486)
VIII. The Function of a Teacher . (1940/452)
  IX. Ideas
       That Have Helped Mankind .. (1946/509)
   X. Ideas
       That Have Harmed Mankind .. (1946/510)
  XI. Eminent Men I have Known .. (1950/567)
 XII. Obituari (Auto-Obituari) .. (1936/406)

R e p r i n t s
1951 (Feb.) Excerpt from
    "Eminent Men I Have Known" (XI)
    under the title
    "Gladstone and Lenin"
    in "Atlantic Monthly", vol. 187, p. 66-68 567.03
  1951 (Mar.) Excerpt from
     "The Future of Mankind" (III)
     under the title
     "Future of Man"
     in "Atlantic Monthly", vol. 187, p. 48-51 567.04

```
1951 New York: Simon & Schuster . . . . . .   567.05
1958 London: Allen & Unwin . . . . . . . .   567.06
1959 "    : "     " "     . . . . . . . .   567.07
1961 Excerpts:
     "Philosophy and Politics" (I)
     "An Outline
     of Intellectual Rubbish" (VII)
     "The Function of a Teacher" (VIII)
     in "The Basic Writings of B. Russell":
     XI/50, II/7, X/48 (BN 659) . . . . . .   567.08
1966 New York: Simon & Schuster . . . . . .   567.09
1968 London: Allen & Unwin . . . . . . . .   567.10
1969 New York: Simon & Schuster . . . . . .   567.11
1976 London: Allen & Unwin . . . . . . . .   567.12
```

T r a n s l a t i o n s
Chinesisch:
```
     "Lo Su Tsa Wên Chi"
     Tr.: Ts'ai Shên Chang
     1970 Taipeh: Youth Book Store . . . .   567.13
```
Dänisch:
```
     "Unpopulære Essays"
     1950 Kopenhagen: Gyldendal . . . . . .   567.14
```
Deutsch:
```
     "Unpopuläre Betrachtungen"
     Ü.: Dr. Ernst Doblhofer
     1951 Zürich: Europa Verlag. 188 S. . .   567.15
     1973 "    : "       "      . . . . .   567.16
```
I n h a l t
```
     (1) Philosophie und Politik
     (2) Philosophie für Laien
     (3) Der Weg zum Weltstaat
     (4) Die tieferen Beweggründe der Phi-
         losophie
     (5) Die höhere Tugend der Unterdrückten
     (6) Auf der Höhe der Zeit
     (7) Zur Genealogie des Unsinns
     (8) Die Aufgaben des Lehrers
     (9) Ideen,
         die der Menschheit genützt haben
     (10) Ideen,
         die der Menschheit geschadet haben
     (11) Berühmte Männer, die ich kannte
     (12) Nachruf (Selbst-Nachruf)
     1961 Auszug (Englisch)
         Frankfurt: Diesterweg. 48 S.  . .   567.17
         1971: 5. Auflage
     1974 Auszug:
         "Die Aufgaben des Lehrers" (8)
         in BN 707/II:7 . . . . . . . . .   567.18
     1975 in BN710/I . . . . . . . . . . .   567.19
```
Finnisch:
```
     "Filosofiaa jokaimiehelle ..."
     1950 Helsinki, Porvoo: W. Söderström .  567.20
     1967 "       ,  "   : "  " (3rd. ed.)  567.21
     1969 "          . "   : "  " (4th. ed.)  567.22
```

Italienisch:
      "Saggi impopulari"
      Tr.: Aldo Visalberghi
      1963 Florenz: La Nuova Italia 567.23
Japanisch:
      "Jinrui no shôrai"
      Tr.: Hideyo Yamada, Saburô Ichii
      1958 Tokio: Risô-sha 567.24
Koreanisch:
      "In'ryu eui jang'rae"
      Tr.: Yang Byeong-taeg
      1958 Seoul: Min'jung'seo'gwan 567.25
      "Jisigsango"
      Tr.: Yang Byeong-taeg, Jeong Bong Hwa
      1970 Seoul: Daeyang-Seojeog 567.26
Portugiesisch:
      "Ensaios impopulares"
      Tr.: Breno Silveira
      1954 Sao Paulo: Ed. Nacional 567.27
Schwedisch:
      "Filosofi för lekmän och andra essayer"
      Tr.: Anders Byttner
      1950 Stockholm: Natur och Kultur . . . 567.28
      1965 "   : "   "   "   . . . 567.29
Spanisch:
      "Ensayos impopulares"
      Tr.: Floreal Mazia
      1952 Mexiko: Hermes 567.30
Sp./Catalanisch:
      "Assaigs impopulars"
      Tr.: August Gil
      1965 Barcelona: Ediciones 62 . . . . . 567.31

George Bernard Shaw

1951 (Jan.) in "VirginiaQuarterly",vol.27, p. 1-7   568.01
     1956 in "Portraits from Memory" (BN 617)   568.02

     T r a n s l a t i o n s
     Chinesisch .... 1967 in BN 617.07 . . . . . 568.03
     Finnisch ...... 1957 in BN 617.09 . . . . . 568.04
     Italienisch ... 1958 in BN 617.10 . . . . . 568.05
     Japanisch ..... 1959 in BN 617.12 . . . . . 568.06
     Portugiesisch . 1958 in BN 617.14 . . . . . 568.07
     Schwedisch .... 1956 in BN 617.15 . . . . . 568.08
     Spanisch ...... 1960 in BN 617.16 . . . . . 568.09

To Face Danger Without Hysteria

1951 (Jan. 21) in "New York Times Magazine",
     p. 7, 42, 44, 45 . . . . 569.01
     1951 in "Worth Reading"
         The New York Times Company, p. 21-24 . 569.02

What's Wrong With Americans

1951 (Apr. 24) in "Look", vol. 15, p. 34-35 . . 570.00

Note nécrologique

1951 in "Mind", vol. 60, p. 297-298 . . . . . . 571.01
    1951 under the title
    "La valeur de l'individualité humaine"
    in "Synthese, 6 / n. 63 / 359-363
    Amsterdam 571.02
    (L. Wittgenstein: 26.4.1889-29.4.1951;
    see also BN 237)

No Funk, No Frivolity, No Fanaticism.

1951 (May 6) in "New York Times Magazine",
    p. 7, 22, 23 . . . . 572.00

Living in an Atomic Age

1951 (May 4) in "Radio Times",
    vol. 111, no. 1434, p. 5 . . . . 573.00

China and History

1951 (Aug. 4) in "Saturday Review of Literature",
    vol. 34, p. 39 . . . . 574.00

Are Human Beings Necessary?"

1951 (Sept. 15) in "Everybody's Weekly", p. 13 . 575.00

The Best Answer to Fanaticism - Liberalism

1951 (Dec. 16) in "New York Times Magazine" . . 576.01
    With "A Liberal Decalogue" (10 commandments)
    1969 in "Autobiography III", p.60 f. (BN 682) 576.02
    1972 in "The Collected Stories of B.R."(BN 701) 576.03
    1975 in Brian Carr (ed.): "Bertrand
    Russell. An Introduction." p. 65 (BN 709) 576.04

My Faith in the Future

1951 in "John o'London's Weekly", vol. 60, p. 706 577.00

John Stuart Mill: "On Liberty"

1951 in "Invitation to Learning",
    vol. 1, p. 356-363 . . . . 578.00

The Political and Cultural Influence

1951 in "The Impact of America On European Culture",
    adapted from the "Third Programme" of the BBC.
    Boston: The Beacon Press, p. 3-19 . . . . 579.00

Nature and Origin of Scientific Method

1951 in "The Western Tradition",
    London: Vox Mundi Books 580.01
    Boston: The Beacon Press, p. 23-28 . . . . 580.02
    British Broadcasting Talks.

Scepticism and Tolerance

1951 in "The Western Tradition",
London: Vox Mundi Books 581.01
Boston: The Beacon Press, p. 100-104 . . . 581.02
British Broadcasting Talks.

NEW HOPES FOR A CHANGING WORLD

1951 London: Allen & Unwin. 218 pp. 582.01
New York: Simon & Schuster. 218 pp. 582.02
C o n t e n t s
Part I: Man and Nature.
I. Current Perplexities. II. Three Kinds
of Conflict. III. Mastery Over Physical
Nature. IV. The Limits of Human Power.
V. Population.
Part II: Man and Man.
VI. Social Units. VII. The Size of Social
Units. VIII. The Rule of Force. IX. Law.
X. Conflicts of Manners of Life. XI. World
Government. XII. Racial Antagonism. XIII.
Creeds and Ideologies. XIV. Economic
Co-operation and Competition. XV. The
Next Half-Century.
Part III: Man and Himself.
XVI. Ideas Which Have Become Obsolete.
XVII. Fear. XVIII. Fortitude. XIX. Life
Without Fear. XX. The Happy Man (Not i-
dentical with "The Happy Man" in BN 363/
XVII). XXI. The Happy World.

C o m m e n t a r y
I suspected that I had too much emphasized,
hitherto, the darker possibilities threat-
ening mankind and that it was time to write
a book in which the happier issues of current
disputes were brought into relief. I called
this book "New Hopes for a Changing World"
and deliberately, wherever there were two possibilities, I emphasized that it might be
the happier one which would be realized.
..... I began to feel that "New Hopes for a
Changing World" needed fresh and deeper examination and I attempted to make this in my
book "Human Society in Ethics and Politics"
(1954/609) (From Bernhard Russell's "Autobiography III").

K o m m e n t a r
"Ich argwöhnte, bislang allzusehr jene dunklen Möglichkeiten betont zu haben, die die
Menschheit bedrohten, und ich meinte, nun-
mehr wäre ein Buch an der Zeit, in dem weniger deprimierende Themen gängiger Ausein-
andersetzungen im Vordergrund stünden. Es

erhielt den Titel "New Hopes for a Changing
World", und jedesmal, wenn zwei Möglichkeiten zur Wahl standen, betonte ich darin nachdrücklich und mit Vorbedacht, es könnte etwa
die Realisierung des glücklicheren Weges be-
vorstehen. .... Allmählich hatte ich aber das
Gefühl, "New Hopes for a Changing World" be-
dürfe einer neuerlichen und tieferen Prüfung; dies versuchte ich mit meinem Buch "Human Society in Ethics and Politics"" (1954/
609) (Aus B. Russell's "Autobiographie III").

R e p r i n t s
1951 Excerpt:
    "Current Perplexities" (I)
    in "The Listener" (May 17) 582.03
1951 Excerpt:
    "The Limits of Human Power" (IV)
    in "The Listener" (June 7) 582.04
1956 London: Allen & Unwin 582.05
1960 " : " " " 582.06
1961 Excerpts:
    "Current Perplexities" (I)
    "World Government" (XI)
    "The Next Half-Century" (XV)
    "Life Without Fear" (XIX)
    in "The Basic Writings of B. Russell":
    XVII/74-77 (BN 659) 582.07
1968 New York: Minerva Press 582.08
1970 Excerpt from "The Happy Man" (XX)
    under the title
    "How to Grow Old"
    in "Bertrand Russell - 1872-1970"
    Nottingham: Russell Peace Foundation
    (The Spokesman) 582.09

T r a n s l a t i o n s
Arabisch:
    "Āmāl Jadīdah Fī'Ālam Mutaghayyir"
    Tr.: 'abd al-Karīm Aḥmad
    1962 Kairo: al-Dar al-Qawmiyyir" . . . 582.10
Chinesisch:
    "Shih Chiai Chih Hsin Hsi Wang"
    Tr.: Chang I
    1952 Taipeh: Cheng Chung Book 582.11
Dänisch:
    "Menneskeheden paa Skillevejen"
    1952 Kopenhagen: Berlingske Forlag . . 582.12
Deutsch:
    "Neue Hoffnung für unsere Welt"
    Ü.: Fischer-Wernecke
    1952 Darmstadt, Genf:
    Holle Verlag. 243 S. 582.13

Inhalt
Teil I: Der Mensch und die Natur
1. Allgemeine Gegenwartsprobleme. 2.
2. Dreierlei Konflikte. 3. Der Sieg
über die Natur. 4. Die Grenzen unserer Macht. 5. Das Bevölkerungs-
problem.
Teil II: Der Mensch u. seine Mitmenschen.
6. **Gesellschaftliche** Gruppen. 7. Um-
fang der gesellschaftlichen Gruppen.
8. Das Recht des Stärkeren. 9. Ge-
setz und Recht. 10. Konflikte durch
Lebensweise. 11. Weltregierung. 12.
Rassengegensätze. 13. Glaubensfra-
gen und Ideologien. 14. Zusammenarbeit und Konkurrenz im Wirtschafts-
leben. 15. Die nächsten 50 Jahre.
Teil III: Der Mensch und sein Ich.
16. Ideen, die heute überholt sind.
17. Angst. 18. Standhaftigkeit. 19.
Leben ohne Furcht. 20. Der glückliche Mensch. 21. Die glückliche
Welt.

Portugiesisch:
"A ultima oportunidade do homem"
Tr.: José Antóni Machado
1955 Lissabon: Guimaraes 582.22
1966   "   : " 582.23
Schwedisch:
"Mänskligheten vid skiljevägen
Tr.: Karl Hylander
1951 Stockholm: Natur och Kultur . . .   582.24
Spanisch:
"Nuevas esperanzas
para un mundo en transformación"
Tr.: Ramon Ulia
1953 Buenos Aires: Hermes 582.25
"Noves esperances
per a un mon que canvia"
Tr.: Ramón Folch i Camarasa
1968 Barcelona: Selecta 582.26

The Impact of Science on Society

Matchette Foundation Lectures at Columbia Univ.

1951 New York: Columbia University Press. 64 pp.   583.00
C o n t e n t s
I. Science and Tradition.   II. Effects of
Scientific Technique.   III. Science and
Values.

THE IMPACT OF SCIENCE ON SOCIETY

This book is based upon lectures originally given
at Ruskin College in Oxford, three of which were
subsequently repeated at Columbia University, New
York. The last chapter in this book was the Lloyd
Roberts Lecture given at the Royal society of
Medicine, London, on Nov. 29, 1949.

1952 London: Allen & Unwin. 140 pp. 584.01
C o n t e n t s
I. Science and Tradition.   II. General Effects of Scientific Technique.   III. Scientific Technique in an Oligarchy.   IV. Democracy and Scientific Technique.   V. Science
and War.   VI. Science and Values.   VII. Can
a Scientific Society be Stable?

C o m m e n t a r y
About "The Impact of Science on Society" the
following can be said: "During the last three
hundred years, science has proved to be an
enormously powerful revolutionary force.
Russell goes about to investigate the changes
caused by science and arrives at the conclusion that the transformation of human life
through science is still at its beginning.
Briefly and concisely he first discusses the

immediate intellectual effect - the disap-
pearance of traditional faith, then the consequences of technological perfection as applied in industry and in war. Finally, it
is because of the newly emerging philosophy
that a different conception of man's position
in the universe develops. (Publisher's note)

K o m m e n t a r
Über "The Impact of Science on Society"ist
folgendes zu sagen: "Während der letzten drei-
hundert Jahre hat sich die Wissenschaft als
eine ungeheuer mächtige revolutionäre Kraft
erwiesen. Russell untersucht nun die durch
die Wissenschaft hervorgerufenen Wandlungen
und stellt dabei die Behauptung auf, daß die
Umformung des menschlichen Lebens durch die
Wissenschaft erst in den Anfängen steckt.
Knapp und klar erörtert er zunächst die
unmittelbaren geistigen Auswirkungen: das
Schwinden traditionellen Glaubens, sodann die
Folgen der technischen Vervollkommnungen, wie
sie in der Industrie und im Kriege angewandt
wurden. Endlich ist es die sich neu bildende
Philosophie, die eine andere Auffassung vom
Standort des Menschen im Weltall entwickelt!"
(Verlagsmitteilung in BN 584.10)

R e p r i n t s
1953 New York: Simon & Schuster 584.02
1959 London: Allen & Unwin 584.03
1961 Excerpt:
      "Science and Values" (VI)
      in "The Basic Writings of B. Russell":
      XVI/69 (BN 659) 584.04
1968 New York: AMS Press 584.05
1968 London: Allen & Unwin 584.06
1976 "   : "   " " 584.07

T r a n s l a t i o n s
Arabisch:
      "Al-Mujtama' al-Basharī fil-Akhlāq
      wal-Siyāsah"
      Tr.: 'abd-al-Karīm Ahmad
      1959 Kairo:
            Maktabit al-Anglo al-Misrivvah . 584.08
Dänisch:
      "Fornuften ellerdøden"
      Tr.: Elsa Gress
      1953 Kopenhagen: Berlingske Forlag . . 584.09
Deutsch:
      "Wissenschaft wandelt das Leben"
      Ü.: Hanns von Krannhals
      1953 München: Paul List. List-Tb. 27 . 584.10

1952

Inhalt
I. Wissenschaft wandelt das Leben. II.
Hauptauswirkungen der wissenschaftlichen Technik. III. Die wissenschaftliche Technik in einer Oligarchie. IV.
Demokratie und wissenschaftliche Technik. V. Wissenschaft und Krieg. VI.
Wissenschaft und Werte. VII. Kann ein
wissenschaftliches Gemeinwesen stabil
sein?

Spanisch:
"El Impacto de la ciensia en la sociedad"
Tr.: J. N. Domingo, Juan Novella
1952 Madrid: Aguilar 584.23
1956 in BN 615 . . . . 584.24
1958 Madrid: Aguilar 584.25
1967 "   : "   5th ed. 584.26
Sp./Catalanisch:
"L'impacte de la ciencia en la societat"
Tr.: Eduard Carbonell
1970 Barcelona: Ediciones 62 . . . . . 584.27

The Corsican Adventures of Miss X

1952 in Magazine "Go" 585.01
1953 in "Satan in the Suburbs" (BN 599) . . 585.02
1961 in BN 599.03 . . . . 585.03
1972 in BN 701 . . . . 585.04

Translations
Dänisch . . . . 1953 in BN 599.05 . . . . . 585.05
Deutsch . . . . 1953 in BN 599.07 . . . . . 585.06
Französisch . . . 1965 in BN 599.09 . . . . . 585.07
Ind./Bengali . . 1962 in BN 599.10 . . . . . 585.08
Ind./ Oriya . . . 1958 in BN 599.11 . . . . . 585.09
Italienisch . . . 1953 in BN 599.12 . . . . . 585.10
Japanisch . . . . . 1954 in BN 599.13 . . . . . 585.11
Niederländisch 1955 in BN 599.14 . . . . . 585.12
Schwedisch . . . . 1953 in BN 599.15 . . . . . 585.13
Serbokroatisch 1964 in BN 599.16 . . . . . 585.14
Spanisch . . . . . . 1953 in BN 599.17 . . . . . 585.15
Türkisch . . . . . . 1965 in BN 599.19 . . . . . 585.16

Preface to Henri Poincaré's "Science and Method"

1952 New York: Dover Publications 586.00

Reason and Passion

1952 in "Listener", vol. 48, p. 495-496 . . . . 587.01
Translations
Italienisch:
1953 in "Rivista critica di Storia della
filosofia" (Mailand), 8/105-107 . . . 587.02

How Near is War?

1952 London: D. Ridgway. 39 pp. 588.00
(A Fleet Street Forum Publication)

The Next Eighty Years

1952 (May 18) in "Observers", p. 4 . . . . 589.00
(Russell's 80th birthday: 18.5.1922.
See also BN 590 und "Reflections on my 80th
Birthday" in BN 617)

My First Eighty Years
1952 (May 25) in "New York Post", Sec. 2, p. 10-11   590.00

Dictionary of Mind, Matter, and Morals.
More than 1000 definitions and opinions selected
from over 100 of B. Russell's books and papers.
Wörterbuch über Geist, Materie und Moral.
Mehr als 1000 Erklärungen und Meinungen aus über
100 Büchern und Aufsätzen B. Russell's.

1952 New York: Philosophical Library. 290 pp. . . 591.01
1965 New York: Citadel Press 591.02

What is Freedom?
1952 London: Batchworth Press. 32 pp. 592.01
1961 in "Fact and Fiction": II:I (BN 660) . 592.02
C o n t e n t s
   I. National Freedom / Freedom of the Group /
     Individual Freedom
  II. Political Freedom / Economic Freedom/
     Mental Freedom
III. Personal Liberty / Government and Liber-
     ty / Liberty and Ideas / Limits of To-
     lerance / Education for Freedom
 IV. The Future of Freedom

T r a n s l a t i o n s
Italienisch ... 1961 in BN 660.06 . . . . . 592.03
Japanisch ..... 1962 in BN 660.08 . . . . . 592.04
Portugiesisch . 1965 in BN 660.10 . . . . . 592.05
Schwedisch .... 1964 in BN 660.11 . . . . . 592.06

What is Democracy?
1953 London: Batchworth Press. 39 pp. 593.01
1961 in "Fact and Fiction": II:II (BN 660) . 593.02
C o n t e n t s
   I. Democracy / What it Means / How it Began /
     Representative Government / American
     Democracy / The Role of Police / The State
     and the Army
  II. Evils of Power / Democratic Freedom /
     Democracy and War
III. The Geographical Problem / Tolerance in
     Democracy / Democracy and Nationalism /
     The Teaching of History
 IV. Revolution / World Government / Excess
     of Government / Democracy and Liberty
  V. Dangerous Idolatry / Diminution of
     Liberty
 VI. Redressing Grievances - Democracy and
     the West

1953

```
Translations
Italienisch ... 1961 in BN 660.06 . . . . .   593.03
Japanisch ..... 1962 in BN 660.08 . . . . .   593.04
Portugiesisch . 1965 in BN 660.10 . . . . .   593.05
Schwedisch .... 1964 in BN 660.11 . . . . .   593.06
```

The Idea of Progress

1953 (Mar. 14) in Manchester "Guardian", p. 4 .   594.00

What Would Help Mankind Most?

1953 (Sept. 27) in "New York Times Magazine" . .   595.01
1961 in "The Basic Writings of B. Russell":
   XVII/73 (BN 659) 595.02

What is an Agnostik?

1953 (Nov. 3) in "Look" Magazine, (c) Cowles M.   596.01
1955 in "The Religion of America"
   New York: Simon & Schuster 596.02
1957 London: Heineman 596.03
1961 in "The Basic Writings of B. Russell":
   XV/62 (BN 659) 596.04
(see also BN 553)

The Cult of "Common Usage"

1953 in "British Journal for the Philosophy of
   Science", vol. 3, p. 103-107 . . . .   597.01
1956 in "Portraits from Memory" (BN 617) .   597.02
1961 in "The Basic Writings of B. Russell":
   III/12 (BN 659) 597.03

```
Translations
Chinesisch .... 1967 in BN 617.07 . . . . .   597.04
Finnisch ...... 1957 in BN 617.09 . . . . .   597.05
Italienisch ... 1958 in BN 617.10 . . . . .   597.06
Japanisch ..... 1959 in BN 617.12 . . . . .   597.07
Portugiesisch . 1958 in BN 617.14 . . . . .   597.08
Schwedisch .... 1956 in BN 617.15 . . . . .   597.09
Spanisch ...... 1960 in BN 617.16 . . . . .   597.10
```

The Good Citizen's Alphabet

1953 London: Gaberbocchus Press
   Illus. by Franciszka Themerson. 28 pp. . .   598.01
1958 New York: Philosophical Library . . .   598.02
1970 in BN 693 . . . .   598.03
1972 in "The Collected Stories of B.R."(BN 701)   598.04

```
Translations
Spanisch:
    "Diccionario del hombre contemporaneo"
    Tr.: Josefina M. Alinari
    1957 Buenos Aires: S. Rueda . . . . .   598.05
```

SATAN IN THE SUBURBS AND OTHER STORIES

1953 New York: Simon & Schuster. 148 pp. 599.01
London: John Lane / The Bodley Head 599.02

C o n t e n t s
Preface / Satan in the Suburbs or Horrors
Manufactured Here / The Corsican Ordeal of
Miss X (1952/585) / The Infra-redioscope /
The Guardians of Parnassus / Benefit of Clergy

C o m m e n t a r y
... Not content with all these activities he
turned to a completely new vocation, the
writing of fiction. He wanted to publish his
short stories under a pseudonym, building up
a new seperate reputation at the age of eighty;
but editors refused to take his stories without his name on them. Eventually "The Corsican
Adventures of Miss X" was published anonymously in the magazine "Go" (BN 585), with
a prize of £25 for anyone who could guess who
had written it. Nobody succeeded in doin so.
His stories appeared in book form as "Satan
in the Suburbs", and "Nightmares of Eminent
Persons" (BN 701). Angus Wilson, called it
"an exceedingly entertaining collection", in
which "the formal eighteenth-century syntax
and language add delightfully to the general
ironic mood" - reminiscent of Swift.

K o m m e n t a r
... Doch alle diese Tätigkeiten genügten ihm
noch nicht - er wandte sich einer völlig neuen
Berufung zu und fing an Erzählungen zu schreiben. Er wollte seine Kurzgeschichten unter
einem Pseudonym veröffentlichen und so im
Alter von achtzig Jahren einen neuen Ruf auf-
bauen. Die Herausgeber aber weigerten sich,
seine Geschichten ohne seinen Namen zu nehmen. Schließlich wurde "The Corsican Adventures of Miss X" in dem Magazin "Go" (BN 585)
anonym veröffentlicht; für jeden, der den
Verfasser erraten könnte, war ein Preis von
25 Pfund bestimmt. Niemand konnte ihn erraten. In Buchform erschienen seine Erzählungen als "Satan in the Surbs" und "Nightmares
of Eminent Persons" (BN 701). Angus Wilson
nannte die Erzählungen "eine überaus unter-
haltsame Sammlung", bei der die "Form von Syntax und Sprache des achtzehnten Jahrhunderts
in reizvoller Weise die allgemein ironische
Stimmung erhöht" - an Swift erinnernd.

R e p r i n t s
1961 Harmondsworth: Penguin 599.03
1972 in "The Collected Stories of B.R."(BN 701) 599.04

T r a n s l a t i o n s
Dänisch:
    "Fanden i forstæderne"
    Tr.: Michael Tejm
    1953 Kopenhagen: Westermann 599.05
    1964 "   : Vinten 599.06
Deutsch:
    "Satan in den Vorstädten"
    1953 Darmstadt, Genf: Holle. 599.07
    1954 Darmstadt: Verlag: Das goldene
         Vlies (Bürgers Tb. 32) 599.08
    I n h a l t
    Vorwort / Satan in den Vorstädten / Die
    Korsische Probe der Miss X / Das Infra-
    rotioskop / Die Hüter des Parnass / Das
    Vorrecht der Geistlichen
Französisch:
    "Satan dans les fauborgs"
    Tr.: Marcello Sibon
    1961 Paris: Mercure de France 599.09
Ind./Bengali:
    "Satavdir šaytan"
    Tr.: Ajit Krishna Basu
    1962 Kalkutta: Rupa 599.10
Ind. / Oriya:
    "Upanagarare sayatan"
    Tr.: Nagendrakumar Ray
    1958 Kattak: Prafulla Chandra Das . . 599.11
Italienisch:
    "Satana nei sobborghi"
    Tr.: Raffaela Lotteri
    1953 Mailand: Longanesi 599.12
Japanisch:
    "Tampenchû"
    Tr.: Tsutomu Uchiyama
    1954 Tokio: Chûô Kôron-sha 599.13
Niederländisch:
    "Satan in de buitenwijk"
    Tr.: Hans de Vries
    1955 's-Gravenhagen:
         Zuid Hollandsche U. M. 599.14
Schwedisch:
    "Satan i sovstaden"
    Tr.: Anders Byttner
    1953 Stockholm: Natur och Kultur . . . 599.15
Serbokroatisch:
    "Davo u predgradu i druge pripovetke"
    Tr.: Dušanka Brajović
    1964 Belgrad: Narodna Knjiga 599.16
Spanisch:
    "Satán en los suburbios"
    Tr.: Luis Conde Vélez
    1953 Barcelona: Caralt 599.17
    1956 in BN 615 . . . . 599.18

Türkisch:
"Varoluşçunun bunalimi"
Tr.: Türkan Arâz
1965 Istanbul: Ataç Kitabevi . . . . . ·599.19

Review of M. St. J. Packe's
"The Life of John Stuart Mill"

1954 (Apr. 4) in "Observer", London, p. 9 . . . 600.00

Review of A. J. Ayer's
"Philosophical Essays"

1954 (Aug. 8) in "Observer", London, p. 7 . . . 601.00

Can Religion Cure Our Troubles?

1954 (Nov. 9, 11) in "Dagens Nyheter", Stockholm 602.01
 1957 in "Why I Am Not a Christian and Other
   Essays" (BN 625) 602.02
 1961 in "The Basic Writings of B. Russell":
   XV/64 (BN 659) 602.03

 T r a n s l a t i o n s
 Dänisch . . . . 1966 in BN 625.11 . . . . . 602.04
 Deutsch . . . . 1963 in BN 625.12 . . . . . 602.05
 Italienisch . . . 1960 in BN 625.19 . . . . . 602.06
 Japanisch . . . . . 1959 in BN 625.21 . . . . . 602.07
 Koreanisch . . . . 1960 in BN 625.23 . . . . . 602.08
 Niederländisch 1966 in BN 625.26 . . . . . 602.09
 Persisch . . . . . . 1970 in BN 625.28 . . . . . 602.10
 Portugiesisch . 1960 in BN 625.30 . . . . . 602.11
 Schwedisch . . . . 1958 in BN 625.32 . . . . . 602.12
 Spanisch . . . . . . 1958 in BN 625.33 . . . . . 602.13
 Türkisch . . . . . . 1966 in BN 625.36 . . . . . 602.14

Review of L. Price's
"Dialogues of A. N. Whitehead"

1954 (Nov. 14) in London "Sunday Times", p. 6 . 603.00

Man's Peril from the Hydrogen Bomb

1954 (Dec. 30) in "Listener", vol. 52, p.1135-1136 604.00

Are the World's Troubles Due to Decay of Faith?

1954 in "Rationalist Annual", p. 7-13 . . . . . 605.00

Do Science and Religion Conflict?

1954 in "Journal British Astronomical Association"
  vol. 64, p. 94-96 . . . . 606.00

History as an Art

1954 Aldington, Kent: Hand and Flower Press. 23 pp. 607.01
 1956 in "Portraits from Memory" (BN 617) . 607.02
 1961 in "The Basic Writings of B. Russell":
   XIII/58 (BN 659) 607.03

```
T r a n s l a t i o n s
Chinesisch .... 1967 in BN 617.07 . . . . .   607.04
Finnisch ...... 1957 in BN 617.09 . . . . .   607.05
Italienisch ... 1958 in BN 617.10 . . . . .   607.06
Japanisch ..... 1959 in BN 617.12 . . . . .   607.07
Portugiesisch . 1958 in BN 617.14 . . . . .   607.08
Schwedisch .... 1956 in BN 617.15 . . . . .   607.09
Spanisch ...... 1960 in BN 617.16 . . . . .   607.10
```

NIGHTMARES OF EMINENT PERSONS AND OTHER STORIES

```
1954 London: John Lane / The Bodley Head. 150 pp.   608.01
     New York: Simon & Schuster. 177 pp. . . . .    608.02
     1960 London: Allen & Unwin . . . . . . . .     608.03
     1961 Excerpt:
          "The Metaphysician's Nigthmare"
          in "The Basic Writings of B. Russell":
          II/8 (BN 659) . . . . . . . . . . . .     608.04
     1972 In "the Collected Stories of B.R."(BN 701) 608.05
     C o n t e n t s
     Preface
     Nightmares of Eminent Persons
          The Queen of Sheba's Nightmare: Put Not Thy
            Trust in Princes
          Mr. Bowdler's Nightmare: Family Bliss
          The Psychoanalyst's Nightmare: Adjustment/
            a Fugue
          The Metaphysician's Nightmare: Retro Me
            Satanas
          The Existentialist's Nightmare: The A-
            chievement of Existence
          The Mathematician's Nightmare: The Vision
            of Professor Squarepunt
          Stalin's Nightmare: Amor Vincit Omnia
          Eisenhower's Nightmare: The McCarthy-
            Malenkov Pact
          Dean Acheson's Nightmare: The Swan-Song
            of Menelaus S. Bloggs
          Dr. Southport Vulpes's Nightmare: The Vic-
            tory of Mind Over Matter
     Zahatopolk
     Faith and Mountains

     T r a n s l a t i o n s
     Italienisch:
          "Incubi ed altre storie"
          Tr.: Lia Formigari
          1956 Florenz: Sansoni . . . . . . . .     608.06
```

HUMAN SOCIETY IN ETHICS AND POLITICS

```
1954 London: Allen & Unwin. 239 pp. . . . . . .     609.01
     1955 New York: Simon & Schuster. XXI, 227pp.   609.02
     1955 New York: New American Library.
          XVI, 200 pp. (Mentor book) . . . . . .    609.03
```

Contents
Preface. Introduction.
Part I: Ethics.
Part II: The Conflict of Passions.

Commentary
"I began to feel that 'New Hopes for a
Changing World' (1951/582) needed fresh and
deeper examination and I attempted to make
this in my book 'Human Society in Ethics and
Politics'" (Russell in "Autobiography III").
     Russell therefore laboured to find some ob-
jective foundation for ethical theory, de-
ciding that "Right desires will be those that
are capable of being compossible with as many
other desires as possible". The importance
of Russell's idea of "compossible desires"
was not so much pedantic as practical: he once
put it that "The wish to harmonize desires
is the chief motive of my political and social beliefs, from the nursery to the international state." At the end of his discussion
in "Human Society in Ethics and Politics"
Russell decided that he had merely found some
guiding principles for use in practice, not
objective knowledge. He said in a broadcast:
"Philosophers are fond of endless puzzles
about ultimate ethical values and the basis
of morals. My own belief is that so far as
politics and practical living are concerned
we can sweep aside all these puzzles, and use
common sense principles." Or, as he put it in
"Human Society in Ethics and Politics": "In
political arguments, it is seldom necessary
to appeal to ethical considerations,since
enlightened self-interest affords a suffi-
cient motive for action in accordance with
the general good."

1954

K o m m e n t a r
"Allmählich hatte ich das Gefühl, 'New
Hopes for a Changing World' (1951/582) be-
dürfe einer neuerlichen und tieferen Prüfung;
dies versuchte ich mit meinem Buch 'Human
Society in Ethics and Politics'". (Russell
in "Autobiographie III").
Russell bemühte sich darum, eine objektive
Grundlage für eine ethische Theorie zu finden. Er kam zu dem Schluß: "Rechtmäßige Wünsche werden solche sein, die mit einer möglichst großen Zahl anderer Wünsche 'compossible' (mit-möglich, vereinbar) sind."
Die Bedeutung der Russellschen Idee von den
"compossiblen Wünschen" war weniger theore-
tisch als praktisch. Er drückte es einmal so
aus: "Das Verlangen, Wünsche miteinander in
Einklang zu bringen, ist die Haupttriebkraft
meiner politischen und sozialen Überzeugungen
- von der Kinderstube bis zum internationalen Staat." Am Ende seiner Ausführungen in
"Human Society in Ethics and Politics" stellte
Russell fest, daß er nicht objektives Wissen
gefunden habe, sondern nur einige Leitsätze
für den praktischen Gebrauch. In einer Radio-
sendung sagte er: "Philosophen befassen sich
gern mit endlosem Rätselraten über letzte
ethische Werte und die Grundlagen der Moral.
Meine eigene Überzeugung ist, daß wir in Din-
gen der Politik und des praktischen Lebens
alle diese Rätsel über Bord werfen können,
um uns nur nach den Grundsätzen des gesunden
Menschenverstandes zu richten." Oder wie er
es in "Human Society in Ethics and Politics"
ausdrückte: "Bei politischen Debatten ist es
selten nötig, ethische Erwägungen heranzu-
ziehen; denn das erleuchtete Selbstinteresse
schafft im Zusammenwirken mit dem allgemeinen Guten eine ausreichende Grundlage für das
Handeln."

R e p r i n t s
1956 Excerpt:
     "Steps Towards a Stable Peace" (II:IX)
     in "Portraits from Memory" (BN 617) . 609.04
1961 Excerpt:
     "Politically Important Desires" (II:II)
     in "The Basic Writings of B. Russell":
     XI/51 (BN 659) 609.05
1962 New York: New American Library.
     XVI, 200 pp. (Mentor book) 609.06
1963 London: Allen & Unwin 609.07
1971 "   : "   " " 609.08

T r a n s l a t i o n s
Deutsch:
"Dennoch siegt die Vernunft"
Ü.: Ruth Gillischewski
1956 Bonn: Athenäum Verlag 609.09
"Moral und Politik"
1972 München: Nymphenburger Verlagshandlung (Nachdruck der deutschen
Erstausgabe von 1956, BN 609.09). 609.10
I n h a l t
Vorwort. Einführung.
Teil I: Ethik.
1. Ursprünge sittlicher Anschauun-
gen und Gefühle. 2. Sittenkodizes. 3.
Die Moral als Mittel. 4. Gut und
schlecht. 5. Partielle und allgemeine Wohlfahrt. 6. Die moralische
Verpflichtung. 7. Die Sünde. 8. Die
moralische Streitfrage. 9. Gibt es
ein sittliches Wissen? 10. Die sitt-
liche Autorität. 11. Erzeugung und
Verteilung. 12. Abergläubische Moral. 13. Moralische Sanktionen.
Teil II: Der Konflikt der Leidenschaften.
1. Von der Ethik zur Politik. 2. Politisch bedeutsame Wünsche. 3. Vor-
sorge und Fertigkeit. 4. Mythos und
Magie. 5. Kohäsion und Konkurrenz.
6. Die wissenschaftliche Technik und
die Zukunft. 7. Wird der religiöse
Glaube uns retten? 8. Eroberung?
9. Wege zu einem dauernden Frieden.
10. Auftakt oder Abgesang.
Finnisch:
"Etiikka ja politiikka"
Tr.: Kai Kaila
1955 Helsinki, Porvoo: W. Söderström . 609.11
Koreanisch:
"Yun'ri wa jeong'chi"
Tr.: Gim Tae-gil
1958 Seoul: Min'jung-seo'gwan 609.12
Persisch:
"Akhlāq o Siāsat dar Jāme'e"
Tr.: Mohammad-e Heydari
1970 Teheran: Vahid 609.13
1973 "   : " 609.14
Portugiesisch:
"A sociedade humana
na ética e na política"
Tr.: Osvaldo de Araujo Souza
1956 Sao Paulo: Ed. Nacional 609.15
Schwedisch:
"Moral och minnen"
Tr.: Anders Byttner
1957 Stockholm: Natur och Kultur . . . 609.16

Spanisch:
"Etica politica en la sociedad humana"
Tr.: Ramón Ulía
1957 Buenos Aires: Hermes 609.17

Promoting Virtuous Conduct

1955 (Feb. 20) in London "Observer", p. 6 . . . 610.00

My Debt to German Learning

1955 (Sept.) Unpublished manuscript in R. Archives
McMaster University, Hamilton/Ontario. 5 pp. 611.00

Science and Human Life

1955 in "What is Science?", ed. by J. R. Newman.
New York: Simon & Schuster, p. 6-17 . . . . 612.01
1961 in "The Basic Writings of B. Russell":
XVII/78 (BN 659) 612.02
1965 in "On the Philosophy of Science": VI:II
(BN 672) 612.03

Review of J. O. Urmson's
"Philosophical Analysis: Its Development Between
the Two World Wars"

1956 in "Hibbert Journal", vol. 54, p. 320-329 . 613.01
1959 in "My Philosophical Development":
Excerpt from "18. Some Replies to Criti —
cism" (BN 648) 613.02

    T r a n s l a t i o n s
    Arabisch . . . . . . 1959 in BN 648.07 . . . . . 613.03
    Deutsch:
        1958 in "Zeitschrift für Philosophische
            Forschung", 12/3-16.
            Schlehdorf am Kochelsee und
            Meisenheim am Glan. 613.04
    Deutsch . . . . 1973 in BN 648.08 . . . . . 613.05
    Französisch . . . 1961 in BN 648.09 . . . . . 613.06
    Italienisch:
        In "Rivista di filosofia", 48 / 243-256
        1957 Turin 613.07
    Italienisch . . . 1961 in BN 648.10 . . . . . 613.08
    Japanisch . . . . . 1959 in BN 648.11 . . . . . 613.09
    Polnisch . . . . . . 1971 in BN 648.12 . . . . . 613.10
    Portugiesisch . 1960 in BN 648.13 . . . . . 613.11
    Schwedisch . . . . 1960 in BN 648.14 . . . . . 613.12
    Spanisch . . . . . . 1960 in BN 648.15 . . . . . 613.13
    Sp./Catalanisch 1969 in BN 648.17 . . . . . 613.14
    Ungarisch . . . . . 1968 in BN 648.19 . . . . . 613.15

John Stuart Mill

Lecture on a master mind, read 19 Jan. 1955

1956 London: Oxford University Press.
From the Proceedings of the British Academy,
vol. 41, p. 43-59 . . . . 614.01
1956 in "Portraits from Memory" (BN 617) . 614.02

T r a n s l a t i o n s
Chinesisch .... 1967 in BN 617.07 . . . . . 614.03
Finnisch ...... 1957 in BN 617.09 . . . . . 614.04
Italienisch ... 1958 in BN 617.10 . . . . . 614.05
Japanisch ..... 1959 in BN 617.12 . . . . . 614.06
Portugiesisch . 1958 in BN 617.14 . . . . . 614.07
Schwedisch .... 1956 in BN 617.15 . . . . . 614.08
Spanisch ...... 1960 in BN 617.16 . . . . . 614.09

Miscellany/Sammelband in Spanisch
under the title
"Obras escogidas"

1956 Madrid: Aguilar. 1140 pp. 615.00
(Bibliotheca de Premios Nobel)
C o n t e n t s
Introducción a la Filosofia Mate-
mática (Introduction to Mathe-
matical Philosophy . . . . 1919/191)
Ensayos sin Optimismo (Sceptical
Essays . . . . 1928/331)
Elogio de la Ociosidad (In Praise
of Idleness . . . . 1935/401)
El Impacto de la Ciensia en la So-
ciedad (The Impact of Science
on Society . . . . 1952/584)
Satan en los Suburbios (Satan in
the Suburbs . . . . 1953/599)

LOGIC AND KNOWLEDGE

1956 London: Allen & Unwin. XI, 382 pp. 616.01
New York: Macmillan. XI, 382 pp. 616.02
C o n t e n t s
(1) The Logic of Relations .... (1901/027)
(2) On Denoting . . . . (1905/056)
(3) Mathematical Logic as Based
on The Theory of Types .... (1908/084)
(4) On the Relations of Univer-
sals and Particulars . . . . . . (1912/114)
(5) On the Nature of Acquaintance (1914/125)
(6) The Philosophy of Logical
Atomism . . . . (1918/178)
(7) On Propositions: What They
Are and How They Mean . . . . . (1919/179)
(8) Logical Atomism . . . . (1924/265)
(9) On Order in Time . . . . (1936/410)
(10) Logical Positivism . . . . (1945/503)

R e p r i n t s
1968 London: Allen & Unwin 616.03
1971 New York: Macmillan 616.04
T r a n s l a t i o n s
Deutsch:
    Auszüge:
    "On Denoting" (2)
    "Logical Atomism" (8)
    1971 in BN 696 . . . . 616.05
    "Mathematical Logic as Based on The The-
      ory of Types" (3)
    "On the Ralations of Universals and Par-
      ticulars" (4)
    "On the Nature of Acquaintance" (5)
    "The Philosophy of Logical Atomism" (6)
    1976 in BN 711 . . . . 616.06
Französisch:
    Excerpt:
    "De la dénotation" (On Denoting)
    in "L'Age de la Science", p. 171-185 . 616.07
Italienisch:
    "Logica e conscenza"
    Tr.: Luca Pavolini
    1961 Mailand: Longanesi 616.08
Portugiesisch:
    "Lógica e conhecimento"
    (With G. E. Moore's "Principios éticos")
    Tr.: Pablo Mariconda
    1974 Sao Paulo: Abril Cultural 616.09
Spanisch:
    Excerpts:
    "Sobre de la denotatión" (On Denoting)
    1962 in BN 665 . . . . 616.10
    "El atomismo logico" (Logical Atomism)
    Tr.: Sari Ali Jafella
    in "Revista de Filosofia", 15/16-78
    1964 La Plata 616.11
    "Ensayos sobre logica y conocimiento"
    Tr.: Javier Muguerza
    1966 Madrid: Taurus. 531 pp. 616.12
    Excerpt:
    "La filosofia del atomismo lógico"
    (The Philosophy of Logical Atomism)
    in "Concepción analitica de la filosofia"
    1974 Madrid: Alianza Editorial. IIvols.
    (vol. I, p. 139-211) 616.13
Tschechisch:
    Excerpts:
    "O označeni" (On Denoting)
    "Logický atomismus" (Logical Atomism)
    1967 in BN 680/ A:1, C:6 . . . . 616.14

PORTRAITS FROM MEMORY AND OTHER ESSAYS

1956 London: Allen & Unwin. 227 pp. 617.01
New York: Simon & Schuster. 246 pp. 617.02
C o n t e n t s
Adaptation: an Autobiographical Epitome
Six Autobiographical Essays:
  I. Why I Took to Philosophy
  II. Some Philosophical Contacts
  III. Experiences of a Pacifist in the First
    World War
  IV. From Logic to Politics
  V. Beliefs: Discarded and Retained
  VI. Hopes: Realized and Disappointed
How to Grow Old (see also BN 582.09)
Reflections on My Eightieth Birthday
    (see also BN 589 and 590)
Portraits from Memory:
  I. Some Cambridge Dons of the Nineties
  II. Some of My Contemporaries at Cambridge
  III. George Bernard Shaw (1951/568)
  IV. H. G. Wells
  V. Joseph Conrad
  VI. George Santayana
  VII. Alfred North Whitehead
  VIII. Sidney and Beatrice Webb
  IX. D. H. Lawrence
Lord John Russell
John Stuart Mill (1956/614)
Mind and Matter
The Cult of "Common Usage" (1953/597)
Knowledge and Wisdom
A Philosophy for Our Time
A Plea for Clear Thinking (1947/514)
History as an Art (1954/607)
How I Write
The Road to Happiness
Symptoms of Orwell's "1984"
Why I Am Not a Communist (1934/391)
Man's Peril
Steps Toward Peace

R e p r i n t s
1957 London: Allen & Unwin 617.03
1961 Excerpts:
    "Adaptation: An Autobiograph. Epitome"
    "Why I Took to Philosophy"
    "The Cult of 'Common Usage'"
    "History as an Art"
    "How I Write"
    "Man's Peril"
    in "The Basic Writings of B. Russell":
    I/3, I/4, III/12, XIII/58, II/5, XVII/80
    (BN 659) 617.04

1963 New York: Simon & Schuster 617.05
1969 Excerpt:
    "Reflections on My Eightieth Birthday"
    under the title
    "Postscript"
    in "Autobiography III" (BN 682) . . . 617.06
T r a n s l a t i o n s
Chinesisch:
    "Lo Shu Hui I Lu"
    Tr.: Ling Hêng Chê
    1967 Taipeh: Chih Wen Pub. Service . . 617.07
Deutsch:
    Auszug:
    "Reflections on My Eightieth Birthday"
    unter dem Titel
    "Postskriptum"
    1971 in "Autobiographie III" (BN 682.18) 617.08
Finnisch:
    "Muotokuvia muistista ja muita esseitä"
    Tr.: J. A. Hollo
    1957 Helsinki, Porvoo: W. Söderström . 617.09
Italienisch:
    "Ritratti a memoria"
    Tr.: Raffaela Pellizzi
    1958 Mailand: Longanesi 617.10
    1969 "   : " 617.11
Japanisch:
    "Jiden-Teki kaiso"
    Tr.: Hidekichi Nakamura
    1959 Tokio: Misuzu-shobo 617.12
    1970 "   : "   " 617.13
Portugiesisch:
    "Retratos de memória e outros ensaios"
    Tr.: Brenno Silveira
    1958 Sao Paulo: Ed. Nacional 617.14
Schwedisch:
    "Möte med minnen"
    Tr.: Anders Byttner
    1956 Stockholm: Natur och Kultur . . . 617.15
Spanisch:
    "Retratos de memoria y otros ensayos"
    Tr.: Manuel Suárez
    1960 Buenos Aires: Aguilar 617.16
    1976 Madrid: Alianza Editorial 617.17

The Great Mystery: Do Men Survive Death?

1957 (Jan. 13) London "Sunday Times", p. 10 . . 618.00
    (see also BN 414)

The Pursuit of Truth

1957 (Apr. 2) in "London Calling", no. 910/14 . 619.01
    1961 in "Fact and Fiction": I:VI (BN 660) . 619.02

```
T r a n s l a t i o n s
Italienisch ... 1961 in BN 660.06 . . . . . 619.03
Japanisch ..... 1962 in BN 660.08 . . . . . 619.04
Portugiesisch . 1963 in BN 660.10 . . . . . 619.05
Schwedisch .... 1964 in BN 660.11 . . . . . 619.06
```

Review of P. F. Strawson's
"On Refering"

```
1957 (July) in "Mind", vol. 66, p. 585-389  . .  620.01
     1959 in "My Philosophical Development":
          Excerpt from "18. Some Replies to Criti-
          cism" (BN 648)  . . . . . . . . . . .     620.02
     1973 in "Essays in Analysis": III:6 (BN 705)  620.03

     T r a n s l a t i o n s
     Deutsch ....... 1973 in BN 648.08 . . . . .    620.04
     Französisch ... 1961 in BN 648.09 . . . . .    620.05
     Italienisch ... 1961 in BN 648.10 . . . . .    620.06
     Japanisch ..... 1959 in BN 648.11 . . . . .    620.07
     Polnisch ...... 1971 in BN 648.12 . . . . .    620.08
     Portugiesisch . 1960 in BN 648.13 . . . . .    620.09
     Schwedisch .... 1960 in BN 648.14 . . . . .    620.10
     Spanisch ...... 1960 in BN 648.15 . . . . .    620.11
     Sp./Catalanisch 1969 in BN 648.17 . . . . .    620.12
     Ungarisch ..... 1968 in BN 648.19 . . . . .    620.13
```

Christian Ethics

```
1957 (Oct. 13) in London "Observer", p. 8  . . .  621.01
     (Oct. 20) in London "Observer", p. 15 . . .  621.02
```

Review of G. F. Warnock's
"Metaphysics in Logic"

```
1957 in "Journal of Philosophy", 54, p. 225 - 230  622.01
     1959 in "My Philosophical Development":
          Excerpt from "18. Some Replies ti Criti-
          cism" (BN 648) . . . . . . . . . . . .     622.02

     T r a n s l a t i o n s
     Deutsch ....... 1973 in BN 648.08 . . . . .    622.03
     Französisch ... 1961 in BN 648.09 . . . . .    622.04
     Italienisch ... 1961 in BN 648.10 . . . . .    622.05
     Japanisch ..... 1959 in BN 648.11 . . . . .    622.06
     Polnisch ...... 1971 in BN 648.12 . . . . .    622.07
     Portugiesisch . 1960 in BN 648.13 . . . . .    622.08
     Schwedisch .... 1960 in BN 648.14 . . . . .    622.09
     Spanisch ...... 1960 in BN 648.15 . . . . .    622.10
     Sp./Catalanisch 1969 in BN 648.17 . . . . .    622.11
     Ungarisch ..... 1968 in BN 648.19 . . . . .    622.12
```

Logic and Ontology

```
1957 in "The Journal of Philosophy"
     New York, 54/225-230 (see also BN 622.01) .  623.00
```

1957

Understanding History and Other Essays

1957 New York: Philosophical Library. 122 pp. . 624.01
C o n t e n t s
How to Read and Understand History (1943/485)
The Value of Free Thought (1944/497)
Mentalism versus Materialism:
The Meaning of Matter / The Nature of
"Maas" / Ups and Downs of the Atomic The-
ory / Quantum Theory / The Behavior of
Matter in Bulk / Physics Is Still Deter-
ministic / Psychology Also Has Changed /
Life As It Appears in Biology / What We
Mean by Habit / Habit Primarily Physical /
Physical Causes of Introspection / The
Physical and Mental Overlap / Definition
of "Physical" / The Relations Between Men-
tal and Physical Events / The Questions
of "Materialism"

T r a n s l a t i o n s
Persisch:
"Dark-e tārix"
Tr.: Yadollāh Tusi
1963 Teheran: Ebne Sinā 624.02

WHY I AM NOT A CHRISTIAN
AND OTHER ESSAYS ON RELIGION AND RELATED SUBJECTS

Edited with an Appendix
on the "Bertrand Russell Case" by Paul Edwards

1957 London: Allen & Unwin. XIII, 225 pp. 625.01
New York: Simon & Schuster. XVII, 266 pp. . 625.02
Don Mills (Ontario): Thomas Nelson. 208 pp. 625.03
C o n t e n t s
(1) Preface by Bertrand Russell
(2) Editor's Introduction
(3) Why I Am Not a Christian .. (1927/314)
(4) Has Religion Made Useful Contributions to Civilization? (1930/357)
(5) What I Believe .... (1925/293)
(6) Do We Survive Death? ...... (1936/414)
(7) Seems, Madam? Nay, It Is ... (1957/625)
(8) A Free Man's Worship ...... (1903/036)
(9) On Catholic
and Protestant Skeptics ... (1929/335)
(10) Life in the Middle Ages ... (1925/288)
(11) The Fate of Thomas Paine .. (1934/392)
(12) Nice People .... (1931/368)
(13) The New Generation .... (1930/356)
(14) Our Sexual Ethics .... (1936/404)
(15) Freedom and the Colleges .. (1940/450)
(16) Can
Religion Cure Our Troubles? (1954/602)
(17) Religion and Morals .... (1957/625)

(18) Appendix by Paul Edwards:
How Bertrand Russell Was Prevented from
Teaching at The College of the City of
New York (see also BN 449).

C o m m e n t a r y
to "What I Believe" (1925/293)
and "(18) Appendix by Paul Edwards: ..."
"What I Believe" was published as a little
book in 1925. In it, Russell wrote in the
preface, "I have tried to say what I think
of man's place in the universe, and of his
possibilities in the way of the achieving the
good life. ... In human affairs, we can see
that there are forces making for happiness,
and forces making for misery. We do not know
which will prevail, but to act wisely we must
be aware of both." In the New York court proceedings in 1940 "What I Believe" was one of
the books presented as evidence that Russell
was unfit to teach at City College. Ex-
tracts from it were also widely quoted in
the press, usually in such a way as to give
quite a false impression of Russell's views.

K o m m e n t a r
zu "Woran ich glaube" (in BN 625.12)
und "(18) Anhang von Paul Edwards: ..."
"What I Believe" wurde 1925 als ein kleines
Buch veröffentlicht. In seinem Vorwort dazu
schrieb Russell: "Ich habe versucht zu sagen, was ich von der Stellung des Menschen
im Universum und von seinen Möglichkeiten,
eine gutes Leben zu führen, denke. .... Wir
können sehen, daß es in menschlichen Angele-
genheiten Kräfte gibt, die Glück, und solche,
die Unglück hervorbringen. Wir wissen nicht,
welche sich durchsetzen werden, aber um weise
zu handeln, müssen wir uns beider bewußt
sein." In dem New Yorker Gerichtsverfahren
von 1940 war "What I Believe" eines von
den Büchern, die als Beweis dafür dienten,
daß Russell untauglich sei, am City College
zu lehren. Auszüge aus dem Buch wurden in
der Presse in einer Weise veröffentlicht,
daß ein ganz falscher Eindruck von Russell's
Ansichten entstand.

R e p r i n t s
1961 Excerpts:
    "Why I Am Not a Christian" (3)
    "What I Believe" (5)
    "Can Religion Cure Our Troubles?" (16)
    in "The Basic Writings of B. Russell":
    XV/63; IX/43; XV/64 (BN 659) 625.04
1963 New York: Simon & Schuster 625.05

1964 London: Allen & Unwin 625.06
1966 New York: Simon & Schuster 625.07
1967 London: Allen & Unwin 625.08
1967 Toronto: Nelson 625.09
1975 London: Allen & Unwin 625.10

T r a n s l a t i o n s
Dänisch:
"Derfor er jeg ikke kristen"
Tr.: Erik Brunn
1966 Kopenhagen: Bilmann & Eriksen . . 625.11
Deutsch:
"Warum ich kein Christ bin"
Ü.: Marion Friedel-Steipe
1963 München: Szczesny Verlag. 269 S. . 625.12
1967 " : " " 7. Aufl. 625.13
1968 Reinbek:Rowohlt. 262 S.
rororo-Taschenbuch 1019/20 . . . 625.14
1972 " " 6. Auflage . . 625.15
I n h a l t
(1) Einführung des Herausgebers der
englischen Ausgabe (Paul Edwards)
(2) Vorwort von Bertrand Russell
(3) Warum ich kein Christ bin
(4) Hat die Religion nützliche Beiträge
zur Zivilisation geleistet?
(5) Woran ich glaube.
(6) Gibt es ein Weiterleben nach dem
Tode?
(7) Es scheint so, meine Dame? Nein,
es ist so.
(8) Über katholische und protestanti-
sche Skeptiker
(9) Das Leben im Mittelalter
(10) Das Schicksal Thomas Paines
(11) Nette Leute
(12) Die neue Generation
(13) Sexualethik
(14) Die Lehrfreiheit
(15) Die Existenz Gottes, eine Diskussion zwischen B.Russell und Pater
F.C.Copleston. (1948/535.04)
(17) Religion und Moral
(18) Anhang von Paul Edwards:
"Wie Bertrand Russell daran gehin-
dert wurde, am City College von
New York zu lehren"
Französisch:
Excerpts:
"Pourquoi je ne suis pas chrétien"
(Why I Am Not a Christian - 3)
"Religion et civilisation"
(Has Religion Made Useful Contributions to civilization? - 4)
"Ce que je crois" (What I Believe - 5)

1957

in "Pourquoi je ne suis pas chrétien et
autres textes"
Tr.: Guy Le Clech
1960 Paris: Pauvert 625.16
1964 " : " 625.17
1972 " : " 625.18
Italienisch:
"Perché non sono cristiano"
Tr.: Buratti Cantarelli
1960 Mailand: Longanesi 625.19
1972 " : " 625.20
Japanisch:
"Shûkyô wa hitsuyô ka"
Tr.: Otake Masura
1959 Tokio: Kochi Shuppan-Sha 625.21
1968 " : Arechi Shuppansha, rev. ed. 625.22
Koreanisch:
"Jong'gyo neun pilyohan'ga"
Tr.: Lee Si-yag
1960 Seoul: Baegjochpansa 625.23
"Naneun woe gidog gyoini aninga"
Tr.: Mu-pyeong Yum
1963 Seoul: Heuimunchulpansa 625.24
"Naneun wae cheuriseuchani aninga"
Tr.: Yang Byeong Taeg, Jeong Boug Hwa
1970 Seoul: Daeyang-Seojeog 625.25
Niederländisch:
"Waarom ik geen christen ben. En andere
essays over religie en verwante onder-
werpen."
Tr.: Addy Kaiser
1966 Amsterdam: Mossault. 625.26
1976 " : Meulenhoff 625.27
Persisch:
"Cherā Masihi Nistam"
Tr.: S. A. S. Taheri
1970 Teheran: Daryā 625.28
Tr.: Abdol'ali-ye Dastgheib
1972 Teheran: Farhang 625.29
Portugiesisch:
"Porque não cristão e outros ensaios
sôbre religão e assuntos correlatos"
Tr.: Brenno Silveira
1960 Sao Paulo: Expsicao do livro . . 625.30
1965 " " : " " " . . 625.31
Schwedisch:
"Varför jag inte är kristen och andra
essäer om religion och besläktade ämnen"
Tr.: Andres Byttner
1958 Stockholm: Natur och Kultur . . . 625.32
Spanisch:
"Por que no soy cristiano ..."
Tr.: Josefina Martinez Alinari
1958 Mexiko, Buenos Aires: Hermes . . 625.33
1962 " , " " : " . . 625.34

Tschechisch:
> Excerpts under the title:
> "Proč nejsem křest'anem a jiné eseje"
> Tr.: František Kejdana
> 1961 Prag: Orbis. 110 pp. 625.35

Türkisch:
> "Neden hiristiyan değilim"
> Tr.: Ender Gürol
> 1966 Istanbul: Varlik Yayinevi 625.36
> 1972 " : " " 625.37

Open Letter to Eisenhover and Krushchev

1957 (Nov. 7) in "New Statesman" 626.01
1958 (Jan. 21) in "Look"-Magazine 626.02
1958 in BN 627 . . . . 626.03
1961 in "The Basic Writings of B. Russell":
    XVII/79 (BN 659) 626.04

> C o m m e n t a r y
> Krushchev replied personally to Russell,
> while foreign secretary John Foster Dulles
> answered in the place of President Eisenhover.
> The "New Statesman" of 2nd April, 1958 printed
> Russell's comment to both replies. The com-
> plete correspondence was later published in
> bookform (BN 627).

> K o m m e n t a r
> Chruschtschow antwortete Russell persönlich,
> während an Stelle des amerikanischen Präsi-
> denten Eisenhower Außenminister John Foster
> Dulles die Beantwortung übernahm. Im "New
> Statesman" vom 2.4.1958 erschien eine Stel-
> lungnahme Russell's zu beiden Antworten. Der
> gesamte Briefwechsel wurde später in Buchform
> veröffentlicht (BN 627).

> T r a n s l a t i o n s
> Deutsch:
> > "Offener Brief
> > an Eisenhover und Chruschtschow"
> > 1972 in BN 703/V:14 . . . . 626.05

The Vital Letters of Russell, Krushchev, Dulles

1958 London: Macgibbon & Kee. 77 pp. 627.01
1967 Xerox reprint of original edition.
    Ann Arbor, Mich.: University Microfilms 627.02
Commentary see under BN 626.

> T r a n s l a t i o n s
> Italienisch:
> > "Lettera ai potenti della terra.
> > Con le risposte N. Kruscev e F. Dulles"
> > 1958 Turin: Einaudi. 627.03

The World and the Observer

1958 (Feb. 2) in "Listener", vol. 59, p. 451 . . 628.00

Sous l'influence de Voltaire

1958 (Feb.) in "Table Ronde", no. 122, p. 159-163 629.00

The Divorce of Science and Culture

1958 (Feb.) in "UNESCO Courier", vol.11, no.2, p.4 630.00

The Role of Science in Society

1958 (Mar.) in "International Affairs" (Moskau)
no. 3, p. 4 . . . . 631.00

Let's Stay Off the Moon

1958 (Aug. 30) in "Maclean's Magazine",
vol.71, p. 7, 45-46 . . . . 632.01
1969 in "The Times" and "Wall Street Journal"
without change 632.02

Prof. G. E. Moore

1958 (Oct. 28) in London "Times", p. 14 . . . . 633.00

Respect for Law

1958 (Winter) in "San Francisco Review",
vol. 1, no. 1, p. 63, 65 . . . . 634.00

Review of G. Williams'
"The Sanctity of Life and the Criminal Law"

1958 in "Stanford Law Review", vol.10, p.382-385 635.00

Review of Gilbert Ryle's
"The Concept of Mind"

1958 in "Journal of Philosophy", 55, p. 5-12 . . 636.01
1959 in "My Philosophical Development":
Excerpt from "18. Some Replies ti Criticism" (BN 648) 636.02

Translations
Deutsch .... 1973 in BN 648.08 . . . . . 636.03
Französisch ... 1961 in BN 648.09 . . . . . 636.04
Italienisch ... 1961 in BN 648.10 . . . . . 636.05
Japanisch ..... 1959 in BN 648.11 . . . . . 636.06
Polnisch ...... 1971 in BN 648.12 . . . . . 636.07
Portugiesisch . 1960 in BN 648.13 . . . . . 636.08
Schwedisch .... 1960 in BN 648.14 . . . . . 636.09
Spanisch ...... 1960 in BN 648.15 . . . . . 636.10
Sp./Catalanisch 1969 in BN 648.17 . . . . . 636.11
Ungarisch ..... 1968 in BN 648.19 . . . . . 636.12

Mathematical Infinity
1958 in "Mind", vol. 67. p. 385 . . . . 637.00

The Will to Doubt
1958 New York: Philosophical Library. 126 pp. . 638.01
London: Allen & Unwin 638.02
C o n t e n t s
Can Men Be Rational? . . . . (1923/262)
Free Thought
   and Official Propaganda . . . . . (1922/236)
On the Value of Scepticism . . . . . (1928/327)
On Youthful Cynicism . . . . (1935/401)
Is Science Superstitious? . . . . . . (1926/304)
"Useless" Knowledge . . . . (1935/401)
What Is the Soul? . . . . (1935/401)
The Ancestry of Fascism . . . . (1935/396)
Stoicism and Mental Health . . . . . (1935/401)
Modern Homogeneity . . . . (1935/401)
Men versus Insects . . . . (1934/390)
On Comets . . . . (1935/401)
(Same contents as in "Let the
People Think", 1941/464)

Bertrand Russell's Best; Silhouettes in Satire
1958 London: Allen & Unwin. 113 pp. 639.01
New York: New American Library. 126 pp. . . 639.02
Toronto: Nelson 639.03
1961 New York: New American Library 639.04
1971 "   "   : "   "   " 639.05
1971 London: Allen & Unwin 639.06
1975 "   : "   " " 639.07
C o n t e n t s
Short-Excerpts from different works under
the titles: I. Psychology. II. Religion.
III. Sex and Marriage. IV. Education. V.
Politics. VI. Ethics.

T r a n s l a t i o n
Italienisch:
   "Bertrand Russell in due parole"
   Tr.: Elisa Morpurgo
   1961 Mailand: Longanesi 639.08
   1972 "   : " 639.09
Japanisch:
   "Rusell meigenshū"
   (Russell Analects
   written by English and Japanese)
   Tr.: Shōda Yoshiaki, Arai Yoshio
   1966 Tokio: Hara-Shobo. 202 pp. . . . 639.10

My Philosophical Development
1958/59 in "The Hibbert Journal", London,
   57, 2-8 . . . . 640.00

Mind

1959 (Mar.) in "Encounter", vol. 12, no. 3, p. 84   641.00

The Influence and Thought of G. E. Moore

1959 (Mar. 30) in "Listener", vol. 61, p. 755-756   642.00

The Expanding Mental Universe

1959 (July 18) in "Saturday Evening Post",
     vol. 232, p. 24-25, 91-93 . . . . 643.01
     1959 in "Adventures of the Mind"
        New York: Alfred A. Knopf, p. 275 - 285   643.02
     1961 in "The Basic Writings of B. Russell":
        IX/44 (BN 659) 643.03
     T r a n s l a t i o n s
     Deutsch:
        "Das sich ausdehnende
        geistige Universum"
        in "Abenteuer des Geistes"
        1961 Gütersloh: Bertelsmann. S.191-199   643.04

Logical Positionen

1959 in "Revue Internationale de Philosophie",
     Brüssel, 4 / 3-19 . . . . 644.00

Introduction to Ernest Gellner's "Words and Things"

1959 London: Victor Gollancz, p. 13-15 . . . . . 645.01
     1960 London: Victor Gollancz 645.02
     1968 Harmondsworth: Penguin 645.03

Miscellany/Sammelband in Japanisch
under the title
"Ken'i to kojin"

1959 Tokio: Nau'undo 646.00
     Excerpts from
     "Sceptical Essays" . . . . (1928/331.28)
     "Authority and the Individual" (1949/554.20)
     Tr.: Kozo Tada

COMMON SENSE AND NUCLEAR WARFARE

1959 London: Allen & Unwin. 94 pp. 647.01
     1960 New York: Simon & Schuster 647.02
     1960 London: Allen & Unwin 647.03
     1960 Toronto: Nelson 647.04
     1961 Excerpt:
        "Methods of Settling Disputes
        in the Nuclear Age" (III)
        in "The Basic Writings of B. Russell":
        XVII/81 (BN 659) 647.05
     1968 New York: AMS Press. 92 pp. 647.06

1959

Contents
Preface
Introduction
I. If Brinkmanship Continues
II. If Nuclear War Comes
III. Methods of Settling Disputes in the
Nuclear Age
IV. Programme of Steps towards Peace
V. New Outlook Needed before Negotiations
VI. Disarmament
VII. Steps Towards Conciliation
VIII. Territorial Adjustments
IX. Approach to an International Authority
X. Some Necessary Changes in Outlook
Appendix:
I. Unilateral Disarmament. II. Inconsistency?

Translations
Arabisch:
"Al-Harb wal-tanzīm"
Tr.: 'Abd-il-Karīm Ahmad
1960 Kairo:
Maktabit al-Anglo al Misriyyah . 647.07
Chinesisch:
"Changshi he hewuqizhanzheng"
(Im Bestand des Instituts für Philoso-
phie der Akademie für Sozialwissenschaf-
ten in Peking. Erscheinungsort und -jahr
waren nicht zu ermitteln.) 647.08
Dänisch:
"Atomkrig og sund fornuft"
Tr.: Mogens Boisen
1960 Kopenhagen: Branner & Korch . . . 647.09
Deutsch:
"Vernunft und Atomkrieg"
Ü.: Hellmut Hilzheimer
1959 München, Wien, Basel: Desch . . . 647.10
Inhalt
Vorwort
Einführung
(1) Verzweiflung ist keine Weisheit
(2) Wenn es zum Krieg kommt ...
(3) Die gemeinsamen Interessen
(4) Erste Schritte zu einem dauerhaf-
ten Frieden
(5) Ein neues politisches Denken
(6) Abrüstung
(7) Die Aufgaben eines internationalen
Schlichtungsausschusses
(8) Territorialfragen
(9) Schaffung einer übernationalen Be-
hörde
(10) Notwendige Standpunktsänderungen
Anhang: (1) Einseitige Abrüstung
(2) Inkonsequenz?

Auszug:
"Ein neues politisches Denken" (5)
(New Outlook Needed before Negotia-
tions - V)
1972 in BN 703/V:15 . . . . 647.11
Ind./Bengali:
"Sabhyatā o āṇavik yuddha"
Tr.: Kalpanā Rāy
1959 Kalkutta: Art and Letters 647.12
Ind./Malayalam:
"Vivekamillenkil vinasam"
Tr.: M. Gonvindan
1963 Kottayam: Sahit ya Pravathaka . . 647.13
Ind./Telugu:
"Anuyugamlō prapanca sānti"
Tr.: V. Nārāyanarāv
1959 Mahilipattanamu: M. Seshachalam . 647.14
Italienisch:
"Prima dell' Apocalisse"
Tr.: Adriana Pellegrini
1959 Mailand: Longanesi 647.15
Japanisch:
"Joshiki to Kaku Senso"
Tr.: Munetaka Iijima
1959 Tokio: Riso-sha 647.16
Portugiesisch:
"Senso comum e guerra nuclear"
Tr.: Alvaro Cabral
1963 Lissabon: Ulisseia 647.17
Singhalesisch (Ceylon):
"Vyawahara Gnanaya Ha
Nyashthika Sangrama"
Tr.: S. H. J. Sugunasiri
1959 Colombo: M. D. Gunasena 647.18
Slovenisch:
"Pamet in atomska vojna"
Tr.: Vladimir Naglič
1961 Ljubljana: Cankarjeva Založba . . 647.19
Spanisch:
"La guerra nuclear ante el sentido
do común"
Tr.: Amando Lazaro Ros
1959 Madrid: Aguilar 647.20
Excerpt:
"Algunos cambios necessarios
de nuestros puntos de vista"
(Some Necessary Changes
in Outlook - X)
1962 in BN 665 . . . . 647.21
Türkisch:
"Sağduyu ve atom savasi"
Tr.: Avni Yakalioğlu
1959 Ankara:
Doğus Ltd. Sirketi Matbaasi . . . 647.22

MY PHILOSOPHICAL DEVELOPMENT

1959 London: Allen & Unwin. 279 pp. 648.01
New York: Simon & Schuster. 279 pp. 648.02
Toronto: Nelson 648.03

C o n t e n t s
1. Introductory Outline
2. My Present View of the World
3. First Efforts
4. Excursion into Idealism
5. Revolt into Pluralism
6. Logical Technique in Mathematics
7. Principia Mathematica:
   Philosophical Aspects
8. Principia Mathematica:
   Mathematical Aspects
9. The External World
10. The Impact of Wittgenstein
11. Theory of Knowledge
12. Consciousness and Experience
13. Language
14. Universals and Particulars and Names
15. The Definition of "Truth"
16. Non-Demonstrative Inference
17. The Retreat from Pythagoras
18. Some Replies to Criticism
    (see also BN 613, 620, 622, 636)
... Russell's Philosophy:
    a Study of its Development
    by Alan Wood

C o m m e n t a r y
In this book Bertrand Russell gives an account
of the development of his philosophical thinking from the initial immature and juvenile
attempts at the age of fifteen right up to
our times. A report, such as the one presented
by one of the greatest thinkers of our age
and covering nearly seventy years of his
philosophical work, is undoubtedly just as
significant as it is fascinating.

K o m m e n t a r
Bertrand Russell gibt in diesem Buch einen
Rechenschaftsbericht über die Entwicklung
seines philosophischen Denkens von den Anfängen unfertiger, jünglingshafter Versuche
im Alter von fünfzehn Jahren bis in unsere
Zeit. Ein Bericht, wie der vorliegende, von
einem der größten Denker seiner Zeit über
beinahe siebzig Jahre seiner philosophischen
Arbeit, ist zweifellos ebenso bedeutend wie
faszinierend.

1959

Reprints
1961 Excerpts:
"Theory of Knowledge" (11)
"Non-Demonstrative Inference" (16)
"The Retreat from Pythagoras" (17)
in "The Basic Writings of B. Russell":
V/27, XVI/70, VI/31 (BN 659) 648.04
1965 Excerpt:
"Non-Demonstrative Inference" (16)
in "On the Philosophy of Science": V/II
(BN 672) 648.05
1975 London: Allen & Unwin (Paperback) . . 648.06
Translations
Arabisch:
"Falsafatī kayfa Tatawwarat"
Tr.: 'abd-al-Rashīd al-Sādiq
1959 Kairo:
Maktabit al-Anglo al-Misriyyah . 648.07
Deutsch:
"Philosophie.
Die Entwicklung meines Denkens."
Ü.: Eberhard Bubser
1973 München:
Nymphenburger Verlagshandlung . . 648.08
Inhalt
1. Ein einleitender Überblick
2. Wie ich die Welt heute sehe
3. Erste Versuche
4. Mein Exkurs in die idealistische
Philosophie
5. Die antiidealistische Revolte und
mein Weg zum Pluralismus.
6. Logik und Mathematik
7. Die "Principia Mathematica":
Philosophische Aspekte
8. Die "Principia Mathematica":
Mathematische Aspekte
9. Die Außenwelt
10. Der Einfluß Wittgensteins
11. Erkenntnistheorie
12. Bewußtsein, Erlebnis und Erfahrung
13. Die Sprache
14. Universalien, Einzeldinge,
Eigennamen.
15. Zur Definition der Wahrheit
16. Schlüsse, die nicht absolut zwingend sind.
17. Mein Abschied von Pythagoras
18. Kriterien und Entgegnungen
... "Die Philosophie Bertrand Russells"
Fragment zu einer Studie über ihre
Entwicklung von Alan Wood.

Französisch:
"Histoire de mes idées philosophiques"
Tr.: Georges Auclair
1961 Paris: Gallimard 648.09
Italienisch:
"La mia vita in filosofia"
Tr.: L. Pavolini
1961 Mailand: Longanesi 648.10
Japanisch:
"Watakushi no tetsugaku no hatten"
Tr.: Fumio Noda
1959 Tokio: Misuzu shobô 648.11
Polnisch:
"Môj rozwoj filozoficzny"
Tr.: Halina Krahelska,
     Czeslaw Znamierowski
1971 Warschau:
     Państwowe Wydawnictwo naukowe . .   648.12
Portugiesisch:
"Meu pensamento filosófico"
Tr.: Breno Silveira
1960 Sao Paulo: Ed. Nacional 648.13
Schwedisch:
"Min filosofiska utveckling"
Tr.: Alf Ahlberg, Anders Byttner
1960 Stockholm: Natur och Kultur . . .   648.14
Spanisch:
"La evolución
de mi pesamiento filosófico"
Tr.: J. N. Domingo
1960 Madrid: Aguilar 648.15
Excerpt:
"Mi abandono de Pitágoras"
(The Retreat from Pythagoras - 17)
1962 in BN 665 . . . .   648.16
"La evolución
de mi pesamiento filosófico"
1976 Madrid: Alianza 648.17
Sp./Catalanisch:
"Le meva concepció del món"
Tr.: Carbonell i Torras
1969 Barcelona: Edicions 62 . . . . .   648.18
1974 "   : "   " 648.19
Ungarisch:
"Filozófiai fejlödśem"
Tr.: Ferenc Fehér
1968 Budapest: Gonddat Kiadó 648.20

WISDOM OF THE WEST

1959 London: Macdonald & Co. in Verbindung   mit
     (c) Rathbone Books, London. 320 pp., illus.   649.01
     Garden City, N. Y.; Toronto: Doubleday . .   649.02

Contents
Foreword
Prologue / Before Socrates / Athens / Hellenism / Early Christianity / Scholasticism / Rise of Modern Philosophy / British Empiricism / Enlightenment and Romanticism / Utilitarianism and since / Contemporary / Epilogue

Commentary
"Wisdom of the West" is an entirely new work; though, of course, it would never have appeared had not my "History of Western Philosophy" preceded it. - An account of the history of philosophy may proceed in one of two ways. Either the story is purely expository, showing what this man said and how that man was influenced. Alternatively, the exposition may be combined with a certain measure of critical discourse, in order to show how philosophic discussion proceeds. This second course has been adopted here. - To support the account, there is a collection of pictures of men, places and documents, which have been chosen as nearly as possible from sources belonging to the period to which they refer. Above all, an attempt has been made, wherever this seemed feasible, to translate philosophic ideas, normally expressed only in words, into diagrams that convey the same information by way of geometrical metaphor. There is little to fall back on here, and the results are therefore not always entirely successful. However, it seems that such methods of presentation are worth exploring. Diagrammatic exposition, so far as it can be achieved, has the further advantage of not being tied to any particular tongue (Excerpt from Russell's Foreword).

Kommentar
"Denker des Abendlandes" ist ein vollkommen neues Werk: Nie hätte es freilich erscheinen können, ohne meine vorausgegangene "Geschichte der Philosophie des Abendlandes". - Die Darstellung einer Geschichte der Philosophie kann auf die eine oder andere Weise geschehen. Entweder ist es ein Bericht, was dieser oder jener Denker sagte, oder die Darbietung wird mit kritischen Bemerkungen verbunden, die zeigen, wie das philosophische Gespräch vor sich geht. Diese zweite Methode wird hier angewandt. - Um das Verständnis zu erleichtern, fügen wir eine Reihe Bilder bei: Menschen, Orte und Dokumente, die möglichst aus

Quellen der jeweiligen Zeit gewählt wurden.
Vor allem ist der Versuch gemacht worden,
philosophische Ideen, die normalerweise nur
in Worten ausgedrückt werden, in graphischen
Darstellungen und in geometrischen Metaphern
zu vermitteln. Allerdings gibt es hier nicht
allzu viele Möglichkeiten; doch scheint die
Methode wert, erprobt zu werden. Die graphische Ausdrucksweise, soweit sie überhaupt verwirklicht werden kann, hat noch den weiteren
Vorteil, daß sie an keine besondere Sprache
gebunden ist (Auszug aus Russell's Vorwort).

R e p r i n t s
1966 Greenwich, Conn.: Fawcett Publications 649.03
1970 London: Macdonald 649.04
1975 "   : " 649.05
T r a n s l a t i o n s
Dänisch:
    "Den vestlige verdens filosofi"
    Tr.: Elsa Gress Wright
    1961 Kopenhagen: Spektrum 649.06
Deutsch:
    "Denker des Abendlandes"
    Ü.: Károly Földes-Papp.
    1962 Stuttgart: Chr. Belser. 320 S. . 649.07
    1970 Berlin: Deutsche Buchgemeinschaft 649.08
    I n h a l t
    Vorwort
    Einführung / Vor Sokrates / Athen / Hel-
    lenismus / Frühchristentum / Scholastik/
    Der Anstieg der modernen Philosophie /
    Englischer Empirismus / Aufklärung und
    Romantik / Utilitarismus / Gegenwart /
    Nachwort
Französisch:
    "L'aventure de la pensée occidentale"
    Tr.: Claude Saunier
    1961 Paris: Hachette 649.09
Italienisch:
    "La sagezza dell' Occidente"
    Tr.: L. Pavolini
    1961 Mailand: Longanesi 649.10
    1975 "   : " 649.11
Japanisch:
    "Seiyô no chie"
    Tr.: Tomriya Takashi
    1968 Tokio: Shakai Shisôsha. 2 vols. . 649.12
Koreanisch:
    "Seoyang eui jihye"
    Tr.: Jeong Bonghwa
    1960 Seoul: Eulyumunhwasa 649.13
    Tr.: Yang Byeong Taeg, Jeong Bonghwa
    1970 Seoul: Daeyang-Seojeog 649.14

Norwegisch:
"Vestens visdom"
Tr.: Arild Haaland
1961 Oslo: Tiden 649.15
Schwedisch:
"Västerländets visdom"
Tr.: Andres Byttner
1961 Stockholm: Forum 649.16
1977 "   : 649.17
Serbokroatisch:
"Mudrost Zapada"
Tr.: Marija + Ivan Salečič
1971 Zagrebß Mladinska knjiga 649.18
Slowenisch:
"Modrost zahoda"
Tr.: Boris Verbič
1972 Ljubljana: Mladinska knjiga . . .   649.19
Spanisch:
"La sabiduria de Occidente"
Tr.: Juan Garcia Puente
1962 Madrid: Aguilar 649.20
1973 in BN 706 ("Obra completa I") .   649.21

Notes on "Philosophy", January, 1960

A reply to Mr. Lijewski: A re-examination
of the Russellian theory of describtion.

1960 (April) in "Philosophy", London,
vol. 35, p. 146-147 . . . .   650.00

University Education: What It Ought to Be

1960 (März) in "Arkansas Alumnus", p. 13-15 . .   651.01
1961 in "Fact and Fiction": II:X (BN 660) .   651.02

Translations
Italienisch ... 1961 in BN 660.06 . . . . .   651.03
Japanisch ..... 1962 in BN 660.08 . . . . .   651.04
Portugiesisch . 1965 in BN 660.10 . . . . .   651.05
Schwedisch .... 1964 in BN 660.11 . . . . .   651.06

The Case for Neutralism

Debate with Gaitskell

1960 (July 24) in "New York Times Magazine"
p. 10, 35-36 . . . .   652.00

Preface to "Einstein on Peace"

1960 New York: Simon & Schuster,
ed. O. Nathan and H. Norden. 653.00

Act or Perish -
A Gall to Non Violent Action (versus Nuclear Warfare)

1960 A Gall by B. Russell and Michael Scott for
    the "Committee of 100" in the autumn 1960.   654.01
    1969 in "Autobiography III", p. 137-139 . .   654.02

    T r a n s l a t i o n s
    Deutsch .... 1971 in BN 682.18, S.191-194   654.03
    Deutsch:
        "Handeln oder zugrunde gehen -
        Aufruf zum gewaltlosen Widerstand"
        (gegen automare Kriegsführung)
        1972 in BN 703/V.:17 . . . .   654.04

BERTRAND RUSSELL SPEAKS HIS MIND

1960 Cleveland, New York: World Pub. Co. 173 pp.   655.01
    London: A. Barker. 173 pp. 655.02
    New York: Avon Book Division. Hearst Corp.   655.03
    New York: Bard Books . . . . , 655.04
    1974 Westport, Conn.: Greenwood Press . . .   655.05
    C o n t e n t s
    1. What Is Philosophy? 2. Religion. 3. War
    and Pacifism. 4. Communism and Capitalism.
    5. Taboo Morality. 6. Power. 7. What Is
    Happiness? 8. Nationalism. 9. Great Britain.
    10. The Role of the Individual. 11. Fanati-
    cism and Tolerance. 12. The H-Bomb. 13. The
    Possible Future of Mankind.

    C o m m e n t a r y
    The following thirteen dialogues with B.
    Russell were filmed for television during
    four and one-half days in the spring of 1959.
    No prepared script was used and no retakes
    were made, since Lord Russell insisted he was
    not an actor. His words were recorded on film -
    and in the pages of this book - as he first
    spoke them.
    Woodrow Wyatt, the interviewer throughout
    the entire series, has had considerable ex-
    perience with the BBC as a television com-
    mentator. He is currently a member of Par-
    liament for the Labour Party.

    K o m m e n t a r
    Die folgenden dreizehn Dialoge mit B.
    Russell wurden während vierundeinhalb Tagen
    im Frühjahr 1959 vom britischen Fernsehen
    aufgenommen. Es wurden kein vorbereitetes
    Manuskript verwendet, und keine Wiederho-
    lungen gemacht, weil Lord Russell betonte,
    er sei doch kein Schauspieler. Seine Worte
    wurden im Film - und in den Seiten dieses
    Buches - so festgehalten, wie er sie gespro-
    chen hat.

Woodrow Wyatt, der Interviewer dieser ganzen Serie, besitzt eine beträchtliche Erfahrung als Fernsehkommentator bei der BBC.
Er ist Abgeordneter für die Labourparty im
englischen Parlament.

T r a n s l a t i o n s
Deutsch:
   "Bertrand Russell sagt seine Meinung"
   Eine Serie von 13 Interviews im Frühjahr
   1959 mit B. Russell von Woodrow Wyatt.
   Tr.: Günter Schwarz
   1976 Darmstadt: Verlag Darmstädter
         Blätter, Schwarz & Co. 224 S. . .   655.06
   I n h a l t
   1. Was ist Philosophie? / 2. Religion /
   3. Krieg und Pazifismus / 4. Kommunismus und Kapitalismus / 5. Tabu-Moral /
   6. Macht / 7. Was ist Glück? / 8. Na-
   tionalismus / 9. Großbritanien / 10. Die
   Rolle des Individuums / 11. Fanatismus
   und Toleranz / 12.Die Wasserstoffbombe /
   13. Die mögliche Zukunft der Menschheit.
Französisch:
   "Ma conception du monde"
   Tr.: Louis Evrard
   1962 Paris: Gallimard 655.07
   1973 "   : " 655.08
Ind./Gujarati:
   "Russell na vartalap"
   1971 Ahmedabad: Balgovind Prakashan .   655.09
Italienisch:
   "Bertrand Russell dice la sua"
   Tr.: Adriana Pellegrini
   1961 Mailand: Longanesi 655.10
Japanisch:
   "Russell wa kataru"
   Tr.: Tômiya Takashi
   1964 Tokio: Misuzu shobô 655.11
Norwegisch:
   "Bertrand Russell på nært hold"
   Tr.: Kjell Billing
   1965 Oslo: Pax 655.12

On Civil Disobedience

1961 (Apr. 15) Speech in Birmingham
   Printed as leaflet 656.01
   1969 in "Autobiography III", p. 139-144 . . 656.02
   T r a n s l a t i o n s
   Deutsch . . . . 1971 in BN 682.18 S.194-204 656.03
                        (Über gewaltlosen Wi-
                        derstand)

Civil Disobedience
==================

1961 in "New Statesman", vol. 61, p. 245-246 . . 657.00

Miscellany / Sammelband in Niederländisch
under the title
"Sententies"
=============

1961 's-Gravenhagen: Boucher. 32 pp.
     Tr.: F. J. Schmit, A. C. Niemeyer 658.00

THE BASIC WRITINGS OF BERTRAND RUSSELL 1903-1959
==

1961 London: Allen & Unwin. 736 pp.
     Ed. by Robert E. Egner and Lester E. Denonn 659.01
     New York: Simon & Schuster 659.02
     Toronto: Nelson 659.03
     1962 London: Allen & Unwin 659.04

     C o n t e n t s
     Vide p. XXII - XL of this Bibliography,
     especially p. XXII above.

     I n h a l t
     Siehe S. XXIII - XLI dieser Bibliographie,
     speziell S. XXIII oben.

     T r a n s l a t i o n s
     Spanisch:
         "Escrito básicos 1903-1959"
         1969 Madrid: Aguilar 659.05

FACT AND FICTION
================

1961 London: Allen & Unwin. 282 pp. 660.01
     Toronto: Nelson 660.02
     1962 New York: Simon & Schuster. 317 pp. .   660.03
     1972 Excerpt:
         "Divertissements" (III: I - VI)
         in BN 701 . . . . 660.04
     C o n t e n t s
     Part I: Books that Influenced Me in Youth
       I. The Importance of Shelley . (1961/660)
      II. The Romance of Revolt . . . . . (1961/660)
     III. Revolt in the Abstract . . . . (1961/660)
      IV. Disgust and Its Antidote . . (1961/660)
       V. An Education in History . . . (1961/660)
      VI. The Pursuit of Truth . . . . . . (1957/619)
     Part II: Politics and Education
       I. What is Freedom? . . . . (1952/592)
      II. What is Democracy? . . . . (1953/593)
     III. A Scientist's Plea
          for Democracy . . . . (1961/660)
      IV. The Story of Colonization . (1961/660)
       V. Pros and Cons of Nationalism (1961/660)
      VI. The Reasoning of Europeans (1961/660)
     VII. The World I should Like to
          Live in . . . . (1961/660)
    VIII. Old and Young Cultures . . . . (1961/660)

Translations
Deutsch:
Auszug:
"Erziehung für eine schwierige Welt"
(Education for a Difficult World - II:IX)
1974 in BN 707/II:8 .... 660.05
Italienisch:
"Parole e cose"
Tr.: Bruno Oddera
1961 Mailand: Il Saggiatore 660.06
"Realta e finzione"
Tr.: Luciano Savoia
1967 Mailand: Longanesi 660.07

Japanisch:
    "Jijitsu to koyokô"
    Tr.: Teiji Kitakawa
    1962 Tokio: Otowa Shobô 660.08
    Excerpts:
    "Minshu-shugi towa nami ka juyû towa
    nani" (What is Freedom? What is Democ-
    racy? - II: I, II)
    Tr.: Antonio Neves Pedro
    1962 Tokio: Riso-Sha 660.09
Portugiesisch:
    "Realidade e ficção"
    Tr.: Antonio Neves Pedro
    1965 Lissabon: Europa-América 660.10
Schwedisch:
    "Fakta och fantasi"
    Tr.: Anders Byttner
    1964 Stockholm: Natur och Kultur . . . 660.11

HAS MAN A FUTURE?

1961 London: Allen & Unwin. 136 pp. 661.01
    Toronto: Nelson 661.02
    1962 New York: Simon & Schuster. 128 pp. . 661.03
    1962 Harmondsworth: Penguin 661.04
    1962 London: Allen & Unwin 661.05
    1964 "   : "   " " 661.06
    1965 "   : "   " " 661.07
    1971 "   : "   " "   . . . .· . . 661.08
C o n t e n t s
1. Prologue or Epilogue? 2. The Atom Bomb.
(Excerpt 1945 in BN 502.02) 3. The H-Bomb.
4. Liberty or Death? 5. Scientists and the
H-Bomb. 6. Long-term Conditions of Human
Survival. 7. Why World Government is Dis-
liked. 8. First Steps Towards Secure Peace.
9. Disarmament. 10. Territorial Problems.
11. A Stable World.

T r a n s l a t i o n s
Arabisch:
    "Hal lil-insan mustaqbal"
    Tr.: 'Ayid Al-Rabbāt
    1962 Kairo: A-Dār al-Qawmiyyah 661.09
Birmanisch (Burma):
    "Lutha myo-pyoke myilaw"
    Tr.: Maung Ne Oo
    1965 Rangoon: Moe Oo Pan Publication . 661.10
Chinesisch:
    "Jên lui ti ming yün"
    Tr.: Hsing Chou Huang
    1967 Taipeh: Cheng Wen Publ. Service . 661.11

Dänisch:
 "Har menesket en fremtid?"
 Tr.: Mogens Boisen
 1962 Kopenhagen: Spektrum 661.12
 1963 " : " 661.13
Deutsch:
 "Hat der Mensch noch eine Zukunft?"
 Ü.: Paul Paudisch
 1963 München: Kindler. Kindler Tb. 11. 661.14
 I n h a l t
 I. Prolog oder Epilog? II. Die Atom-
 bombe. III. Die Wasserstoffbombe. IV.
 Freiheit oder Tod? V. Wissenschaftler
 und die Wasserstoffbombe. VI. Unter
 welchen Bedingungen kann die Menschheit
 auf die Dauer fortbestehen? VII. Warum
 der Gedanke einer Weltregierung nicht
 beliebt ist. VIII. Erste Schritte zur
 Sicherung des Friedens. IX. Abrüstung.
 X. Territoriale Probleme. XI. Eine sta-
 bile Welt.
 Auszüge:
 "Atomwaffen und atomare Kriegsführung"
 (From "The Atom Bomb" - 2)
 1972 in BN 703/V:12 . . . . 661.15
 "Freiheit oder Tod" (Liberty or
 Death - 4)
 1972 in BN 703/V:16 . . . . 661.16
 "Aufruf zur Zusammenarbeit nichtkommu-
 nistischer und kommunistischer Wissen-
 schaftler" (From "Scientist's and the
 H-Bomb" - 5)
 1972 in BN 703/V:13 . . . . 661.17
Französisch:
 "L'homme survivra-t-il?"
 Tr.: Yves Massip
 1962 Paris: J. Didier 661.18
Ind./Gujaratî:
 "Manav tarun bhavi?"
 Tr.: Subhadra Gandhi
 1962 Baroda: Yajna Prakašan 661.19
Ind./Hindi:
 "Manav ka bhavisya"
 Tr.: Anima Singha, Sušilkumar Dhar
 1972 Kalkutta: Educational Enterprisers 661.20
Italienisch:
 "E domani? ..."
 Tr.: Adriana Pellegrini
 1962 Mailand: Longanesi 661.21
Japanisch:
 "Jinrui ni mirai wa aru ka"
 Tr.: Ikki Hidaka
 1962 Tokio: Risô-Sha 661.22

Koreanisch:
  "Ilyu-ege Jangrega Isseulga"
  Tr.: Ilchyeol Sin
  1962 Seoul 661.23
Niederländisch:
  "Heeft de mens een toekomst?"
  Tr.: F. Bijlsma
  1962 Amsterdam: J. M. Meulenhoff . . . 661.24
Portugiesisch:
  "Tem futuro o homem?"
  Tr.: Brenno Silveira
  1962 Rio de Janeiro:
       Civilização Brasileira 661.25
Schwedisch:
  "Har mäniskan en framtid?"
  Tr.: Anders Byttner, Sten Söderberg
  1962 Stockholm: Natur och Kultur . . . 661.26
Singhalesisch (Ceylon):
  "Mānava Sanhatiyē Iranama Kumagda?"
  Tr.: Wilson Siriwarnasinghe
  1963 Colombo: Gunasēna & Co. 661.27
Spanisch:
  "Tiene el hombre un futuro?"
  Tr.: Juan Novella Domingo
  1963 Madrid: Aguilar 661.28
Türkisch:
  "Insanliğin geleceği"
  Tr.: Memduh Balaban
  1964 Istanbul: Ataç Kitabevi 661.29
  Tr.: Ismail Hakki Oğuz
  1965 Ankara: Ajans Türk Matbaasi . . . 661.30
  "Insanliğin yarini"
  Tr.: Aksit Göktürk
  1972 Ankara: Bilgi Yayinevi 661.31

<u>For and Against Being 90</u>

1962 (May 13) in "Observer", p. 10 . . . . 662.00
     (Russell's 90th birthday: May 18, 1972)

<u>History of the World in Epitome</u>

1962 London: Gaberbocchus. 14 pp.
     Illus. by Franciszka Themerson 663.01
     1970 in BN 693 . . . . 663.02
     1972 in "The Collected Stories of B.R." (BN 701) 663.03

     "They (Gaberbochus) also published my 'yeu
d'esprit' on the End of the world, a short
"History of the World", for my 90th birthday
in a little gold volume."(Autobiography III)
     "Meine kurze "History of the World", ein
kleines 'jeu d'esprit' über das Schicksal
der Welt, kam zu meinem 90. Geburtstag als
Goldbändchen gleichfalls im Privatverlag
(Gaberbocchus) meiner Freunde heraus."

Miscellany/Sammelband in Türkisch
under the title
"Düyamizin sorunlari"

1962 Istanbul: Büyük Kervan Basimevi. 180 pp.
    Tr.: Sabahattin Eyüboğlu, Vedat Günyd . . .   664.00

Miscellany/Sammelband in Spanisch
under the title
"La filosofia en el siglo XX y otro ensayos"

1962 Montevideo: Editorial Alfa. 125 pp. 665.00
    C o n t e n t s
    La filosofia en el siglo XX (Phi-
        losophy in the Twentieth Century 1924/278)
    Mi abandono de Pitágoras (The Re-
        treat from Pythagoras . . . . 1959/648)
    Sobre la denotación (On Denoting 1905/056)
    Algunos cambios necesarios de
        nuestros puntos de vista (Some
        Necessary changes in Outlook ... 1959/647)

Comunismo y Capitalismo

1963 in "Cuadernos", Paris, no. 69 / 21-24 . . .   666.00

Civil Disobedience

1963 in "A Matter of Life", ed. Clara Urquhart
    Boston: Little, Brown 667.01
    London: Cape, p. 189-196 . . . .   667.02
    T r a n s l a t i o n s (?)
    Deutsch:
        "Die Pflicht zum bürgerl. Ungehorsam"
        1963 (June) in "Friedensrundschau" . .   667.03
        vol. 17, no. 6, p.

Unarmed Victory

1963 London: Allen & Unwin. 155 pp. 668.01
    New York: Simon & Schuster 668.02
    Toronto: Nelson 668.03
    Baltimore, Harmondsworth: Penguin 668.04
    C o n t e n t s
      I. The International Background
     II. The Cuban Crisis
         a. The Castro Regime in the USA
         b. The Days of Crisis
         c. The Settlement
    III. The Sino-Indian Dispute
         a. Outline of the Genesis of the Dispute
         b. The Dispute
         c. The Aftermath
     IV. Lessons of the Two Crisis

T r a n s l a t i o n s
Birmanisch (Burma):
    "Letnet mê Aung Naing Yay",
    Tr.: San Myint Aung
    1967 Rangun: Pon Nya Pub. 668.05
Hebräisch:
    "Niẓẓaḥon we-lo be-nešek"
    Tr.: B. Evron
    1964 Tel-Aviv: Amikam 668.06
Italienisch:
    "La vittoria disamata"
    Tr.: Lidia Locatelli
    1965 Mailand: Longanesi 668.07
Japanisch:
    "Buki naki shôri"
    Tr.: Makino Tsutomu
    1964 Tokio: Risôsha 668.08
Singhalesisch (Ceylon):
    "Nirāyudha Vijayagrahanaya"
    Tr.: M. D. N. Austin
    1964 Colombo: M. D. Gunasena 668.09

Semantics and the Cold War

1964 (Dec.) in "Playboy", vol. 11, p. 175,206,251 669.00

The Ethos of Violence

1965 (Jan.) in "Minority of One",
    vol. 7, no. 1, p. 6-7 . . . . 670.00

Letters to Meinong

1965 in "Philosophenbriefe aus der Wissenschaft-
    lichen Korrespondenz von Alexius Meinong".
    Graz: Akademische Druck- und Verlagsanstalt 671.00
Bertrand Russell
On the Philosophy of Science

A Miscellany (Sammelband), edited with an introduction by Charles A. Fritz, Jr.

1965 Indianapolis, Ind.: Bobbs-Merill. 232 pp. . 672.00
    C o n t e n t s
    Part I: Formal and Empirical Science
        1. What Is an Empirical Science?
           (From "The Analysis of Matter",
           BN 315/XVII)
        2. Mathematics and Logic
           (From "Introduction to Mathematical
           Philosophy",
           BN 191/18)
        3. Interpretation
           (From "Human Knowledge",
           BN 536/IV:I)

4. Minimum Vocabularies
   (From "Human Knowledge"
   BN 536/IV:II)
Part II:
Sense Data and the Philosophy of Science
   1. The World of Physics
      and the World of Sense
      (From "Our Knowledge of the External
      World",
      BN 133/IV)
Part III: Physics and Perception
   1. Physics and Experience
      (From "Human Knowledge",
      BN 536/III:IV)
   2. Structure
      (From "Human Knowledge",
      BN 536/IV:III)
   3. Time and Space
      (From "Human Knowledge",
      BN 536/IV:V+VI)
   4. Space-Time
      (From "Human Knowledge",
      BN 536/IV:VII)
   5. Space-Time and Causality
      (From "Human Knowledge",
      BN 536/IV:X)
Part IV: Psychology
   1. Mental Phenomena
      (From "The Analysis of Mind",
      BN 213/XV)
Part V: Causation and Inference
   1. On the Notion of Cause
      (From "Mysticism and Logic",
      BN 172/IX)
   2. Non-demonstrative Inference
      (From "My Philosophical Development",
      BN 648/16)
Part VI: Science and Culture
   1. The Place of Science in a Liberal
      Education
      (From "Mysticism and Logic",
      BN 172/II)
   2. Science and Human Life
      (From "What is Science?",
      BN 612)

War and Atrocity in Vietnam

1965 London: B. Russell Peace Foundation 673.01
     1967 in "War Crimes in Vietnam" (BN 678/2) 673.02
     T r a n s l a t i o n s
     Deutsch:
        "Krieg und Grausamkeit in Vietnam"
        in G. Grüning "Bruderkrieg in Vietnam"
        1965 Frankfurt: Verband der
             Kriegsdienstverweigerer 673.03

1966/1967

Appeal to the American Conscience

1966 (Sept.) in "The Minority of One",
    vol. 8, p. 12-14 . . . . 674.01
    London: B. Russell Peace Foundation 674.02
    1967 in "War Crimes in Vietnam" (BN 678/12) 674.03
    T r a n s l a t i o n s
    Deutsch:
        "Appell an das Gewissen Amerikas"
        in "Plädoyer für einen
        Kriegsverbrecherprozeß"
        1968 Berlin: Edition Voltaire 674.04
        1972 in BN 703/18 . . . . 674.05

False and True

1967 (Mar. 12) in "Observer", London, 33 . . . . 675.00
    A letter correcting the statement in his "Au-
    tobiography", vol. I, of the paradox in-
    volving "The statement on the other side of
    this piece of paper is false".

Preface to Wilfred Burchett's "Hanoi sous les bombes"

1967 Paris: F. Maspern 676.00

Is the Notion of Progress an Illusion?

1967 in Malcolm Muggeridge: "Muggeridge through
    the Microphone".
    London: British Broadcasting Corp., p. 25-31 677.00

WAR CRIMES IN VIETNAM

1967 London: Allen & Unwin. 179 pp. 678.01
    New York: Monthly Review Press. 178 pp. . . 678.02
    Toronto: Nelson 678.03
    C o n t e n t s
    Introduction
        Background to the American Involvement
        (Hintergrund der Verwicklung Amerikas)
    1. The Press and Vietnam
        (Die Presse und Vietnam)
        Some early attempts to make known the
        character of the war and the role of the
        USA in it, including exchanges with the
        "New York Times" in early 1963.
        (Einige frühe Versuche den Charakter des
        Krieges und die Rolle Amerikas bekannt-
        zumachen, einschließlich Korrespondenz-
        Austausch mit der "New York Times" im frü-
        hen 1963)
    2. War and Atrocity in Vietnam (1965/673)
        (Krieg und Gräßlichkeit in Vietnam)

- 236 -

An early account of the barbarous nature
of the war
(Ein früher Bericht über die barbarische
Natur des Krieges)
3. Free World Barbarism
(Barbarismus der Freien Welt)
Gold War myths which obscure the issues
at stake in Vietnam.
(Der Mythos des Kalten Krieges verdunkelt
Veröffentlichungen über Vietnam)
4. Danger in South-East Asia
(Gefahr in Südost-Asien)
A brief examination of the claim that only
"non-lethal" gases were in use South Viet-
nam
(Eine kurze Ausführung über das Anrecht,
daß nur "nicht-tödliche"-Gase in Süd-
Vietnam eingesetzt wurden)
5. The Cold War: A New Phase?
(Der Kalte Krieg: Eine neue Phase?)
How the USA has replaced former colonial
powers in Asia and elsewhere
(Wie die USA frühere Kolonialmächte in
Asien und anderswo ersetzte)
6. The Selection of Targets in China
(Die Wahl der Zielscheiben in China)
US escalation of the war
(US-Eskalation des Krieges)
7. The Labour Party's Foreign Policy.
(Die Außenpolitik der Labour Party)
A speech on the bankruptcy of the Labour
Party's foreign policy, leading to resig-
nation from the Party
(Eine Rede über den Bankrott der Außen-
politik der Labour Party, der zur Resig-
nation der Partei führte)
8. Peace Through Resistance to US Imperialism
(Friede durch den Widerstand gegen US-
Imperialismus)
The world context in which the war occurs
(Der Weltzusammenhang in dem der Krieg
erscheint)
9. The Only Honourable Policy
(Die einzige ehrenvolle Politik)
A comparison of the peace terms of the
Vietnamese and those of Churchill in World
War II
(Ein Vergleich der Friedensbedingungen des
Vietnamkrieges mit denen von Churchill
im 2. Weltkrieg)
10. Broadcast on National Liberation Front
Radio to American Soldiers
(Sendung für amerikanische Soldaten im
Radio der Nationalen Befreiungsfront)

An appeal to American soldiers, urging
them to refrain from further war crimes
(Eine Aufforderung an amerikanische Soldaten von weiteren Kriegsverbrechen Ab-
stand zu nehmen)
11. Speech to the National Conference of Solidarity
(Rede an die Nationale Solidaritäts-Kon-
ferenz)
The necessity for solidarity with the
people of Vietnam
(Die Notwendigkeit der Solidarität mit
dem Volk von Vietnam)
12. Appeal to the American Conscience (1966/
674)
(Appell an das amerikanische Gewissen)
The character of the war and the respon-
sibility of the American people
(Der Charakter des Krieges und die Ver-
antwortlichkeit des amerik. Volkes)
Postscript:
The International War Crimes Tribunal
Appendix:
Report from North Vietnam by Ralph Schoenman

C o m m e n t a r y
"War Crimes in Vietnam" is comprised of a
few of the innumerable letters, statements,
speeches and articles delivered by me since
1963. To these are added an Introduction
giving the general background of the situation et the beginning of 1967 and of my own
attitude to it; a Postscript describing
briefly the War Crimes Tribunal for which I
had called; and an appendix containing some
of the findings of Ralph Schoenman during
one of his visits of many weeks to Vietnam.
(Russell: "Autobiography III")

K o m m e n t a r
"War Crimes in Vietnam" stellt eine Auswahl
meiner unendlich vielen Briefe, Erklärungen,
Reden und Artikel seit dem Jahre 1963 dar.
Hinzu kommt eine Einleitung, worin die allgemeine Situation Anfang des Jahres 1967 sowie meine Haltung zu dieser Lage beschrieben
sind, weiters ein Nachwort, in dem ich eine
kurze Beschreibung des von mir einberufenen
Vietnam-Tribunals gebe, und einen Anhang,
der manches von dem enthält, was R. Schoenman
während einer seiner mehrwöchigen Reisen in
Vietnam festgestellt hatte.

T r a n s l a t i o n s
Arabisch:
    "Jarā'im al-ḥarb al-amrīkīyah"
    Tr.: Ismā'il al-Mahdāwī
    1967 Kairo: Dār al-Kātib al-'Arabī . .   678.04
    "....................."
    (War Crimes in Vietnam)
    Tr.: M. Fallaha
    1968 Damaskus: Min. de la Culture . .   678.05
    "Jarā'im al-ḥarb fi fiyitnam"
    Tr.: Muhamad yaḥyā 'uways
    1970 Kairo:
    Al-sharikah al-Muttabdah lil Nashr   678.06
Birmanisch (Burma):
    "Vietnam sit yazawat kaun myar"
    Tr.: Kyaw Aung, Nyunt Kyuu
    1968 Rangun: Yamiry Sarpay Pinya . . .   678.07
Dänisch:
    "Krigsforbrydelser i Vietnam"
    Tr.: Harry Mortensen
    1967 Kopenhagen: Spektrum 678.08
Deutsch:
    Auszüge:
    "Krieg und Grausamkeit in Vietnam" (War
    and Atrocity in Vietnam - 2)
    1965 in BN 673.03 . . . .   678.09
    "Rede an die amerikanischen Soldaten in
    Süd-Vietnam" (Broadcast on National
    Liberation Front Radio to American
    soldiers - 10)
    1968 in "Plädoyer für einen
        Kriegsverbrecherprozeß"
    Frankfurt: Edition Voltaire, S. 18   678.10
    "Ansprache auf der englischen Vietnam-
    Solidaritäts-Konferenz" (Speech to the
    National Conference of Solidarity - 11)
    1968 ebenda, S. 39 . . . .   678.11
    "Appell an das Gewissen Amerikas"(Appeal
    to the American Conscience - 12)
    1968 ebenda, S. 24 (1972 in BN 703/18)   678.12
    "Post Skriptum: An das Gewissen der
    Menschheit" (Postscript: The Interna-
    tional War Crimes Tribunal)
    1968 ebenda, S. 43 . . . .   678.13
Französisch:
    "Nuremberg pour le Vietnam"
    Tr.: Guillaume Carle
    1967 Paris: Maspero 678.14
Italienisch:
    "Crimini de guerra nel Vietnam"
    Tr.: Giangiacomo Cascella
    1967 Mailand: Longanesi 678.15

Japanisch:
"Vietnam no sensô hanzai"
Tr.: Suzuki Yoshirô
1967 Tokio: Kawade shobô 678.16
Niederländisch:
"Oorlogsmisdaden in Vietnam"
Tr.: Hermien Manger
1967 Amsterdam: Bezige Bij 678.17
Norwegisch:
"Krigsforbrytelser i Vietnam"
Tr.: Einar Kleppe, Morten Krogstad
1967 Oslo: Cappelen 678.18
Polnisch:
"Zbrodnie wojenne w Wietnamie"
Tr.: Antoni Wyda
1967 Warschau: Wydawn. Min. Obrony Narod 678.19
Spanisch:
"Crímenes de guerra en Vietnam"
Tr.: Manuel Aguilar
1967 Madrid: Aguilar 678.20
1968 "   : "   3rd ed. 678.21
Türkisch:
"Vietnam da savas suçlari"
Tr.: Niyazi Atakôglu
1967 Ankara: Bilgi Yayinevi 678.22

Miscellany/Sammelband in Italienisch
under the title
"Il pensioro di Bertrand Russell"

Una antologia dagli scritti a cura di E. Musacchio.

1967 Turin: Loescher. XXXVIII, 347 pp. 679.00

Miscellany/Sammelband in Tschechisch
under th title
"Logika, jazyk a věda"

1967 Prag: Svoboda 680.00
    C o n t e n t s
    A. Logika a matematika
       (Logic and Mathematics)
          1. "O označeni" (On Denoting 1905/056)
          2. "Popisy" (Description ... 1919/191)
          3. "Teorie logických typu"
             (Theory of Logical Types 1910/098)
          4. "Matematika a logika"
             (Mathematics and Logic .. 1919/191)
    B. Jazyk a teorie poznáni
       (Language
       and the Theory of Acquaintance)
          5. "Jazyk" (Language from
             "Human Knowledge" II:II-X 1948/536)

1967

C. Filosofie a věda
   (Philosophy and Science)
   6. "Logický atomismus"(Logi-
      cal Atomism .... 1924/265)
   7. "O pojmu příčiny" (On the
      Notion of Cause .... 1913/119)
   8. "Vědecké pojmy" (Scien-
      tific Concepts from "Human
      Knowledge" IV:I-III ..... 1948/536)

A detailed catalogue of
The Archives of Bertrand Russell

(The Archives of B.Russell, 1280 Main Street West,
McMaster University, Hamilton, Ontario, L8S 4L6)
Archive administrator & editor: Barry Feinberg.
Chief archivist: Miss P. M. Fisher; archive & edi-
torial unit: David Ash, Kenneth M. Blackwell, Ro-
nald Kasrils.

1967 London: Continuum 1 Ltd. 343 pp. 681.00
     This edition is limited to 300 copies.

THE AUTOBIOGRAPHY OF BERTRAND RUSSELL

1967 Vol. I, 1872-1914
     London: Allen & Unwin. 230 pp. 682.01
     Boston: Little, Brown 682.02
     Toronto: McClelland & Stewart 682.03
     C o n t e n t s
     Prologue: What I have lived for.
     I. Childhood. II. Adolescence. III.Cambridge.
     IV. Engagement. V. First Marriage. VI."Prin-
     cipia Mathematica". VII. Again Cambridge.
1968 Vol. II, 1914-1944
     London: Allen & Unwin. 268 pp. 682.04
     Boston: Little, Brown 682.05
     Toronto: McClelland & Stewart 682.06
     C o n t e n t s
     Preface.
     I. The First War. II. Russia. III. China.
     IV. Second Marriage. V. Later Years of Tele-
     graph House. VI. Amerika 1938-1944.
1969 Vol. III, 1944-1967
     London: Allen & Unwin. 232 pp. 682.07
     New York: Simon & Schuster 682.08
     C o n t e n t s
     Preface.
     I. Return to England. II. At Home and Abroad.
     III. Trafalgar Square. IV. The Foundation.
     Postscript.

     C o m m e n t a r y
     Russell's "Autobiography" in three volumes
     is one of the really important autobiogra-
     phies of our time which embraces almost a

whole century of social and intellectual
changes. In the first two volumes that world
is described which ended with World War Two,
and those struggles of a political and social
nature are depicted which had almost, or even
entirely, been won. The third volume, however,
may be the most important, especially for
the younger reader, because it concerns the
struggle which still has to be won and which
filled the last twenty years of Russell's
life: the struggle for world peace and nuclear
disarmament.

K o m m e n t a r
Russell's "Autobiographie" in drei Bänden
ist eine der wirklich bedeutenden Autobio-
graphien unserer Zeit, die fast ein ganzes
Jahrhundert gesellschaftlicher und intellek-
tueller Veränderungen umspannt. In den ersten
beiden Bänden wurde jene Welt dargestellt,
die mit dem zweiten Weltkrieg endete, und
jene Kämpfe auf politischem und gesellschaft-
lichem Gebiet, die bereits fast oder sogar
ganz gewonnen waren. Der dritte Band mag jedoch vor allem für die jüngeren Leser der
wichtigste sein, weil er jenen Kampf betrifft,
der noch gewonnen werden muß, der die letzten zwanzig Jahre in Russell's Leben erfüllte:
der Kampf für den Weltfrieden und die auto-
mare Abrüstung. (Mitteilung des Insel-Verla-
ges über "Autobiographie III", BN 682.18)

R e p r i n t s
1968 Vol. I, 1872-1914
    New York: Bantam Books 682.09
1969 Vol. I - III
    London: Allen & Unwin 682.10
    New York: Simon & Schuster 682.11
1971 London: Allen & Unwin. Vol. I - III . . 682.12
1975 "   : "   " " .
    1 vol., Paperback, 752 pp. 682.13

T r a n s l a t i o n s
Chinesisch:
    "Lo Su Chih Chuan"
    Tr.: Yin Jang Tsê
    Taipeh: Wen Yuan Book
    1968 I/1872-1914 . . . . 682.14
    "Luosu zizhuan"
    Taipeh
    1973 ?/ 682.15
Deutsch:
    "Mein Leben"
    Ü.: Harry Kahn. / Nachwort: Golo Mann
    Zürich: Europa Verlag. 360 S.
    1967 I/1872-1914 . . . . 682.16

Deutsch:
 "Autobiographie"
 Tr.: Julia Kirchner
 Frankfurt: Insel Verlag.
 1970 II/1914-1944 . . . . 682.17
 "Autobiographie"
 Tr.: Rudolf Ways
 Frankfurt: Insel Verlag
 1971 III/1944-1967 . . . . 682.18
 "Autobiographie"
 Frankfurt: suhrkamp taschenbuch
 1972 I/1872-1914. Tb. 22 . . . . . 682.19
 1973 II/1914-1944. Tb. 84 . . . . . 682.20
 1974 III/1944-1967. Tb. 192 . . . . . 682.21
 Auszüge aus "Autobiographie III"
 unter dem Titel
 "Handeln oder zugrunde gehen"
 1972 in BN 703/V:17 . . . . 682.22
Finnisch:
 "Elämäni"
 Tr.: Eila Pennanen
 Helsinki, Porvoo: Söderström
 1967 I/1872-1914 . . . . 682.23
 1968 II/1914-1944 . . . . 682.24
 1969 III/1944-1967 . . . . 682.25
Französisch:
 "Autobiographie"
 Tr.: A. + Michel Berveille
 Paris: Stock
 1968 I/1872-1914 . . . . 682.26
 1969 II/1914-1944 . . . . 682.27
 1970 III/1944-1967 . . . . 682.28
Italienisch:
 "L'autobiografia;
 Tr.: Lucia Krasnik
 Mailand: Longanesi
 1969 I/1872-1914 . . . . 682.29
 1969 II/1914-1944 . . . . 682.30
 1970 III/1944-1967 . . . . 682.31
Japanisch:
 "Russell jijoden"
 Tr.: Hidaka Kazuteru
 Tokio: Risōsha
 1968 I/1872-1914 . . . . 682.32
 1970 II/1914-1944 . . . . 682.33
 1973 III/1944-1967 . . . . 682.34
Koreanisch:
 "Ginagin sarang-eui osolgil"
 Tr.: Bong-Cheon Jin
 Seoul: Sina Chulapansa
 1967 I/1872-1914 . . . . 682.35
 Tr.: O Jong Hwa
 Seoul: Namchang
 1969 I/1872-1914 . . . . 682.36

Niederländisch:
    "Autobiografie"
    Tr.: M. + L. Coutinho
    Amsterdam: Bezige Bij
    1968 I/1872-1914 . . . . 682.37
    1970 II/1914-1944 . . . . 682.38
    1973 III/1944-1967 . . . . 682.39
Norwegisch:
    "Memoarer"
    Tr.: Louise Bohr Nilsen
    Oslo: Tiden
    1967 I/1872-1914 . . . . 682.40
    1968 II/1914-1944 . . . . 682.41
    1969 III/1944-1967 . . . . 682.42
Polnisch:
    "Autobiografia"
    Tr.: Bronislaw Zieliński
    Warschau: Czytelnik
    1971 I/1872-1914 . . . . 682.43
Portugiesisch:
    "Autobiografia"
    Tr.: José Laurênio de Melo,Alvaro Gabral
    Rio de Janeiro: Civilização Brasileira
    1967 I/1872-1914 . . . . 682.44
    1970 II/1914-1944 . . . . 682.45
    1972 III/1944-1967 . . . . 682.46
Rumänisch:
    "Autobiografie"
    Tr.: Adina Arsenescu
    Bukarest: Editura politică
    1969 I/1872-1914 . . . . 682.47
Schwedisch:
    "Memoarer"
    Tr.: Anders Byttner, Roland Adlerberth
    Stockholm: Natur och Kultur
    1967 I/1872-1914 . . . . 682.48
    1968 II/1914-1944 . . . . 682.49
    1969 III/1944-1967 . . . . 682.50
Spanisch:
    "Autobiografia"
    Tr.: Manuel de la Escalera
    Madrid: Aguilar
    1968 I/1872-1914 . . . . 682.51
    1975 II/1914-1944 (Mexiko: Aguilar) . 682.52
    1971 III/1944-1967 . . . . 682.53
Ungarisch:
    "Önéletrajz"
    Tr.: Pál Vámosi
    Budapest: Europa Kiadó
    1970 I/1872-1914 . . . . 682.54

Bertrand Russell on the Afterlife

1968 (Sept.-Oct.) in "Humanist" (Buffalo, N.Y.)
vol. 28, no. 51, p. 29 . . . . 683.00

Open Letter to Wladyslaw Gomulka (1968, Dec. 9)

1968 (Nov./Dec.) in "World Jewry" (London) . . . 684.01
T r a n s l a t i o n s
Deutsch:
   "Offener Brief an Wladyslaw Gomulka"
   in H. Abosch "Antisemitismus in Rußland"
   1972 Darmstadt: Melzer 684.02
   1972 in BN 703/V:19 . . . . 684.03

The Art of Philosophizing and Other Essays

1968 New York: Philosophical Library. 119 pp. . 685.01
1974 Totowa, N.J.: Littlefield, Adams & Co. 685.02
1977 " , " " : " , " " " 685.03
C o n t e n t s
The Art of Rational Conjecture . (1942/474)
The Art of Drawing Inferences .. (1942/475)
The Art of Reckoning .... (1942/476)

Miscellany/Sammelband in Italienisch
under the title
"Saggi"

1968 Mailand: Fabbri. Tr.: D.Barbone, G.Sardelli 686.00
C o n t e n t s
"Saggi scettici" (Sceptical Essays 1928/331)
"Principi di reforma sociale"(Prin-
   ciples of Social Reconstruction 1916/159)
"......................."
   (The Essence of Religion ..... 1912/113)

Miscellany/Sammelband in Chinesisch
under the title
"Lo Su San Wen Chi" (Essays)

1968 Taipeh: Chi Wen Pub. Ser.
Tr.: Mou Chih Chung 687.00

Labour's Goldwater

1969 (Nov. 28) in "Tribune", p. 1 . . . . 688.00

Miscellany/Sammelband in Italienisch
under the title
"Il pensiore filosofico"
Antologia dagli scritti.

1969 Bologna: Calderini. 190 pp.
Tr.: Giuseppe Magnano 689.00

DEAR BERTRAND RUSSELL ...

A Selection of His Correspondence
with the General Public, 1950-1968,
ed. by B. Feinberg and R. Kasrils.

```
1969 London: Allen & Unwin. 196 pp.  . . . . . . .  690.01
     Boston: Houghton Mifflin  . . . . . . . . .  690.02
     1970 New York: Simon & Schuster . . . . . . .  690.03
     1970 London: Allen & Unwin  . . . . . . . .  690.04
```

T r a n s l a t i o n s
Deutsch:
"Briefe aus den Jahren 1950-1968"
Ü.: Burkhardt Kiegeland
1970 Frankfurt: Josef Melzer. 198 S. . 690.05
Hebräisch:
"Bertrand Russell ha-yaqar; misvhar
mittokh halifat ha-mikhtavim shello
im ha-qehal ha-rahav, 1950-1968"
Tr.: Arye Shor
1971 Jerusalem: Y. Marcus 690.06
Italienisch:
"Caro Bertrand Russell"
Tr.: Rosanna Pelà
1971 Mailand: Longanesi 690.07
Niederländisch:
"Beste Bertrand Russell .... een keuze
uit zijn correspondentie met het publick
1950-1968"
Tr.: Marluce Goos
1971 Antwerpen, Utrecht: A. W. Bruna . 690.08
Schwedisch:
"Bäste Bertrand Russell ...
Urval ur hans brevväxling."
Tr.: Roland Adlerberth
1970 Stockholm: Natur och Kultur . . . 690.09

Open Letter to U Thant (1969, Dec. 1)

1970 (May) in "Bertrand Russell. 1872-1970"
Nottingham: B. Russell Peace Foundation
(The Spokesman) 691.00

On American Violence

1970 (Mar.) in "Ramparts", vol. 8, p. 55-57 . . 692.00

The Good Citizen's Alphabet (1953/598)
and History of the World in Epitome (1962/663)

1970 London: Gaberbocchus 693.01
     1972 in "The Collected Stories of B.R." (BN 701) 693.02

Miscellany/Sammelband in Italienisch
under the title "Linguaggio e realtà"

1970 Bari: Laterza. 222 pp.
     Antologia a cura di Massimo A. Bonfantini . 694.00

The Russell Memorandum

Private Memorandum concerning Ralph Schoenman

C o m m e n t a r y
Russell dictated the private memorandum on
8 Dec. 1969, about two months before his death.
He furnished it with the following signed note:
"This is my memorandum. I told my wife what
I wished her to type and she has typed it.
I have raed it over to myself twice carefully
and she has read it aloud to me once. I entirely endorse it as being mine and what I
wished to say." - Russell's memorandum clari-
fies the history of his relationship with
Ralph Schoenman. Russell writes in his "Autobiography III":"Towards the end of July, 1960,
I received my first visit from a young American called Ralph Schoenman. I had heard of
some of his activities in relation to CND
(Campaign for Nuclear Disarmament = Kampagne
für Nukleare Abrüstung) so I was rather cu-
rous to see him." The result was a close
co-operation concerning Vietnam, the Bertrand
Russell Peace Foundation and other matters,
which, however, was broken off with a letter
by Russell of 19th July 1969.

K o m m e n t a r
Russell diktierte das private Memorandum am
8. Dez. 1969, ungefähr zwei Monate vor seinem Tod. Er versah es mit der folgenden sig-
nierten Notiz: "Dies ist mein Memorandum. Ich
sagte meiner Frau, was sie schreiben sollte
und sie schrieb es. Ich habe es mir zweimal
sorgfältig durchgelesen und sie las es mir
einmal laut vor. Ich erkenne es vollständig
als mein an und als das, was ich zu sagen
wünschte." Russell's Memorandum bringt Klarheit in die Geschichte seiner Beziehung mit
Ralph Schoenman. Russell schreibt in seiner
"Autobiography III": "Ende Juli 1960 besuchte
mich erstmalig ein junger Amerikaner namens
Ralph Schoenman. Ich hatte einiges über seine
Tätigkeiten im Zusammenhang mit der CND (Campaign for Nuclear Disarmament = Kampagne für
Nukleare Abrüstung) gehört und war deshalb
neugierig, ihn zu treffen." Die Folge war
eine enge Zusammenarbeit betreffend Vietnam,

Bertrand Russell's Friedensstiftung und an-
deres, die aber mit einem Brief Russells vom
19. Juli 1969 abgebrochen wurde.

Miscellany/Sammelband in Deutsch
unter dem Titel
"Philosophische und politische Aufsätze"

1971 Stuttgart: Reclam. 222 S. (RUB 7970-72) . .   696.00
     I n h a l t
     "Über das Kennzeichen" (On Denoting 1905/056)
     "Der logische Atomismus" (Logical
        Atomism .... 1925/265)
     "Über den Gegenstand der Physik.
        Aus: Antwort auf Kritik." (Re-
        ply to Criticism .... 1944/496)
     "Der Pragmatismus" (Pragmatism .. 1909/090)
     "Über die Natur von Wahrheit und
        Falschheit" (On the Nature of
        Truth and Falsehood .... 1910/100)
     "Die geistigen Väter des Faschis-
        mus" (The Ancestry of Fascism;
        also: The Revolt Against Reason 1935/396)
     "Was für den Sozialismus spricht"
        (The Case for Socialism ...... 1935/401)
     "Lob des Müßiggangs" (In Praise of
        Idleness .... 1932/376)
     "Ethik" (Ethics .... 1927/316)
     "Über d. Verbindlichkeit ethischer
        Urteile. Aus: Antwort auf Kritik"
        (Reply to Criticism .... 1944/496)

Russell's Logical Atomism

1972 London: Fontana, ed. by David Pears 697.00
     C o n t e n t s
     The Philosophy of Logical Atomism (1918/178)
     Logical Atomism (1924/265)

The Life of Bertrand Russell
in pictures and his own words

Compiled by Christopher Farley and David Hodgson
for the Bertrand Russell Centenary

1972 Nottingham: B. Russell Peace Foundation
     (Spokesman Books) 698.00

My Own Philosophy

1972 Hamilton, Ont.:
     McMaster University Library Press 699.00

Atheism

Collected Essays, 1943-1949

1972 New York: Arno Press 700.00

C o n t e n t s
Am I An Atheist or an Agnostic? (1949/553)
An Outline of Intellectual Rubbish (1943/486)
Can Men be Rationalist? .... (1923/262)
The Faith of a Rationalist ..... (1947/517)
Ideas That Have Harmed Mankind (1946/509)
Ideas That Have Helped Mankind (1946/510)
On the Value of Scepticism ..... (1928/327)
The Value of Free Thought ...... (1944/497)
What Can A Free Man Worship? ... (1903/036)

THE COLLECTED STORIES OF BERTRAND RUSSELL

Compiled and edited by Barry Feinberg

1972 London: Allen & Unwin. 349 pp. 701.01
1973 New York: Simon & Schuster 701.02

C o n t e n t s
Preface
    Notes for a speech to the Au-
      thors' Club, 11 February 1953 (1972/701)
Part I: Longer Stories
    The Perplexities of J. Forstice (1972/701)
    Satan in the Suburbs .... (1953/599)
    Zahatopolk .... (1954/608)
    Faith and Mountains .... (1954/608)
Part II: Short Stories
    The Corsican Ordeal of Miss X (1952/585)
    The Infra-redioscope .... (1953/599)
    The Guardians of Parnassus .. (1953/599)
    Benefit of Clergy .... (1953/599)
    The Right Will Prevail or
      The Road to Lhasa .... (1961/660)
Part III: Nightmares
    The Queen of Sheba's Nigthmare (1954/608)
    Mr. Bowdler's Nightmare ...... (1954/608)
    The Psychoanalyst's Nightmare (1954/608)
    The Metaphysician's Nightmare (1954/608)
    The Existentialist's Nightmare (1954/608)
    The Mathematician's Nightmare (1954/608)
    Stalin's Nightmare .... (1954/608)
    Eisenhower's Nightmare ...... (1954/608)
    Dean Acheson's Nightmare .... (1954/608)
    Dr. Southport Vulpes's
      Nightmare .... (1954/608)
    The Fisherman's Nightmare .... (1961/660)
    The Theologian's Nightmare ... (1961/660)
Part IV: Anecdotes
    Family, Friends and Others .. (1972/701)
    Reading History
      As It Is Never Written ... (1972/701)
Part V: Medley
    Dreams .... (1961/660)
    Parables .... (1961/660)
    Cranks .... (1961/660)

The Boston Lady .... (1972/701)
Children's Stories .... (1972/701)
Newly Discovered Maxims
    of La Rochefoucauld ...... (1961/660)
A Liberal Decalogue .... (1951/576)
"G" is for Gobbledygook ..... (1972/701)
The Good Citizen's Alphabet (1953/598)
    and History of the World in
    Epitome .... (1962/663)
Auto-Obituary .... (1936/406)

Miscellany/Sammelband in Türkisch
under the title
"Düsünceler"
_____

1972 Istanbul: Cem Yayinevi. 247 pp.
      Tr.: Sabahattin Eyüboğlu, Vedat Günyol . . 702.00

Miscellany/Sammelband in Deutsch
unter dem Titel
"Politische Schriften I. Was wir tun können."
_____

1972 München: Nymphenburger Verlagshandlung
     (Russell Studienausgabe. Dialog 110) . . . 703.00
       I   n   h   a   l   t
       Einleitung
   I. Marxismus und Kapitalismus
      1. Die deutsche Sozialdemokratie
         und das Problem der politischen
         Strategie (German Social Democ-
         racy as a Lesson in Political
         Tactics .... 1896/002)
      2. Die deutsche Sozialdemokratie:
         Auszüge (German Social Democ-
         racy .... 1896/007)
  II. Der erste Weltkrieg
      3. Ein Appell an die Intellektuel-
         len Europas (An Appeal to the
         Intellectuals of Europe ...... 1915/141)
      4. Grundlagen für eine soziale Um-
         gestaltung(Principles of Social
         Reconstruction .... 1916/159)
      5. Politische Ideale (Political
         Ideals .... 1917/171)
 III. Das bolschewistische Rußland
      6. Praxis und Theorie des Bolsche-
         wismus (The Practice and Theory
         of Bolshevism .... 1920/207)
  IV. Kapitalismus - Sozialismus -
      Demokratie
      7. China und das Problem des fernen
         Ostens (The Problem of China 1922/238)
      8. Die Kultur des Industrialismus
         und ihre Zukunft (The Prospects
         of Industrial Civilization ... 1923/263

1972/1973

Bertrand Russell's America,
his transatlantic travels and writings

A documented account by B. Feinberg and R. Kasrils
Vol. I, 1896-1945 (see also BN 708)

1973 London: Allen & Unwin. 356 pp. 704.01
     1974 under the title
          "Bertrand Russell's America"
          New York: Viking Press 704.02

ESSAYS IN ANALYSIS

Edited by Douglas Lackey

Misceallany/Sammelband in Spanisch
under the title
"Obras completas"

1973 Madrid: Aguilar. II vols., 1073, 1390 pp. . 706.00
    C o n t e n t s
  I. Historia de la Filosofia
    "Historia de la Filosofia Occi-
    dental"(History of Western Phi-
    losophy .... 1945/504)
    "La Sabiduria de Occidente"(Wisdom
    of the West .... 1959/649)
  II. Ciencia y Filosofia 1897 - 1919
    "Ensayo sobre los Fundamentos de la
    Geometria" (An Essay on the
    Foundations of Geometry ...... 1897/010)
    "Exposición Critica de la Filoso-
    fia de Leibniz" (A Critical Ex-
    position of the Philosophy of
    Leibniz .... 1900/019)
    "Los Principios de la Matemática"
    (The Principles of Mathematics 1903/037)
    "Ensayos Filosóficos" (Philosophi-
    cal Essays .... 1910/100)
    "Misticismo y Lógica" (Mysticism
    and Logic .... 1917/172)
    "Principia Mathematica" / Excerpts
    (Principia Mathematica .... 1910/101)
    "Los Problemas de la Filosofia"
    (The Problems of Philosophy .. 1912/118)
    "Nuestro Conocimiento del Mundo Ex-
    terrior" (Our Knowledge of the
    Extern World .... 1914/133)
    "Introducción a la Filosofia Mate-
    mática" (Introduction to Mathe-
    matical Philosophy .... 1919/191)

Miscellany/Sammelband in Deutsch
unter dem Titel
"Erziehung ohne Dogma"

1974 München: Nymphenburger Verlagshandlung
    (Russell Studienausgabe. Dialog 108) . . . 707.00
    I n h a l t
  I. Erziehung und Gesellschaft:
    16 Unter-Titel siehe BN 378.11
    (Education and the Social Order 1932/378)
  II. Probleme der Erziehung
    1. Erziehung als politische Insti-
    tution (Education as a Politi-
    cal Institution .... 1916/159)
    2. Sozialismus und Erziehung (So-
    cialism and Education .... 1925/292)
    3. Die Ziele der Erziehung (The
    Aims of Education .... 1926/308)

Mortals and Others
Bertrand Russell's American Essays 1931-1935

Edited by Harry Ruja. Volume I.

1975 London: Allen & Unwin. 176 pp. 708.00
(see also BN 704)

C o m m e n t a r y
In the arly 1930s, the "New York American" and other newspapers owned by W. R. Hearst published a literary page to which a large number of writers and artists contributed. Bertrand Russell was one of the regulars, contributing a total of 156 essays from 22 July 1931 to 2 May 1935. His essays made frequent reference to the events and problems of the day, but to a large extent the themes are perennial. They were written by a philosopher, by a man who by the end of his long and full life had pursued with vigour and even distinction five or six careers in addition to that of philosopher: mathematician, logician, educator, moralist, propagandist for social reform, and agitator for peace - and all these roles to a degree find expression in these essays. - When the essays first appeared, Lord Russell was no stranger to America. He had first visited the United States in 1896 with his first wife, herself

an American, staying for three months, meeting
her relatives and lecturing at Bryn Mawr College and at Johns Hopkins University. He had
come to the States again in 1914, 1924, 1927,
1929, and 1931 (From the Preface).

K o m m e n t a r
In den frühen 1930er Jahren publizierten die
"New York American" und andere Zeitungen im
Besitz von W. R. Hearst eine literarische Seite, bei der eine große Anzahl Schriftsteller
und Künstler mitwirkten. Bertrand Russell war
einer der regelmäßigen, der eine Gesamtzahl
von 156 Essays beisteuerte, in der Zeit vom
22. Juli 1931 bis 2. Mai 1935. Seine Essays
bezogen sich häufig auf Ereignisse und Probleme des Tages, aber zu einem großen Teil
waren es immerwährende Themen. Sie wurden
von einem Philosophen geschrieben, von einem
Mann, der am Ende seines langen und reifen
Lebens mit Kraft und Würde fünf oder sechs
Laufbahnen zusätzlich zu der des Philosophen
verfolgt hat: Mathematiker, Logiker, Erzie-
her, Moralist, Propagandist sozialer Reformen und Agitator für Frieden - und alle diese Rollen finden ihren deutlichen Ausdruck
in diesen Essays. - Als die Essays zum erstenmal erschienen, war Lord Russell den
Amerikanern kein Fremder mehr. Er hatte die
USA 1896 zum erstenmal besucht zusammen mit
seiner ersten Frau, selbst Amerikanerin, und
blieb drei Monate, um Verwandte zu treffen und
Vorlesungen am Bryn Mawr College und an der
Johns Hopkins Universität zu halten. 1914,
1924, 1927, 1929 und 1931 kehrte er jeweils
in die Staaten zurück.

Bertrand Russell - An Introduction

which is a school book containing selections from
Russell's Writings as a basis for group discussion classes in secondary schools and comparable
institutions. Edited by Brian Carr, Lecturer in
Philosophy, University of Exeter.
(... ist ein Schulbuch enthaltend eine Auswahl aus
Russell's Schriften als Basis für Diskussionsgrup-
pen in Oberschulklassen und vergleichbaren In-
stitutionen.)

1975 London: Allen & Unwin. 149 pp. • • • • • • 709.00

Miscellany/Sammelband in Deutsch
unter dem Titel
"Freiheit ohne Furcht"

1975 Reinbek bei Hamburg: Rowohlt
rororo Sachbuch 6900. Hg.: Achim von Borries 710.00

1975/1976

Miscellany/Sammelband in Deutsch
unter dem Titel
"Die Philosophie des Logischen Atomismus"

1976 München: Nymphenburger Verlagshandlung
     (Russell Studienausgabe. Dialog 104) ... 711.00
     Hg.: Johannes Sinnreich
     I n h a l t
     Vorwort
     Einleitung

ANHANG

APPENDIX

1. Chronologisches Verzeichnis der Hauptwerke
Chronological Index of Main Works

3. Sekundär-Literatur / Secondary Literature (SL)

Die Nachweisungen des Schrifttums über Bertrand Russell,
d. h. die Sekundär-Literatur, beschränkt sich auf eine
charakteristische Auswahl von Büchern über Russell's Werke und Wirkungen; sie dürfte zunächst als erster Zugang
zum Werk und zur Persönlichkeit Russell's ausreichend
sein. Durch eine solche Auswahl soll andererseits indi-
rekt angedeutet werden, daß eine optimal vollständige
Erfassung der Sekundär-Literatur, wegen ihres großen und
schwer überschaubaren internationalen Umfanges, allzuoft
Wunschgedanke bleiben muß.

The recording of writings on Bertrand Russell, i. e. of
secondary literature, has been limited to a representa-
tive selection of books about Russell's works and effects;
it should suffice for a first approach to Russell's work
and personality. By such a selection it is indicated,
that the complete registration of secondary literature
is likely to remain a disederatum because of its vast and
hardly surveyable international volume.

1918 Jourdain, P. E. B.
"The Philosophy of Mr. Bertrand Russell" ... SL 01

1928 Wood, Herbert G.
"Bertrand Russell Is Not a Christian"
London: Student Christian Movement .... SL 02

1931 Thalheimer, Ross.
"A Critical Examination of the Epistemologi-
cal and Psycho-physical Doctrines of Russell"
Baltimore, Md.: John Hopkins Press .... SL 03

1941 Dewey, J. and Kallen, H. M. (eds.)
"The Bertrand Russell Case"
Essays by various writers on the revocation of
B. Russell's appointment to a chair of phi-
losophy in the College of the City of New York.
New York: The Viking Press .... SL 04

1942 Hardy, G. H.
"Bertrand Russell and Trinity" (Siehe SL 31)
Cambridge, Engl.: Author .... SL 05

1944 Schilpp, Paul A. (ed.)
"The Philosophy of Bertrand Russell"
(A Collection of Critical Essays)
Evanston, Chicago: Northwestern University
1951 La Salle, Ill.: Open Court

1949 Darbon, André
"La philosophie des mathématiques;
étude sur la logistique de Russell"
Paris: Presses Universitaires de France .... SL 07

1949 Leggett, Harry W.
"Bertrand Russell, O. M."
London: Lincolns-Prager .... SL 08
1950 New York: Philosophical Library
1950 Toronto: MyLeod

1951 Dorward, Alan
"Bertrand Russell;
a Short Guide to His Philosophy"
London: Longmans .... SL 09

1952 Fritz, Charles A., Jr.
"Bertrand Russell's Construction of the Ex-
ternal World"
London: Routledge & Kegan Paul .... SL 10
New York: Humanities

1952 Gotlind, Erik
"Bertrand Russell's Theories of Causation"
Uppsalla: Almquist & Wiksell .... SL 11

1957 Edwards, Paul
"How Bertrand Russell Was Prevented from
Teaching at the College of the City of New
York." In Russell: "Why I Am Not a Christian",
p. 207-259.
London: Allen & Unwin .... SL 12
New York: Simon & Schuster
Don Mills (Ontario): Thomas Nelson

1957 Wood, Alan
"Bertrand Russell, the Passionate Skeptic"
London: Allen & Unwin .... SL 13
1958 New York: Simon & Schuster
1959 Deutsch:
        "Bertrand Russell,
        Skeptiker aus Leidenschaft"
        Thun: Otto Verlag

1958 Clark, Cecil H. D.
"Christianity and Bertrand Russell"
London: Butterworth .... SL 14

1958 Warnock, Geoffrey J.
"Bertrand Russell"
'English Philosophy Since', Chap. 3
New York, London: Oxford University Press .. SL 15

1959 Wood, Alan
"Russell's Philosophy:
a Study of its Development"
In Russell 'My Philosophical Development',
p. 255-276.
London: Allen & Unwin .... SL 16
New York: Simon & Schuster
Toronto: Nelson
1973 Deutsch:
        "Die Philosophie B. Russell's. Fragmente
        zu einer Studie über ihre Entwicklung."
        Siehe BN 648.08.

1960 Purcell, Victor (Myra Buttle, pseud.)
"Bitches' Brew;
or, The Plot Against Bertrand Russell"
New York: Watts .... SL 17

1962 Gottschalk, Herbert
"Bertrand Russell"
Berlin: Colloquium Verlag .... SL 18
1965 Englisch:
      "Bertrand Russell, a Life"
      London: Baker
1966 New York: Roy

1963 Aiken, Lillian W.
"Bertrand Russell's Philosophy of Morals"
New York: Humanities .... SL 19

1963 Park, Joe
"Bertrand Russell on Education"
Columbus, Ohio: Ohio State University Press SL 20
1965 London: Allen & Unwin

1967 Devaux, Philippe
"Bertrand Russell ou la paix dans la vérité"
Paris: Seghers .... SL 21

1967 Edwards, Paul; Alston, W. P. and Prior, A. N.
"Russell, Bertrand Arthur William"
In 'The Encyclopedia of Philosophy',
vol. 7, p. 235-258
New York: Macmillan & Free Press .... SL 22
London: Collier-Macmillan

1967 Feinberg, Barry (ed.)
"The Archives of Bertrand Russell"
London: Continuum. (Siehe BN 681.00) .... SL 23

1967 Pears, David F.
"Bertrand Russell
and the British Tradition in Philosophy"
New York: Random House .... SL 24
London: Collins
1972 2nd ed.

1967 Schoenman, Ralph (ed.)
"Bertrand Russell, Philosopher of the Century"
London: Allen & Unwin .... SL 25
1968 Boston: Little Brown

1968 Lewis, John
"Bertrand Russell: Philosopher and Humanist"
London: Lawrence & Wishart .... SL 26
New York: International Publishers

1969 Clack, Robert J.
"Bertrand Russell's Philosophy of Language."
The Hague: Martinus Nijoff .... SL 27

1969 Eames, Elizabeth R.
"Bertrand Russell's Theory of Knowledge"
London: Allen & Unwin .... SL 28

1969 Ready, W.
"Necessary Russell"
Toronto .... SL 29

1970 Crawshay-Williams, Rupert
"Russell Remembered"
Oxford University Press .... SL 30

1970 Hardy, G. H.
"Bertrand Russell and Trinity"
Cambridge University Press .... SL 31
A College Controversy of the Last War, i. e.
1914-1918, by G.H.Hardy, Cambridge (1942, siehe SL 05). The story of the controversy about
pacifism between B. Russell and the Fellows
of Trinity College, Cambridge, as a result of
which he was ejected from his Lectureship.

1970 Klemke, E. D. (ed.)
"Essays on Bertrand Russell"
Urbana, Ill.: University of Illinois Press . SL 32

1970 Watling, John
"Bertrand Russell"
            Oliver & Boyd .... SL 33

1971 Ayer, A. J.
"Russell and Moore: The Analytical Heritage"
London: Macmillan .... SL 34
Cambridge: Harvard University Press
1972 Ayer, A. J.
"Russell" (Fontana Modern Masters)
London: Fontana (Collins) .... SL 35

1972 Jager, Ronald
"The Development of Bertrand Russell's
Philosophy"
London: Allen & Unwin .... SL 36

1972 Pears, D. F. (ed.)
"Bertrand Russell:
A Collection of Critical Essays."
(With a Bibliography by Harry Ruja)
New York, Toronto: Doubleday and Co. .... SL 37

1974 Nakhnikian, George (ed.)
"Bertrand Russell's Philosophy"
                    .... SL 38

1975 Carr, Brian
"Bertrand Russell. An Introduction"
London: Allen & Unwin (siehe BN 709.00) .... SL 39

1975 Clark, Ronald W.
"The Life of Bertrand Russell"
London: Jonathan Cape and
Weidenfeld und Nicolsen. 750 S. .... SL 40

1975 Thomas, J. E. and Blackwell, Kenneth (eds.)
"Russell in Review,
The McMaster Russell Centenary Celebrations,
1972." Toronto: .... SL 41

4. Alphabetisches Werkverzeichnis / Index of Works

Normalschrift:
 a) Titel eines kleineren Werkes.
 b) Inhalts-Titel zum Titel eines Hauptwerkes, wenn
    vor der Bibliographie-Nummer (BN) ein "in" steht.
Großbuchstaben:
 Titel eines Hauptwerkes.
Normalschrift eingeklammert:
 Kein Russell-Titel, sondern Titel eines rezensierten
 Werkes oder eines Werkes mit einer Einleitung oder
 einem Vorwort von Russell.

Standart letters:
 a) Title of a smaller work.
 b) Title of the contents to a main work, incase "in"
    before bibliographical number (BN).
Big letters:
 Title of a main work.
Standart letters in brackets:
 No Russell title, but title of a reviewed work or of
 a work with a introduction or with a preface by Russell.

- 285 -

                        - 297 -

R e v i e w
of C. D. Broad's
"A General Notation for the Relation
of Numbers" (Note on ...) 181/059
of C. D. Broad's
"The Mind and Its Place in Nature" 298/093
of J. Percy Bruce's
"Chu Hsi and His Masters" 255/080
of N. Bukharin's
Historical Materialism" 303/094
of Burrt's
"The Metaphysical Foundation
of Modern Physics" 304/094
of Paul Carus's
"The Foundations of Mathematics" 091/023
of E. Cassierer's
"Leibniz' System in seinen wissenschaftlichen Grundlagen"(Critical notice ...) . 033/010
of L. Couturat's
"De l'infini mathematique" 008/005
of L. Couturat's
"La Logique de Leibniz d'après des
documents inédits" (Critical notice ...) 033/010
of L. Couturat's
"Opusculus et fragments inédits de Leibniz" 044/017
of L. J. Delaporte's
"Essai philosophique sur les géometries
non-Euclidiennes" 045/017
of J. H. Denison's
"Emotion as the Basis of Civilization" ..
of J. Dewey's
"Studies in Logical Theory" 090/023
of J. Dewey's
"Columbia University Essays, Philosophical and Psychological in Honor
of William James" 090/023
of J. Dewey's
"Essays in Experimental Logic" 180/059
of A. S. Eddington's
"The Nature of the Physical World" 337/112
of A. S. Eddington's
"New Pathways in Science" 399/137
of K. Geissler's
"Die Grundsätze und das Wesen des Unendlichen in der Mathematik und Philosophie" 034/010
of E. Goblot's
"Essai sur le classification des sciences" 013/007
of J. A. Gunn's
"Modern French Philosophy" 232/074
of A. Hannequin's
"Essai critique sur l'hypothese des atoms
dans la Science contemporaine" 006/003
of W. Hastie's
translation of Kant's "Cosmogony" 025/009
of G. Heymans'
"Die Gesetze und Elemente
des Wissenschaftlichen Denkens" 001/003

R e v i e w
of C. H. Hinton's
"The Fourth Dimension" 047/017
of Johan Huizinga's
"The Waning of the Middle Ages" 288/089
of Hu Shih's
"The Development of the Logical Method
in Ancient China" 252/079
of "Essays Philosophical and Psychological
in Honor of William   J a m e s " 089/022
of W. James's
"The Will to Believe and Pragmatism" 090/023
of W. James's
"Memories and Studies" 105/030
of W. James's
"Essays in Radical Empiricism" 115/032
of H. H. Joachim's
"The Nature of Truth".................. 075/021
of H.H. Joachim's
"Immediate Experience and Mediation" 192/064
of C. E. M. Joad's
"Essays in Common-Sense Philosophy" 188/060
of J. M. Keynes's
"A Treatise on Probability" 226/074
of Josef Wood Krutch's
"The Modern Temper" 338/113
of John Laird's
"Recent Philosophy" 408/144
of G. Lechalas
"Étude sur l'espace et le temps" 005/003
of H. Levy's
"A Philosophy for a Modern Man" 434/149
of N. O. Lossky's
"The Intuitive Basis of Knowledge" 187/060
of A. E. H. Love's
"Theoretical Mechanics: an Introductory
Treatise on the Theory of Mechanics" 012/006
of A. Luce's
"Bergson's Doctrine of Intuition" 229/074
of H. MacColl's
"Symbolic Logic and Its Applications" ... 069/020
of H. S. Macran's
"Hegel's Doctrine of Formal Logic" 111/031
of G. Mannoury's
"Methodologisches und Philosophisches
zur Elementar-Mathematik" 097/024
of A. Meinong's
"Über die Bedeutung
des Weberschen Gesetzes" ....: 015/007
of A. Meinong's
"Untersuchungen zur Gegenstandstheorie
und Psychologie" 058/019
dasselbe / the same .... II:2 in 705/252
of A. Meinong's
"Über die Erfahrungsgrundlagen
unseres Wissens" 071/020

- 318 -

R e v i e w
    of A. Meinong's
       "Über die Stellung der Gegenstandstheorie
       im System der Wissenschaften" 078/021
       dasselbe / the same .... II:3 in 705/252
    of C. Mercier's
       "A New Logic" 108/030
    of G. E. Moore's
       "Principia Ethica" 040/016
    of G. E. Moore's
       "Philosophical Studies" 227/074
    of C. K. Ogden's
       "The Meaning of Meaning" 248/079
    of R. Osborn's
       "Freud and Marx" 424/147
    of M. St. J. Packe's
       "The Life of John Stuart Mill" 600/199
    of A. Pastore's
       "Logica formale dedotta dalla
       considerazione di modelli meccanici" 070/020
    of Pigou's
       "The Riddle of the Tariff" 038/016
    of H. Poincaré's
       "Science and Hypothesis" 055/018
    of Eileen Power's
       "Medieval People" 288/089
    of L. Price's
       "Dialogues of A. N. Whitehead" 603/199
    of "Proceedings of the Aristotelian Society" 189/060
    of S. Radhakrishnan's
       "Indian Philosophy" 255/080
    of E. P. Ramsey's
       "Foundations of Mathematics
       and other Logical Essays" 370/124
    of A. Reymonds's
       "Logique and Mathématiques" 092/023
    of I. A. Richards'
       "The Meaning of Meaning" 248/079
    of A. Ruge's
       "Encyclopaedia of the Phisophical Sciences" 123/037
    of Gilbert Ryle's
       "The Concept of Mind" 636/215
    of G. Santayana's
       "Reason in Science" 062/019
    of G. Santayana's
       "Soliloquies in England" 234/074
    of G. Santayana's
       "Life of Reason" 247/079
    of G. Santayana's
       "Scepticism and Animal Faith" 250/079
    of F. C. S. Schiller's
       "Philosophical Essays" 090/023
       "Studies in Humanism" 090/023
    of F. C. S. Schiller's
       "Formal Logic" 109/030
    of J. Schulz's
       "Psychologie der Axiome" 018/007

R e v i e w
   of Norman Kemp Smith's
     "A Commentary
     to Kant's 'Critique of Pure Reason'" 174/055
   of K. Stephen's
     "The Misuse of Mind" 227/074
   of P. F. Strawson's
     "On Refering" 620/209
     dasselbe / the same .... III:6 in 705/252
   of J. O Urmson's
     "Philosophical Analysis:
     Its Development Between the Two World Wars" 613/204
   of Freda Utley's
     "Japan's Feet of Clay" 409/144
   of G. P. Warnock's
     "Metaphysics in Logic" 622/209
   of Weiss's
     "Principles of Mathematics" 375/127
   of A. N. Whitehead's
     "Science and the Modern World" 302/094
     dasselbe / the same 304/094
   of G. Williams'
     "The Sanctity of Life and the Criminal Law" 635/215
   of J. Z. Young's
     "Doubt and Certainty
     in Science" (Comments on ....) 562/183
Revival of Puritanism, The 257/080
Revolt Against Reason, The 396/137
Revolt in the Abstract .... I:III in 660/228
Revolt into Pluralism .... 5 in 648/220
Revolution .... III in 400/138
"   IV in 593/195
Revolution and Dictatorship .... II in 204/065
"   "   " ....II:IV in 207/066
Revolutionary Power .... VII in 436/149
Rewars of Philosophy 523/173
Rex versus Bertrand Russell 149/043
Ricardo .... II:B:XI in 395/133
(Riddle of the Tariff) 038/016
Right Will Prevail
   or The Road to Lhasa, The .... III:II in 660/229
"   II in 701/249
Rings of Electrons .... VIII in 264/083
Rise of Greek Civilization, The   Book One:I:I in 504/162
Rise of Modern Philosophy .... in 649/223
Rise of Science, The .... Book Three:I:VI in 504/163
ROADS TO FREEDOM:
   SOCIALISM, ANARCHISM AND SYNDICALISM 177/055
Road to Happiness, The .... in 617/207
Role of Individuality, The .... III in 554/180
Role of Induction, The .... VI:II in 536/175
Role of Police, The .... I in 593/195
Role of Science in Society, The 631/215
Role of the Intellectual in the Modern World .. 437/152
Romance of Revolt, The .... I:II in 660/228

5. Quellennachweis / List of Sources

Periodika
1. National Union Catalog
   a) Pre 1956 London: Mansel Information
                The American Library Association
   b) 1956-1967 Totawa, N.J..: Littlefield, Adams & Co.
   c) 1968-1972 Ann Arbor, Mich.: J. W. Edwards
   d) 1973 ff. Washington: Library of Congress
2. Cumalative Book Index
   a) 1928-1932 The United States Catalog
   b) 1933 ff. World list of books
                in the English Language
3. British National Bibliography
   a) 1950-1970 London: The Council
                of the British National Bibliography
   b) 1971 ff. London: The British Library,
                Bibliography Services Division
4. British books in print
   London: J. Whitaker & Son
5. Répertoire Bibliographique de la Philosophie.
   Publié sous les auspices de L'Institut International
   de Philosophie avec le patronage de l'Unesco.
   Löwen (Belgien): Institut supérieur de Philosophie
6. Index translationum
   Paris: Les Presses de l'Unesco
7. Bibliographie de la Philosophie
   Paris: Librarie Philosophique, J. Vrin
8. Deutsches Bücherverzeichnis (Leipzig)
9. Deutsche National-Bibliographie (Leipzig/DDR)
10. Deutsche Bibliographie (Frankfurt/BRD)

Einzelwerke / Individual works
11. a) B. Russell: "A History of Western Philosophy"
       1945 New York: Simon & Schuster (Introduction)
       1946 London: Allen & Unwin   ("   )
    b) B. Russell: "Philosophie des Abendlandes"
       1950 Zürich: Europa Verlag (Vorwort)
12. a) Alan Wood:
       "Bertrand Russell, the Passionate Sceptic"
       1957 London: Allen & Unwin
    b) Alan Wood:
       "Bertrand Russell, Skeptiker aus Leidenschaft"
       1959 Thun: Otto Verlag
13. a) Bertrand Russell:
       "My Philosophical Development"
       1959 London: Allen & Unwin
       (Appendix: "Russell's Philosophy.
       A study of its Development." by Alan Wood)
    b) Bertrand Russell:
       "Philosophie. Die Entwicklung meines Denkens."
       1973 München: Nymphenburger Verlagshandlung
       (Anhang: "Die Philosophie Bertrand Russell's.
       Fragmente zu einer Studie über ihre Entwick-
       lung." von Alan Wood.)

14. a) Bertrand Russell: "Wisdom of the West"
       1959 London: Macdonald and Jane's (Foreword)
    b) Bertrand Russell: "Denker des Abendlandes"
       1962 Stuttgart: Belser (Vorwort)
15. "The Basic Writings of Bertrand Russell"
    1961 London: Allen & Unwin
         New York: Simon & Schuster
16. "Complete Catalogue"
    1977 London: Allen & Unwin
17. Paul A. Schilpp (ed.)
    "The Philosophy of Bertrand Russell"
    1944 Evanston, Chicago: Northwestern University.
    1951 La Salle, Ill.: Open Court
    (Bibliography by Lester E. Denonn)
18. "Encyclopaedia Britanica", vol.19
    1962 London
19. "Essays in Analysis by Bertrand Russell"
    1973 London: Allen & Unwin (Bibliography)
20. D. F. Pears (ed.)
    "Bertrand Russell. A Collection of Critical Essays"
    1972 New York, Toronto: Doubleday and Co.
    (Bibliography by Harry Ruja)
21. "Philosophen Lexikon", Bd. 2
    1950 Berlin: W. de Gruyter. 2. Auflage
22. Herbert Gottschalk: "Bertrand Russell"
    1962 Berlin: Colloquium Verlag
23. Bertrand Russell
    "Autobiography I - III"
    1967 ff. London: Allen & Unwin
    "Autobiographie I - III"
    1967 ff. Zürich: Europa V., Frankfurt: Insel V.
24. Kindlers Literatur-Lexikon
    1974 München: Deutscher Taschenbuch Verlag